CONTENTS

VOLUME I

LIST OF ILLUSTRATIONS

PLATES

VOLUME I

TEXT-FIGURES

VOLUME I

I. THE ENGLISH LANDSCAPE

1. *England in 1066*

WHEN William of Normandy landed at Pevensey, the unconquered England that rolled away northwards before him had already been colonized and settled by the Old English for some six hundred years, and by the Scandinavians for nearly two hundred. Twenty generations had gone by since the *Adventus Saxonum*: there were now between a million and a million and a half people in England. Nearly all of them were countrymen and farmers, dwelling in compact villages, in hamlets, or in scattered farmsteads. Only about one in ten lived in the boroughs, and few of these boroughs had much that was recognizable as town life. London, always paramount, may have had twenty thousand people within its Roman walls (about sixty to the acre), but in the provinces only three towns—York, Norwich, and Lincoln—had as many as a thousand houses, with Oxford and Thetford not far behind. Ipswich had about eight hundred houses, Gloucester rather more than six hundred. About a score of towns had from two to five hundred houses each, perhaps one to two thousand five hundred people.

The eastern side of England, the first to be colonized and settled by the Old English, was the most densely peopled. A good quarter of the total population lived in the four coastal counties between Humber and Thames. Norfolk and Suffolk were the most populous with an average of between forty and fifty people to the square mile, rising to over eighty on the Norfolk coast to the north of Yarmouth. In the south midlands lay another tract of favoured country: the three adjacent counties of Oxfordshire, Berkshire, and Wiltshire each had an average of more than thirty people to the square mile; and about half the English counties had between twenty and thirty. But the inclement northern parts, so far as we have any satisfactory

knowledge of them, had barely more than five. This dearth of people arose in part from the geography of the north, but much of it was the consequence of the terrible and deliberate devasta/tion by the Conqueror in 1069–70, above all in Yorkshire where the vales at least must have been fairly thickly colonized and settled in late Saxon times.

Even by 1066 the English landscape was, in many regions, a palimpsest, as it were, of human activity. The Scandinavian settlement between the ninth and eleventh centuries had in part overlain the Old English, though much of it filled in the gaps between the Anglo/Saxon patches. The Old English settle/ment had in places overlain the Romano/British; the Romano/British layer covered, to some extent, the landscape created by prehistoric farmers back to the bronze age. The palimpsest was still patchy, but there were some parts of England where one could have uncovered layers extending backwards for ten or twenty centuries.

Villages had made their appearance in the bronze age. They became more numerous in the iron age, and by Romano/British times were dotted fairly thickly over the chalk and lime/stone uplands of southern England. They may also have ex/isted in the lowlands, but if so, centuries of later cultivation have obliterated them here, and it is only on the downlands, where they were given over to sheep/pastures at an early date, that their farms and fields may be recognized. Besides the native villages of Roman Britain there were possibly a thousand country/houses (villas), each surrounded by a cultivated estate extending in all probability to several hundred acres. Most of these villas perished in the disturbances of the fourth century and their estates were abandoned to nature once more. But their fields, tended for so many generations, must have been clear enough to the first Saxon settlers a hundred years later, and would have been taken over at once, however weed/grown and submerged in scrub, in preference to the still untouched natural woodland that lay around. The close proximity of Romano/British villa sites to so many English villages today is surely not accidental. Not a few Old English villages were established

within a few hundred yards of the derelict walls of a Romano-British country-house, and the nucleus of their open fields laid out upon the reclaimed ploughland of the villa estate. That the remains of some Roman buildings were still clearly visible in the countryside as late as the tenth century is shown by a Saxon charter relating to (Water) Eaton in Oxfordshire, in which a *faga flora* ('tesselated pavement') is referred to as a landmark. The village of Fawler in Oxfordshire, which is not recorded as a name until the early thirteenth century, derived its name from a similar origin, and a tesselated pavement was discovered here in the year 1865. It yet remains to be proved that any English village has had a continuous existence since Romano-British times, but the evidence in certain places is at least suggestive.

The Saxon farmers, entering a new country, were not geologists, but they were, from a long practical experience, sensitive to the lie of the land and to the varying qualities of soils, and they knew where to halt their march and build their first huts. Doubtless they made mistakes in choosing some of their sites. Villages which appear to be static or decaying when we read of them in medieval records represent some of these ill-chosen sites, and others may well have disappeared without record before the Norman Conquest, and lie buried and unknown, awaiting accidental discovery by deep ploughing, as at Butley in Suffolk.[1] But in the main the colonists chose well: a dry subsoil for building, a steady supply of water from wells or springs or an adjacent stream, and easily workable loams for their arable farming. On such sites in the eastern lowlands of England they planted their first villages. Most of the earliest villages lay east of a line joining the upper Trent with Southampton Water: they are particularly numerous in East Anglia and Essex, and on the coastal plain of Kent and Sussex. They are numerous also in Oxfordshire, along the upper Thames and its tributaries, a region that had been much favoured in earlier centuries by the owners of villas and by humbler Romano-British farmers.[2]

[1] *Proc. Suffolk Inst. Arch.* xxv (1950-2), pp. 207-8.
[2] See Map X (*b*) in Collingwood and Myres, *Roman Britain and the English Settlements*, 2nd ed. (1937), and the Ordnance Survey *Map of Roman Britain*.

By the eleventh century villages were spread unevenly all over England. The Old English had founded most of them in the course of time, but from the late ninth century onwards the Scandinavian settlers, following up a successful conquest, had partitioned a good deal of northern and eastern England and had established some hundreds of villages of their own. In some districts, like the Wreake valley in east Leicestershire, nearly every village bears a Danish name for some miles on either side of the valley. Lincolnshire was even more heavily influenced by Scandinavia. Here we find some hundreds of Danish place-names, of which those ending in -by and -thorpe are the most easily recognizable. In the north-west of England, in the Lake District, and along the Lancashire coast, it was the Norwegians, coming across from Ireland and the Isle of Man in the tenth century, who first settled this mostly in-hospitable country. Their *thwaites*, or clearings, give us one of the most distinctive place-name elements in this part of England.

It is likely that the settlements of the Old English, for some generations after the Conquest, invariably took the form of more or less compact villages, both for reasons of security and for the co-operative clearance of woodland on a large scale with very limited equipment. The margin between life and death from starvation was narrow: land had to be cleared quickly if the new village was to survive. The shortage of plough-teams also required a co-operative agriculture after the ground had been won. Even in such a predominantly arable county as Oxfordshire there was only one plough-team to every two-and-a-half rural households in 1086, and in Norfolk there were nearly five rural households to every team. Where, therefore, arable farming was important, the development of open fields, cultivated in common and subject to communal rules, was an economic necessity. No other method of cultivation was possible in an economy which suffered so gravely from a short-age of capital equipment.

We still know very little of the plan of the early villages. The suggestions thrown out by Maitland in *Domesday Book and*

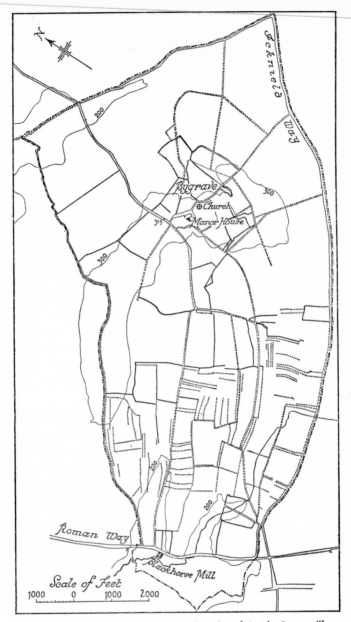

FIG. I. Bygrave (Hertfordshire), a small nucleated Anglo-Saxon village
which survived intact in the midst of its open fields until the twentieth
century. The village, grouped around the church and manor-house, was
planted on the highest ground in the parish, where water was also
available. Every farmstead lies in the village, none in the fields. The
territory of the village extended to about 1,800 acres

Beyond have not been followed up, and the study of village plans has advanced hardly a step since he wrote at the close of the nineteenth century. It seems likely that there were at least two distinct types from the beginning, the street-village and the village grouped around a large green or a 'square'. We hear in a life of St. Cuthbert of a fire in a seventh-century village, the houses of which seem to have been aligned along a single east–west street. On the other hand, the Devonshire villages grouped around a large open square, with the church at the end or to one side, seem too to represent an aboriginal type, and to be similar in origin and antiquity to the 'green-villages' of north-eastern England. These fundamental types could probably arise in later centuries also; and there may be other plans of which we are at present ignorant, such as the rather formless village, still roughly nucleated but with its houses scattered about in no discoverable relationship to each other or to any centre. Such a formless type may be the result of medieval (or later) 'squatting' on the waste. Whatever the shape of the village, in the open-field parishes all the farmsteads were gathered together in its lanes and streets; and the village lay as near the centre of its territory as possible, so as to minimize the distances to be traversed between the widely scattered strips belonging to each farm (Fig. 1).

The open fields that stretched away from the medieval village towards the horizon have been described so often that it is hardly necessary to dwell upon their layout again. The map of the Nottinghamshire parish of Laxton (made in 1635), of which a small portion is reproduced in Fig. 2, shows the complex pattern of arable strips or selions, their grouping into blocks or furlongs (the *culturae* of the medieval documents), and the broad green common balks that ran here and there through the fields to form a system of occupation roads. Beside the streams lay the village meadows, and round the edge of the parish (for the most part) lay the common pastures. The direction and size of the arable strips was determined by the slope of the ground and the nature of the soil. Only a small proportion reached the 'standard' size of one acre: most were between a quarter and half an acre in size. It was a more complex pattern

Fig. 2. The lay-out of a Midland open-field parish; Laxton (Nottinghamshire) as it was in 1635. The map shows only a small part of the parish—the West Field and Westwood Common

than is often thought, and open-field farming, too, was more flexible and varied than we are inclined to imagine.

In the midlands, the classic home of open-field farming, where it lasted longest and therefore struck the deepest roots, the open fields generally numbered either two or three, though by Tudor times there was a tendency for their number to increase by subdivision. Each field extended to several hundred hedge-less acres, and was often separated from its fellows by an earthen bank which can still sometimes be identified. Similarly, in many places we can still trace, in the ridge-and-furrow of the modern pastures, the very ridges of the Saxon and medieval strips cast up long ago by the action of the plough (see Pl. 1). Not all open-field strips were ridged in this way (it all de-pended on the type of plough in use in the region), and not all ridge-and-furrow is the result of medieval strip-ploughing. How much of it reflects the fossilized medieval landscape we do not yet know, but that a good deal of it does so in the mid-lands is quite certain.

The Old English and the Scandinavian settlers established their open fields wherever they founded villages, whether it was in Cornwall or Kent or Lancashire, or anywhere between.[1] But well before the Norman Conquest it is evident that pioneers had also begun to establish isolated farmsteads away from any village. These single farmsteads were probably the result of woodland clearance by individual peasant house-holds. Their little fields lay in severalty from the beginning, hacked out of the waste yard by yard, acre by acre, and en-closed with high hedgebanks to keep out the animals of the adjacent forest. We find such isolated farmsteads recorded in the later Anglo-Saxon charters, and they occur in considerable numbers in Domesday Book. Queen Hoo Hall, remote among the tangled lanes of Hertfordshire, is recorded in a charter of *c.* 1060 as *Quenildehaga*: it is 'the *haga* (hedge) or enclosure of a

---

[1] Gray, in *English Field Systems* (1915), considered that the open-field system, in its commonly understood form, was confined to the northern and southern mid-lands. Detailed regional studies since that date have shown, however, that open fields existed in medieval Cornwall, Devon, Kent, and Essex, and there is good evidence from Lancashire also.

PLATE I

Great Stretton, an abandoned village-site in Leicestershire, showing the rectangular enclosures of the medieval farmsteads and the pattern of ridge-and-furrow which represents the arable farming of the old open fields

PLATE 2

A frontier-farm in upper Swaledale (Yorkshire), probably on a medieval site but rebuilt at a later date. The sycamore tree is a characteristic later addition to the scene

woman named Cwēnhild'; and many of the small *worthys* of western Devon have the same origin in the work of a single peasant household. It is possible that the hamlet type of settlement, consisting of two or three houses clustered together, is the result of additional farmsteads being built by the sons or kinsmen of the original founder upon the ancestral site. There was more than enough land for all in the surrounding waste, and there would be a natural tendency to keep the homesteads together however far away the clearances went on.

In 1066 much of England was still a natural wilderness, though there was vastly more waste in some parts than others. Such land as had been brought into use presented two different faces. One typical landscape was that of a nucleated village lying in the centre of its territory, with large unenclosed expanses of land all around it, in which the holdings of individual peasants lay dispersed in single strips and across which ran unfenced and unmade tracks from the village outwards in all directions. The other landscape was that of farmsteads and hamlets, dispersed in the woodland clearings or on the coastal marshes in eastern England, with small fields cultivated outside any communal organization. The former landscape was to be found most widely in the midlands and eastern England; the latter most commonly in the west and north. But there were few counties where one would not have found both landscapes to a greater or a less degree, as, for example, in Hertfordshire, or Berkshire, or Warwickshire.

2. *The Woodland and Forest*

It is impossible to say how much of the English landscape remained under its natural woodland, fen and marsh, moorland and heath, in 1086, for the measurements given in Domesday Book do not lend themselves to exact interpretation; but when we reflect that even at the end of the seventeenth century Gregory King reckoned more than one-quarter of England and Wales to be 'heaths, moors, mountains, and barren land' (probably an overestimate) we should be safe in assuming that a half of

England was 'waste' in the eleventh century, and that of this enormous area some millions of acres were potentially valuable land. There were far too few people in the country to develop its natural resources to the full. England was still at an early colonial stage of development, and was to remain so, indeed, until the end of the sixteenth century.

It is easy to dismiss generations of human effort in an abstract phrase, to say that the twelfth century was the most formative century (as it was) in the making of the English landscape; but behind this abstraction there lies a daily, blinding sweat, blood at times, and backbreaking toil with axe and spade and saw. It was a slow world, a hand-made world, created yard by yard, at times almost inch by inch, by the labour of countless human beings out of the primordial chaos of timber, rock, and water. Such a hand-made world reveals itself in a characteristic pattern on the map (Fig. 3). It was a world without power other than that of human muscles and of draught animals. Only the water-mill existed to lighten the burden of hard labour, and that could not help with the labour of colonization.

The process of colonization went on slowly all the time. Possibly the Norman Conquest halted it for a few seasons while men wondered what was going to happen next in their remote farms and villages, but the work did not pause for long. Reading between the lines of Domesday Book, we see the conquest of forest and marsh, and of the sea, going on actively very soon after the political conquest. As the twelfth century passed the reclamation of new land—the clearing of the woods, the draining of marsh and fen, the walling-off of the sea, the breaking-up of the lower moorlands and the walling of the higher for pasture—acquired an immense impetus. In this endless struggle with Nature the conquest of the woodlands was the most important single element. Old villages enlarged their open fields continually by co-operative felling, clearing, and ploughing around the woodland edges, pushing slowly outwards towards the still-distant frontiers of their territory (Pl. 2). New villages were still being founded in some of the more dis

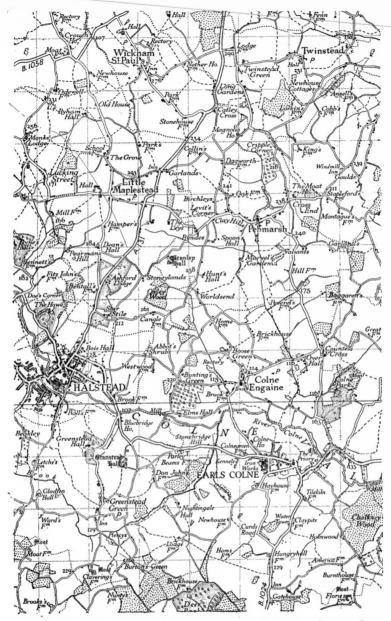

FIG. 3. The characteristic landscape of medieval colonization: direct enclosure from primeval woodland in North Essex. This type of country is characterized by a network of winding lanes, scores of scattered farmsteads, and frequent hamlets with names that betray their woodland origin

tant clearings. Of Eardisley, in western Herefordshire, we are told in Domesday Book that it pays no geld, renders no customary payment or service, does not belong to any hundred. 'It lies in the middle of a forest and there is one house.' It was 'Aegheard's clearing', which must have come into existence since the Conquest. Within a hundred years, or a little more, it had developed into a parish, and had acquired a church of its own to serve the farmsteads that were now dotted over its four to five thousand acres on the old red sandstone.

The heavy labour of forestclearance was carried out mostly by free tenants, with the licence of the lord of the manor to whom the 'waste' belonged. We find such men at work all over Devon, for example, and in Warwickshire the Arden woodlands to the north of the Avon were being opened up by free peasants at the same period, with the encouragement of their lords. By the closing years of the thirteenth century about onehalf the manorial tenants in the Arden country were free tenants, most of whom had originated in this colonization movement of the immediately preceding generations. On the Essex manor of Woodham Ferrers there had been a great wood at the time of Domesday. An Elizabethan survey shows less than sixty acres left. Nearly threequarters of the manorial tenants at this date were freeholders, and the manor consisted mostly of small enclosed fields and crofts. Woodham Ferrers had been enclosed direct from the forest and waste, without the introduction of open field, by the ancestors of the Elizabethan freeholders.[1] One would find a similar picture in all those parts of England where much woodland remained at the time of Domesday.

The disafforestation of some of the numerous royal forests and warrens at the close of the twelfth century and the beginning of the thirteenth gave a renewed impetus to the colonizing movement. The royal forests and warrens were not necessarily wooded or waste land. They were large tracts of country set aside for royal hunting and subject to special and severe laws

[1] 'Survey of the Manor of Woodham Ferrers, 1582', in *Trans. Essex Arch. Soc.* xxiv (1951), pp. 6–16.

against trespass and poaching. The Norman kings had extended such forest laws to much of the country (possibly a
third of the whole), beginning with the New Forest created by
William I before 1086. Considerable parts of many counties,
like Cornwall and Devon, Essex, Northampton, and others,
were placed under forest law in the twelfth century. Much
land already cleared was thereby made difficult to cultivate.
Only three counties (Norfolk, Suffolk, and Kent) are known
to have contained no land subject to forest law. On the other
hand, the whole of Essex may have been subject to it.

The royal forests reached their greatest extent under Henry II
and thereafter diminished gradually in extent as Richard and
John sold their rights in order to relieve their finances. The
whole of Cornwall and Devon (except Dartmoor) was disafforested in 1204 in return for large sums of ready cash. In
1227 the men of Middlesex were granted

that the warren of *Staines* shall be no more a warren and shall be disafforested, so that all men may cultivate their lands and assart their woods
therein, nor shall any warrener, forester, or justice interfere therein for any
woods, lands, vert, venison, or cultivation, or summon any man before them,
but all men there shall be free of all things pertaining to the said warren.[1]

In 1228 all the land between the Severn and the top of Cotswold was similarly disafforested, and in 1230 the forest of
Kesteven in Lincolnshire. Much royal forest still remained—
the forest of Rossendale in Lancashire remained as such until
1507, and not until then could it be effectively opened up and
settled—but great tracts of England had been freed by the middle of the thirteenth century, with a consequent stimulus to
settlement and cultivation.

The direct reclamation of land from the primeval woods
produced a landscape that is at once recognizable on the
modern Ordnance Survey map: a landscape of narrow, winding lanes, indicative of a yard-by-yard approach through difficult country, of scattered farms with names embodying those of
medieval owners or occupiers, of hamlets like little knots in the
pattern, named 'End' or 'Green' or 'Street', and of smallish

[1] *Calendar of Charter Rolls*, i, p. 56.

fields of irregular shape (Fig. 3). And if we walked over the ground itself we should see massive earthen hedgebanks crowned by big timber. It is a purely medieval landscape, and one can find more or less substantial pieces of it in nearly every English county. Much of south-western England is such a landscape, most of the Welsh border country also. We find it very markedly even in the midlands and in the south-east of England. The Kent and Sussex Weald is above all a landscape of medieval colonization, and so is most of Hertfordshire except the chalk uplands in the north. The deep Hertfordshire country between Sawbridgeworth and Much Hadham is formed in this way. In the Wheathampstead country, which is of the same type, we know that the abbot of Westminster, to whom the manor belonged, was dividing it up in the thirteenth century into what we should call roughly one-hundred-acre farms.

3. *Marshland and Fen*

Besides the attack on the woodlands, there was both small- and large-scale drainage of marshland and fen. Something had already been done long before by the Romans, notably in Romney Marsh. In a charter of Offa (772) relating to land at Bexhill, we already read of 'the old marsh ditch' on the Pevensey Levels. This may be a piece of early Saxon drainage, but is more likely, perhaps, to be Roman. By the middle of the tenth century the Saxon abbots of Glastonbury had begun the reclamation of their vast marshland endowment in mid-Somerset. According to the persistent tradition of the abbey, a certain bridge in the marshes at Baltonsborough, five miles away, had been built in Abbot Dunstan's time, and a certain ditch, possibly his work, named after him. Thurstan, the first Norman abbot of Glastonbury, seems to have brought in what we should call a drainage engineer (he is called *Girard Fossarius* in Domesday Book), who held the manor of Greinton and other property under the abbot and seems to have been responsible for the large-scale reclamation of moor and marsh of which we see indirect evidence. Under his eye the great

PLATE 3

Rich grazing land near Glastonbury (Somerset), reclaimed by Glastonbury abbey from waste and marsh at some period between the tenth century and the thirteenth

coastal manor of Brent Marsh had more than trebled in value within a few years before 1086. Such a spectacular rise in value could only be the result of the construction of a sea-bank along the Bristol Channel coast, or at least of the substantial repair of an earlier work which had fallen into decay. Several inland manors more than doubled in value in the same years. They are all in the Levels, and must have been the scene of much em-banking and ditching, The wild, wet moors were turned into valuable marshes for grazing, and later some of them grew fine crops of corn (Pl. 3).

Throughout the twelfth and thirteenth centuries the abbey lands down in the Levels were being embanked, ditched, and drained, and little fields were being created whose boundaries were not earthen hedgebanks, as in former woodland, but winding ditches lined with willow trees. Most of the 160,000 acres of the Somerset Levels belonged to ecclesiastical land-lords in medieval times—to the see of Wells, and to the abbeys of Glastonbury, Muchelney, and Athelney—and in the records of all of them we can read of large-scale transformation of the wet moors by ditching and draining, and the deliberate planting of osiers. Much draining was done in later centuries down to the nineteenth, but we can usually recognize the work of the medieval landlords in the narrow, winding ditches, especially those near the sites of the monastic houses, in contrast to the broad, straight drains of later periods. Around the isolated hill of Brent Knoll, near the Somerset coast, the pattern of fine blue winding lines is very evident on the 2½-inch map, the pattern of medieval drainage. In the Kent and Sussex marshes we hear of the same organized reclamation by the great ecclesi-astical landlords from the twelfth century down to the eve of the Dissolution; and the cartularies of the Lincolnshire monas-teries are full of references to land newly won from the sea or the fen in this period.

Nor were the wealthy ecclesiastical corporations the only agents by which marsh and fen were rescued from the water. We find lay magnates like the earl of Chester enclosing and draining the West Fen in southern Lincolnshire in the first

quarter of the thirteenth century; and the remarkable terrier of Fleet shows us the same ceaseless activity in the country to the south of the Wash on land belonging to the family of de Multone. In all the inland marshes and along the coastal and estuary tidal flats we find free peasants, too, carrying out their own small-scale schemes. Such were the curious family of Sokespitch, on their marshland farm between Exeter and the sea, who made it so fertile that they dwelt there undisturbed from the twelfth century down to the nineteenth.

In the coastal marshes of Lincolnshire the individual pea-sant did much to rescue farmland from the sea. The Lincoln-shire marshland in the twelfth century was full of free peasants (descendants, very largely, of the Danish settlers of pre-Con-quest times) who lived not in the inland villages founded by their forefathers but in dispersed farmsteads within sight of the sea, surrounded by small enclosures of arable, meadow, and salt-marsh. The same pressure of a rising population, and perhaps of a rising standard of living, which had driven the young Warwickshire peasant out into the woods of Arden to make a new home and win new land for himself, also drove the young Lincolnshire peasant down from the Wolds and the clay vales to the North Sea marshes, to fashion there the landscape that Tennyson saw long afterwards:

> Stretch'd wide and wild the waste enormous marsh,
> Where from the frequent bridge,
> Like emblems of infinity
> The trenchéd waters run from sky to sky.

Many of the smaller banks and ditches that we see in the Lin-colnshire marshland must be the work of these early medieval peasant households, but the sea-banks that separate the villages around the Wash from the tidal waters—most notably the so-called Roman Bank—are the result of large-scale co-operative effort by whole villages or whole hundreds, much of it in pre-Conquest times. The line of these ancient sea-dikes is often marked today by a minor road, raised several feet above the surrounding fields, and running with many abrupt bends a mile or two back from the present shore-line (Fig. 4).

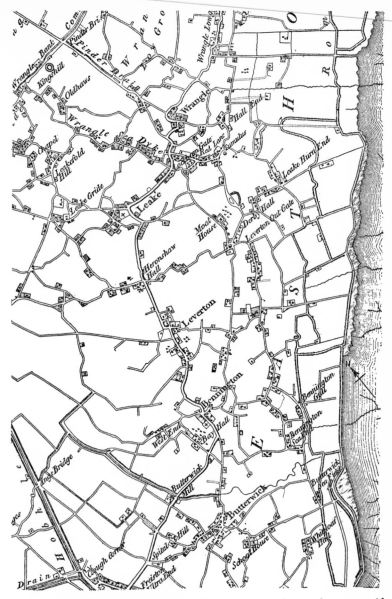

FIG. 4. The landscape of reclamation from coastal marshes on the western side of the Wash. Some of this reclamation is of pre-Conquest date, but much more was accomplished in the twelfth and thirteenth centuries

4. The Moorlands

The high moorlands called for another method of attack. Neither timber nor standing water were the enemies, but an inclement climate, a thin infertile soil, and in some parts great blocks of stone strewn about the surface. Such were the granite moorlands of south-western England. These had been abandoned by farmers since the late iron age, probably as a result of climatic changes. By late Saxon times, settlers were again nibbling along the more sheltered edges: on the western side of Dartmoor cattle farms had crept up in places to 900 feet above the sea (as at Willsworthy), and on the drier eastern side sheep-farms (called Shapleigh today) up to 1,100 or 1,200 feet. By the closing years of the thirteenth century the sheltered slopes of the inner moor had been colonized again after a break of some fifteen centuries, and we find thirty-five 'ancient tenements' named in the records of medieval Dartmoor. Some of the original peasant farmsteads of this period, built of natural blocks of moorstone, as the surface granite was called, survive in a ruined state—at Yardworthy, Challacombe, and Cholwich Town, for example—and are among the very few early medieval farmsteads left to us. They are probably thirteenth or early fourteenth century in date (Pl. 4). These remote Dartmoor farms were mostly pastoral, but some oats and peas were grown, the ground having been prepared for cultivation by a process known locally as 'beating'. The surface was cleared of its granite blocks, which went to build field-walls, farmsteads, and gateways, and the thick, leathery turf was skimmed off with a spade, stacked up, and burnt slowly until it was reduced to a fine ash. This was then thrown back on to the pared ground and dug well in, so lightening the subsoil and fertilizing it at the same time, and the ground was then ready for three or four successive grain-crops before reverting to rough pasture once more.

Only at the edges or in sheltered valleys, however, could the high moors be broken up like this. The open stretches on the higher levels were mostly used for rough grazing, and in

PLATE 4

Cholwick Town (Devon), a frontier-farm below the edge of Dartmoor, first settled about 1200–25. The farmstead shown here dates from about 1500, but in the farmyard below the house (not visible here) stand the remains of the first peasant-dwelling on the site. The word 'town' is used here in its original Old English sense of 'homestead'

the twelfth and thirteenth centuries townships on either side of these windy uplands were coming into conflict on the summits over pasture rights. The solitary home of the curlew had been invaded by quarrelsome man and made the subject of property rights. In 1279 the tenants of Fountains abbey in Yorkshire on the Kilnsey moors, and those of Salley abbey on the Arncliffe and Litton moors, accused each other of trespassing with their cattle on the other's ground. The grangers at Stainforth on the one side of the moor, and at Kilnsey on the other, were ordered to mark the boundary with great stones, and to mark the stones with bold crosses. Near by, on the Malham moors, we read of walls in several places, erected by Fountains, or Bolton abbey, or Salley about this time. Some of those dark gritstone walls that undulate across these upland wastes, or the silvery Craven limestone walls, both very characteristic elements in the west Yorkshire landscape today, go back, then, to these monastic disputes of the thirteenth century; and it is in this way that the boundaries of the Dales parishes were finally determined.

5. *The Monastic Contribution*

The monastic contribution to the making of the English land-scape was considerable, from Cornwall up to Northumber-land. Well before the Norman Conquest monks had been clearing the woodlands (especially in the Severn valley), drain-ing the marshes and fens (above all on the fenland estates of Peterborough, Ely, and Ramsey), and founding new towns at their gates (as at St. Albans). And after the Conquest their activity in all these fields is even more evident. New monas-teries were established in the wilds of the north, for example at Furness (1127) in the far north of Lancashire. Most important were the Cistercians, whose rule required that they should be remote from the habitations of man and that they should till the soil themselves. After a start at Waverley in Surrey (1118), they resettled the devastated dales of Yorkshire and brought them back to life. Rievaulx, Jervaulx, Byland, and Kirkstall were all founded in the beautiful and empty valleys of the

Yorkshire rivers; and the abbey of St. Mary of Fountains began as a collection of huts beneath an elm tree in Skeldale.

In more settled parts of England, as in Lincolnshire, where the Old English and Scandinavian villages were clustered so thick on the ground that barely a mile of fields separated them, the Cistercian houses were obliged to make an artificial wilder-ness for themselves. At the southern end of the Lincolnshire Wolds the foundation of Revesby abbey in 1142 uprooted three villages—Revesby itself, *Toresbi*, and *Scithesbi*. Revesby survives, possibly a resettlement on a new site, but Toresbi and Scithesbi seem to have disappeared at once and their very sites have been lost. In Warwickshire, Upper Smite was swept away by the foundation of Combe abbey in 1150, and Dishley in Leicestershire was probably wiped out by the Cistercian house of Garendon. Villages became monastic granges, and in many places—especially on the limestone uplands—their open arable fields were converted into wide sheep-pastures. One may often detect these sites on the Ordnance map today in the word 'Grange' standing alone in an empty white space on an otherwise crowded map.[1] Thus the wilderness was restored to use, but it was a different kind of landscape.

Most of the Cistercian foundations were, however, made in wild or waste districts, nominally the property of an overlord but economically undeveloped. The monks were therefore inserted, as it were, into the countryside without dislocation or disturbance of any kind; they proceeded to reduce the wilderness to cultivation and to live upon their labour. When they had developed the land within the immediate neighbour-hood of the monastery, granges were constructed or adapted on more distant parts of the property, and the abbey became the centre of a wider economic unit, such as we can see by glimpses in working order at Rievaulx under Ailred. These granges multiplied rapidly. Meaux, founded only in 1151, had seven granges already by c. 1170, and Wardon twelve by 1190, and neither of these was an abnormally large house; Furness came gradually to be the nerve-centre of a far-flung system of exploitation.[2]

Many of these granges were cultivated as arable farms for the

---

[1] It was the extensive enclosed fields of Dishley grange that gave Robert Bakewell a suitable milieu for his revolutionary experiments in stock-breeding in the second half of the eighteenth century.

[2] Knowles, *The Monastic Order in England*, pp. 349–50.

sustenance of the abbey, but it was probably the extensive sheep-walks of the pastoral granges that made the most marked impression upon the medieval landscape, above all in York-shire, Lincolnshire, and Wales. The importance of the mon-asteries as sheep-farmers is revealed by the fact that in 1193-4 the whole of the wool of the Cistercians and Premonstraten-sians for that year was taken as a contribution towards the ransom of Richard I.

Sheep-farming on a considerable scale was, however, no-thing new even when the Cistercian monasteries were being founded. Ely abbey had 13,400 sheep on its estates at the time of Domesday, and the coastal marshes of Essex carried heavy flocks of sheep at the same date, mostly the property of lay land-lords. Nor can there be any doubt that the famous sheep-walks of the Cotswold uplands, and to a lesser extent of the adjoining limestone country of north Oxfordshire, were grazed by many thousands of sheep in Saxon times. Both Shipton-under-Wychwood and Shipston-on-Stour are recorded in eighth-century charters, and several other Shiptons ('sheep village') are recorded in the same area by the eleventh century. Indeed, the existence of a considerable fulling establishment at the Roman villa of Chedworth, near Cirencester, takes Cotswold sheep-farming back to the third or fourth century. Doubtless it was somewhat more localized at that date, and was extended during Saxon times with the clearance of the original wood-land cover and the foundation of monastic houses in the region. But from late Saxon times at least the Cotswolds must have looked much the same as they did before 1939 when the sheep-walks could still be seen. The chalk downlands of Wiltshire are probably of similar antiquity as sheep-pastures, though Domesday Book is uninformative on the subject and we get no clear picture until the early thirteenth century. In 1225 the village of South Damerham and its hamlet of Martin, on the south Wiltshire Downs, pastured well over four thousand sheep between them; and at Dinton and Teffont, not far away, there were more than fifteen hundred. We also observe that though many of the sheep belonged to important

monastic houses like Glastonbury and Shaftesbury, the great majority belonged to the peasantry.[1] Thus, though the development of the medieval sheep-pastures owed much to the monastic houses, to great ecclesiastics like the bishop of Winchester, and to lay magnates like the dukes of Lancaster with their ranch-like farms in the Peak District, the sheep of the English peasantry may well have appeared first on the scene and were, in sum total, often more numerous even in the great sheep-raising regions.

The colonization of the English landscape reached its climax, so far as the medieval period is concerned, round about the year 1300, though it did not cease even then. One sees the visible expression of this climax, in various ways, in the thousands of medieval churches that have come down to us. Many parish churches had been built in Saxon and early Norman times, especially in eastern England, but it was in the twelfth century and the early thirteenth that the majority were built for the first time, above all in the west and north. Here they set the seal upon many generations of toil, providing a physical as well as a spiritual centre for the new communities that had come into existence in hamlets and farmsteads scattered over thousands of acres of new land. And at the same time the fine network of parish boundaries was completed, except for odd corners here and there, until the multitudinous towns of the Industrial Revolution came into being and created new communities. The demarcation of parish boundaries had certainly begun in pre-Conquest times, but it took several centuries to complete the process.

The little church of rubble masonry from the local quarry, built in the two generations after 1150, was the symbol of the birth of a new community in the woods or along the moorland edge. Many of these original Norman buildings come down to us more or less intact, such as Fingest, a parish carved out of the Buckinghamshire woods, and first recorded in the year 1163. In hundreds of others only the font, a blocked doorway or window or a fragment of walling remains as evidence of the twelfth-

[1] Eileen Power, *The Medieval English Wool Trade*, pp. 30–31.

century church destroyed in a later rebuilding. In the long-settled east of England, and most of all where the deep rich soils of the marshland and the fens had been rescued from the water, the original small churches were pulled down to make way for something much more splendid. One contrasts the emptiness of the scenery of the Lincolnshire fens in the late eleventh cen-tury with the tremendous constellation of Decorated Gothic churches in the same region only two or three centuries later—Heckington, Ewerby, Swaton, and Sleaford. Or one thinks of the wealth of the Northamptonshire soils, especially on the oolitic limestone, as reflected in Warmington, and of the Oxfordshire ironstone symbolized in the glory of Bloxham.

6. The Changing Landscape, 1066–1348

The Black Death, which broke out in the late summer of 1348, brought all this great activity to a standstill for many years, and slowed down the work of colonization for generations. It is therefore a convenient point at which to pause and assess the changes that had taken place in the 280 years since the Norman Conquest.

Scores of new villages had been founded in the woodland country, but more important than this was the great expansion of the open fields around the villages that had already been established at the time of the Conquest. Here the growth of population, and of a higher standard of living, had probably brought into use all the available land of the parish. The open-field villages had reached their frontiers by the closing years of the thirteenth century. This does not mean that they had cleared and ploughed up all their 'waste', for the 'waste'—yielding as it did common pasture for animals and firing for villagers—was an essential part of the peasant economy, and it was necessary to strike a balance between the claims of arable, pasture, and woodland. As it was, too much woodland was destroyed over most of England in the urge to win new agri-cultural land, and by the sixteenth century a serious timber famine developed.

Besides the new villages, and the expansion of the old, many hamlets and isolated farmsteads had also come into existence since 1066. Some of these hamlets developed their own miniature open-field systems, but in the main they, like the dispersed farmsteads, created a landscape of small, hedged fields, cultivated independently from the beginning. In some parts of England, notably perhaps in the south-west and the south-east, the extent of country so cultivated seems to have led indirectly to the early extinction of such open fields as once existed. The open fields that had stretched around the ancient Saxon villages of Essex, Kent, and Devon, for example, had nearly all disappeared by the middle of the sixteenth century. In Devon it is known that they were being enclosed during the thirteenth century and the early fourteenth, and the same would probably be true of other counties where, in Tudor times, the arable is described as wholly enclosed.

Already, then, by the eve of the Black Death, open fields in some regions were giving way to a landscape of hedged enclosures. Some of these closes were of considerable size, perhaps thirty or forty acres, and probably represent the hedging around of a complete block of demesne land, an old *cultura* in the open fields. Others are minute, strip-like enclosures, so narrow at times (as in the Exe valley north of Exeter) that the roots of trees growing in the opposite hedgebanks meet underground; and these probably represent the hedging around by peasants of single arable strips. These little enclosures differ from the small fields enclosed directly from ancient woodland in having straight hedges and in being narrow and rectangular in shape.

There were far more buildings in the English countryside by 1348. Over the country as a whole the population had risen from under 1½ million to about 3½ million. Norfolk and Suffolk now had more than a hundred people to the square mile; and the belt of dense population stretched westwards through the Norfolk marshland into the fens of Lincolnshire, and thence back over the stone belt of Rutland and Northamptonshire to the claylands of Leicestershire and southwards to include Bed-

fordshire. The whole of this rich agricultural region had on an average rather more than a hundred people to the square mile in 1348. In general, a line joining Flamborough Head on the Yorkshire coast with the head of the Severn estuary divided the populous half of England from the less populous. East of this line the population numbered everywhere more than fifty to the square mile, except in Hampshire, Surrey, and Sussex, where the great tracts of sandy heath and woodland reduced the average. Still, the coastal plain of Sussex must have been one of the most densely peopled regions of England. The least populated counties were those of the extreme north, except the East Riding, which had filled up remarkably since the devastations that had followed the Conquest. Northumberland, Cumberland, and Westmorland prob-ably had fewer than thirty people to the square mile in 1348, and Lancashire and the West and North Ridings of Yorkshire hardly more.[1] The east of England was still the richest in all respects in the first half of the fourteenth century, not only in its farmlands but also in its towns. Of the twenty-five most highly assessed towns in the tax assessment of 1334, no fewer than sixteen lay in the eastern lowlands, the other nine being distributed fairly equally between the midlands, the west, and the south.[2]

Not only were there far more houses in the English country-side but there were more mills, castles, and churches also. There were some six thousand water-mills in England at the time of Domesday, and many more had come into exis-tence since then. We do not know how many there may have been by the early fourteenth century, but can only judge from the number of manors where mills appear in the later medieval

[1] No information is available for the counties of Durham and Cheshire, but they would certainly have fitted into this general picture of the north. The belt of thinly peopled country extended southwards to include Shropshire and Staffordshire.

[2] Public Record Office, Exchequer K.R., E. 164/7. For this purpose, New-castle (4th) and York (3rd) are counted as in the eastern lowlands. The southern towns are Salisbury, Winchester, and Southampton; the western towns Bristol, Gloucester, and Exeter; and the midland towns Oxford, Shrewsbury, and Coventry.

extents and inquisitions and not in 1086. Since the thirteenth century, too, the fulling-mill had become a fairly common sight along the streams, more so in some parts than others. By the fourteenth century, several hundred windmills were at work all over England, more commonly in the east and south, for the many swift streams of the west and north made the water-mill more practicable. Like so much else, the windmill made its appearance in the twelfth century. We hear of two almost simultaneously in the last decade of the century—at Tandridge in Surrey in the time of Richard I, and at Bury St. Edmunds, where Herbert, the dean, erected a windmill in 1191, only to have it destroyed by the orders of Abbot Samson, who feared the competition with his own water-mills. We also hear of a windmill in Sussex during the time of Bishop Seffrid II of Chichester (1180–1204).

As to the churches, they were not only much more numerous but also more conspicuous in the landscape. Over a good deal of England the original churches had been rebuilt on a grander scale with the advancing prosperity of the thirteenth century. On the stone belt that crosses the country from south-west to north-east, where settlement had been early and medieval pros-perity consequently greater, the parish churches were very largely rebuilt between about 1150 and 1250, many of them with fine spires, another element in the English scene.[1] On the claylands to the east and west of the stone country, the great period of rebuilding—from south Yorkshire down to War-wickshire, if no farther—had been between about 1280 and 1330, so that whereas the Early English is the glory of North-amptonshire and Rutland, it is the Decorated style that gives the most beautiful village churches to Leicestershire or Not-tinghamshire or south Lincolnshire. The amount of money employed in the rebuilding of churches was remarkable. In the small county of Rutland there cannot have been more than six to nine thousand people all told during the chief building period of 1150–1250. Yet this population, about that of an

[1] The earliest spires appear in the first years of the thirteenth century in North-amptonshire.

average country-town today, erected no fewer than fifty-two parish churches, some of them (like Ketton) superb, and most of them handsome. Rutland had a church to every two thou- sand acres of land, one to every forty or fifty households. Every mile or so in eastern England one would have seen spires and towers rising from the fields, and fields populous with men, women, and children tending the strips. From many midland fields the peasant could have looked up from his work and seen half a dozen spires around the horizon, and by climbing his own church tower he could have counted fifteen to twenty.

England was not everywhere as crowded as this. Lincoln- shire had 620 medieval churches; but Derbyshire, one of the poorer counties, had only 109. Allowing for the difference in size between the two counties, Derbyshire had only half as many churches and villages as Lincolnshire. The paucity of churches in the uplands of Derbyshire and Staffordshire is brought out in a conversation in Part II of *The compleat Angler*, which was published in 1676:

Viator: What have we here, a church? As I'm an honest man, a very pretty church! Have you churches in this country, sir?
Piscator: You see we have: but had you seen none, why should you make that doubt, sir?
Viator: Why, if you will not be angry, I'll tell you; I thought myself a stage or two beyond Christendom.

There were, too, many more towns, main roads, and bridges. The twelfth century, and the thirteenth, had seen 'the fever of borough creation', when the lords of rural manors all over the country had optimistically speculated upon founding market- towns upon their lands, so enhancing their incomes from urban rents, market tolls, and the revenues of fairs. And the creation of hundreds of little market-towns, each serving a radius of three to five miles, perhaps up to ten miles in the remoter parts, brought into existence, or perhaps we should say solidified, a great number of main roads for the first time, and led to the erection of many bridges all over the country.

7. *Decay and Retreat, 1348–1485*

The tremendous loss of life occasioned by successive outbreaks of the Black Death left its mark upon the face of the country. According to one estimate, the population of England had fallen to about 2,200,000 by 1377, a fall of some forty per cent. in a single generation.[1] The first impact of the pestilence had been even heavier: in many places a half to three-quarters of the population had died, in a few there was a total extermination. The north Oxfordshire parish of Steeple Barton is typical of many in these years. Round about the year 1300 it had rebuilt its church in a large and handsome way, as befitted a flourishing community; and an extent of the manor, made a few years before the Black Death, enumerated sixty tenants. Another extent made in 1349–50 reveals the first effects of the pestilence. The water-mill—that king-post of the peasant economy—was in ruins and worth nothing. Thirty-two of the thirty-six customary tenants were dead, and over six hundred acres of their land lay uncultivated. Cottagers' rents had dropped from fifty-four shillings a year to 6s. 9d., and the perquisites of the manor court had fallen from forty shillings a year to forty pence. Three years later the manor-house itself was 'worth nothing', the dove-house ruinous, and nearly twelve hundred acres lay uncultivated for lack of tenants. The village seems never to have recovered from this blow. Today only the vicarage, a farmhouse, and two cottages remain near the church; the lines of the old streets can be traced in the fields immediately around; and one picks up broken medieval pottery in the hedge, but nothing of later date than the early fourteenth century. After 1349–50 silence fell upon the place, and the survivors moved to another site a mile away. Life returned eventually, and the fields were cultivated once more; but the old village had gone for ever.

Many hundreds of villages disappeared in the course of the next two centuries. Few were wiped out at one dramatic stroke, though this seems to have happened occasionally. Of the tiny parish of Middle Carlton in Lindsey it was reported in 1398

[1] Russell, *British Medieval Population*, pp. 246, 263.

that there had been no parishioners for forty years. Tilgarsley, near Eynsham in Oxfordshire, had been a sizeable place in the late thirteenth century: on the Hundred Rolls of 1279 fifty-two tenants' names are listed. But in 1359 the tax-collector was obliged to report that no one had lived there for the past nine years, and today its very site is unknown. At Shoby, in the north Leicestershire Wolds, the parish was united with its neighbour in 1395, the reason given for the union being the decrease of population through pestilence and the consequent diminution in the value of the benefice.

Here and there, then, a village disappeared entirely from the map. Sometimes it was refounded on a new site (perhaps at one of its hamlets) either from fear of infection among the debris or because of the difficulty of grappling with a half-ruined village swarming with rats. But in a great number of places there was no wholesale abandonment, only a slow and deepening decay extending over two or three generations, so that the majority of lost villages disappeared in the course of the fifteenth century and the early sixteenth. Altogether more than thirteen hundred deserted village-sites are now known in England. Of these, some had disappeared before the Black Death, such as those wiped out in the making of the New Forest[1] or in the making of the Cistercian granges. Others have disappeared in more recent times, as in the making of an eighteenth-century park around a country-house. But the great majority of these deserted villages—perhaps a thousand in all— were abandoned during the two centuries after 1350, most of them in the first half of this period. These sites are most numerous on the eastern side of England. There are sixty lost villages in Leicestershire, nearly a hundred in Warwickshire, nearly eighty in Northamptonshire. In the East Riding of Yorkshire there are ninety-nine sites, in Norfolk about one hundred and thirty.

The visible changes in the landscape were the complete dis-

---

[1] F. Baring, 'The Making of the New Forest', *E.H.R.* xvi (1901), pp. 427–38. Some of the New Forest villages were refounded later, but ten remained completely lost.

appearance of a great number of villages and the falling into ruin of their churches (Pl. 5), the shrinking of a great number of other villages to a fraction of their former size, the abandon/ ment of cultivation on the marginal lands that had been re/ claimed from the waste in the 'land/hunger' of the thirteenth century and the conversion of a great deal of arable land to sheep and cattle pastures for want of sufficient labour to keep it under tillage.

The retreat from the marginal lands is most apparent on the Lincolnshire Wolds, and above all on the sandy heaths of Nor/ folk. One finds clear evidence of it in north Norfolk, where tiny thirteenth/century churches were built by the pioneers of the twelfth and thirteenth centuries, and abandoned before the middle ages were over. Around Colkirk, to the south of Fakenham, lie no fewer than four ruined churches.[1] On the breckland of south/west Norfolk and its margins there was a similar retreat: here, as many as twenty/eight villages—mostly small—were deserted, nearly all before 1450. Santon—'the *tun* on sandy soil' in Domesday Book—is a good example of an abandoned village in this area, though its ruined church was rebuilt in 1628. In the Colkirk district, Pudding Norton is the most revealing, with a ruined church and a well/marked cause/ way running between the mounds and banks where the village/ houses formerly stood.[2] Some English villages and hamlets had a life of only two or three centuries. Asterleigh in Oxfordshire was 'the eastern clearing' on the edge of Wychwood, first settled during the twelfth century. It acquired a church and became a separate parish, but as early as 1316 we find it united with its neighbour Kiddington, and by 1466 it had been com/ pletely abandoned.

The four generations or so after 1350 were not entirely a time of retreat and decay. The decline in agriculture and trade, that affected the midlands above all, had no counterpart in Devon,

[1] J. Saltmarsh, 'Plague and Economic Decline in the later Middle Ages', Cam/ bridge Hist. Jnl. (1941).

[2] I take my Norfolk information by permission from K. J. Allison, 'The Lost Villages of Norfolk' (University of Leeds dissertation, 1952).

PLATE 5

The remains of the old parish church of Pickworth (Rutland). The village, which had nearly a hundred taxpayers in 1377, was probably abandoned in the late fifteenth century

where a great number of parish churches were rebuilt or sub-
stantially enlarged, and where many squires and franklins rebuilt their houses in a new style and stone bridges replaced the
timber bridges of the thirteenth century all over the county.
There was, similarly, a good deal of church building going on
in Suffolk all through the fifteenth century. Nor did the work of
colonization entirely cease. In the woodlands of Buckinghamshire and Hertfordshire, fifteenth-century assarts are common,
though on nothing like the scale of the twelfth and thirteenth-
century colonization movement; and we find large-scale re-
clamations of marshland continuing in south-west and eastern
Kent under the priors of Canterbury. Prior Thomas Goldston
I (1449–68) spent twelve hundred pounds on the 'inning' of
Appledore Marsh, and Prior William Petham (1471–2) a
further three hundred pounds on reclaiming six hundred acres.
New lands and new farms were still coming into existence (but
no new villages), and new churches were being built, in many
parts of the country; but generally speaking it was a time of
abandoned villages, falling population, contracting cultivation, and of conversion of arable to pasture. Much of the depopulation of arable villages for sheep- and cattle-pastures
that was so vehemently complained of in Tudor sermons and
pamphlets occurred in fact during the fifteenth century, a
good deal of it before 1450, and a good deal of it forced upon
both lay and monastic landlords by the shortage of labour for
arable farming and a general shortage of tenants for their lands
(Pl. 1). The emergence of these extensive closes of pasture
was the most conspicuous change in the English landscape
during the fifteenth century. It had begun before the end of
the fourteenth, for when a Leicestershire squire was proceeded
against in 1545 for depopulating four arable farms on his
estate and converting them to pasture, his son was able to
prove that this had been done as long ago as the autumn of
1378 and was no doubt a belated consequence of the Black
Death.

8. *The Early Tudor Landscape*

It is sometimes said that in 1485 the English countryside still resembled a sort of archipelago 'with innumerable islands of cultivation set in a sea of "waste" '. It would be truer to regard it rather as already a sea of cultivation lapping around islands of 'waste', some of them still large—like Dartmoor and Exmoor in the south-west or the Lincolnshire heath in the east—and some of them small, a mere half-dozen miles across, like the ancient rocky landscape of Charnwood in Leicestershire. There were still moorlands, dense woods, and marshes, and many thousands of fenland acres awaiting a Vermuyden generations ahead; but a very large area of wilderness had been reclaimed and transformed since the Norman Conquest and there was little 'waste' left in many counties. Such natural cover-ing as remained in these parts was an essential element in the village economy: indeed, there was not enough of it in a great number of places in the highly-cultivated midlands. All this was especially true of England south of the Trent; north of it the moorlands still stretched unbroken for a hundred miles, though all but their highest summits were criss-crossed with the dry stone-walling of the sheep-pastures.

The woodlands were still extensive in places: the forest of Arden was a reality to Shakespeare, and the forests of Dean, Epping, Sherwood, and the rest were still recognizable forests. But they were thinner than of old, and the age of the timber famine was only just ahead. The English had been felling their timber as recklessly as the Americans in the nineteenth century. By Leland's time the iron-workers of Sussex were eating rapid-ly into the woods of the Weald, those of Dean into the forest around them, and they were to be found also in the woods of the Black Country, around Sheffield, and in the Clee hills of Shropshire.[1] Over considerable tracts of England, wood was already so scarce and dear that the peasantry were burning

---

[1] By the closing years of the century the rate of destruction in the woods was enormous: one Durham man was said in 1629 to have felled more than thirty thousand oaks in his lifetime (Nef, *The Rise of the British Coal Industry*, i, p. 194).

dried cow-dung (as in Leicestershire and the Isle of Portland), bean-haulms, and furze.

The population of England had been rising slowly during the fifteenth century, but there were still fewer than three million people in 1500, well below the numbers of the early fourteenth century. Not until the end of the sixteenth century was the plague level reached again. The demand for land was still sluggish among tenants: only after the middle of the century do the symptoms of land-hunger begin to manifest themselves once more. There was little new colonization therefore: only in the forest of Rossendale, disafforested in 1507, do we find any such activity, and even there it is not conspicuous until the second half of the century.[1]

There were three sheep to every human being in the England of Leland's time. No wonder the opponents of enclosure could say that sheep ate up men. 'Sheep have become so great de-vourers and so wild', wrote Sir Thomas More, 'that they eat up and swallow down the very men themselves. They consume, destroy, and devour whole fields, houses, and cities.' Most of the depopulation of villages in the past had been gradual and the result of natural processes; but by the closing years of the fifteenth century some landlords were hastening the processes of extinction and change, and evicting their tenants from their arable farms in order to create large pasture-closes. At Stretton Baskerville, on the borders of Warwickshire and Leicestershire, Henry Smith in 1494 evicted eighty persons from a dozen farmsteads and some cottages. They 'were constrained to depart thence and live miserably'. The parish church crumbled, and cattle sheltered inside its broken walls. Other inquisitions taken before Wolsey's commissioners in 1517 tell us over and over again that the inhabitants of midland villages had departed in tears from their homes.

Other changes were visible in the landscape, some of them as melancholy to men of sensibility as the destruction of the open-field villages. The monastic houses were dissolved be-tween 1536 and 1539. Their lead roofs and stone walls were

---

[1] Tupling, *The Economic History of Rossendale*, esp. chaps. ii and iii.

too valuable to leave, and after a few years became shattered, bird-haunted ruins standing in silent glades. In some places a wealthy layman, purchaser of the site from the Crown, built himself a country-house with the old materials or trans-formed part of the monastic buildings into a mansion, like Sir John Thynne who built the first house at Longleat in Wiltshire some time between 1540 and 1567, or the Beau-mont who transformed Gracedieu nunnery in Leicestershire into a country-house about the same time.

There were more ruins to be seen in early Tudor England than at any time for centuries: monastic houses, medieval castles, chantry chapels, town walls, all were crumbling or 'clean fallen', as Leland would have said. These were the visible signs of the passing of an age, of medieval civilization; and the new civilization had yet to be born. Compton Wyn-yates, Thornbury, Hengrave, and other large houses were being built during the first half of the century; but the splendours of Burghley and Hardwick, Holdenby, Kirby and Wollaton, and of their timbered parks, had yet to be seen. Much secular build-ing was going on in the English countryside, but it was nothing like the exuberant flowering that was to come in the last quarter of the century, a flowering that extended down to the village houses themselves. For it was in the two generations between about 1570 and 1640 that rural England was almost entirely rebuilt and almost the last traces of medieval peasant habita-tions were obliterated. In the history of the English land-scape the years before Elizabeth I formed a kind of meditative pause: a great age of secular building lay ahead; the transforma-tion of the northern and the midland scene by mining and manufacturing industry was so far visible only in scratches on the surface; the towns were still half-medieval inside their broken walls. Here and there new landlords were transforming the landscape, but this—though a disaster to those on the spot— did not amount to much in the whole picture. Even in the midlands, where these changes were most frequent, in most parishes the immemorial open-fields still stretched far and wide to the horizon.

WORKS FOR REFERENCE

ALLISON, K. J. 'The Lost Villages of Norfolk' (unpublished dissertation, University of Leeds, 1952).

BARGER, E. 'The Present Position of Studies in English Field Systems', *Eng. Hist. Rev.*, liii (1938).

BAZELEY, M. L. 'The Extent of the Royal Forest in the Thirteenth Century', *Trans. Roy. Hist. Soc.* 4th ser. iv (1921).

BERESFORD, M. W. 'Ridge and Furrow and the Open Fields', *Econ. Hist. Rev.* 2nd ser. i (1948); 'The Deserted Villages of Warwickshire', *Trans. Birmingham Arch. Soc.* 66 (1950); 'The Lost Villages of Yorkshire', *Yorkshire Arch. Jnl*, Parts 148, 149, 150 (1951–3); *The Lost Villages of England* (1954).

CONZEN, M. R. G. 'Modern Settlement (of North-East England)', *Scient. Survey of North-Eastern England* (1949).

CRAWFORD, O. G. S. *Archaeology in the Field* (1953).

DARBY, H. C. *The Medieval Fenland* (1940); 'Domesday Woodland', *Econ. Hist. Rev.* 2nd ser. iii (1950); *The Domesday Geography of Eastern England* (1952).

GRAY, H. L. *English Field Systems* (1915).

HELM, P. J. 'The Somerset Levels in the Middle Ages, 1086–1539', *Journal Brit. Arch. Assoc.* 3rd ser. xii (1949).

HILTON, R. H. *Social Structure of Rural Warwickshire in the Middle Ages* (Dugdale Soc., Occ. Papers no. 9, 1950).

HOSKINS, W. G. *Essays in Leicestershire History* (1950); (and H. P. R. FINBERG) *Devonshire Studies* (1952); *The Making of the English Landscape* (1955).

KERRIDGE, E. 'Ridge and Furrow and Agrarian History', *Econ. Hist. Rev.* 2nd ser. iv (1951).

MESSENT, C. J. W. *The Ruined Churches of Norfolk* (1931).

NEILSON, N. *A Terrier of Fleet* (British Academy, Records of Social and Econ. History, iv. 1920).

NIGHTINGALE, M. 'Open Field Agriculture in Kent' (unpublished Oxford thesis, B.Litt. 1952).

ORWIN, C. S. and C. S. *The Open Fields* (1938).

PAGE, W. 'The Origins and Forms of Hertfordshire Towns and Villages', *Archaeologia*, lxix (1917–18).

PEAKE, H., *The English Village* (1922).

POWER, E. *The Medieval English Wool Trade* (1941).

RAISTRICK, A. *The Story of the Pennine Walls* (2nd ed., 1952).

SALZMAN, L. F. 'The Inning of the Pevensey Levels', *Sussex Arch. Collections*, liii (1910).

SMITH, R. A. L. 'Marsh Embankment and Sea Defence in Medieval Kent', *Econ. Hist. Rev.* x, no. 1 (1939–40); *Canterbury Cathedral Priory* (1943).

THORPE, H. 'The Green-Villages of County Durham', *Inst. Brit. Geographers* (1951).

TUPLING G. H. *The Economic History of Rossendale* (1927).

II. DOMESTIC ARCHITECTURE AND TOWN-PLANNING

1. *Halls and Manor-Houses*

IN the middle ages it was only the king, the Church, and the aristocracy who could habitually afford to build in stone, and consequently it is their halls and manor-houses which are the chief surviving examples of medieval domestic architecture today. Over eight hundred houses with recognizable medieval features are listed in Turner and Parker's great work on *The Domestic Architecture of the Middle Ages*, and in many cases their architectural history has been the subject of careful investigation by archaeologists and local historians. The main developments in the history of the English manor-house between the twelfth and fifteenth centuries are therefore well established. Moreover, in a small country such as England, with a ruling aristocracy closely united by family ties and common political loyalties, changes in architectural taste spread rapidly from one part of the kingdom to another, and the castles and manor-houses of the great follow a uniform evolution which corresponds closely to the parallel development of ecclesiastical architecture. Regional variations there are, but whether it is built of Northamptonshire stone, East Anglian brick, or west midland timber framing, it is generally possible to date a medieval manor-house within twenty or thirty years in a way which is hardly possible in the case of humbler dwellings.

Whatever its size or period, the 'invariable, and indeed, the only essential feature of the English medieval house' was (as the late Sir Alfred Clapham pointed out) the great hall. It was the centre alike of the royal palace and of the manor-house, the nucleus round which the lesser buildings were grouped. Its origins go back to Anglo-Saxon times, and although no pre-

Conquest example survives, documents suggest a time when the terms 'house' and 'hall' were virtually synonymous, and the whole round of daily life took place beneath its ample roof. But as early as the eighth century references are found to small, detached buildings known as 'bowers', which contained the domestic offices and served as bedrooms for the lord and his family. There might also be a private chapel, such as the one at Deerhurst in Gloucestershire which was built by Earl Odda not long before the Conquest, and in the eleventh century the possession of a private church and a belfry was regarded as one of the attributes of thegnly rank. So was the ownership of a *burh-geat*, or defensible gateway, for the whole site was often surrounded by an earthwork and palisade, and was then known as a *burh*, or fortified residence. All the buildings within it were generally, though not invariably, built of wood, and the Anglo-Saxon hall is usually supposed to have 'closely re-sembled in form and structure the great aisled barns which have carried on the old tradition without a break almost to the pre-sent day'.[1] From *Beowulf* we learn of the shining ornaments which decorated the roof of a royal hall of the heroic age, and of the 'gold-inwoven tapestries' which hung from its walls on special occasions; while Bede, in a famous passage of his *Ecclesi-astical History* (Bk. II, cap. xiii), tells us of the central hearth by which it was warmed. But for knowledge of its plan and structure we are at present dependent on the enigmatic testi-mony of a single aerial photograph,[2] and it is only when the literary evidence has been supplemented by archaeological in-vestigation that we shall have any clear idea of the great halls in which Anglo-Saxon kings held their councils and drank their mead.

. Of the halls of earls and thegns we know even less; but they must have been a not uncommon feature of the Anglo-Saxon countryside, for in Domesday Book the existence of a lord's

[1] A. W. Clapham, 'The Origin of the Domestic Hall', in *Some Famous Build-ings and their Story*, p. 69.

[2] Of the *villa regalis* at Yeavering in Northumberland, reproduced in D. Knowles and J. K. St. Joseph, *Monastic Sites from the Air* (1952), pl. 126.

house is regarded as one of the essential features of a manorial estate, and it was here that the 'hall-moot' met to do justice and to declare the custom of the manor. In villages where the lordship was divided there must often have been more than one hall—just as there was sometimes more than one church—and even quite humble men might possess their own *aula*. In Normanton-on-Trent, for instance, in the time of King Edward, there were five thegns, each of whom had his hall, though their combined estates were worth no more than ten shillings.

By the time of King William, earls and thegns had given way to Norman barons and knights, but the hall and the manor remained. It is well known that the Normans brought about a revolution in English military architecture, but how far domestic architecture was affected by the Conquest is uncertain. It is generally agreed that in the twelfth century English manor-houses conformed to one of two prevailing types—the aisled hall, which resembled the nave of a church, and the 'first-floor' hall, which was raised on a basement. The former presumably derived from Anglo-Saxon timber building, while the latter has sometimes been regarded as a specifically Norman innovation. But there is evidence that the 'first-floor' hall was not unknown in pre-Conquest England, and Harold's hall at Bosham is depicted as such in the Bayeux Tapestry. It had its counterpart in the monastic frater, or refectory, which was almost invariably raised on a vaulted undercroft, just as the aisled hall had its parallel in the infirmary halls of the religious houses, as at Canterbury and Ely. But until more is known of the Anglo-Saxon hall from archaeological investigation it would be unwise to seek a monastic origin for either the aisled hall or the 'first-floor' hall. There must have been halls in England long before there were regularly planned monasteries, and it would have been remarkable if in the course of five hundred years the Anglo-Saxon builder had not devised more than one type of house. It may, however, be observed that the 'first-floor' hall is a type unsuited to wooden construction, and that it probably became common only when stone came into general use for domestic building in the

twelfth century. The greatly increased use of masonry after the Conquest was undoubtedly connected with the importation of Norman methods of building, and to this extent the 'first-floor' hall may be regarded as characteristic of Norman rather than of Anglo-Saxon England.

Excellent examples of the 'first-floor' plan survive at Boothby Pagnell in Lincolnshire (Fig. 5), at the house in Cambridge

FIG. 5. Boothby Pagnell, Lincolnshire: the twelfth-century manor-house.

known as 'The School of Pythagoras', and within the castles of Richmond and Christchurch. The entrance was usually placed in one of the side walls at the lower end of the hall, and had to be approached by an external staircase. At the other end there might be a second doorway leading, as at Boothby Pag-nell, to a 'solar', or private chamber for the lord and his lady. The windows were generally placed high up, perhaps in order to carry the draughts from unglazed windows over the heads of those sitting at table, and there may have been a partition at the lower end to shelter the body of the hall from draughts when the entrance-doors were opened. The cellar was presumably used for storage, and the kitchen must have been in a separate building. The first-floor plan had its advantages: it was free

from damp, and the storage/space must have been useful. But it was apt to be cramped, and it must always have been ex/ pensive to build. Though it survived into the thirteenth century (e.g. at Little Wenham in Suffolk), and was not unknown even in the later middle ages, its obvious incon/ venience led to its gradual abandonment in favour of the 'ground/floor' hall, with or without aisles.

The earliest examples of the aisled hall of which we have specific evidence date from the twelfth century. Until 1928 there stood at Stansfield in Suffolk a barn which, originally the hall of a manor/house, retained its timber columns with the scalloped capitals characteristic of the mid/twelfth century. At Leicester (on the site of the castle), and at Hereford (in the bishop's palace), aisled timber halls of the same sort actually survive, though in both cases much disguised by later altera/ tions: and a fine example in stone still exists at Oakham in Rutland (Fig. 6). These are the only survivors of what must have been a large class of twelfth/century aisled halls, but the plans of several others of later date are given in Fig. 7. Aisled halls such as these were generally buildings of some size, and were seldom found save in houses of considerable importance such as royal and episcopal palaces or the residences of tenants/in/chief. For the lesser man an unaisled hall usually sufficed, and as roofing methods improved it became possible even for royal halls to be spanned without the aid of columns. The most famous example of all is the great hammer/beam roof with which Richard II covered Westminster Hall, dis/ pensing with the posts or arcades which had supported the original roof built by William II.

By the later middle ages the aisled hall was therefore a rarity, and the normal hall was a building of the type made familiar by the college halls of Oxford and Cambridge. At one end was the dais, at the other the two lateral doorways which gave access to the body of the hall through the 'screens passage'. The latter was formed by a stout wooden screen pierced by one or two openings, and usually handsomely ornamented by mouldings and traceried panels. In Lancashire and Cheshire, where

FIG. 6. Oakham Hall, Rutland.

timber halls were usual throughout the middle ages, two of the main trusses were sometimes built out into the hall in such a way as to form the two end sections of a screen, while the centre was occupied when required by a movable wooden barrier (Fig. 8). It has been suggested that this arrangement may possibly be a survival from the earlier type of aisled hall, the

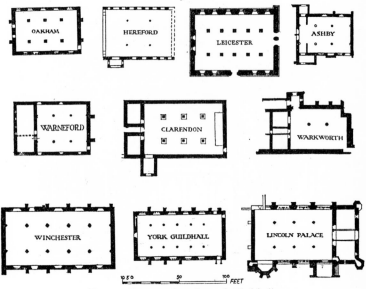

FIG. 7. Comparative plans of aisled halls.

aisle posts being retained only in the case of the truss dividing the 'screens passage' from the body of the hall.

In the centre of the hall was the hearth, and above it was an aperture in the roof covered by a louvre with openings through which the smoke escaped into the open air without admitting the rain. These arrangements can still be seen at Penshurst in Kent, and elsewhere blackened beams and traces of a vanished louvre are evidence of their former existence. But even in the twelfth century wall-fireplaces with flues were a not uncommon alternative to the open hearth, and in 'first-floor' halls they were the normal rule. They became common in halls of all types in the fifteenth and sixteenth centuries, and thereafter it was only

in the Inns of Court and the colleges of Oxford and Cam⁄
bridge that the open hearth survived. The mantels and chim⁄
ney⁄breasts of the new stone fireplaces provided excellent
opportunities for carving and painting, especially of a heraldic
character, while externally their chimneys added a new feature

FIG. 8. Baguley Hall, Cheshire: interior of a timber⁄framed hall.

to English domestic architecture of which full advantage was
taken, from the tall cylinders of the twelfth century (Fig. 9) to
the elaborately moulded brickwork of the sixteenth.

In the end wall of the hall, behind the screen, one or more
doorways gave access to the buttery, pantry, and kitchen. The
commonest arrangement was for a central doorway to lead to
the kitchen by way of a passage flanked by the buttery and
pantry (Fig. 7). In the largest houses the kitchen sometimes
took the form of a detached building with a lofty pyramidal
roof containing louvres through which the smoke and fumes of
cooking were dispersed. A fine example of the fifteenth century

survives at Stanton Harcourt in Oxfordshire, and the recent excavation of the great kitchen at Clarendon Palace in Wilt-shire shows that the type goes back at least to the twelfth century. At Glastonbury it is reproduced in stone, and when the kitchen formed the lower part of a two-storied building it was often vaulted in stone for securi-ty against fire. But kitchens were sometimes of very slight con-struction, and, on royal manors at least, temporary buildings were often erected as occasion required. In 1232 the royal kit-chen at Oxford was blown down by a strong wind, and in many manor-houses of the twelfth and thirteenth centuries cooking must have been done in timber buildings with stone hearths and plaster chimneys of the type referred to in the London Building Assize of 1212.

FIG. 9. Thame, Oxon: A twelfth-century chimney (now destroyed).

While the lower end of the hall thus gave access to the domestic offices, the upper was traditionally connected with the lord's private apartments. These tended to become more numerous as the desire for privacy increased, and by the fifteenth century a wealthy man might have two or three private chambers where his Norman ancestor had had only one. This was convenient when, as not infrequently happened, a manor-house was physically divided between two or three co-heirs, or when a widow claimed as her dower one-third of the accom-modation in the 'capital messuage' in addition to one-third of the landed estate of her late husband. Thus the dower

assigned in 1330 to Joan, widow of Richard Cifrewas of Clewer, included a chamber with a cellar and a privy, all the cellarage beneath the hall, free access to the kitchen, a 'long house next to the Thames' containing two chambers and two privies, a stable, and 'all the garden called the Eldergardyn'.[1] In 1386, after the death of Sir Nigel Loring of Chalgrave in Bedfordshire, his manor-house was carefully apportioned be-tween his two daughters, one taking the hall and screens, the chapel, and all the chambers to the east of the hall, the other the buttery, pantry, and wine-cellar together with various cham-bers to the west of the hall.[2]

The hangings and other furniture (which included win-dow-glass and fittings which would nowadays be regarded as fixtures) with which great men and ladies adorned their private apartments were frequently carried about with their baggage as they proceeded from one manor to another, but wall-paintings provided a form of permanent decoration, and the king was not the only magnate who had his 'painted chamber'. A par-ticularly fine example, decorated with heraldry and a 'wheel of the five senses', can be seen at Longthorpe in Northampton-shire, and there are traces of a scheme of painted drapery in the solar at Luddesdown Court in Kent. By the fifteenth century wainscoting was beginning to be common, and in the Tudor period the form of panelling known as 'linen-fold' became ubiquitous.

A private chapel in which the lord and his family might hear mass was a common feature of the medieval manor-house, as numerous episcopal licences testify, and the chapels even of small houses were sometimes buildings of considerable archi-tectural distinction (Fig. 10). A characteristic feature of the private chapel, common in the later middle ages, was the division of the west end into two floors, of which the upper communicated with the great chamber and formed a gallery

---

[1] P.R.O., E. 315/36, no. 126. For another example, see *Cal. Inq. post mortem*, vii, p. 145.
[2] *The Court Roll of Chalgrave Manor*, ed. M. K. Dale (Beds. Hist. Rec. Soc.), xxviii (1950), pp. xxxi–xxxii.

used by the master of the house and his family, while the servants worshipped below. For whether or not the hall was of the
'first-floor' type the great chamber was usually at first-floor
level, and access to it was gained by means of a staircase, either
internal or (as at Stokesay Castle, Shropshire) external. Occasionally, as at Fyfield in Berkshire, it was placed over the service

FIG. 10. Horne's Place, Appledore, Kent: a fourteenth-century domestic chapel.

apartments, and in semi-fortified houses such as Stokesay and
Longthorpe it might occupy an upper room in a tower. Often,
as at Luddesdown Court, the solar occupied a cross-wing, thus
creating an L- or T-shaped plan, but in the twelfth and
thirteenth centuries the disposition of the various chambers was
subject to great variation, and even palaces were apt to consist
of a loose assemblage of buildings, separately roofed, independently planned, and added to when required. The internal
corridor (though common in castles) was seldom found in
purely domestic building, and the various apartments which
formed a palace or a large manor-house were linked by pent-
houses or covered ways which have rarely survived to the

present day, though the marks of their roofs can often be seen on the stone walls which remain.

In the course of the fourteenth century, however, the planning of English manor-houses became less incoherent, and in houses such as Markenfield Hall, Yorkshire, or Sutton Courtenay manor house, Berkshire, the various buildings are closely integrated so as to form an architectural composition in which art as well as convenience is apparent. Often the hall and solar occupy one side of a courtyard entered through a gateway. At first the gateway was a detached building joined to the house only by a wall, which might or might not be provided with the parapet-walk and battlements whose erection required a royal licence to 'crenellate'. But as the demand for additional accommodation grew—especially in the houses of great men who 'maintained' large numbers of retainers—the sides of the courtyard tended to be filled by lodgings, stables, and other apartments, thus creating the quadrangular plan which became characteristic of the fifteenth century. The process of accretion by which it was achieved is perfectly illustrated by the history of Haddon Hall in Derbyshire (Fig. 11). In the beginning this was 'probably no more than a tower or small manor-house, with an open courtyard attached and fenced with timber'.[1] In the reign of John a defensive wall was built round this courtyard, which was enlarged so as to include in its south-west corner the chapel of the neighbouring hamlet. Early in the fourteenth century the existing hall was built across the courtyard, dividing it into two. The front court was entered by a gatehouse at its north-west corner, and the inner or upper court was reached through the screens-passage of the hall, to which a porch was added later in the same century. Towards the close of the fifteenth century a suite of first-floor rooms, entered from the great chamber, was built on the south side of the front court, with cellars beneath which enclose part of the original boundary wall. Early in the sixteenth century various lodgings were built on the north and west sides

[1] A. H. Thompson, *The English House* (1936), pp. 18–19, from which the account of Haddon which follows is largely taken.

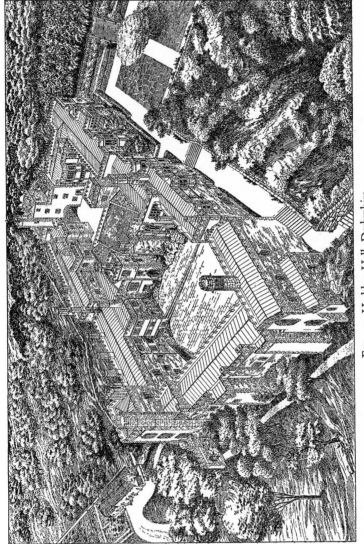

Fig. 11. Haddon Hall, Derbyshire.

of the front court, and the gatehouse was rebuilt. At about the same time a similar range was built along the north side of the base-court, terminating in a second gatehouse whose lower portions may incorporate part of the original twelfth-century tower or house. Finally, in the reign of Elizabeth I, the enclosure of the base-court was completed upon the east side, and the south side was occupied by one of the long galleries so characteristic of the period.

By the fifteenth century the quadrangular plan, which at Haddon had been attained piecemeal by successive additions, was normally adopted from the start when building a house of any size. A good example of the smaller sort is seen at Icomb Place in Gloucestershire, built in the latter part of the fifteenth century by a gentleman of moderate estate (Fig. 12). Here, as elsewhere, the hall has retained its central importance, and the great chamber is lighted by one of the projecting 'oriel' windows which were so popular in the later middle ages. Externally, the gateway is the most striking feature, and, although incapable of serious defence, is buttressed and battlemented in an attempt to emulate the entrance-towers of more pretentious mansions. For in many fifteenth-century houses the gatehouse was given a prominence which, while no doubt reflecting the insecurity of life in a country dominated by 'over-mighty subjects', also bears witness to the national fondness for tower-building which is so evident in the church architecture of the period. This semi-military style of architecture must have appealed to those who had grown rich on the spoils of warfare in France, and there were many soldiers of fortune who, like Lord Stourton of Stourton in Wiltshire, built themselves houses of 'two courtes', whereof one was, as Leland put it, 'high embatelid castelle lyke'. The fifteenth century, in fact, produced a kind of mansion, half house and half castle, which cannot easily be classified as either. Sometimes, as at Tattershall, Buckden, or Ashby-de-la-Zouche, a great keep-like tower dominated the fifteenth-century landscape as the towers of the Norman barons had done three centuries earlier, though its real purpose may have been rather to provide its owner with a

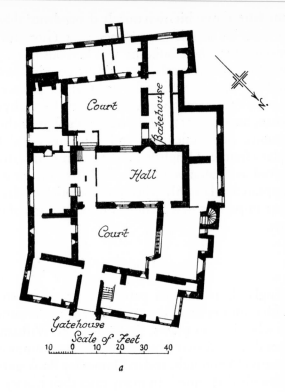

Court

Bakehouse

Hall

Court

Gatehouse
Scale of Feet
10 0 10 20 30 40

a

b

Fɪɢ. 12. Icomb Place, Gloucestershire.

secure retreat from his own unruly dependents[1] than to stand a siege from his enemies: sometimes, as at Thornbury or Hurst-monceux, the whole building was laid out like a fourteenth-century concentric castle, but with large windows and other unmilitary features which showed that the posture of defence was more apparent than real. Thornbury, begun by the duke of Buckingham in 1511, was perhaps the last of these fortified mansions, but battlements and gatehouses had become so regular a feature of English domestic architecture that they long survived as decorative features, and (like the great hall itself) disappeared at last only when the discipline of classical archi-tecture imposed a new formula on the builders of the English house.

2. Town Houses and their Setting

In England, as in other parts of Europe, the eleventh and twelfth centuries brought a great increase in the number of per-sons who lived in towns. By the time of William the Con-queror there were over a hundred urban communities enjoying the status of a borough, and in Domesday Book sixteen of these are described as 'cities'. In many cases their history went back to Roman times: in others to the foundation of a fortified 'burh' by an Anglo-Saxon king. Some were of quite recent founda-tion, having grown up under the protection of a castle or that of a great Benedictine abbey. There was, naturally, considerable variety in their planning: each had an individuality which directly reflected its historical development, and which can, in many cases, still be detected in the layout of its streets today. Contrary to what might be expected, those which were of Roman foundation were not usually those whose streets were straightest or most regularly spaced, for many of them had been almost, if not wholly, depopulated during the Dark Ages. Their public buildings had been allowed to fall into decay, blocking the adjacent streets with debris, round which men

---

[1] As argued by W. D. Simpson, ' "Bastard Feudalism" and the later Castles', *Antiquaries Jnl.* xxvi (1946).

had made new paths which came in time to determine the streets of the medieval town. Even in those cities such as London and Canterbury, where some semblance of civic life may be presumed to have lingered on, the careful work of the Roman surveyors had been almost totally obliterated. Some' times, as at York (Fig. 13) or Chester (Fig. 15), the Roman defences still served in part to define the boundary of the medieval city: sometimes, as at Gloucester (Fig. 14) and Chi' chester, the principal thoroughfares still followed the approxi' mate line of the axial streets of the Roman layout. In many cases it was the Church which, by selecting a former Roman city as a seat for a bishopric, ensured its survival:[1] but it was also the Church whose buildings often provide the most strik' ing instances of the medieval disregard for Roman planning. At York the minster, carefully orientated east and west, lies athwart the centre of the Roman legionary fortress in such a way as utterly to confuse its original layout (Fig. 13); at Lincoln the Norman cathedral stood wholly within the walls of the Roman city, but late in the twelfth century a section of them was taken down by St. Hugh in order to rebuild the choir on a larger scale, and ultimately the ecclesiastical authorities created an irregular walled close which lies partly within and partly without the limits of the Roman *colonia* (Fig. 16). Here, as else' where, the construction of a Norman castle still further ob' scured the Roman plan: 166 houses were pulled down to make way for the great mound with its encircling ditch, and the same ruthless policy entailed the destruction of many houses in York, Norwich, Shrewsbury, Cambridge, Huntingdon, Stamford, and other towns.

While the picturesque irregularity of many medieval city centres can thus be traced to the intrusion of church or castle, a more gradual process of suburban expansion was often lead' ing to unplanned development outside the walls. Already in the reign of Edward the Confessor Lincoln had its flourishing suburb in Wigford, on the other side of the River Witham, and

---

[1] Of the seventeen medieval English bishoprics, ten possessed a cathedral church on the site of a Roman town.

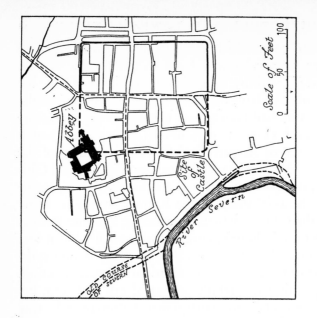

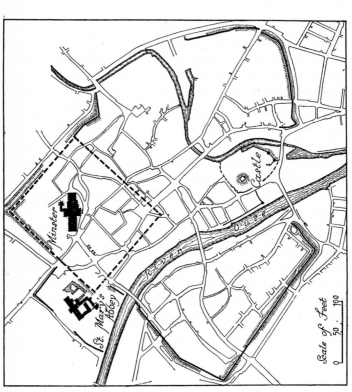

FIG. 13. York.

FIG. 14. Gloucester.

The broken lines indicate Roman walls and streets.

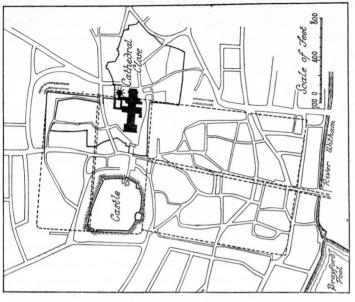

Fig. 16. Lincoln.

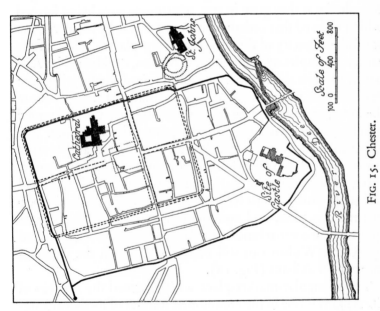

Fig. 15. Chester.

The broken lines indicate Roman walls and streets.

in all the towns which profited from the increase of trade in the eleventh and twelfth centuries there is evidence that new streets were being formed outside the ancient fortifications (as at Gloucester and Chester), or where water circumscribed the original site, on the opposite bank (as at Norwich, Cambridge, and Bristol). Such spontaneous growth was rarely controlled by any considerations other than those imposed by local topography, and often took the form of 'ribbon development' along one or more of the main roads leading to the city gates. In some towns it was the policy of the Norman conquerors to plant a rival French colony alongside the existing Saxon borough, thus creating a new quarter with its own marketplace and church, and adding still further to the existing urban complex. It was the settlement of 125 French burgesses at Norwich which led to the establishment of what later became the Mancroft ward: and at Nottingham the original Saxon borough, occupying less than 40 acres, was duplicated by the building of a French borough between its western boundary and the castle.

While the more ancient English cities were thus increasing in complexity as they grew in size, new towns were being formed which showed that orderly development was by no means beyond the capacity of the medieval townplanner. One of the earliest examples is the town of St. Albans, established by Abbot Wulsin in about 950. It was built round a long, triangular marketplace formed by widening the road on the north side of the abbey precincts. The frontages on this road were divided into lots, which were taken up by prospective burgesses. The abbot assisted by providing building materials, and himself erected three parish churches for the benefit of the townspeople. Here, as elsewhere, the marketplace was occupied by booths and stalls which, at first only temporary, gradually became permanent structures, and eventually houses and shops. But in spite of these encroachments the layout of the town established by Abbot Wulsin can still be traced today in the streets of modern St. Albans (Fig. 18).

The triangular marketplace which formed the nucleus of St. Albans is one of the commonest features of medieval Eng

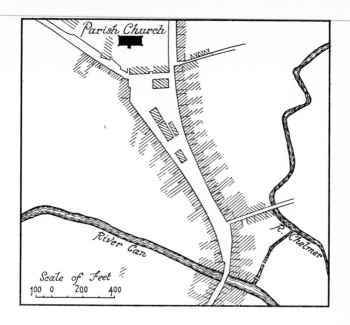

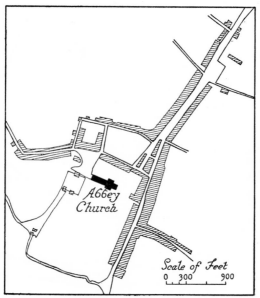

FIGS. 17 and 18. Triangular market-places: Chelmsford (*above*) and St. Albans (*below*).

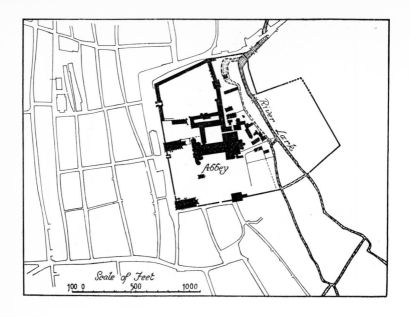

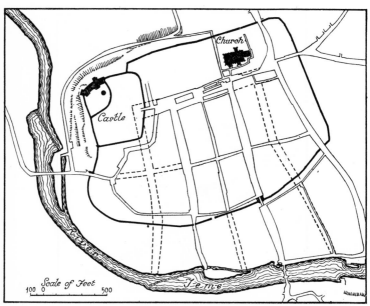

FIGS. 19 and 20. Planned medieval towns: Bury St. Edmunds (*above*) and Ludlow (*below*).

lish town-planning. Another is the chessboard pattern formed by a regular grid of intersecting streets. The earliest French examples date from the second half of the eleventh century, and there is no definite evidence of its occurrence in England before 1066. It was adopted by Abbot Baldwin of Bury St. Edmunds (1065–97) when he enlarged the town of Bury soon after the Norman Conquest (Fig. 19), and the late Sir William St. J. Hope showed that it was followed at Ludlow when that town was laid out at the end of the eleventh century or early in the twelfth by one of the Lacys (Fig. 20). The most striking examples, however, date from the thirteenth century. In 1220 Richard Poore, bishop of Salisbury, tired of living under military surveillance in Old Sarum, laid out a complete new town on his own meadows by the Avon (Fig. 21). Edward I did the same at Winchelsea in 1283 (Fig. 23), and after the conquest of Wales he built a series of fortified towns at Conway, Caernarvon, Flint (Fig. 22), and Beaumaris, which both in purpose and in planning recall the contemporary *bastides* of southern France.

But in spite of the examples of Bury and Salisbury and Winchelsea, regular planning was always exceptional. The twelfth and thirteenth centuries were a great period of town-building in England. Landowners all over the country were seeking to share in the economic prosperity of their time by obtaining a grant of market rights and establishing a trading community on their estates. Sometimes, as at Sherborne (Fig. 24) and Eynsham (Fig. 25), they added a new street or a 'new land' to an existing town or village, offering low rents and other inducements to those who were willing to become their tenants: sometimes, as at Newtown, near Sandleford in Berkshire, or at 'Francheville' near Swainston in the Isle of Wight, they created an entirely new settlement on an uninhabited site. The total number of these urban plantations was considerable, but there are very few in which any sign of deliberate planning can be detected. The reason for this is clear. Town-building was a speculation, and like all speculations it involved the investment of capital. To lay out the site of a new town complete

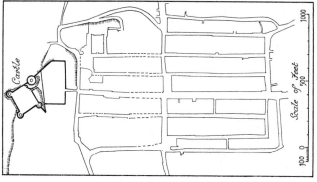

FIG. 22. Flint.

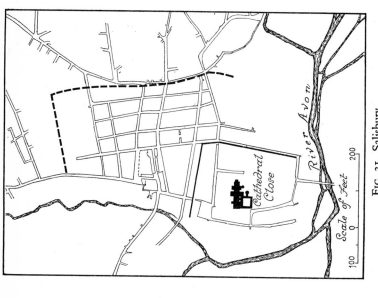

FIG. 21. Salisbury.

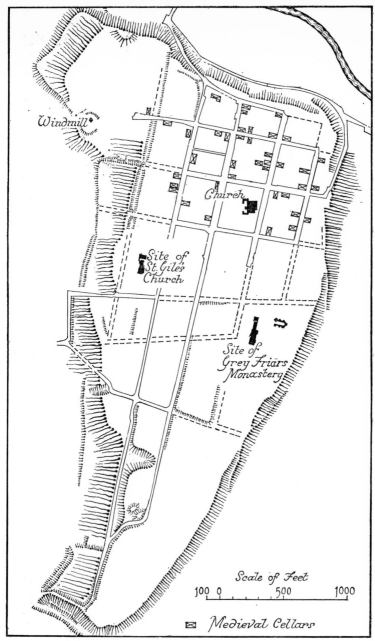

Windmill

Church

Site of
St. Giles
Church

Site of
Grey Friars
Monastery

Scale of Feet
100 0   500   1000

⊠ Medieval Cellars

FIG. 23. Winchelsea, as laid out by King Edward I.

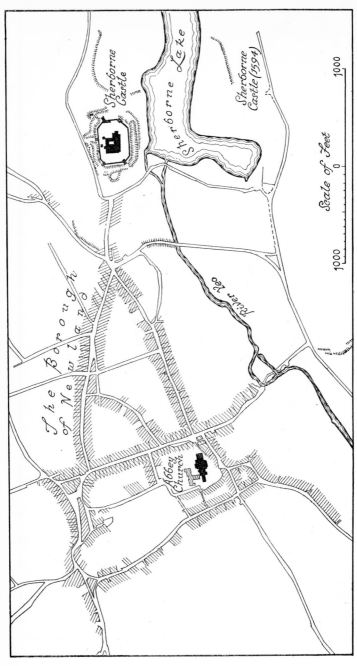

FIG. 24. Sherborne, Dorset, showing the Borough of Newland established by the bishops of Salisbury, whose castle is on the right. The remainder of the town was controlled by the Abbey.

with streets, market-places, churchyards, and house-plots involved the expenditure of more capital—and perhaps more
confidence in the future—than the average landowner possessed. It was only the greatest landowners—kings, bishops, and
abbots—who had the resources to create a planned town and
who were prepared to take the risk of doing so. That there was

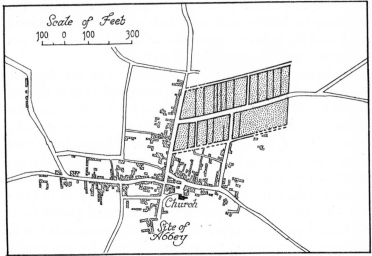

FIG. 25. Eynsham, Oxon, showing the new borough founded by the abbot in
1215.

a risk is shown by the history of Edward I's new town on Poole
Bay, which failed to compete successfully with the town of
Poole founded some forty years earlier by William Longespée,
earl of Salisbury, and is now represented by a solitary farmhouse: and it is significant that those planned towns whose
layout has been best preserved are precisely those whose population was guaranteed from the first—Salisbury, which took
the place of Old Sarum as Winchelsea did of Old Winchelsea, and the Welsh bastides, whose colonization was part of
Edward I's plan for the subjugation of Wales. Even at Winchelsea a number of the plots into which the town was divided
were never built upon, but have remained unoccupied to the

present day. Elsewhere many of these speculative boroughs re-
lapsed to the status of villages or vanished away altogether:
others survived long enough to become the 'rotten boroughs' of
the eighteenth century. It is not surprising, therefore, that those
who founded towns in the twelfth and thirteenth centuries
usually did little more than provide a site, grant a charter, and
leave the rest to private enterprise. In any case it is doubtful
whether they attached great importance to formal planning.
Symmetry for its own sake made little appeal to the medieval
mind, and the military importance of straight streets was not
appreciated until the invention of artillery.

The layout of most medieval English towns can therefore
best be interpreted in terms of local topography rather than of
human foresight, and recurring features such as the triangular
market-place formed by the junction of two converging roads,
if not accidental, were at least so simple as to demand little conscious contrivance on the part of their planners. Even the apparently artificial plan of a town such as Oxford—sometimes
regarded as the earliest example of a rectilinear layout in England—is as likely to have been the result of natural growth from
two roads intersecting approximately at right angles as it is of
deliberate setting out on the ground. 'Given the rectangular
house plot as the unit of settlement and the street as the axis of
expansion, lateral and linear growth will be the natural modes
of expansion, to form a rectangular pattern of streets and
blocks.'[1] Elsewhere—as at Ludlow and Salisbury and Winchelsea—the evidence of planning is undeniable, but it is not
necessary to seek a Roman precedent for the simple pattern of
intersecting streets which appealed so strongly to the medieval
English town-planner. If it commended itself to Richard Poore
and Edward I, it did so for the practical reason that it enabled
their new towns to be divided up into rectangular building plots whose superficial area could easily be calculated.
Market places and churchyards could be created by the simple
expedient of leaving one or more blocks vacant, and the risk of

[1] R. E. Dickinson, 'The Morphology of the Medieval German Town', Geographical Rev. xxxv (1945), p. 76.

fire was minimized by the insulation of the housing-blocks. The largest and most imposing buildings were still—as in older cities—those of the Church, though the friars had taken the place of the monks, and the new towns of the twelfth and thirteenth centuries were rarely as liberally provided with parish churches as the older cities, whose haphazard growth had re-sulted in the parochial anarchy of London, Norwich, or York. In Salisbury there were only three parish churches besides the cathedral; in Flint and Ludlow there was only one. Architec-turally impressive though these great town churches might be, they were rarely sited so as to close vistas or to form the focal point of a formal layout of streets in the way which became common in Europe in the seventeenth century. The greater churches, indeed—those of the collegiate and monastic cor-porations—were often enclosed in a walled precinct which set them apart from the rest of the town. But their towers and spires none the less dominated its architecture, rising visibly above its roofs (Fig. 26), while the sound of their bells reiterated the claims of ecclesiastical authority. Beside those of the Church, the civil buildings of all but the greatest English cities were comparatively insignificant. Their guildhalls rarely equalled the 'hôtels de ville' of northern France and the Netherlands in architectural distinction, and only in Scotland was it usual for the town hall or 'tollbooth' to be provided with a steeple and belfry on the continental model.

Another difference between English and continental towns was the comparative absence of fortifications. As Frederick, duke of Würtemberg, observed in 1592, English towns, 'even when they are walled, are neither fortified nor defensible'.[1] The contrast was probably more striking in the sixteenth century than it had been at an earlier date: nevertheless, the political unity of England from the Conquest onwards made it possible for many towns to dispense with elaborate defences unless they were situated in the marches or on the coast, and comparatively few English towns grew up under the protection of a castle in the way which was common in France and Germany. Some

[1] W. D. Robson-Scott, *German Travellers in England 1400–1800* (1953), p. 57.

F

Fig. 26. Coventry: a medieval city as seen from its fields.

had castles thrust upon them at the Conquest, but many were for long protected by no more than an earthen rampart and ditch. It was not until the end of the thirteenth century that even so prosperous a city as Norwich began to replace its primitive defences by a stone wall broken by towers and gates. In the disturbed conditions of the fourteenth and fifteenth centuries many towns found it expedient to strengthen their defences, but such considerable places as Reading, Derby, Salisbury, and Bedford were never walled, and England probably contained more unwalled market-towns than any other country in Europe.

A part from their cost, walls had the disadvantage of restricting the habitable area of a town or, if suburban building was permitted, of requiring periodical extensions in order to bring the new houses within the fortified *enceinte*. But even among walled towns there are few examples in England of that progressive expansion and consequent rebuilding which was so characteristic a feature of the great continental cities. By the time that most English towns had completed their walls, plague and economic decline had begun to reduce both their population and their trade, and no English city except Bristol can show a history of continuous expansion comparable to that of Cologne or Amsterdam. Most English towns, indeed, still had considerable areas of unoccupied land within their walls, and although there might be crowding at the centre (in London, Bristol, and York houses were even built on the bridges) there were open spaces close at hand, while the walls themselves rose straight from the surrounding fields (Fig. 26). Many of the citizens were, indeed, farmers who spent their lives tilling these same fields, and the sight and smell of cattle and agricultural produce must have been familiar to the inhabitants of every medieval town. Barns and granges were to be found within its walls, and in the smaller towns the 'broad gates' mentioned in surveys of medieval houses were often intended for the reception of farm wagons rather than carriages.

It was, however, the presence of merchants and tradesmen which distinguished a town from a village, and it was their

houses which lined its main streets. Of their appearance and construction before the Norman Conquest very little is at present known. That they were nearly all of wood can be in/ferred from later examples, and from the strictness of Anglo/Saxon laws about the responsibility for fire. At Chester a man in whose house it started was fined four shillings, and had in addition to pay two shillings to his nearest neighbour. That they often stood gable to gable in the streets is implied by a ninth/century Canterbury charter recording the sale of a small plot of land in that city which mentions that by customary law two feet had to be left between houses to allow for 'eavesdrip'. Recent excavations at Thetford have shown that some of the inhabitants of that populous pre/Conquest town lived in huts of an extremely primitive character. Nearly all of them were partly dug out of the sand to a depth of one or two feet, and some of them were surrounded by 'walls' of sand faced with turves. Others had walls formed by posts set upon a wooden sleeper/plate and intertwined with withies like a sheep/hurdle: in others the roof/joists seem to have sprung direct from the top of the sand surrounding the dug/out hut space. There was no regular planning, and the space between the huts was honey/combed with latrine/ and storage/pits. But the houses ex/cavated 'probably represent the industrial slum on the western outskirts of the town', and it cannot be supposed that a thegn or a merchant lived in such squalid surroundings.[1] We know nothing about the *domus mercatorum* which Domesday Book mentions in its account of Nottingham, but the stone houses which survive at Lincoln, Southampton, and Bury St. Ed/munds indicate the standard of domestic comfort to which Jewish financiers and other wealthy citizens could aspire in the reign of Henry II. Of two stories, with stone fireplaces and two/light windows elaborately moulded in the style of con/temporary ecclesiastical architecture, they represent a type of house which was also to be found in French cities, and which in England may plausibly be regarded as a Norman importa/

---

[1] This supposition is borne out by the subsequent discovery of a larger house with timber walls and a wooden floor.

tion. Owing to later alterations the internal arrangements of these houses are not easy to reconstruct, but at Lincoln both the surviving houses have handsomely decorated doorways, placed approximately in the centre of the ground floor, from which a through passage may have led to an external staircase at the back. The rooms on the ground floor may have been used for storage, and the first floor was presumably occupied by a small hall and solar. Stone-built houses of this sort were sufficiently uncommon for their material to be specified in contemporary documents, but examples were to be found in most of the principal towns. Their value as a protection against fire is recognized in the London Building Assize of 1189, which points out that in past conflagrations many dwellings had been saved by the presence of a single stone house which stood in the way of the flames. But the Assize itself[1] did no more than encourage the building of stone party-walls three feet thick, and it was not until after a disastrous fire in 1212 that roofs of reeds, rushes, straw, or stubble were forbidden.[2] Wooden chimneys were illegal in London in the fourteenth century, but it was not until the reign of Henry VII that chimneys of 'tree' were forbidden in Nottingham and Worcester, and the great majority of town houses continued to be constructed wholly or partially of timber throughout the middle ages. In the reign of Henry VIII Leland noted that 'the hole toune of Leircester at this tyme is buildid of tymbre: and so is Lughborow after the same rate'. The same might have been said of many towns which, like Leicester itself, have since been rebuilt in stone or brick, but often a considerable number of timber-framed town-houses dating from the fifteenth and sixteenth centuries survive behind the later façades. Houses of this sort usually had a comparatively narrow frontage and presented a gabled elevation to the street. Frequently they stood on a vaulted basement, which formed a fire-proof cellar and elevated the 'ground' floor of the house up to three feet above the level of the street. If so, a flight of

---

[1] Printed in *Munimenta Gildhallae Londoniensis*, ed. H. T. Riley (Rolls Series), i, pp. 319 et seq.
[2] Ibid. ii (i), pp. 86–87.

steps was necessary in order to reach the entrance to the house
(Fig. 27). At Chester the space between the steps was occupied
by stalls which in the course of time became permanent struc‐
tures attached to the houses. Eventually the fronts of the houses
were brought forward to take in the stalls, narrowing the street
by four or five feet on either side, but providing a covered foot‐

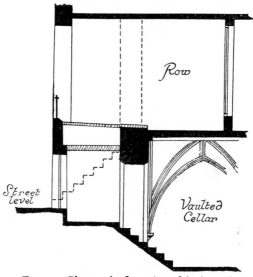

FIG. 27. Chester: the formation of the 'Rows'.

way at what now became first‐floor level, and so creating the
'Rows' which are so characteristic a feature of the city. The
Rows are referred to in the city records as early as the four‐
teenth and fifteenth centuries, but in their present form they
date chiefly from the seventeenth and eighteenth centuries.

Where there was no cellar, or where the street level was the
same as that of the ground floor, the frontage of those houses
which stood on the main streets was commonly occupied by
shops. A medieval shop was a workshop rather than a store,
and its occupant generally needed no more space than was
necessary to carry on his craft. Consequently medieval shops
were of very modest size. How small they sometimes were may
be gathered from the dimensions of eight stone shops in the

FIG. 28. Fifteenth-century shops in Butchers' Row, Shrewsbury.

neighbourhood of Ironmonger Lane, London, which were given to the nuns of St. Mary, Clerkenwell, early in the thirteenth century. The largest had a frontage of 11 feet 5 inches, the smallest of 8 feet 6 inches, and the average floor-space was less than 200 square feet.[1] In Oxford there were many shops less than 8 feet wide, and a fifteenth-century shop in Burford High Street was only $17\frac{1}{2}$ feet long, 7 feet broad, and 7 feet high.[2] It is possible that this was a lean-to erection against the front of a house, though such structures were usually described as stalls (*seldae*) rather than as shops (*schopae* or *sopae*). In most large towns certain trades and types of shop were associated by custom with particular streets which came to bear their names, but how far this occupational specialization was reflected in the external appearance of the shops it is now impossible to say, for very few accurate representations of English medieval shop-fronts have been preserved. In the fifteenth-century shops in Butchers' Row, Shrewsbury, illustrated in Fig. 28, the meat was displayed on hinged flaps projecting outside the ground-floor window openings.

The room over the shop is usually designated in medieval documents as the solar, where the occupant lived, but where the shops were very small it was not uncommon for there to be only one solar to two shops. This would be occupied by one of the two shopkeepers, while the other would have his house in some other part of the town. Many shops occupied the ground floor of buildings intended for other purposes, such as inns and (in Oxford and Cambridge) academic halls (Fig. 29a). The building of shops was in fact a recognized form of investment at a time when speculative building for residential purposes was apparently unknown. In such cases the freehold was often divided among two or more parties: when Oseney Abbey built the Golden Cross Inn in Oxford shortly before 1200, it re-tained four shops on the ground floor, each measuring 6 feet by 15 feet, but 'sold the inn which was behind and above, the

[1] *The Cartulary of St. Mary Clerkenwell*, ed. W. O. Hassall (Camden Soc. 1949), pp. 140–1.
[2] R. H. Gretton, *The Burford Records* (1920), p. 173.

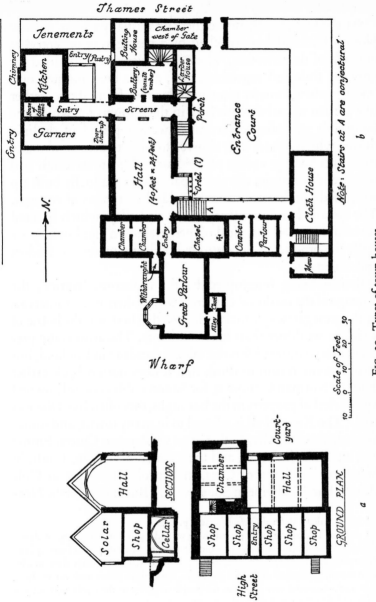

FIG. 29. Types of town houses.

a. Timber-framed house with stone basement and shops (Tackley's Inn, Oxford).
b. The inn of a wealthy London merchant (Brown's Place, London).

abbey covenanting to maintain posts and pillars in their shop adequate for the story above'.[1]

At the rear of each house there was usually a long, narrow plot or 'back-side' approached by a passageway or 'entry' at one side of the tenement. These plots were generally used for growing fruit and vegetables, and, as has been pointed out, 'most medieval towns must have looked, from above, rather like garden suburbs', especially in those towns for which the fourteenth and fifteenth centuries were a period of decline, during which houses were allowed to fall into decay and many tenements became vacant plots.[2] But in the late sixteenth and seventeenth centuries the open spaces were gradually built up with sheds, outhouses, workshops, and even rows of cottages. The crowded and insanitary courts and alleys which resulted are often regarded as typical of medieval town life: but they are really the product of uncontrolled building under the Tudors and Stuarts.

Besides being interrupted by the numerous 'entries', the frontage of the medieval city street was broken at rarer intervals by the great gateway which indicated that here was the house of a citizen wealthier than his neighbours. The aristocratic preference for a country life is one of long standing in England, but there is some reason to think that it does not go back earlier than the Norman Conquest, for Saxon nobles not only owned a good deal of property in the boroughs, they often lived there as well. 'The King's hall is referred to in many towns, and sometimes there were halls of other great personages; Queen Emma had one in Winchester, and the Confessor's queen, Edith, in Stamford, Toki, son of Outi, in Lincoln, Thurbert in Colchester, Earl Godwine in Southwark.'[3] But after 1066 the Nor-

---

[1] H. E. Salter, *Medieval Oxford* (1936), p. 82.

[2] Acts of Parliament were passed in 1536 and 1540 'for reedyfyeng of dyvers Townes in the Realm', in many of which it was stated that there had formerly been 'beautyfull dwellyng Howses there welle inhabited whyche at thys daye moche parte thereof is desolate and void groundys, with pittys sellers and vaultes lying open and uncoveryd very peryllous for people to go by in the nyght without jeopardy of lyfe' (*Statutes of the Realm*, iii, pp. 531, 768).

[3] Dorothy Whitelock, *The Beginnings of English Society* (1952), p. 131.

man barons lived in their castles and manor-houses, leaving
the towns to become predominantly bourgeois. Only in London did they and the ecclesiastical tenants-in-chief have those
'lordly habitations' whither, as William fitz Stephen wrote in
the reign of Henry II, 'they repair and make lavish outlay
when summoned to the City by our lord the king or by
his metropolitan to councils and great assemblies, or drawn
thither by their own affairs'. The 'inns' or town houses of the
bishops and abbots alone numbered over thirty. These aristocratic residences were to be found in every part of the city, for
the tendency for rich and poor to be segregated into different
quarters was little in evidence in medieval English towns. The
inns of the abbots and priors were often situated near the gates
by which their owners would enter the city, and the medieval
merchant lived as a rule where his business was. But the larger
houses were usually placed well back from the street, and in
planning they resembled country manor-houses rather than the
humbler town dwellings among which they stood. Inside the
great gateway there would be a paved courtyard with a hall,
kitchen, chamber, and other apartments, and the ecclesiastical
inns often contained a chapel as well. The bishop of Ely's
house in Holborn, rebuilt in the fourteenth century, had a great
hall 72 feet long and 32 feet wide, with six Gothic windows, a
screen, and a dais. At one end were the bishop's lodgings,
with a small cloister for him to walk in round a garden. The
large and handsome chapel of St. Etheldreda was a separate
building standing on a vaulted undercroft. The abbot of Waltham's inn was less pretentious, but he too had his paved
courtyard entered through a great gate, his chamber, and his
chapel.

The wealthier merchant, who wished to be thought 'estatly
of his governance', built in much the same style as his social
superiors. Indeed, of the two houses which belonged to one of
the most famous of all London merchants, Sir John Pulteney
(d. 1349), one, the 'Cold Harbour' in Dowgate, was rented
in his lifetime by the earl of Hereford, and afterwards came into
the possession of John Holland, earl of Huntingdon and half-

brother of Richard II, while the other, Pountney's Inn in
Candlewick Street, was occupied first by Edward the Black
Prince, then by Richard, earl of Arundel, and later by William
de la Pole, duke of Suffolk. To be the possessor of two such
houses may have been unique: but there were other merchants
who housed themselves with equal magnificence. The stone
tower of William Servat's house in Bucklersbury was still a
landmark in Elizabethan London, and Sir John Crosby's
great hall in Bishopsgate, happily saved from destruction in
1908 to become the nucleus of a London University hostel, is
the equal of any collegiate hall in Oxford or Cambridge.
Fig. 29b shows the plan of another London house of this sort—
Browne's Place in the Parish of St. Dunstan-in-the-East, as it
stood in about 1463. It was built in the reign of Richard II by
a tallow-chandler named Willysdon, and the original speci-
fication has by chance been preserved. The hall and adjoining
buildings, which were constructed of oak timber, stood on a
vaulted basement intended, with other 'chambrys and howses'
above ground, for the storage of merchandise, and there was a
small 'counter' or counting-house between the chapel and the
parlour. The frontage to Thames Street was chiefly occupied
by subordinate tenements, but at the back there was a stone
wharf with a crane and a 'water-house'.

The courtyard plan of Browne's Place was usual even in
lesser merchants' houses, and sometimes there was a small
garden which was used for recreation as well as for growing
herbs. The amount of private accommodation was, however,
often extremely limited even in houses of considerable size, and
before the sixteenth century very few people had a bedroom
to themselves. In the reign of Edward IV a wealthy London
mercer with a wife and seven children had only one chamber
which could be used as a bedroom, and an inventory taken in
a haberdasher's house in 1499 showed that only two bedrooms
were in use, one containing two beds, the other five. Not all
merchants were content with these rather primitive conditions,
and in the reign of Edward III there were four bedrooms
in the house of Richard Lyons, the hated monopolist. But in

general it would seem that the city merchant, faced with the problem of housing both himself and his stock on a contracted site, was usually content with somewhat less privacy than the gentry whose style of living he otherwise emulated. Occasionally a very wealthy man like Sir John Pulteney would have a country house as well as a town house, but although many London merchants bought up manors and tenements in the Home counties, it was for investment rather than out of a desire to establish themselves as country squires. Only in the seventeenth century did the growth of London induce the city merchant to divorce his private life from his business affairs by taking up permanent residence in some suburban village.

3. *Farmhouses and Cottages*

The architecture of the past can never be studied satisfactorily except in relationship to the society for which it was built. This is especially true of the peasant architecture of the middle ages, which was for the most part built by craftsmen of conservative habits for men living in communities no less governed by custom. Only in the houses of the aristocracy can the changing fashions of ecclesiastical architecture be paralleled in contemporary domestic architecture, and although a slow evolution can be traced in the planning and construction of the peasant's dwelling, it is notoriously difficult to establish its chronology. In any case that chronology cannot be constant for the country as a whole, for until quite modern times the character of English farm and cottage architecture in any given locality has been largely determined by the types of building material which were to be found in the immediate vicinity. Moreover, the prehistorian's distinction between the Highland and Lowland zones of Britain is still valid for the student of her medieval domestic architecture, and primitive types of house continued longer in the north and west than they did in the south and east. There is the further difficulty that very few authentic examples of medieval peasant architecture survive in any part of England, and that such as there are date chiefly from the fifteenth

and early sixteenth centuries. For those of an earlier period it is necessary to turn to documentary and archaeological evidence, neither of which has as yet been fully exploited. Archaeology, in particular, may be expected to throw new light on the origins of English peasant architecture as a result of the scien/ tific excavation of deserted villages. For although many Anglo/ Saxon cemeteries of the pagan period have been excavated, very few 'habitation/sites' of the same era have so far been identified, and less is at present known about the domestic arrangements of our Saxon forefathers than about those of their prehistoric predecessors.

At Sutton Courtenay in Berkshire, at Bourton/on/the/ Water in Gloucestershire, and at one or two places elsewhere, dwellings of the fifth and sixth centuries have, however, been excavated. Out of thirty/three examined at Sutton Courtenay, the majority were very small, more or less rectangular huts with their floors sunk into the ground to a depth of about five feet. The roof was supported by a single post at either end, and the walls were probably made of clay, or of wattle and/daub. Their general appearance cannot have been very different from that of the extraordinarily primitive dug/out huts which were in use at Athelney in Somerset a hundred years ago (Fig. 30). At Sutton Courtenay one of the huts had a paving of rough stones, and pebbles were used for the same purpose in Anglo/Saxon huts recently excavated at Wykeham in the North Riding of Yorkshire. There was evidence in one case that a pit deeper than the rest had been used as a potter's workshop, and that weaving was carried out in others, recalling the statement of Pliny that in Germany the women worked at the loom in underground apartments. According to Tacitus the occupants of these semi/subterranean houses covered them with dung in order to keep out the cold. At Sutton Courtenay the roof, whatever its material, rested against a ridge/pole sup/ ported on uprights at each end of the hut: but at Bourton/on/ the/Water the framework was formed by a number of poles inclined inwards to meet over the centre of the hut (Fig. 31), a form of construction which was still in use for charcoal/

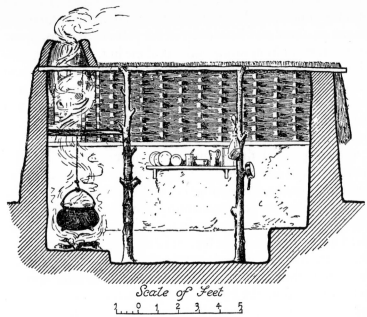

Scale of Feet

2 . 0 1 2 3 4 5

FIG. 30. Athelney, Somerset: nineteenth-century hut.

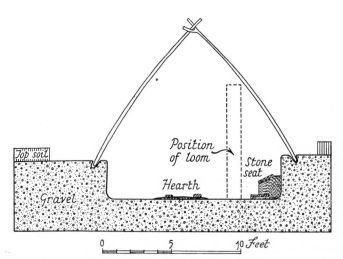

FIG. 31. Reconstruction of Anglo-Saxon hut excavated at Bourton-on-the-Water, Gloucestershire.

burners' huts in modern times. Like the charcoal-burners, the Saxon peasants may have covered the poles with overlapping sods of turf cut from inside and round the hut. How long huts of this primitive type remained in general use in Anglo-Saxon villages it is at present impossible to say (though one containing pottery of the eleventh or twelfth century has been recorded at Aylesbury), for a long gap separates these excavated examples from the earliest surviving medieval dwellings.

It is a gap which the documentary evidence does little to fill, for the charters and surveys of the eleventh and twelfth centuries are uninformative on the subject of the humble dwellings of the English peasantry. It is noteworthy, however, that two of the most numerous classes of unfree peasantry should have de-rived their names from the type of house which they occupied: they were the *bordarii* and *cotarii*, of whom over 80,000 are recorded in the Domesday Survey. The word 'bordar' appears to be derived from the Frankish *borda*, meaning a wooden hut, while a 'cottar' is a person who lives in a 'cot' or cottage. Apart from the fact that the former is of French, the latter of Anglo-Saxon derivation, the two terms are almost interchangeable, and it is doubtful whether they imply any significant difference in architectural form. What the home of an eleventh-century cottager was like only excavation can show, but it is possible that in its simplest form it was a tent-like booth of the kind illustrated in Fig. 32 from a fourteenth-century Flemish manu-script. A cottage of similar form, though of comparatively recent construction, survived at Scrivelsby in Lincolnshire until 1944 (Fig. 33). Its wooden framework stood directly on the ground, and consisted of four straight members at the corners support-ing a ridge-tree. The vertical walls were composed of wooden 'studs' or uprights, with twigs or branches of trees interwoven, the whole being overlaid with mud and plaster. The length, breadth, and height of the building were each approximately 19 feet, corresponding closely to the recorded dimensions of a fourteenth-century booth in the village of West Auckland in Durham.[1] But 'Teapot Hall' (as it was called) was a late and

---

[1] *Bishop Hatfield's Survey* (Surtees Soc. 1856), p. 32.

isolated example of its type, and too much reliance should not be placed upon it as an indication of medieval building methods.

In any case, a wooden framework was by no means univer-sal, and in many parts of the country cottages were built of

FIG. 32. Fourteenth-century booth.

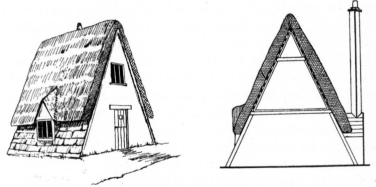

FIG. 33. 'Teapot Hall', Scrivelsby, Lincs.

mud or clay without the support of timber. This form of con-struction was especially common in the west country. The royalist Richard Symonds, writing in his diary (Camden Soc. 1859) in 1644, says that in Devonshire 'the ordinary howses are of the soyle mingled with straw, without posts', and that in the Plymouth region 'almost all the howses be clay, without any timber in the wall, except the doores, roofe and windowes, which is the fashion of the country'. This method of construc-tion was also in use in Yorkshire in comparatively recent times,

and must have been even more widespread in the middle ages. The walls of a mud house formerly existing at Great Hatfield in the East Riding of Yorkshire were made of layers of mud and straw five to seven inches in thickness. The way in which these mud walls used to be built was still remembered in the neighbourhood at the end of the nineteenth century, and was recorded by S. O. Addy.

A quantity of mud was mixed with straw, and the foundation laid with this mixture. Straw was then laid across the top, whilst the mud was wet, and the whole was left to dry and harden in the sun. As soon as the first layer was dry another layer was put on, so that the process was rather a slow one. Finally the roof was thatched, and the projecting ends of straw trimmed off the walls.

The result was surprisingly durable, the walls of a well-built mud house having the consistency of sun-burnt bricks. The 'cob' walling of Devonshire was built up in precisely the same way, the vertical face being trimmed with a spade or 'cob-parer' before being given its characteristic coat of whitewash. In other parts of the country (especially in Dorset and Wiltshire) the hard chalk known as 'clunch' fulfilled the same function, and if protected from the wet by overhanging thatched roofs, proved equally efficient as a walling material. The extent to which turves were used for building in the middle ages is uncertain, but in the fourteenth century turf was being dug in the Isle of Axholme for walling as well as for fuel,[1] and the practice was probably general throughout the fenland area.

By far the most common type of rural dwelling in medieval England was, however, the timber-framed house which re-mained in general use until the end of the seventeenth century, when the decreasing supply of timber encouraged the use of bricks, hitherto confined almost exclusively to the towns and the great country houses; we have William Harrison's testi-mony that in the sixteenth century 'the greatest part of our building' still consisted 'onelie of timber, for as yet few of the howses of the communaltie (except here and there in the west countrie tounes) are made of stone', although in his opinion

---

[1] W. B. Stonehouse, *History of the Isle of Axholme* (1839), p. 233.

they might 'in diverse other places be builded so good cheape of the one as of the other'. In the middle ages, however, cottages and farmhouses were habitually built of wood even in areas where good building stone was available: in the Cotswolds, for instance, it is difficult to find a stone-built house of an earlier date than the late sixteenth century, and the documentary evidence shows that here, as elsewhere, timber had been the normal building material in the past. The same is true of Yorkshire, where, until the end of the sixteenth century, timber-framed houses were 'almost universal, and many an existing stone building is merely a covering of such an early framework'.[1]

While timber was thus the characteristic building material of the medieval peasantry, there was considerable regional variation in its use. In the midlands the commonest type of timber house was the one in which pairs of 'crucks' or 'forks' supported the ridge-pole (Fig. 34). As a form of construction this is of unknown antiquity, but it is found throughout north-west Europe, and in England it appears to have been well established by the beginning of the fourteenth century. It has often been claimed that in its most primitive form it is repre-sented by the house at Scrivelsby described above. But in all the surviving medieval examples the straight and comparatively slight timbers of 'Tea-pot Hall' have been replaced by stout curved principals sawn from the trunk of a tree. These are known as 'crucks' in the north midlands and Yorkshire, as 'siles' or 'sile-trees' in Cumberland, Durham, and Scotland, as 'blades' in Gloucestershire, and as 'couples' or 'forks' else-where. Wherever possible each pair of crucks was sawn from the same tree-trunk in order to obtain principals of equal size and curvature. When set up the butt-end was usually placed at the ridge and not at the sill, apparently because it was believed that damp would be less liable to rise in timbers so inverted.

The purpose of using curved timbers was, of course, to give

[1] J. Walton, 'Cruck framed buildings in Yorkshire', *Yorkshire Archaeological Jnl.* xxxvii (1951), p. 49.

greater head-room than would be possible in a house of the 'Teapot Hall' type. Even so, the space enclosed by a simple cruck framework was somewhat restricted, and various modi/ fications were introduced to allow the construction of vertical

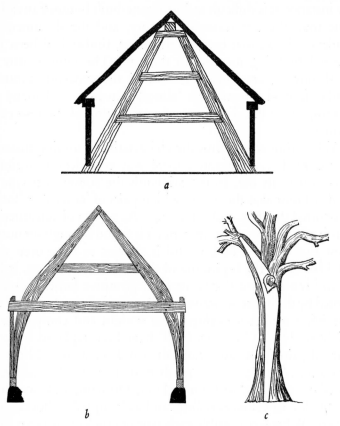

FIG. 34. Cruck construction.

a. Primitive cruck construction; *b.* A pair of crucks with tie-beam; *c.* Cruck cut from the trunk of an oak-tree.

side walls. To some extent this could be accomplished by the use of angular rather than curved crucks, and Sir Cyril Fox has demonstrated how timbers of the desired shape could be obtained from the trunk of an oak-tree (Fig. 34c). The common/ est device, however, was to extend the tie-beams beyond the

junction with the crucks, as in Fig. 34b. In some cases the crucks were virtually independent of the walls, and did little more than support the ridge-tree. But normally the pairs of crucks were the basis of the whole structure, and being set at regular intervals, formed an index to the size of a house. Thus a fifteenth-century Derbyshire lease specifies 'a house with eight pairs of crucks, another with five pairs of crucks, a barn with six pairs of crucks, and a hayhouse with ten pairs of crucks'.[1] The space between two pairs of crucks was known as a 'bay', and it was not uncommon to measure corn stored in a barn by the 'bay'. In some cases the crucks rested directly on the ground, but in better-built houses and barns they stood on stone foot-ings. A later development was to raise the whole framework on to a wall, the feet of the crucks being tenoned into the main ceiling beams. Finally, there is a type of false cruck in which the roof-trusses no longer consist of single curved timbers but are built up of two pieces of wood 'scarfed' at the curve. This, however, was the final development in the history of cruck construction, and as such barely falls within the chrono-logical limits of this chapter.[2]

The walls of a cruck-built house might be of rubble stone-work or even of mud, but were most commonly of the type known variously as 'stud and mud', 'clam stuff and daub', or 'wattle and daub'. The studs were stout timbers tenoned into the sill and wall-plate at top and bottom. Although they were not essential to the stability of a cruck-built house—and may, indeed, have been absent in its most primitive form—they were frequently strong enough to give effective support to the wall-plate (and so to the roof), and even to the crucks which they protected from the weather. The space between them was filled by oak or hazel rods 'sprung' into holes or grooves in the horizontal timbers, interlaced with riven oak slats, and finally 'daubed' or plastered externally. It is likely that in the earliest cruck houses these wattle-and-daub walls were little better

---

[1] F. Williamson in *Notes and Queries* (5 Aug. 1939), p. 97.
[2] On 'false crucks' see Sir Cyril Fox in *Proc. Somerset Arch. Soc.* xciv (1950), pp. 58–59.

than hurdles applied to domestic use, and it has been suggested that (in Monmouthshire at least) the studding represents the intrusion of a 'half-timber' technique from the mid-

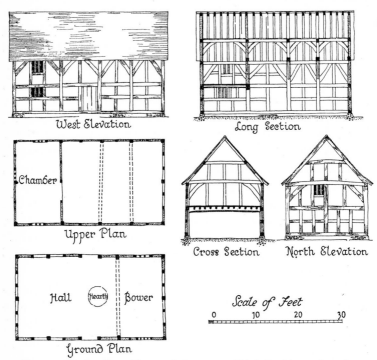

West Elevation
Long Section
Upper Plan
Chamber
Cross Section
North Elevation
Hall   Hearth   Bower
Ground Plan

Scale of Feet
0   10   20   30

FIG. 35. Timber-framed house of about 1500 (Little Bookham, Surrey).

lands. At first the studs were quite closely spaced, but by the sixteenth century in most cases (and earlier in others) they had been set farther apart in such a way as to create the rectangular 'post and panel' construction so characteristic of English timber building in its final form (Fig. 35).

Whether it was 'half-timbered' or built on crucks, the posts and panels of a medieval house were fitted together on the ground or in the carpenter's workshop before being placed in position, and are often found to bear Roman (and in one case Arabic)[1] numerals to guide those who assembled them. A

[1] *Surrey Archaeological Collections*, lxv (1924), p. 66.

statute of 37 Henry VIII refers to 'the secret burnynge of frames
of tymber prepared and made, by the owners thereof, redy to be
set up, and edified for howses', and made it a felony to commit
this particular form of arson. The setting up of a timber-framed
house in this way was known as 'rearing', and in Yorkshire in
the nineteenth century a wooden house was still known as a
'reared house' to distinguish it from one built of stone. The
assistance of many men was required to 'rear' the massive framework of a house built on the cruck principle, and considerable
sums were often spent on ale 'for those who came to the rearing'.
On most manors the customary tenants were allowed to take
timber for the repair and building of houses, though the right
(known as 'housebote') was often restricted to one oak at a
time, and by the sixteenth century some lords were insisting
that a new tree should be planted to replace every one felled.
Stone slates, wooden shingles, and pottery tiles were all employed for roofing in medieval England, but for the peasantry
the usual 'thacking' was reed or straw. This necessitated the
steep-pitched roof characteristic of medieval building, for if a
thatched roof is pitched too low it does not throw the water off
properly. The medieval habit of reaping the ears with a sickle
instead of cutting the corn close to the ground in the modern
fashion left long straw for the thatcher's use, and the provision
of so many acres of stubble for this purpose is sometimes included in medieval leases. Though inferior in some respects
to slate and tile, straw thatch forms an excellent insulating
material, and, living as he did in a house which was three parts
roof, the medieval cottager was doubtless glad of the protection
which it gave him against extremes of heat and cold.

A house whose principal timbers could be framed on the
ground and reared into position could also be taken to pieces
and moved elsewhere with comparative ease, and there is documentary evidence, from Domesday Book onwards, that the
practice was not uncommon. In 1086 a Berkshire tenant was
reported to have removed 'a hall and other houses' from one
manor to another, and in 1274 a tenant of the abbot of Ramsey
was fined two shillings for transferring a solar and a barn from

one place to another without his lord's permission.[1] In 1234 the sheriff of Oxfordshire was ordered to allow Richard earl of Cornwall to take away certain houses at Headington which belonged to the rebel Richard Siward, and to re-erect them on his own manor of Beckley in order to replace houses burned down by Siward.[2] Contracts exist for the peaceable removal of timber houses in the same way,[3] and the practice was not unknown even in the seventeenth century.[4] In view of the portability of the timber-framed house it behoved the medieval landlord to keep careful watch on his tenants, and it was prob-ably for this reason that the dimensions of their farmyard build-ings are so carefully set out in the twelfth-century leases of the canons of St. Paul's.[5]

Unfortunately the documents rarely give similar details of peasants' houses, and the probate inventories which are so valuable a guide to the domestic arrangements of the sixteenth-and seventeenth-century house do not exist for the medieval period. It is probable, however, that the typical cruck-built house of a midland villein often consisted of only two 'bays of building'. In 1281 a villein living at Ridgeacre near Hales-owen in Worcestershire undertook to build for his widowed mother a house thirty feet long within the walls, and fourteen feet wide, with posts, three doors, and two windows,[6] and under a Leicestershire lease dated 31 December 1405 the lessee was, among other things, required to 'make or cause to be made a house upon the said tenement of three pairs of forkes' within the term of three years under penalty of 20s. Both these dwell-ings probably contained two rooms: one, known in the six-teenth and seventeenth centuries as the 'house-part', corre-sponded to the hall of more imposing mansions, while the adjoining 'bower' or 'chamber' served as a bedroom. Both

[1] *Court Rolls of the Abbey of Ramsey*, ed. Ault (1928), p. 269.
[2] *Close Rolls 1231-1234*, p. 363.
[3] Salzman, *Building in England* (1952), pp. 4, 7-8, 452-3; cf. Hist. MSS. Comm., *Sixth Report*, p. 598.
[4] *Records of Bucks*. xi (1922), p. 195.
[5] *The Domesday of St. Paul's*, ed. Hale (Camden Soc. 1857), pp. 122-52.
[6] *Halesowen Court Rolls*, ed. Amphlett (Worcs. Hist. Soc. 1910), i, p. 167.

apartments were open to the roof, and the smoke from the fire in the house part no doubt pervaded the whole dwelling. The poor woman in Chaucer's *Nun's Priest's Tale* was not unique in the sootiness of 'hire bour, and eek hire halle', and the skin of the medieval peasant, exposed alternately to all weathers with out and to peat reek and wood smoke within, must have been prematurely brown and wrinkled. In the case of a cottage the single fire no doubt served for both heating and cooking, but there is reason to think that in the medieval farmhouse the kitchen was often a separate building, and it should not be for gotten that in the early middle ages the maintenance of a com munal baking-oven was a recognized seigneurial right.

In many parts of Europe it was usual for the same roof to shelter both man and beast. The advantage of this arrangement was that it gave the farmer access to his cattle in all weathers, and in many cases it was possible to pass straight from the living-rooms into the cowshed without going out into the open air. How far this type of farmhouse was common in medieval England is uncertain, though it survived until modern times in Wales and Scotland, and Mr. E. M. Jope has excavated a thirteenth-century example at Great Beare in Devonshire. According to Daniel King, the Cheshire farmers still 'used the old manner of the Saxons in Building, and Furniture of their Houses' until early in the seventeenth century, 'for they had their fire in the midst of the house, against a hob of clay, and their Oxen also under the same Roof'.[1] But Harrison, whose *Description of England* was pub lished in 1577, asserts that

the mansion howses of our countrie tounes and villages are builded in such sort generallie, as that they have neither dairie, stable, nor bruehouse annexed unto them under the same roofe (as in manie places beyond the sea & some of the north parts of our countrie), but all separate from the first, and one of them from another.

An example of the type of north-country farmhouse which Harrison had in mind survived until recently at Hurst, near Reeth, in Swaledale (Fig. 36). Here a long, low, cruck-sup

[1] *The Vale-Royall of England* (1656), p. 19.

ported roof sheltered both the farmer and his cows.[1] Addy also records the existence in Yorkshire of a type of rectangular 'shippon' or cowhouse with quarters at one end for the cow-herd, and gives the plan of one at Upper Midhope, near Peni-stone.[2] All these examples are of post-medieval date, but there can be little doubt that they represent a type of farm-building which must have been common in the Highland zone of Britain in medieval times.

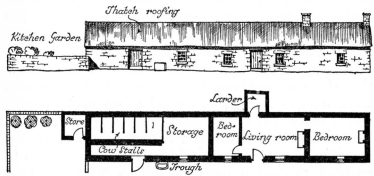

FIG. 36. Farmhouse in Swaledale with house and cattle under the same roof.

It is remarkable that, despite the social and tenurial peculiari-ties which, even in the twelfth and thirteenth centuries, still distinguished the ancient Danelaw, no corresponding differ-ences have yet been observed in its medieval domestic archi-tecture, though excavation may yet demonstrate their former existence. The three south-eastern counties, however, were notable in the later middle ages for a type of house intermediate between the manor-house of more manorialized areas and the comparatively humble dwelling of the midland villein. Its characteristic feature was a miniature great hall rising to the full height of the roof, but flanked at either end by a two-storied wing containing a parlour on the ground floor and one or more rooms above. The angles of the house were supported by massive corner-posts formed out of the butt-ends of trees, turned upside-down and crudely carved with capitals and

[1] R. Clough in *Country Life* (22 Feb. 1952), p. 508.
[2] S. O. Addy, *The Evolution of the English House*, ed. Summerson (1933), p. 89.

bases. The first-floor rooms were 'jettied out' over the lower ones, so that the upper floor of the hall was recessed between them. The difficulty of recessing the roof in corresponding fashion was avoided by carrying the wall-plate across the gap and supporting it at either end by a great curved bracket-piece. In the interior the most striking feature was the great tie-beam across the hall, upon which stood the king-post which sup-ported the ridge of the roof. The fire was made on a hearth in the middle of the floor, and unless there was a louvre the un-glazed windows served the dual purpose of admitting light and emitting smoke.

This type of 'hall-house' appears to have been fully de-veloped by the end of the fourteenth century, and a consider-able number of fifteenth- and early sixteenth-century examples survive. Some of them are to be found in the streets of Kentish villages, but most of them stand on their own in what were originally clearings in the Wealden woodland. For, unlike the midland villein, whose gable-end fronted on to the street of a 'nucleated' village, set among open fields which he cultivated in common with his neighbours, the Kentish freeholder lived in scattered hamlets or isolated farms in whose cultivation the common field played little or no part, and whose descent was regulated by the form of partible inheritance known as 'gavel-kind'. It is possible that it is in these customs that the explanation of the Kentish hall-house is to be found: for there is docu-mentary evidence that, although legally partitioned among the sons of each successive holder, the estate of a Kentish yeoman was in many cases held by his heirs in common and cultivated by their joint labours. The hall-house, with its parlour or solar at either end of a common hall, would certainly fit in admirably with the historian's picture of a group of heirs, descended from a common ancestor, 'living in one large house or in a small group of adjoining houses and holding a domain in common'.[1] That a single dwelling, even in the manorialized midlands, often sheltered more than one couple is indicated by the not infrequent agreements made before manorial courts whereby

[1] G. C. Homans, *English Villagers of the Thirteenth Century* (1942), p. 112.

the holder of a tenement would undertake to give his father and mother a room at one end of his house in which to dwell in their old age, and the curious duality in the planning of the Kentish hall-house may perhaps represent a deliberate attempt to give each of two heirs his own share of the family dwelling.

Whatever their origin, the hall-houses of Kent and Sussex represent the most elaborate type of peasant architecture to be found in medieval England, and fully bear out the traditional superiority of the Kentish freeman over his servile neighbour. By the end of the sixteenth century, however, Kent had ceased to be unique in its peasant aristocracy of yeoman farmers, and in every part of England, from the Yorkshire dales to the Devonshire combes, prosperous countrymen were busy im-proving the medieval houses in which they had been brought up. In the words of their historian, 'there is one respect in which all contemporary writers who dealt with the homes of the com-moners agreed, namely that in regard to both size and comfort the lesser folk of the Elizabethan period had better homes to live in than had their ancestors'.[1] It was not only noblemen and prosperous gentry who were adding to their ancestral homes: such phrases as 'the newe parlour', the 'newe chamber', and 'the parlour I had latelie built' occur in scores of yeoman wills and inventories of the sixteenth century, and there were many among them who, like the Martindales of Lancashire, 'pulled downe the old house quite to the ground', and built 'that strong and large stone house that now stands in its place'.[2]

Building has always been a conservative trade, and much that was medieval in building practice persisted throughout the sixteenth and seventeenth centuries. But the increasingly general use of stone and brick, the universal division of new houses into two stories, and the frequent insertion of floors and ceilings into old ones, as well as the addition of new chambers and parlours, each with its own fireplace and chimney, all contributed to introduce a new and more comfortable phase

[1] M. Campbell, *The English Yeoman* (1942), p. 228.
[2] Quoted by Campbell, op. cit.

into the history of the English house. At Sutton Coldfield in Warwickshire a Tudor bishop even built a model village of two-story houses for his tenants, and by the early seventeenth century it was possible for Bishop Hall to write with some contempt of that 'silly cote of one bay's breadth' which had once been the home of so many English villagers.

WORKS FOR REFERENCE

Building Technique

ARKELL, W. J. *Oxford Stone* (1947).

CROSSLEY, F. H. *Timber Building in England* (1951).

INNOCENT, C. F. *The Development of English Building Construction* (1916).

KNOOP, D., and JONES, G. P. *The Mediaeval Mason* (1933); 'The English Medieval Quarry', *Econ. Hist. Rev.* ix (1938–9).

LLOYD, N. *History of English Brickwork* (1925).

SALZMAN, L. F. *Building in England down to 1540* (1952).

Halls and Manor-houses[1]

AMBLER, L. *The Old Halls and Manor-Houses of Yorkshire* (1913).

BUCKLER, J. C. Drawings of Norman Domestic Architecture (British Museum, Add. MS. 24434).

CLAPHAM, A. W. 'The Origin of the Domestic Hall', in *Some Famous Buildings and their Story* (n.d.).

DOLLMAN, F. T., and JOBBINS, J. R. *An Analysis of Ancient Domestic Architecture*, 2 vols. (1861–3).

HEMP, W. J. 'Early Timber Work at Henblas, Llandderfel and Penarth Fawr, Llanarmon', *Archaeologia Cambrensis*, xcvii (1943).

LLOYD, N. *A History of the English House* (1937).

ROUSE, E. CLIVE, and BAKER, AUDREY. 'The Wall-paintings at Longthorpe Tower, near Peterborough', *Archaeologia*, xcvi (1955).

ROYCE, Rev. D. 'Icomb Place', *Trans. of the Bristol and Gloucestershire Arch. Soc.* vii (1882–3).

TAYLOR, H. *Old Halls in Lancashire and Cheshire* (1884).

THOMPSON, A. H. *The English House* (Historical Association Pamphlet no. 105, 1936).

TIPPING, H. A. *English Homes*, Period 1, 2 vols. (1921–37).

TURNER, T. HUDSON, and PARKER, J. H. *Domestic Architecture of the Middle Ages*, 3 vols. in 4 parts (1851-9).

TWOPENY, W. Drawings of medieval English domestic architecture (British Museum, Print Room).

WOOD, M. E. 'Norman Domestic Architecture', *Archaeological Jnl.* xcii (1935); 'Thirteenth-Century Domestic Architecture in England', *Archaeological Jnl.*, *Supplement* to vol. cv (1950).

Town Houses and their Setting

ANDREWS, F. B. 'Town Houses of Timber Structure in Worcestershire', *Trans. of the Birmingham and Midland Institute*, xxxviii (1912).

BEECHENO, F. R. 'The Sucklings' House at Norwich', *Norfolk Archaeology*, xix (1917), xx (1918).

CAM, H. M., 'The Origin of the Borough of Cambridge', *Proc. of the Cambridge Antiquarian Soc.* xxxv (1933-4).

CHAMBERS, G. E. 'The French Bastides and the Town Plan of Winchelsea', *Archaeological Jnl.* xciv (1937).

DICKINSON, R. E. 'The Distribution and Functions of the Smaller Urban Settlements of East Anglia', *Geography*, xvii (1932); 'The Town Plans of East Anglia', ibid. xix (1934).

EDWARDS, J. G. 'The Building of Flint', *Pubs. of the Flint Historical Soc.* xii (1951-2).

FOX, L. *The Borough Town of Stratford-upon-Avon* (1953).

GODFREY, W. H. 'The Rebuilding of Crosby Hall at Chelsea', in *Some Famous Buildings and their Story*, by A. W. Clapham and W. H. Godfrey (n.d).

HARVEY, J. H. 'Four Fifteenth-Century London Plans', *London Topographical Record*, xx (1952).

HAVERFIELD, F. *Ancient Town-Planning* (1913).

HEWITT, J. 'Notes on the Mediaeval Architecture of Chester', *Jnl. of the Chester Arch. Soc.* N.S. i (1887).

HILL, J. W. F. *Medieval Lincoln* (1948).

HOMAN, W. M. 'The Founding of New Winchelsea', *Sussex Archaeological Collections*, lxxxviii (1949).

HONEYBOURNE, M. J. 'The Abbot of Waltham's Inn', *London Topographical Record*, xx (1952).

HOPE, W. H. ST. JOHN. 'The Ancient Topography of the town of Ludlow', *Archaeologia*, lxi (2) (1909).

HOSKINS, W. G. 'The Landscape of Towns', *The Listener*, xlviii, 18 and 25 Sept. and 2 Oct. 1952.

HUDSON, W. *How the City of Norwich grew into Shape* (1896).

HUGHES, J. H., and LAMBORN, E. A. G. *Towns and Town-Planning* (1923).

JONES, S. J. 'The Growth of Bristol', *Trans. and Papers of the Institute of British Geographers*, 1946.

JOPE, E. M. 'Excavations in the City of Norwich in 1948', *Norfolk Archaeology*, xxx (1952).

KINGSFORD, C. L. 'Historical Notes on Mediaeval London Houses', *London Topographical Record*, x–xii (1916–20); 'On some London Houses of the Early Tudor Period', *Archaeologia*, lxxi (1920–1); 'Bath Inn or Arundel House', ibid. lxxii (1921–2); 'A London Merchant's House and its Owners, 1360–1614', ibid. lxxiv (1923–4); 'London in the Fifteenth Century', in *Prejudice and Promise in XVth Century England* (1925).

KNOCKER, G. M., and HUGHES, R. G. 'Anglo-Saxon Thetford', *Archaeological News Letter*, ii, no. 8 (1950).

LAVEDAN, P. *Histoire de l'Architecture Urbaine* (1926).

LEE, F. 'The Origins of Northampton', *Archaeological Jnl.* cx (1953).

Liber Luciani de Laude Cestrie, ed. M. V. Taylor (Lancashire and Cheshire Rec. Soc. lxiv, 1912).

NORMAN, P. 'Sir John de Pulteney and his two Residences in London', *Archaeologia*, lvii (2) (1901).

PAGE, W. 'The Origin and Forms of Hertfordshire Towns and Villages', ibid. lxix (1917–18).

PANTIN, W. A. 'The Development of Domestic Architecture in Oxford', *Antiquaries Jnl.* xxvii (1947).

RICHMOND, I. A. 'The Four *Coloniae* of Roman Britain', *Archaeological Jnl.* ciii (1946).

SALTER, H. E. *Medieval Oxford* (1936).

SALUSBURY, G. T. *Street Life in Medieval England* (2nd ed. 1948).

SHILLABER, C. 'Edward I, Builder of Towns', *Speculum*, xxii (1947).

SKELTON, R. A. 'Tudor Town Plans in John Speed's *Theatre*', *Archaeological Jnl.* cviii (1951).

SMITH, J. T. 'A Note on the origin of the Town-Plan of Bury St. Edmunds', *Archaeological Jnl.* cviii (1951).

SPEED, JOHN. *Theatre of the Empire of Great Britaine* (1611).

STENTON, F. M. *Norman London, An Essay*, with a translation of William fitz Stephen's *Description* by H. E. Butler, and a Map of London under Henry II by M. B. Honeybourne (Historical Association Pamphlet nos. 93–94, 1934).

STEPHENSON, C. *Borough and Town* (1933), chap. vii.

STEWART, C. *A Prospect of Cities* (1952).

THRUPP, S. L. *The Merchant Class of Medieval London* (Chicago, 1948).

TOUT, T. F. *Mediaeval Town Planning* (1934).

WHEELER, R. E. M. *London and the Saxons* (London Museum Catalogue, no. 6, 1935).

Wood, M. E. 'A Late Fifteenth-century House in George Street, St. Albans', *St. Albans and E. Herts. Architectural and Archaeological Soc. Trans.* N.S. v (1937).

Farmhouses and Cottages

Addy, S. O. *The Evolution of the English House*, ed. Summerson (1933).

Andrews, F. B. 'Half-timbered houses in Worcestershire', *Trans. Birmingham and Midland Institute*, xxxvi (1910).

Baily, C. 'Remarks on Timber Houses', *Surrey Archaeological Collections*, iv (1869).

Baring-Gould, S. 'An Ancient Settlement on Treworth Marsh', *Jnl. of the Royal Institution of Cornwall*, xi (1892-3).

Barley, M. W. 'The Lincolnshire Village and its Buildings', *The Lincolnshire Historian*, no. 7 (1951); *Farmhouses and Cottages in Lincolnshire and Nottinghamshire* (1952) (unpublished thesis in Bodleian Library: MS. Top. Lincs. d. 5).

Campbell, M. *The English Yeoman* (1942), chap. 6.

Chatwin, P. B., and Harcourt, E. G. 'The Bishop Vesey Houses and the other old Buildings in Sutton Coldfield', *Birmingham Archaeological Society's Trans.* lxiv (1941-2).

Cocks, A. H. 'A Semi-Underground Hut in Walton Road, Aylesbury', *Records of Bucks.* ix (1909).

Cooper, H. S. 'Timber-framed Houses in the Kentish Weald', *Archaeologia Cantiana*, xxix (1911).

Dawber, E. G. *Old Cottages and Farm-houses in Kent and Sussex* (1900); *Old Cottages, Farm-houses and other stone buildings in the Cotswold District* (1905).

Dunning, G. C. 'Bronze Age Settlements and a Saxon Hut near Bourton-on-the-Water', *Antiquaries Jnl.* xii (1932).

Fox, Sir Cyril, and Lord Raglan, *Monmouthshire Houses*, i (National Museum of Wales, 1951).

Hoskins, W. G. *Midland England* (1949), chap. 6.

Johnston, P. M. 'Civil and Domestic Architecture', *V.C.H. Sussex*, ii (1907); *Kent* ('Little Guides', 1935). Appendix VII on 'Kentish Timber Houses'.

Laver, H. 'Ancient Type of Huts at Athelney', *Proc. Somerset Arch. Soc.* lv (1909).

Laycock, C. H. 'The Old Devon Farm-House', *Trans. Devonshire Association*, lii-liv (1920-2).

Lethbridge, T. C. 'An Anglo-Saxon Hut on the Car Dyke, at Waterbeach', *Antiquaries Jnl.* vii (1927); 'Huts of the Anglo-Saxon Period', *Proc. Cambridgeshire Antiquarian Soc.* xxxiii (1938).

Morgan, F. C. 'The Cruck Buildings of Herefordshire', *Woolhope Club's Trans.* for 1936-8.

Musson, R. 'A Thirteenth Century Dwelling at Bramble Bottom, Eastbourne', *Sussex Archaeological Collections*, xciii (1955).

NEVILL, R. *Old Cottage and Domestic Architecture in South-West Surrey* (1889).

OLIVER, B. W. 'The Devonshire Cottage', *Trans. Devonshire Association*, lxxxi (1949).

OSWALD, A. S. *Country Houses of Kent* (1933), chap. 3.

PARKINSON, J. and OULD, E. A. *Old Cottages Farm-Houses and other Half-Timber Buildings in Shropshire, Herefordshire and Cheshire* (1904).

PEATE, I. C. *The Welsh House* (1944).

SINGLETON, W. A. 'Traditional Dwellings in the Cheshire Countryside', *The Cheshire Historian*, i (1951); 'Traditional Dwellings in the South Manchester Area', *Jnl. of the Manchester Geographical Soc.* lv–lvi (1949–52); 'Traditional House-types in Rural Lancashire and Cheshire', *Trans. of the Historical Society of Lancashire and Cheshire*, civ (1952).

WALTON, J. *Homesteads of the Yorkshire Dales* (1947); 'The Development of the Cruck Framework', *Antiquity*, xxii (1948); 'Cruck-framed Buildings in Yorkshire', *Yorkshire Archaeological Jnl.* xxxvii (1951).

WEBSTER, V. R. 'Cruck-Framed Buildings of Leicestershire', *Trans. Leicestershire Arch. Soc.* xxx (1954).

WORTH, R. H. 'The Dartmoor House', *Trans. of the Plymouth Inst.* xviii (1944).

No attempt has been made to list the numerous articles on individual houses: full references for those of twelfth to thirteenth-century date will be found in the two articles by Miss Wood cited above.

III. MILITARY ARCHITECTURE

A S, after the Norman Conquest, the authority of lordship became the most significant element in medieval
society, so the castle, which at once symbolized lordship and gave it material expression, was amongst the
most familiar features of the medieval scene. From the late
eleventh century, when castles were being established through
the length and breadth of England as the instruments of the
new feudal order, to the late fifteenth, when political and social
change combined with the developing use of firearms to render
them obsolete, their building and rebuilding was a continuing
process. The architectural achievement which it represented,
and of which so much is still left to us, reached its highest point
in the reign of Edward I, when there was scarcely an English
shire that did not contribute its quota to the labour levies and to
the enterprise of mason- and timber-craft required for erecting
the king's new castles in Wales. It was indeed fitting that at
such a time even the toys of the six-year-old heir to the throne,
Edward of Caernarvon, should have included a model castle,
made of wood and painted in colours, contrived by one of the
officers of his household.[1]

Two and a half centuries earlier, however, the castle, properly so called, had been unknown here. For the Anglo-Saxon

[1] Magistro Johanni Brodeye, coco domini Edwardi filii Regis, pro quodam
castello tantissimo [*sic*] facto de lignis et aliis diversis aptaturo ad modum castri cum
diversis coloribus et aliis rebus emptis ad id, quod quidem castrum delatum fuit
coram Regina in magna aula Westmonasterii die feste et nuptiarum domine Mar-
garete filie Regis, pro sumptibus quos fecit circa facturam et empcionem dictarum
rerum dicti castri, denunciante domino Waltero de Bello Campo senescallo, xliiij.s.
vj.d.' P.R.O., Chancery Miscellanea, 4/5, f. 53. The marriage of the princess
Margaret to the heir of John, duke of Brabant, was solemnized on 8 July 1290.
Prince Edward's elder brother Alphonso had also had a toy fort made for him: the
Pipe Roll of 1279 (E. 372, 123, m. 21) records payment for 'maeremium emptum
ad quoddam castellettum inde faciendum ad opus Alfunsi filii Regis et cariatum
usque Windesoram'.

burh was essentially a walled or palisaded town, a fencible enclosure for the protection of a community, not a defended strong point for securing the power of an individual. That was the special role of the castle, and the castle was first introduced into England about the year 1050 by the Norman element at the court of Edward the Confessor. Ralf, the Confessor's nephew, whose father was Drogo, count of the French Vexin, and who held the earldom of Herefordshire from 1053 to 1057, promoted the construction of castles in his border territory to protect it against the incursions of Welsh raiders. To him and his Norman followers can be assigned with reasonable certainty the establishment of Ewias Harold, Richard's castle, and the castle of Hereford itself, and these three sites may accordingly be regarded as the prototypes of the 'motte-and-bailey' pattern, to be described in a moment, which the Norman Conquest was soon to carry to every part of the land. It is not improbable that other castles of this pattern in Herefordshire similarly date from Ralf's tenure of the earldom, but except in the three cases named documentary evidence is lacking. There are in addition two castles in eastern England whose origins can with fair probability be traced to a date before the Conquest. One, the motte-and-bailey at Clavering in Essex, is likely to be the castle that Robert FitzWimarc, the Norman staller, is recorded to have possessed to the north of London in 1052. The other is on Dover cliff, where earthworks, ringing the Roman pharos and the Saxon church of St. Mary and forming the nucleus of the great stronghold of later ages, are held to be those of the castle built by Earl Harold in 1064-5 in pursuance of his oath to Duke William of Normandy.

If, as an example of one of these earliest structures, we look at the remains of Ewias Harold (Fig. 37), we can see at a glance the two essential and most permanent features of the Norman castle design. These are the elevated, flat-topped, earthen mound or 'motte' and its associated forecourt or 'bailey'. The mound is nearly circular, with a diameter of some 75 feet at its summit and a height of 50 feet above the enclosing court; the latter is a crescent-shaped area embracing about one-half of the mound's

circumference. A ditch or moat encloses the outer side of the
mound. The bailey has a rampart and ditch on the north, and
elsewhere is defended by a steep scarp. The plan is exceptional

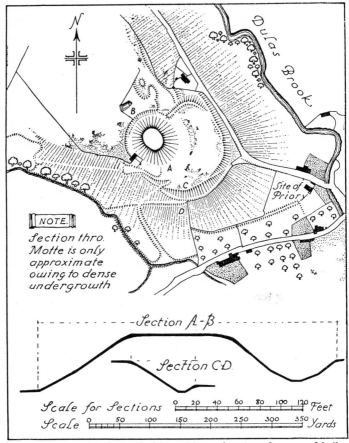

FIG. 37. Ewyas Harold, Herefordshire. Plan and section of motte-and-bailey
castle.

in that the ditch outside the mound is not continued on the inside so as to divide it from the bailey, and this does not appear to
be due, as is so often the case, to later obliteration. The siting of
the castle on the edge of a steep slope falling to a stream is very
typical.

We have hitherto depended for our knowledge of the further

defences of these early castles on the descriptions of the chroniclers and the delineation of four mottes in Brittany and Normandy which appear on the Bayeux Tapestry. The picture of
Duke William's mounted knights assaulting the castle of
Dinan (Pl. 6), though highly conventionalized, is particularly
instructive. The mound is shown with its encircling bank and
ditch towards the entrance (i.e. on the side where the bailey
would be) as well as towards the field. It is approached by a
stepped wooden bridge which rises, as its spans the ditch, from
the counterscarp bank to the level of the structures which ring
the upper part of the motte. Of these the most prominent is a
palisade of heavy upright timbers to which the besiegers are
trying to set fire. Projecting from it at a rather lower level are
what seem to be intended for a pair of small flanking towers,
each containing a window. Rising from within the palisade is
a timber tower of two storeys. The lower level is apparently
open, so that only the corner posts impede movement on the top
of the mound. The upper part of the structure is difficult to interpret; it appears to be roofed and to contain a window. There is
a gateway at the foot of the bridge, and the timber work generally is shown with much decorative detail. The keys of the
castle, which Duke Conan offers in surrender by holding them
on his lance from the parapet of the right-hand tower, themselves imply that this fort of earth and timber was no makeshift
structure. The evidence of the Tapestry corresponds closely
with an early twelfth-century account of castle-building in
Flanders:

It is the custom of the nobles of that region, who spend their time for the
most part in private war, in order to defend themselves from their enemies to
make a hill of earth, as high as they can, and encircle it with a ditch as broad
and deep as possible. They surround the upper edge of this hill with a very
strong wall of hewn logs, placing towers on the circuit, according to their
means. Inside this wall they plant their house, or keep, which overlooks the
whole thing. The entrance to this fortress is only by a bridge, which rises from
the counterscarp of the ditch, supported on double or even triple columns,
till it reaches the upper edge of the motte.[1]

[1] Quoted by Mrs. E. S. Armitage, *The Early Norman Castles of the British Isles*
(London, 1912), p. 88.

In 1949 the excavation of a motte at Abinger, Surrey, brought to light much confirmatory archaeological evidence.[1] Clearance of the top of the mound disclosed the whole circuit of post-holes which had held the twelfth-century palisade, while near the centre a rectangular layout of deeper holes for baulks supporting a structure of greater height indicated the position of the surmounting tower (Pl. 7a). Four symmetrically placed slots within the rectangle suggest the framework of an internal stair to the upper part of the tower. Two or three feet back from the perimeter a second circle of rather slighter holes, concentric with the first, suggests the presence of a form of wall-walk running round the inside of the palisade. The mound was so sited that its moat was water-filled from a spring. Evidence from pottery fragments showed that the first defences dated from c. 1080 to c. 1120; the timber work appeared to have been entirely renewed about the middle of the twelfth century. Evidence as to the defences of the bailey is wanting both in the Bayeux Tapestry and in the chronicle descriptions, nor have the banks of the presumed bailey at Abinger survived for investigation. It is reasonable to infer that they were generally palisaded in the same way as the mottes to which they were related.

With such a consensus of evidence, pictorial, literary, and archaeological, there can be no doubt that these motte-and-bailey, earth-and-timber structures were the most typical castles seen in England in the first century after the Conquest. Where they have not been incorporated and masked in later works of stone, their bare or tree-clad banks are still to be seen in every part of the country from East Anglia to Anglesey and from the Solent to beyond the Solway. At Ewias we have looked at the type in its earliest and simplest form, but innumerable variants of shape and scale survive, as may be seen from the many comparative plans figured in Mrs. E. S. Armitage's *Early Norman Castles*, in the *Inventories* of the Royal Commissions on Historical Monuments, and in some of the *Victoria County Histories*. Instead of one bailey there may be two or more of

---

[1] See report by B. Hope-Taylor in *Archaeological Jnl.* (1950), pp. 15–43.

PLATE 6

Duke William's soldiers assault the castle of Dinan. From the Bayeux tapestry

PLATE 7

a. Abinger, Surrey. Top of motte showing excavated post-holes of timber defences

'*Country Life*'

b. Restormel, Cornwall. A circular shell keep

varying dimensions. Sometimes, as at Windsor or Arundel, the motte is set midway between two baileys of roughly equal size. Often, as at Castle Acre or Kilpeck, additional earthworks will enclose the dwellings of a borough, attached to the castle from the time of its foundation. At Berkhampstead, where the castle was probably established in the earliest stages of the Conquest, there are double banks and ditches, an elaboration which occurs also at the great border motte-and-bailey of the Corbets at Caus in Shropshire, at Llanstephan near Carmarthen, and at Penrhos near Monmouth. Lewes and Lincoln are rare instances of early castles with two mounds. The size of the motte might itself vary greatly both in height and surface area. Sometimes it is developed into a circular or oval earthwork, forty to eighty yards in diameter, giving sufficient space for the inclusion upon it of the hall and the ancillary buildings which in the more normal plan would generally have occupied the bailey. Such treatment is common in South Wales, where good examples of it are to be seen at Ogmore, Llawhaden, White Castle, and Grosmont. The last-named probably owes its foundation to William FitzOsbern, the Conqueror's closest friend and collaborator, and can accordingly be dated to the years 1067–71; the castle of Monmouth, likewise founded by him, is of the same type, with the borough occupying what is in effect the position of the castle bailey.

The advantages of the earth-and-timber castle were that it could be constructed relatively quickly, in almost any type of country, and with little call for skilled labour. The height of the motte above the bottom of its ditch must have rendered sapping extremely difficult, while the steepness of its sides, now generally diminished by centuries of silting, would present a most formidable obstacle to direct assault. Earthwork also has the advantage of permanence; it is probable that comparatively few mottes raised in Britain in the eleventh and twelfth centuries have been entirely obliterated, while there are innumerable cases in which their initial presence, no longer immediately apparent, has in fact determined a castle's development through the rest of its history. The weakness lay in the material used to

complete the defences. Not only is timber ill suited to withstand attack, but it also requires constant repair and renewal in the face of natural decay. While it is true that halftimbered buildings in the bailey might rest for generations on stonesleeper walls, the essence of the palisade is that its main members are stepped into the ground. That, sooner or later, meant their progressive deterioration, a condition which probably explains the need for the replacement of the Abinger defences, already referred to, within about fifty years of their construction. If such a castle were successfully subjected to direct attack by fire, a weapon which the Norman assailants of Dinan evidently included in their armoury in 1064 (Pl. 6), its defences would soon be consumed; if it were captured intact, they could be readily dismantled and their materials carried off for use elsewhere. In the early 1150's the Cistercians of Meaux, for example, built a bakehouse, a stable, and some of their first conventual offices out of timber presented to them from the recently demolished *castellum ligneum* of Mountferaunt near Birdsall.[1] The grant, soon after 1146, to the Austin Canons of Old Buckenham of the site of Old Buckenham castle *et castellum diruendum* may well have conveyed a similar material advantage.[2] When we consider the inherently unsatisfactory properties of wood for military works, it is the more surprising to find how long its use was continued. The new borough of Montgomery, founded in 1223, was merely enclosed with a palisade; not until 1278 was this replaced with a wall of stone, and even then such of the wood as could be reused was taken to the castle to enclose one of the baileys.[3] At the height of the Welsh War of 1282–3, timber was deemed to provide a sufficient form of protection for the refounded English borough of Rhuddlan.[4] As the result of a change of plan at Linlithgow in 1302, intended stone gates and towers were ordered instead to be built in wood.[5]

[1] *Chron. de Melsa* (Rolls Series), i, p. 105, and *Early Yorkshire Charters* (ed. C. T. Clay), pp. 89–90.
[2] J. H. Round, 'The Castles of the Conquest' (*Archaeologia*, 1902), p. 21, note c.   [3] *Archaeologia Cambrensis* (1947), pp. 281–3.
[4] *Calendar of Ancient Correspondence concerning Wales*, ed. J. G. Edwards (Cardiff, 1935), p. 262.   [5] *Eng. Hist. Rev.* (1950), pp. 449–51.

The removal of a timber hall from Conway for re-erection in-side Caernarvon castle in 1316 reflects the persistence of wood construction as an element in military architectural practice side by side with stone building of the highest quality.[1]

Although the use of timber for fortification works was thus widespread in the early years of the Conquest and of long dura-tion thereafter, it would nevertheless be remarkable if those same early years which saw the initiation of such notable achievement in the building of great stone churches should not have witnessed the execution of castle works in stone from the beginning also. The number of such works datable with certainty to the eleventh century is, however, exceedingly small and, as might be expected, they are limited to districts where building stone lay readily to hand or could be easily transported by water. At Richmond in Yorkshire most of the curtain wall with its rectangular flanking towers and projecting gatehouse (later embodied in a magnificent keep), and likewise the great hall, are the work of Count Alan of Brittany, who held the Honour of Richmond from 1071 to 1089. Probably parts of the enclosing walls of Peveril castle in the Peak district, and of Brough-under-Stainmore in Westmorland, are as early. On the Welsh marches Ludlow is another great castle which, like Richmond and Peveril, is founded on the rock, and whose in-ner ward never had earth-and-timber defences. Begun by Roger de Lacy between 1085 and 1095, its curtain is flanked by four small rectangular towers and ridden by a rectangular gatehouse, afterwards altered and incorporated, like its Yorkshire counter-part, in a late twelfth-century keep. Within the ward stands the castle's unique round-naved chapel, probably begun in about 1090 though perhaps not finished till a generation later. Exeter castle has also preserved the remains of an eleventh-century stone entrance gate. Another building which has, with much probability, been assigned to the earliest years of the Conquest is the great hall at Chepstow, for it is believed to be a part of the castle which Domesday records as having been established there by William FitzOsbern. Yet another work of hardly less

[1] P.R.O., Ministers' Accounts, 1211/17.

early date is the small four-storey tower of Oxford castle; it was built, as was the now much-reconstructed undercroft of the adjacent chapel of St. George, by Robert d'Oilli in the 1070's. The base of a detached stone tower excavated in 1946 on the site of the Oxfordshire castle of Ascot d'Oilli[1] has closely similar dimensions (35 feet by 35 feet, compared with the Oxford tower's 35 feet by 37 feet 6 inches), and may go back to the same early period. The curtain wall at Rochester preserves masonry which is almost certainly part of the stone castle recorded to have been built by Bishop Gundulf and dated by Round to the years 1087–9. The base of the keep at Pevensey, a structure altogether *sui generis* by virtue of its six round-ended projections, one of them part of the third-century Roman wall against which it is built, may well be of the time of William of Mortain (1091–1101).

Foremost amongst all these early works stands the great tower which gives its name to the castle of the capital. Begun by the Conqueror and finished under his successor, the Tower of London may be looked on in its general conception as providing the model for those many rectangular stone keeps which, while varying greatly in dimension and detail, were to become as a class the most typical product of the military architecture of the following century. The purpose of the Tower was to provide complete accommodation, secure and of great strength, for the king and his treasure, his family and the principal members of his household. With the exception of Colchester, where only the lower part of the tower now remains, no other eleventh-century keep was conceived on quite so grand a scale. But there are twelfth-century examples, such as Rochester (1126–39) or Dover (*c.* 1180–91), which approach very closely to them. Both these great Kentish towers are notable for the large buildings covering their entrance stairs and each containing a chapel, an arrangement followed in a number of other keeps, as for example at Portchester (*c.* 1165) and Newcastle upon Tyne (1167–77). Very many such towers, which constituted the most characteristic pattern of fortified residence from

---

[1] *Oxoniensia* (1946–7), pp. 165–7.

PLATE 8

Castle Keeps
(a) Hedingham, Essex; (b) Pembroke

the Conquest to the time of the loss of Normandy, survive—
some larger, as at Kenilworth or Carlisle; some smaller, as at
Goodrich or Brough; some nearly intact, as at Hedingham
(Pl. 8 a), and some much ruined, as at Corfe; some obscured
almost beyond recognition by later alteration, as in the little
keep at Hay, between Hereford and Brecon. Their military
potency lay in the innate strength of their masonry, which has
enabled them to resist the ravages of time and assaults of man
alike; this is particularly well seen in such an example as the
tower at Bridgnorth, the bulk of which, though tilting over at
an angle of 50–60° since its undermining in the Civil War in
the seventeenth century, remains today as solid as when it was
built.

The majority of the rectangular tower keeps were placed
within the castle bailey, whose outer defences were in many
cases not renewed in stone until the thirteenth century. The
made ground of mottes was not suited to bear the concentrated
weight of such great structures; consequently, though examples
exist (e.g. at Lydford, Clun, or Norham), it is rare to find stone
towers added to artificial mounds much before the year 1200.
It is much more common to find instead the timber pali-
sades of mottes being replaced in the twelfth century by a
roughly circular or polygonal curtain wall following the crest of
the mound and forming what is usually termed a 'shell-keep'.
It seems highly probable that some of the more important
mottes, especially those scarped from largely natural elevations
where stone lay close at hand, may have been ringed in this
way from the first. It has been claimed that this is the case at
Durham, where the mainly fourteenth-century octagonal shell
structure is held to be a rebuilding incorporating masonry of
the eleventh century.[1] On general grounds one would similarly
expect an earlier date than that usually given (c. 1172) for the
lowest part of the best known of all shell-keeps, the Round
Tower at Windsor, and it may well be that it should more
properly be assigned to the time of the Conqueror. Other early
examples, likely to date at least in part from the years before

[1] S. Toy, *The Castles of Great Britain* (London, 1953), p. 56.

1100, are at Warwick, Tamworth, Arundel, and Lewes, the half-octagon flanking towers at the last-named being additions of *c*. 1260. The development of the form was general and widespread, reaching by the middle of the twelfth century from Tonbridge in Kent to Rothesay in the Isle of Bute. In the west country there are well-preserved examples at Launceston, Trematon, and Restormel (Pl. 7*b*), with more fragmentary remains at Totnes, Plympton, and Barnstaple. In Wales and its marches there is an imposing, if much restored, shell-keep at Cardiff, and the fragments or traces of others at Caus, Brecon, Crickhowell, Kilpeck, and Richard's Castle. At Carisbrooke in the Isle of Wight, both the shell on the motte and the curtain of the bailey were probably already standing in 1136, when Baldwin de Redvers is said to have had there 'a stately castle built of hewn stone'. Remains of what are likely to be slightly later examples survive at Berkhampstead and Pickering. Perhaps the most complete and least altered structure of this type is the shell which crowns the larger mound at Lincoln. It is polygonal, with a flat pilaster buttress at each angle; the steep stairs by which it is approached from the bailey up the face of the mound probably preserve the original arrangement.

In all the cases cited the shell wall is built on the flat top of the mound, along or a little way in from its circumference. Within the area thus enclosed there would be either a simple tower, no doubt often long in the traditional timber construction, or, where the mound was large enough, a hall and its ancillary apartments. Less commonly the shell was built up from the base of the mound so as to provide it with a strong stone revetment. Of this treatment there are outstanding examples at Berkeley in Gloucestershire and Farnham in Surrey. In Wales it appears to have been employed at Carmarthen and Cardigan, while there is also a partially revetted early mound at Castell Prysor in Merioneth. The shell wall at Tretower in Breconshire, where the mound was a low one, is of the same class.

These round shell-keeps, in spite of their name, are not, properly speaking, towers, but curtain walls for the protection of the small but vital areas comprised within the tops of

mottes. Towers, whether keep towers or the flanking towers of bailey curtains (of which those at Framlingham, Suffolk, built 1190–1200, afford the most striking example), tended throughout the twelfth century to remain rectangular in plan. But there were exceptions, and by the end of the century one or two less orthodox designs were already pointing the way to the round or round-fronted tower which was to be the most characteristic component of castle construction for the next two hundred years. Most notable among them are the keeps at Orford in Suffolk and Conisborough in Yorkshire. Orford, a royal building of 1166–73, is a polygonal tower flanked by three projecting square turrets, set so as to command its whole face and make hazardous any attempt to assault it directly. Conisborough, built in the 1180's, has a magnificent round tower, probably the earliest in England, from which are symmetrically projected, like cogs on a wheel, six solid wedge-shaped turrets. They serve the double purpose of buttresses and fenders, adding alike to the structural strength and military invulnerability of the building. Here, as at Orford, direct approach to the tower proper was made more difficult than was the case with the straight-walled, pilaster-buttressed, rectangular keep, the exposed corners of which moreover offered profitable quarry to the siege miner. Both buildings foreshadow the increasing emphasis which was to be placed, throughout the following century, on the flanking cover of continuous wall faces, as well as heralding a transition from square to circular keeps or tower houses.

Both these developments have now to be followed out. An intermediate stage between the rectangular and the round keep is to be seen in such a tower as that at Helmsley in the North Riding. Built about 1200, it is of traditional rectangular form towards the bailey but round-fronted towards the field. Towers of similar pattern were favoured in Wales by Llywelyn the Great, who presumably employed a French or English architect; a good example is at Ewloe, Flintshire (c. 1210), and there are remains of others at Dinas Bran, Denbighshire, and Castell-y-Bere (c. 1225) and Castell Carn-Dochan, both in Merioneth.

It is interesting, too, to see what is essentially a highly developed form of the same plan being employed as late as 1285–
90 by Master Ralf the Mason who during those years was
building for Roger Bigod III at Chepstow the great D-shaped
tower-residence now known as Marten's Tower.[1] Much earlier,
probably soon after 1200, the architect employed by Roger's
great-grandfather, William the Marshal, had built at Pembroke the finest of all English round keeps, a great unbuttressed
free-standing tower, four storeys high, and still preserving intact
its original stone saucer-vault (Pl. 6). At Cilgerran in the same
county, likewise, at the time of building, a Marshal lordship, are
two similar towers, somewhat later in date and now roofless,
both set astride the curtain of the inner ward. Round keeps on
the line of the curtain also occur at Barnard Castle, Co.
Durham, and at several native castles in Wales; of these the
best preserved is the tower at Dolbadarn, Caernarvonshire,
but there were others, some partly remaining, at Rhyd Castell
(Pentrevoelas), Bere, Carn Dochan, and Dolforwyn. The last-
named, built to offset the neighbouring royal castle at Montgomery, was in course of erection in 1273,[2] and this may well
indicate an approximate date for some of the others.

Already by the early part of the thirteenth century, when
sufficient time had elapsed to allow for settlement, it was also
being found feasible to build round keep towers on the tops of
mottes. The southern Welsh marches provide a regional group
of such structures in the surviving towers at Caldicot, Long-
town, Skenfrith, Bronllys, and Tretower, and in the foundations of another at Maes-celyn near Crickhowell. An interesting motte-tower belonging to the last decades of the century is
that at Hawarden, near Chester, a squat two-storey building
with a series of wall-chambers. That there were, however,
serious risks inherent in imposing heavy masonry structures
on purely artificial mounds, even after the lapse of more than
170 years, is apparent from the case of the great tower at York

[1] P.R.O., Ministers' Accounts, Bundle 922.
[2] *Foedera*, I. ii, p. 504; *Littere Wallie*, ed. J. G. Edwards (Cardiff, 1940), pp.
23–24.

castle. This remarkable building was begun in 1245.[1] It was designed on an almost unique quatrefoil plan by Henry III's master mason Henry de Reyns, the architect of the West-minster chapter-house, and may well have been intended to carry a third storey which in the event it was found inadvisable to erect, for a record of 1358 shows that the fractures which the walls exhibit today were then already in evidence, and it is therefore not unlikely that signs of weakness may have appeared while building was still in progress.

If the abiding glory of twelfth-century military architecture is the simple dignity of the rectangular keep, that of the succeed-ing century is the curtain with its flanking half-round towers, the great double-towered gateways, and the turreted tops of the English castles of Snowdonia. As the power of siege weapons increased, there was a tendency to widen and throw forward the area of defence and multiply the obstacles in the way of the attacker. In other words, while, as we have seen, new keeps or tower-residences for lords or constables continued to be built intermittently all through the 1200's, the emphasis shifted to making more and more elaborate the outward defences through which approach to the keep or other residential apart-ments of the castle could alone be gained. In some of the more important castles this meant the addition of an outer ring of defence concentric with but lower than the inner, enclosing a narrow enveloping ward interposed between the main curtain and the surrounding moat; but even in the reign of Edward I, the climacteric of English castle-building, there was nothing sacrosanct about the concentric plan, and for reasons which will appear in a moment at least two of the greatest Edwardian castles, Conway and Caernarvon, do not adopt it.

The activity of the thirteenth century in castle-building was tremendous, and the effort expended in terms of labour and money represented a high proportion of the national resources. This is brought home by the published figures for the construc-tion of eight new royal castles in North Wales between 1277

[1] For the dating of the York keep, generally known as Clifford's Tower, see the present writer's paper in *Archaeological Jnl.* cxi (1954), pp. 153-9.

and 1301.[1] The cost of these buildings alone, as derived from data which may not be altogether complete, amounted to nearly £62,000—say £6¼ millions in modern values. Yet this was but a fraction, albeit a very important one, of the military building in progress during those years over England and Wales as a whole. Moreover, as the Liberate Rolls from about 1220 onwards make abundantly clear, the concentrated effort evoked by the two final Welsh wars was but the culmination of a long sequence of improvement, enlargement, embellishment, and entirely new building which had been going on at royal and baronial castles alike all through the long reign of Henry III.

Detailed analysis of so great a body of material is beyond the scope of this essay, and it is only possible to indicate some of the major examples of the developments which took place. Wards and baileys, for the defence of which throughout the twelfth century palisaded banks had often gone on sufficing, were now enclosed by thick stone curtains strengthened at all salient points with projecting towers, from which the defenders, banked at two or three levels, could sweep the intervening stretches with bolts and arrows from bow or cross-bow. Such are the defences of the outer wards at Corfe and at Pembroke, or, on a smaller scale, the curtain and towers built on to an earlier hall to complete the enclosure of the courtyard at Grosmont in Monmouthshire. Not far from Grosmont, at White Castle, a simple curtain of the 1180's was equipped a generation or so later with four flanking towers and twin-towered gate, while a new outer ward with its own line of defending wall and towers was created to mask the approach to the castle proper. At Kenilworth the original castle was encircled, partly under John and partly under Henry III, by a new outer wall related to an extensive system of water defences. The Norman keep of Pevensey, whose only outer line had hitherto been the Roman wall of Anderida, now developed a strongly protected inner ward with a double-towered gateway (c. 1120) and a line of

[1] J. G. Edwards, 'Edward I's Castle-Building in Wales' (*Proc. Brit. Academy*, xxxii (1946)), pp. 66–73.

curtain and massive D-shaped towers completed for Peter of Savoy in about 1250. Along the borders of Wales entirely new castles were built at Beeston, Montgomery, and Dyserth. Beeston, of which alone substantial remains survive, shows in what is left of the multi-towered curtain of its outer bailey as fine an example as any of this type of defence in the early thirteenth century. The main curtain at Scarborough, stretched across the neck of a promontory, serves a similar purpose, but here the towers, like those at White Castle, appear to be early thirteenth-century insertions in a wall of much earlier date. At Dover the twelfth-century defences, already formidable, were doubled between 1230 and 1260 by the addition of a parallel outer curtain, the main gate through which is noteworthy for its unusual plan.[1] Finally, in the capital, the Tower of London assumed, by works long continued through the successive reigns of Henry III and Edward I, its familiar concentric pattern; the inner curtain, with its dozen attached towers, belongs mainly to the earlier reign; the outer line, with its Water Gate in St. Thomas's Tower (Traitors' Gate), the moat system with the Byward Tower and Middle Tower gates, and the barbican, are all the work of the later.

Dover and the Tower are both remarkable as medieval buildings still in use; for this to be possible, however, they have undergone in post-medieval times much alteration and adaptation. The least-altered monuments to the skill of the thirteenth-century military architect are accordingly not these two great southern fortresses but the series of castles built by Edward I in North Wales. In them every aspect of the art of castle-building can be studied at the very summit of its development. They were engineered under the direction of a builder of genius, Master James of St. George, whose services the king appears to have obtained by arrangement with his kinsman Count Philip of Savoy.[2] They may be conveniently dealt with in two chronological groups, the earlier (1277–82) comprising Flint,

---

[1] Figured in Toy, op. cit., p. 148.
[2] *Eng. Hist. Rev.* lxv (1950), pp. 433–57; *Antiquaries Jnl.* xxxiii (1953), pp. 33–47.

Rhuddlan, Builth, and Aberystwyth, the later Conway and Harlech (1283-90), Caernarvon (begun 1283), and Beau/ maris (begun 1295).

Of Builth, a refortifying in masonry of an early motte-and/ bailey, no stone is now left standing. Flint, so sited and ditched that its walls were washed by the tidal waters of the Dee, had in consequence no need of a concentric outer ring; it is chiefly notable for its detached Great Tower, which in the plan bears the same relationship to the main ward of the castle as does the Tour de Constance to the walled town of Aigues Mortes. But the resemblance ends there, and this much ruined but highly individual structure, with its suite of segment-shaped rooms ranged like a self-contained flat round a small open central space, has no exact parallel in Britain. Aberystwyth and Rhuddlan, by contrast, both follow the concentric form, and the latter, the better-preserved of the two, can today be studied as an instructive example of it (Fig. 38). The castle is built at the top of a low bank beside the tidal river Clwyd, which was canal/ ized for a distance of over two miles in order to provide a direct link for sea-going shipping. The main ward is a quadrilateral bounded by curtains 9 feet thick and 30 feet high, with twin/ towered gates on the diagonal axis and three-quarter-round towers at the other two corners. Rhuddlan was intended as a royal residence, and the halls, chambers, and chapel for the king and queen and their circle were disposed, with store-rooms below, in ranges of timber-framed buildings set against the curtains. Apart from loops at the level of the courtyard, where there was covering protection from the concentric outer wall, the curtains' massive solidity is unbroken by any kind of open/ ing, the windows of the royal apartments having all taken their light from within the quadrangle. Except where the ground slopes down to the river the main enclosure is encircled by a parallel curtain, originally rather less than half the height of the inner line and set some 50 feet outside it. Immediately beyond and below this is a wide, dry moat, with steep revetted sides, which could be swept from end to end from banks of arrow slits placed at alternating levels throughout the length of the wall

above it. The flat ground beyond the moat was likewise commanded by fire from two levels, namely the battlemented wall-
walks of both the higher and the lower curtains. Thus, given
sufficient men and weapons, the more vulnerable sides of the
castle could greet an assailing force with a four-tiered broadside; the dry moat, set well out from the ultimate and strongest
line of defence, would be a death-trap to any who found their
way into it, besides being a sure protection against the operations
of the sapper and miner.

As Rhuddlan was conceived as a royal headquarters in advance of Chester in the conditions arising from the Welsh war
of 1277, so Conway, a stage farther along the sea route which
governed both campaigns, was destined to fulfil the same role
in the new circumstances presented by the war of 1282. Here,
however, a fundamentally different site, a site militarily so good
as to be deemed to justify the uprooting and removal of the
principal Cistercian abbey of Gwynedd, dictated an altogether
different plan for the castle. The position chosen was an isolated
spur of rock, washed by the tidal waters of the Conway river
and its tributary the Gyffin and commanding an age-old cross-
ing-point on the coastal route into Snowdonia. A castle so
poised, and so girt with natural strengths, had no need of man-
made outer defences, and at Conway, as at Flint, the concentric
envelope is accordingly absent. Instead, the main curtain is
thrust out to the lateral edges of the rock platform, so as both to
allow the maximum use of its limited area and present wall and
rock together in a continuous front to the attacker. Eight massive,
stately towers, four on either face, jut out to flank the curtain,
their outer circumference carried down in perfect gradation as
a buttress to the rock and a support to themselves (Pl. 9); all
bear easily discernible evidence of their helicoidal construction.[1] The possibility of direct assault, difficult as it would have
been, was not overlooked: provision was made to equip the
wall-tops throughout the castle with the traditional projecting
wooden fighting galleries or hourds, which may here be re-

[1] Cf. Viollet-le-Duc, *Dictionnaire raisonné de l'architecture française*, v (Paris, 1854–
68), pp. 103–6, s.n. *échafaud*.

garded as compensating for the absence of an outer walled enclosure. Such a site did not lend itself to the large quadrangles of
Rhuddlan, Flint, and Aberystwyth or their great south Wales
contemporary, Caerphilly. The castle was therefore divided
longitudinally into two wards of unequal size, the inner and
smaller of which was given over to the royal apartments (here
built in stone *ab initio*) and distinguished by the addition of turrets
to the heads of its corner towers. The plan of the great hall in the
outer ward, intended for the use of officials of the household and
officers of the garrison, necessarily subordinates convenience to
the irregularities of the site and is accordingly shaped like a
boomerang. Yet despite this underlying need to conform to the
ins and outs of a rugged promontory, the planning of Conway
is for all that infused with a certain overriding symmetry already
displayed at Rhuddlan and shortly to be repeated with un-
inhibited directness at Harlech and Beaumaris. The long,
straight, inflexible north façade with its equally spaced towers,
the four turreted tops to the east grouped to balance their four
uncrowned fellows on the west, the barbicans at either end and
the pairing of towers north and south along the whole length of
the building—all these subtle dispositions make their contribution to Conway's superb effect. The great grey walls still bear
traces of the white rendering in which they once gleamed from
afar, and only the conical caps of the towers are now completely
wanting.[1] Moreover, beside the castle there survive, in the as
yet unbroken circuit of the town wall and its gates, the most
complete and least-altered defences of a medieval castellated
borough now remaining in Britain. It has been justly said that
at Conway the castle and town walls combine together to compose what is 'incomparably the most magnificent of Edward
I's Welsh fortresses'.[2]

During the 1280's the same standards of skill in design and

[1] A good impression of the appearance of a late thirteenth-century castle with
whitened walls and conical roofs to its towers is afforded by the castle of Champvent, near Lake Neuchâtel. The castle was the home of Sir Peter de Champvent
who, at the time Conway was building, was with Edward I in Wales, being one of
the stewards of the king's household.

[2] J. G. Edwards, op. cit., p. 38.

PLATE 9

Flanking towers, Conway Castle

PLATE 10

Beaumaris, Anglesey. The fullest realization of the concentric castle plan

strength in execution were applied to the construction of two more royal castles in the same territory, Harlech and Caernarvon. The former, planned, like Rhuddlan, concentrically on three sides, is especially notable for its well-preserved keep-gatehouse. This structure is the core and centre of the castle, at once the key to its defence and the residence of its constable, the king's deputy. The gate passage, above and around which it is built, is heavily protected with flanking towers, meutrières, double doors, and portcullises. In its residential capacity, with its two suites of apartments on successive floors, the gatehouse fulfils the function of the twelfth-century keep; in its defensive capacity it is set astride the principal curtain at the castle's one inevitable weak point, namely the gateway, against which any land-based attack would be directed, and where treachery from within or guile from without might be expected to seek to operate. There is a marked and interesting contrast between the gracious aspect of its inward elevation and the uncompromising militancy of the outward drum-towers and their attendant foreworks.

Caernarvon, aesthetically perhaps the most satisfying secular building of its size which the middle ages have left to us, stands altogether apart. Unlike the majority of its contemporaries, it has polygonal instead of rounded towers and is further distinguished by a degree of finish and decorative treatment which in the others is for the most part either lacking or exhibited only in particular apartments. There is little doubt that the explanation of these differences is to be sought in the probability that the castle was conceived from the beginning as the *caput* and future royal residence of the English principality of Wales. The later stages of its building, like those of Beaumaris (begun in 1295), were prolonged into the third decade of the fourteenth century. The contrast between the ground-plans of these two structures is due, as always, primarily to differences of site. Caernarvon, on a low tongue of rock, benefited from the natural protection of the Menai strait and the Seiont and Cadnant rivers and therefore, like Conway and Flint, required no concentric defence. Beaumaris, on the other hand, occupying flat ground

with few natural advantages, demanded all the outer protec'
tion that military artifice could afford. It was consequently
furnished with a concentric outer ward and wet moat, and in
the design of the whole, which was never fully completed,
James of St. George produced a symmetrical plan of classic
perfection (Pl. 10). Features common to the two castles are the
provision of internal wall galleries, the universal employment
of the shouldered arch, and the presence in each case of not one
but two keep-gatehouses—all four of them unfortunately left
unfinished.

One of the Caernarvon gatehouses, the King's Gate, is of
exceptional interest. While in the disposition of its parts it is
fundamentally similar to the gatehouse at Harlech, its defensive
apparatus is infinitely more elaborate. The character and pur'
pose of the castle itself, the absence of an outer curtain, the
impossibility, owing to the restricted area of the adjacent walled
town, of constructing a barbican, and above all the bitter ex'
perience of a successful Welsh insurrection in 1294, demanded
that here more than anywhere all the tricks and stratagems of
the engineer's armoury should be brought into play. The result
is a castle entrance of unusually formidable design (Fig. 39). To
reach the inner or lower bailey from the outside it would have
been necessary to cross a drawbridge (the present fixed bridge is
modern) and pass through five doors and under six port'
cullises, with a right-angled turn as one passed from the main
gate passage to a smaller passage (possibly never completed), at
the end of which there was to be a second drawbridge. At each
successive obstacle arrow-slits and spy-holes commanded the
approach from different levels, while in the vaulting above
groups of 'murder holes' threatened assailants and allowed
water to be poured down to extinguish any fire that might be
started against the gates. Well might Dr. Johnson exclaim,
when he visited Caernarvon in 1774, 'I did not think there
had been such buildings. It surpassed my ideas'.

In these noble structures of the Edwardian period the art of
castle-building attained its highest realization. It was not
possible to bring to the war in Scotland anything like the same

amassing of labour and treasure, and English castle-works
there were generally on a less ambitious scale. Henceforward
what the Crown could no longer find the means to do was even
less within the power of any but the greatest barons. Moreover,
at a time when the feudal levy was giving place to the paid field

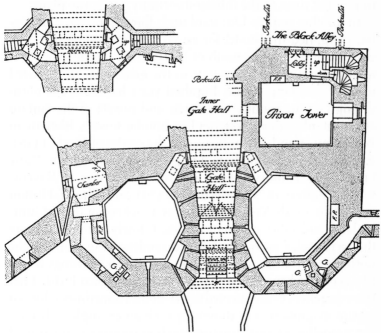

FIG. 39. Caernarvon Castle, North Wales. Plan of King's Gate.

army, the baronial castle was itself beginning to lose its *raison
d'être*. Nevertheless the early years of the fourteenth century continued to produce new works of importance. The spurred
towers of the outer gatehouse and of the great barrage to the
northern lake at Caerphilly, for example, are likely to date from
a little after 1300. Probably contemporary with them is the less
well-known castle of Tregrug in the vale of Usk. Here, at one
corner of a single ward of vast proportions, is a keep-gatehouse
of the first rank, its plan closely similar to that at Tonbridge and
to the principal east gatehouse at Caerphilly; all three were
Clare castles and may reflect the mind of a single architect. At

Dunstanburgh, on the Northumberland coast, a new castle was begun for Thomas of Lancaster in 1313. It was planned to con, sist, like Tregrug, of an immense single ward dominated by a powerful gatehouse/residence placed at one of the angles. The gate's massive twin round towers represent the final expression, in point of time, of the thirteenth/century gatehouse plan.

In another respect Dunstanburgh foreshadowed, and per, haps supplied the model for an architectural form that was widely adopted in the north of England all through the four, teenth century. For in contrast to the gatehouse, and, indeed to what for more than a hundred years had been the norm throughout the country, the turrets and towers of the curtain at Dunstanburgh are rectangular. Similar towers, likewise in Northumberland, are to be seen at the castles of Ford (1338), Etal (1340), Chillingham (1344), and Langley; at Raby (1378) and Lumley (1392) in County Durham; at Ravens, worth, Bolton in Wensleydale (1379) and Sheriff Hutton (1382) in north Yorkshire; and at Cockermouth in Cum, berland and other northern castles. Closely akin to them are the rectangular peels, the fortified residence built all over the northern shires as a defence against Scottish burnings in the two centuries between Bannockburn and Flodden Field. That these detached, battle/mented tower/houses sometimes achieved a grim magnificence is shown by such an example as Belsay; but a smaller, plainer structure, such as survives in the ruined Westmorland/north Lancashire towers of Arnside or Wrays, holme, is more typical.

The peel towers, like Edward I's Welsh castles, were the re, sponse to a particular military problem. So, in the south and east, were a number of castles and town defence works, built mainly in the second half of the fourteenth century in the face of the growing menace of French raids on the Thames estuary and the coasts of Kent and Sussex. The lower storeys of the Land Gate at Rye, built after the burning of the town by the French in 1339, provide an early instance of such activity, and exhibit a decline from earlier standards of strength and security which is apparent in much later fourteenth, and fifteenth/century work.

The forms are preserved, but there is a diminution of substance. Superficially the Land Gate is much like any twin-towered gateway of the previous century; but if we compare it with, say, the Upper Gate at Conway, built sixty years earlier, we find that a wall-thickness of 6 feet has given place to one of 4 feet, while the Conway gate opening of 9 feet has been expanded at Rye to one of 12 feet. By 1340 questions of economy and convenience are evidently influencing purely military considerations, to the detriment of the latter. Later examples of gateways built under the shadow of the French threat to the south-east survive at Canterbury (1378), Cowling (1380), and Saltwood (1383) (Pl. 11a). Of these the Canterbury west gate, with its vaulted passage and well-lit upper room, is a structure of great architectural merit perhaps attributable to the royal architect Henry Yevele. Certainly the Cowling gate was built by a Maidstone mason, Thomas Crump, under Yevele's direction.[1] Donnington castle in Berkshire has a graceful gate of the same period.

Bodiam, situated some 13 miles inland on a formerly navigable reach of the river Rother, is the best-preserved of the later southern castles. It was begun, in or about 1386, for the express purpose of defending the neighbouring countryside against the attacks of the French enemy. Its buildings are ranged round a single square ward with strong curtain walls and round corner towers; there are rectangular-towered gatehouses on the north and south, and single rectangular towers on the other two sides. The castle stands in a sheet of water, a setting which, besides being the ideal defence for a lowland site, makes it one of the most picturesque of English ruins. While in plan and design it shows no significant advance on its thirteenth-century predecessors, it is notable as one of the earliest buildings to be equipped with gun ports. In the arrangement of its accommodation it reflects very clearly the fact that, even within a single ward, it was customary to isolate the private apartments from the quarters of the soldiery; but one has only to recall the elemental separation of motte from bailey, or the sharp division

[1] J. H. Harvey, *Henry Yevele* (London, 1944), p. 39.

of the outer from the inner ward at Conway, to realize that a desire for lordly privacy was not altogether a novelty born of the age of livery and maintenance.

Nevertheless, the outstanding contribution of that age to the unfolding sequence of our theme lies in the magnificent dwell-ings erected by the wealthier noblemen, and their imitators, who had seen service and improved their fortunes in the French wars and who, when their fighting abroad was ended, continued to maintain an armed following clothed in the garb of their house. Such a society postulates the evolution of the private palace for the accommodation of the 'overmighty subject' who was its principal figure, and this is precisely the develop-ment that took place. The fifteenth century is accordingly the time when we witness the growth of the castellated house as a transition between the medieval castle and the Tudor mansion. In the new castle-building the emphasis is henceforward on the residence, on ample planning for comfort, on light and large windows, on making a brave, even a flamboyant show: defence, castellation, is of secondary importance. Of many a building of the period it could be well said, as Thomas Hearne, the painter, said of Michael de la Pole's fortified manor of Wing-field in Suffolk (1384), 'upon the whole, this Fabrick seems to have been formed rather to inspire the idea of dignity, and to oppose a popular tumult, than to resist an enemy'.[1] Two elements are dominant, namely the tower house, providing for the requirements of the lord and his family, and the rectangular courtyard, whose buildings would afford the requisite rooms for guests and retinues. Both elements are found, either separ-ately or in combination, throughout the century; but the ten-dency is for domestic considerations more and more to efface military, until the castle has merged almost imperceptibly into the great country mansion, with its moat or deerleap often the last echo of a defensive tradition.

Tattershall, the finest of the late medieval tower houses (Pl. 11 *b*), has been noted[2] for its resemblance to the splendid tower

---

[1] Thomas Hearne, *Antiquities of Great Britain* (London, 1786), Plate xxx.
[2] W. Douglas Simpson in *Jnl. of Brit. Arch. Assn.* (1935), pp. 184-5.

PLATE II

b. Tattershall Castle, Lincs. The Great Tower, *c.* 1435

a. Salrwood Castle, Kent. The Gatehouse, *c.* 1383

erected after 1395 at the castle of Poitiers for Charles V's brother the duke of Berry, and there is nothing unlikely in sup-posing that Lord Treasurer Cromwell's work in Lincolnshire, begun in 1434, may have been directly influenced by a French model he must almost certainly have seen. But the Tattershall tower is by no means the earliest of its class. The series might be said to begin with Nunney, in Somerset, where Sir John de la Mare was granted licence to crenellate in 1373 and where French influence is apparent in the machicolated tops of the pairs of round towers at either end of the main oblong structure. A forerunner of the Nunney tower, however, had already been built half a century earlier at Dudley. Both buildings are wholly self-contained residences, that at Dudley being placed on the motte of an earlier castle. Earlier still than Dudley, perhaps of *c.* 1300–10, is the square tower built on a motte at Hopton in Shropshire, an important but little-known monument which seems to provide a true intermediate link between the rect-angular keep of the twelfth century and the tower house of the fifteenth. The inference would seem to be that the builders of the later towers may not have been so much concerned with the possibility, at worst a remote one, of having to protect them-selves from their own paid retainers as with the consciousness of being heirs of a tradition, never altogether broken, of the strong tower as the habitation proper to nobility, reflecting in its very height and separateness the difference of station between the wealth and power of lordship and the relative dependence of followers and households.

A striking feature of some of the later buildings is their originality of design. The keep at Warkworth, for example, probably built by the first earl of Northumberland between 1380 and 1390, is a self-contained three-storey tower-house laid out on a plan to which there is no known parallel. Built round a small central light-well, it has been described as a square with canted angles, from the middle of each side of which projects a small square, also having its angles canted. No less remarkable is Wardour in Wiltshire, a castle begun by John, Lord Lovel, in 1392. Here the tower takes the form of a hexagon, with two

of the adjacent angles carried forward to make rectangular pro
jections flanking and thereby giving the semblance of defence
to its entrance. But the reality here is in the pair of large
mullioned and traceried windows over the gate itself rather than
in the narrow line of machicoulis above them or the slight barti
zans surmounting the tower's rearward angles. Wardour, in
its geometric plan and in the arrangement of its rooms round
a polygonal courtyard, strongly recalls Castel del Monte,
Frederick II's famous hunting castle in Apulia. But the re
semblance must surely be fortuitous. There is, on the other hand,
a similarity between Wardour and the great detached hexa
gonal tower of Raglan in Monmouthshire, built by Sir
William ap Thomas between 1430 and 1445, which might
easily be attributable to a direct relationship. Amongst less
exotic but not less impressive tower-houses are Lord Crom
well's other creation at South Wingfield, Derbyshire (c. 1440),
the tower of the bishops of Lincoln at Buckden, Hunts.
(c. 1480), and the grandiose addition made by Lord Hastings
to his castle of Ashby-de-la-Zouch, Leicestershire, after 1474.

Side by side with the towers went the growth of quad
rangular courtyards. Bodiam, already mentioned, was the
archetype of this development in the south. Other examples are
at Farleigh Hungerford in Somerset, Wingfield and Metting
ham in Suffolk, and Caister in Norfolk. Loveliest of them all
as an architectural composition is the great rectangular moated
castle built by Sir Roger Fienes in the 1440's at Hurstmonceux
in Sussex, its mellow brickwork as serene a memorial of its age
as are Hedingham or Caernarvon of the building achievement
of earlier centuries. Brick construction is, indeed, a characteristic
of many of the later buildings, and in such instances as the
fortified gateway of Thornton abbey (1382) or the great tower
at Tattershall it is employed with consummate skill and artistry.
At Raglan, where ashlar facing was easy to obtain, bricks were
used extensively for lining vaults and as a component in the
rubble core of stone-faced walls. Lord Wenlock's unfinished
castle of Someries, near Luton (after 1464), was to be a wholly
brick structure, as was also the moated courtyard castle begun

in 1480 by Lord Hastings at Kirby Muxloe in Leicestershire, of which more substantial remains survive. It is interesting to note that Hastings's master mason at Kirby was a Tattershall man, possibly the son of the master brickworker employed there by Lord Cromwell.

By the time Kirby Muxloe was building the middle ages were drawing to a close. The strong government of the Tudors, together with the solution of the Welsh problem inherent in the succession of their dynasty, did much to remove the principal causes of conflict, while the constitutional struggle which was for a few short years to bring English castles into their own again had as yet hardly appeared on the horizon. By abolish- ing livery and maintenance Tudor legislation put an end also to the need of nobles to fortify their residences and denied the authority of lordship, which, as we suggested at the beginning, was the castle's ultimate sanction, to all except the king. It was his failure to recognize the new state of affairs that in 1521 cost Edward Stafford, duke of Buckingham, his head and left his overweening castle of Thornbury, in Gloucestershire, begun ten years earlier, unfinished. Castles henceforward cease to be houses and houses cease to be castles. Military architecture, in- deed, goes on. But its next manifestation, seen in such a build- ing as the English citadel at Tournai (1515-17),[1] or in the chain of artillery forts established by Henry VIII along our southern and south-eastern shores between 1538 and 1540, is something wholly different from all that has gone before. After Thornbury it is no longer, even in reflection, the architecture of medieval England.

[1] Adolphe Hocquet, 'Tournai et l'occupation anglaise (1513-19)', in *Annales de la Soc. Hist. et Archéol. de Tournai* (Tournai, 1904), pp. 302 ff.

WORK FOR REFERENCE

The subject of English medieval military architecture has a large and growing literature, of which only the barest summary is here possible:

General Works

BROWN, R. ALLEN, *English Medieval Castles* (London, 1954), is a good modern study with excellent illustrations.

THOMPSON, A. HAMILTON, *Military Architecture in England during the Middle Ages* (Clarendon Press, 1912), still remains, after 40 years, the best general treatment of the subject.

The same author's 'Military Architecture', in *Cambridge Medieval History*, vi (Cambridge, 1929), pp. 773–84 and SIR FRANK STENTON's *The Development of the Castle in England and Wales* (Historical Association Leaflet no. 22, 1910, revised edn. 1933) provide useful summaries.

Special Aspects and Period Studies

(i) *Before 1200*

ARMITAGE, E. S., *The Early Norman Castles of the British Isles* (London, 1912).

BROWN, R. ALLEN, 'Royal Castle Building in England 1154–1216', *Eng. Hist. Rev.* lxx (1955), pp. 353–98.

ROUND, J. H., 'The Castles of the Conquest', in *Archaeologia*, lviii (1902), pp. 1–28.

ROUND J. H., 'Tower and Castle', in *Geoffrey de Mandeville* (London, 1892), pp. 328–46.

STENTON, F. M., 'Castles and Castle Guard', being chap. vi of *The First Century of English Feudalism* (Oxford, 1932).

(ii) *The Thirteenth Century*

EDWARDS, J. G., 'Edward I's Castle-Building in Wales', in *Proc. Brit. Academy*, xxxii (1946), pp. 15–81.

TAYLOR, A. J., 'Master James of St. George', in *Eng. Hist. Rev.* lxv (1950), pp. 433–57.

(iii) *The Later Castles*

SIMPSON, W. DOUGLAS, 'Castles of Livery and Maintenance', in *Jnl. of Brit. Arch. Assn.* (1939), pp. 39–54.

SIMPSON, W. DOUGLAS, ' "Bastard Feudalism" and the Later Castles', in *Antiquaries Jnl.* (1946), pp. 145–71.

Studies of Particular Sites and Buildings

Comments on twelfth-century works are often to be found in the introductions to the publications of the Pipe Roll Society.

There are many monographs, varying widely in scale and quality, on individual castles. The following are among the more important:

HOPE, W. H. ST. JOHN, *Windsor Castle*, 2 vols. (London, 1913); 'The Castle of Ludlow' and 'The Ancient Topography of the Town of Ludlow', in *Archae-ologia*, lxi (1909), pp. 257–328 and 383–8.

PERKS, J. C., 'The Architectural History of Chepstow Castle during the Middle Ages', in *Trans. of the Bristol and Gloucestershire Arch. Soc.* lxvii (1946–8), pp. 307–46.

SIMPSON, W. DOUGLAS, 'The Moated Homestead, Church and Castle of Bodiam', in *Sussex Archaeological Collections*, lxxii (1931), pp. 69–99; 'Wark-worth: a Castle of Livery and Maintenance', in *Archaeologia Aeliana*, 4th ser. xv (1938), pp. 115–36; 'Hurstmonceux Castle', in *Archaeological Jnl.* xcix (1943), pp. 110–22; 'Buckden Palace,' in *Jnl. of Brit. Arch. Assn.* (1937), pp. 121–32.

THOMPSON, A. HAMILTON, *Tattershall Castle*, National Trust Handbook (1926).

WOOD, MARGARET E., 'Stokesay Castle' (pp. 64–70) and 'Acton Burnell Castle' (pp. 62–64), in *Thirteenth-century Domestic Architecture in England* (*Archaeological Jnl.* cv (1950), Supplement).

Historical and descriptive guides, each with a dated development plan, are published by H.M. Stationery Office for over sixty castles in England and Wales which are in the care of the Ancient Monuments Branch of the Ministry of Works; *Castles*, by B. H. St. J. O'NEIL (H.M.S.O. 1953), traces in summary form the sequence of English military architecture as illustrated by these buildings.

IV. ART OF WAR

1. *Anglo-Saxon England*

THROUGH much of its history, medieval England was a well-governed kingdom less afflicted by warfare than many other parts of Europe. Yet there were military occasions enough. The invasions of these islands by the English peoples and the ensuing struggles for power were followed, from the ninth into the eleventh century, by attacks from Scandinavia. The process of invasion and conquest was brought to an end by Duke William and the Normans. Thereafter England was herself the base for attacks which her rulers delivered outside her own frontiers. Not only was there continual warfare on the Welsh border until the thirteenth century and on the Scottish border in the fourteenth and fifteenth, but the kings of England on many occasions crossed these borders on major expeditions of conquest. The counter-attack of the early twelfth century which A. L. Poole has called 'the English conquest of Normandy' was continued in campaigns to defend or recover the Angevin possessions in continental Europe, culminating in the great passages of warfare against France waged by Edward III, the Black Prince, and Henry V. Nor was any medieval century after the Conquest free from the alarms of private or civil war; the events of Stephen's reign, the contests of Henry III and Simon de Montfort, and the Wars of the Roses are all familiar episodes of English history.

The middle ages span a millennium, yet it is possible to discuss its warfare as a whole in a single brief survey because certain prime characteristics remained comparatively constant. Weapons changed little, especially when the length of the epoch is borne in mind. Certainly there was nothing to compare with the astonishing developments of the modern world. Lance, spear, sword, and bow were the main personal weapons

at the beginning of the period and remained so at its end. Nor was it an age when elaborate theories of war were practised in the field. Bookish rulers might consult or reproduce in writing the wisdom of Vegetius and other authors of the ancient world, but tradition and physical conditions played a greater part than ideas in moulding military methods. And even if there had been highly developed theories of war, they could hardly have been translated into effective action. Medieval armies, compared with those of the past two hundred years, were on a less permanent footing, were neither so expertly organized nor so thoroughly trained. There were, of course, fighting units who remained together over a period and who must have developed powers of concerted action: the ships' crews of the Vikings, the Great Army of the Danes, the housecarles of the Old English kings, feudal households, mercenary bands, indentured retinues. Organization for war, too, as the financial and administrative records of royal government in medieval England abundantly show, was maintained for important periods at a high level of efficiency. At the same time, it remains true that armies of the period were often kept in the field only with difficulty and that military operations were sometimes indifferently planned and poorly executed because of the inexperience and amateurishness of the troops and their leaders.

On the other hand, continuity does not preclude change: and once the fact of continuity is accepted change can be perceived —often change of a decisive kind which marks the main stages of historical development of warfare in medieval England. Although some weapons were used throughout the middle ages, the bow developed in efficiency and assumed new forms. There were inventions, especially of siege appliances: and by the end of the period gunpowder had been used not only to batter down fortresses but on the field of battle. While a developed art of war may have been lacking, there were tactical changes of the first importance. Not only were great commanders like the Conqueror and Cœur de Lion able to devise tactical measures to meet particular situations but a new system of tactics could be evolved within a generation or two, like that

combination of archers with dismounted men-at-arms which brought England her victories in the Hundred Years War. There were changes too in the social groups from whom the government exacted service, and in the type of army which it attempted to organize.

The armies of the Old English kingdoms were based on the obligation of the peasantry to serve in arms. From the earliest times, however, there were more purely military elements in English society, for kings and magnates were attended by sworn companions whose privilege it was to follow their lords in peace and war. Even when the primitive tribal chieftain and his war band were no more, a society grew up in which there was an aristocracy of service, whose duties were partly military, and in which magnates maintained households which in-cluded armed retainers. After the Danish conquests of the eleventh century there was a closely knit body of royal house-carles whose duties were purely military and who were paid by means of an annual tax levied on the whole kingdom. Beside these developments, peasant service as such may have declined in importance. There are signs that by the eleventh century only a fraction of the whole free population was summoned, while many of the ceorls who came to the host did so as the depen-dants of greater men rather than as members of a militia. But the popular element in military organization was never extin-guished. In an emergency, then as now, every free man might be called upon to defend his home and family and this ancient obligation can be traced throughout the medieval history of England.

The resistance which Alfred and his brother organized against the Danish invasion of Wessex has been called 'the first clearly recorded campaign in England' and his reign is certainly the earliest to reveal an English king who appreciated the nature of his military problems, who sought a solution by the intelligent application of his available military resources, and who, when these resources were proved defective, re-organized or modified them.

The Danish settlement in England was made possible by the

military successes of the Great Army in the years which followed
its first appearance in 865. During this period that army was on
a permanent footing. For this reason it enjoyed an overwhelm-
ing advantage against English peoples, who were not able to
keep a force continuously in the field, and many of its greatest
successes were achieved when there was no effective opposition.
From the first it was a feature of Alfred's policy, however, to
present to every Danish thrust the challenge of a field force.
The penalty of failure to do so was made clear to him in 878,
when most of Wessex submitted to the Danes, and when he
became a fugitive in the isle of Athelney. This episode was an
exception. Alfred's usual practice was demonstrated in 860
when for the first time the Great Army entered Wessex, and
established a camp at a point near Reading where the river
Kennett flows into the Thames. Within a week they had been
challenged not only by the ealdorman of Berkshire but by King
Æthelred of Wessex and his brother Alfred, who made an
unsuccessful attempt on the Danish camp. A few days later the
royal pair led the West Saxons to decisive victory in a pitched
battle on the Berkshire Downs; and although soon afterwards
they suffered two defeats, they never relaxed their resistance to
the invaders. Alfred succeeded his brother as king in 871, and
of the first year of his reign it was recorded in the Chronicle
that 'nine general engagements were fought against the [Dan-
ish] host to the south of the Thames, besides those innumerable
forays which Alfred, the king's brother, and ealdormen and
king's thegns rode on, which were never counted'. Twenty
years later, in meeting the last Danish attacks of his reign,
Alfred showed that he had lost nothing of his speed and re-
soluteness.

The king's success in resisting Danish conquest was also due
in part to his effective use of fortification. A document known
as 'the Burghal Hidage', which was probably drawn up in the
last years of Alfred's life, or soon after his death, provides not
only a list of fortified *burhs* in Wessex, but sets out the arrangements for their defence in time of war. The inhabitants of
neighbouring districts were responsible for providing members

of the garrison on the basis of the number of hides at which each village was assessed. These *burbs* were placed not only on the borders, but in the heart of the kingdom. Manned by a garrison in time of war, and providing a refuge for the local population, they immensely strengthened powers of resistance to an invader, and rendered more difficult his task of enforcing permanent submission.

Nor were they only instruments for defence. Alfred's son and daughter showed how they could be used to support recon/ quest. Like her father before her, Æthelflaed, 'the Lady of Mercia', provided that province with a number of fortified places. With her own lands thus firmly secured, she was able to co/operate with her brother, Edward the Elder, in his reduction of the Danelaw. In 917 and 918 Edward forced the submission of the Danish leaders in East Anglia and the midlands and advanced the boundary of his kingdom to the Humber. These military operations were centred in the strong places, so that every advance was supported by a fortress. In 917 he had armies in the field which fortified first Towcester and then, within Danish territory, 'Wigingamere'. In Essex another force stormed Colchester, occupied it and repaired its walls later in the year, and defended Maldon against counter/attack. In the meantime his sister took Derby in 917 and Leicester in the fol/ lowing year. These operations were marked by a breadth, co/ ordination, and thoroughness which make them 'one of the best sustained and most decisive campaigns of the Dark Ages'.

The successes of the West Saxon kings were based partly on the effective organization of their resources. In military crises, whether of attack or defence, they needed to be able to keep forces in the field for prolonged periods, which was no simple matter in a peasant society. Farmers were not easily kept from their homes and fields for protracted campaigns. It is true that the thegns constituted a military class, and the army which in 893 followed the Danish raid along the Thames valley to Butting/ ton on the Severn seems to have been recruited wholly from that class; but the raising of a sufficiently numerous army usu/ ally required the service of the ceorls. Alfred attempted to over/

come the difficulty by calling out only half the peasant force, which was available when the fortresses had been manned, leaving the remainder free for their normal pursuits, and ulti, mately to relieve those who had first been summoned. In follow, ing generations the selective principle was carried still further.

Development in military organization was not accompanied by tactical changes. Throughout the Anglo-Saxon period warriors were armed with the same shock weapons, sword, spear, and axe. Battles were often begun by an exchange of missiles in which bowmen played their part, but archery was never developed as a tactical device of the first importance. Horses were used as means of transport on the march, and there must have been individuals who could fight on horseback. But mounted combat had certainly not become normal for gentlemen as it had on the Continent, and it was the lack of horsemen and an inferiority in archery which contributed to the English defeat at Hastings in 1066. The point has recently been made with success that the outcome of this battle does not in itself prove that English warfare was in all respects inferior to the continental. The dramatic events of 1066 did not allow Harold to deploy his full strength. When, on or about 1st Octo, ber, he received news of William's landing, Harold was at York. It was just a week after his great victory over the Norse, men at Stamfordbridge. Without delay he set out for London, which he reached probably on 6th October. On 11th he left it again, and crossed the weald into Sussex. William received news of his movements on the 13th, and early on the following day led his army from Hastings to seek out the English. Seven miles north-west of the town he found Harold's force estab, lished on a low ridge.

Harold, fighting on his home ground against a sea-borne in, vader, should have had the advantage in numbers. The north, ern shires, however, were only lukewarm in their loyalty; their military resources had been depleted in the heavy fighting against the Norsemen during September; in his headlong march from York Harold can have brought only small forces with him. The very rapidity of his preparations in London can

scarcely have given him time to mobilize more than a fraction
of the potential military strength even of southern England; so
that on 14th October Harold had probably no more men under
his command than had William. Both armies were of the order
of 6,000–7,000 men.

Harold's best troops were his housecarles, and those of his
two brothers; with these were thegns and free men of some
military experience who had been able to answer his summons.
There were also peasants hastily recruited from the more immediate neighbourhood. The whole force fought on foot, and
it was drawn up in a strictly defensive formation. Its flanks
were protected by steep hillsides: to its front was a gentle slope,
falling fifty feet in some 400 yards, up which any attacks would
need to advance (Fig. 40).

William had at his disposal both mounted and dismounted
troops. Those on horseback constituted the most effective
weapon known to the European warfare of the day. Clad in
mail shirt and iron cap, and defended by the long kite-shaped
shield, they fought from the saddle with lance and sword.
These were the warriors to whom, on the Continent, the Latin
word *miles* had come to be specially applied. Among the foot-
soldiers there were many archers and crossbowmen. The best
contemporary accounts make clear the main stages of the battle.
The Normans advanced on the English position, the foot-
soldiers leading and the mounted men in the rear. The archers
inflicted some loss on the English, but could not break their
formation. After this preliminary attack the mounted knights
came through the archers to carry the fight into the English
lines. They were met by missiles—spears, axes, and even stones
tied on sticks; and hampered as they were by the adverse slope,
they could neither loosen the close array of the English, nor
break through the 'shield wall' which faced them.

The firm resistance on the part of Harold's men depressed the
morale of the enemy, and many of the Bretons on the Norman
left broke off the hand-to-hand fighting; as they fell back others
were infected by the example. The English who had driven off
the Bretons followed in pursuit. This was the first crisis of the

battle. The sight of men seeking safety in retreat is contagious, and the Bretons' withdrawal carried with it the threat of a general and uncontrolled flight. The situation was saved by William himself. At that stage he appears not yet to have entered the fight, but now he rode forward and personally rallied his

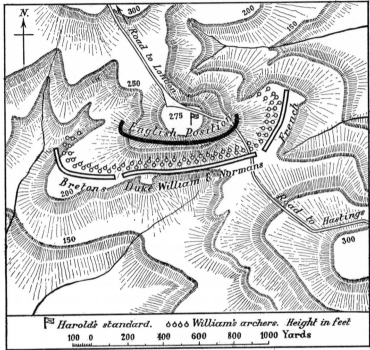

N.

Road to London
300
200
150
250
275
English Position
Bretons
200
Duke William & Normans
French
Road to Hastings
300
150

⚐ Harold's standard. ♦♦♦♦ William's archers. Height in feet
100 0   200   400   600   800   1000 Yards

FIG. 40. The Battle of Hastings

men. His success affected the battle in two ways: not only did it steady his wavering army, but it threw the pursuing English into extreme danger. In pursuit they had yielded up their principal advantages: they were no longer at the top of the slope, and they were no longer in close order; they were a number of individuals on foot and an open target for horsemen who had been once more turned towards them. They suffered heavy losses, and the position of the English as a whole was considerably weakened.

During the day the Normans repeated this success, but their

retreats were no longer a matter of necessity, but were a tactical device. On at least two more occasions groups of knights broke off the battle, drew in pursuit the English who were opposite them and then, wheeling their horses, destroyed their pursuers. These feigned retreats were the principal contributions to a process of attrition which lasted for many hours until, in the late afternoon, with Harold and his brothers dead, the English position was overcome. Pursuit in the gathering darkness destroyed any possibility of reforming the English army. Such was the course of 'one of the battles which at rare intervals have decided the fate of nations'.

2. The first two centuries of English feudalism
(1066–1272)

William's settlement of his newly conquered kingdom was closely related to his military needs. Victory in a single battle, however complete, did not free him from the dangers of renewed English resistance or of invasion from Scandinavia. He needed to provide himself as quickly as possible with the two most effective instruments for making war which he knew—mailed horsemen and adequately manned castles. He achieved this by dispossessing nearly all the English landowners in the upper ranks of society and replacing them with the greater men among those who had followed him to England, most of whom were Normans. The necessity of rewarding these men and the persistence of native revolt obliged him to take this course, while his success as an invading leader gave him the power to carry it through with maximum effect. This new aristocracy held their lands as vassals and tenants of the king on the condition that they rendered him services which included military services. They had not only to answer a summons to join the royal host in person, but they were bound to take with them a contingent of knights, armed and equipped for war. The strength of the contingent had been specified by the king when he first granted the lands. It was usually a multiple of five or ten, and the service owed by the greatest vassals was con-

siderable. Altogether about 180 lay tenants were bound in this way, and to them must be added the bishops and greater abbots, who also held their lands by knight service. By these arrangements William provided himself with a force which probably exceeded 6,000 knights. The method of raising and supporting these warriors was, with few exceptions, left to the lord concerned. In the early days of the Norman settlement, many knights were maintained in the lord's household, but in course of time it became increasingly common for them to be enfeoffed with land on condition of rendering military service and castle guard.

The hierarchy of feudal relationships so created provided a framework within which much of the government of England was carried on, including its military aspect. Too often, however, it is discussed as if it were the only framework of government in general and of military organization in particular. In fact it provided only a part of that organization, and one which steadily decreased in importance. Even from the late eleventh century, when English feudal institutions were still in process of formation, the Conqueror and his sons after him relied on non-feudal sources of recruitment. The Angevin kings of the twelfth and thirteenth centuries did so to an even greater extent, and an understanding of warfare in this period demands some attention to this process. For the time being this will be concentrated on the period before 1272. The still more rapid developments under Edward I and his son will be considered later.

It is doubtful whether the military needs of the English kings could ever have been met from feudal sources alone. The tenant was bound to serve only for a limited period, and indirect evidence indicates that the most commonly accepted spell was forty days in each year. While this may have sufficed for the summer forays of a petty seigneur, it was less useful to a king whose purposes might require a lengthy campaign. The kings of England were further handicapped by the vigorous denial of most of their vassals that they owed service beyond the sea in the continental lands of the Angevin house. There were other

difficulties. When fiefs were divided among co-heirs, the services were divided with them, and each stage of subdivision
made the exaction of service a harder matter. And when a fief
passed by inheritance from father to son, there could be no
guarantee that personal military qualities were part of the
heritage. The fief, as an estate which was the basis of its tenant's
material wealth and social status, could provide the main focus
for his interest and activities, and contemporaries speak of the
rustic knights in whose place the king prefers to hire mercenaries.

During the thirteenth century there was a further change.
The service fixed by the Conqueror remained as the basis on
which financial obligations, like aids and scutages, were paid;
but when corporal service was rendered the number of knights
brought to the muster was drastically less, especially when the
tenant owed the service of more than ten knights or so. There
was no uniform scale of reduction, but the feudal contingents
from the time of Henry III were a fraction, often of the order of
one-twelfth or one-fifteenth, of the old. The circumstances in
which such quotas were first agreed between king and tenants
are imperfectly known, but they were almost certainly connected with the greater cost of maintaining a knight and his
horse. The knight was more completely covered in mail; his
weight was increased by the pot helm and later by pieces of
plate armour; a larger and stronger horse, itself more fully protected, was needed to carry the more ponderous equipment.
The quotas were so much smaller than the original *servitia*,
however, that they seem to be insufficiently explained even by
the enhanced cost of horse and armour, and their reduction
may have been connected also with the king's need for knights
to serve for longer than the customary forty days, and especially
beyond the sea.

Throughout this period troops could be found in Europe
who were more experienced than most feudal tenants and who
would, if paid, serve for longer periods. The habit of employing mercenaries has been associated with the development of
scutage by Henry II and his sons, but both practices date back

to an earlier age. Scutage was already known by that name in the time of Henry I; and the chroniclers of the period provide an impressive array of evidence that not only Henry, but Rufus and the Conqueror before him, used other means for raising money in order to pay troops, and that such commitments were already a heavy charge on the king's resources.

There was as well a source of recruitment older than either feudal or mercenary service, and this was the general obligation on the free population. The fyrd was preserved and called out by the Norman kings and by their Angevin successors, who also reorganized it so as to ensure that an effective reserve of adequately equipped men was always available. In his Assize of Arms of 1181 Henry II ordered that every freeman in the country should maintain a set of military equipment, and should be prepared to use it in the king's service. In 1252 Henry III issued a more elaborate Assize, and in 1285 his son repeated many of its most important provisions in the Statute of Winchester. They provide excellent evidence about the weapons in popular use. Henry II, for example, divided the free population into three classes. All who held a knight's fee, or who possessed goods or revenues to the value of sixteen marks, were required to maintain the full equipment of a knight: the mail hauberk, helmet, shield, and lance. Those whose possessions were worth ten marks were obliged to keep a mail shirt, an iron headpiece, and a lance. The third grade, which included all other freemen in the kingdom, were to equip themselves with a metal cap and a lance, but instead of mail body armour they were allowed a shirt of leather or of quilted cloth. The documents of the thirteenth century imposed a similar, if more elaborate organization. The possession of a horse by the better-armed classes (implied in the Assize of Arms) was specified and, by the lesser men, 'all others that are able shall have bows and arrows'.

The twelfth and thirteenth centuries are an age in which the feudal horsemen are a military *élite*, yet the armies of the period are neither wholly feudal nor wholly mounted. The known facts of military organization are confirmed by reference to

military operations which show that the men who fought on foot had not, as is so often stated, lost their importance in war. The Norman Conquest of England was continued into the hill country of Wales and the bogs and woodland of Ireland. The natives of both lands were elusive foes who could rarely be pinned down to receive a charge of horse; and the necessity of adapting tactics to circumstances, and of employing auxiliaries on foot, especially archers who could be recruited in South Wales became well understood. Nor were special conditions needed to ensure the use of infantry elsewhere. Dismounted troops, with the field commander on foot among them, were a familiar sight on the battlefields of this period. At Tinche- brai, where Henry I fought against his brother Robert in 1106, the king had many *pedites* in the field. He regarded them as sufficiently valuable not only to brigade them with horsemen in each of his two leading divisions, but he himself dismounted and took his place on foot among them *ut constantius pugnarent*. As a result his army stood up to the cavalry charge with which Robert began the action, and the day was decided in Henry's favour by a mounted attack delivered by the men of Brittany and Maine, whom he had posted out to a flank for that very purpose. In a minor en- counter at Brémule in 1119 King Henry dismounted the majority of his knights and himself commanded them; only a minority were left horsed, and it was the group on foot which defeated the unco-ordinated mounted attack of the French. At Bourg Théroulde (1124) the force loyal to Henry won a victory in the same way, with the addition of a number of archers who took the charging enemy in the flank and made their defeat still more decisive. The English force which threw back the Scots at the battle of the Standard (1138) was partly made up of shire levies—the fyrd was still alive— and the whole force, knights and peasants, all fought on foot and were drawn up in a single close formation. Three years later King Stephen, when captured at Lincoln, had arrayed part of his army on foot and was himself fighting on foot among them.

Nevertheless, the mailed horsemen remained the most powerful type of warrior on the battlefield. At Lewes and Evesham in the thirteenth century the decisive blows were struck by mounted knights. But the age well knew the military value of a mass of foot-soldiers. Such a force was useless in attack, and it could not be manœuvred; but when its morale was high and formation close, it had a tough defensive quality which enabled it with bow and spear to withstand the onset of mounted knights. Their value was recognized in the measures taken to organize them in units and to place them under effective command. It was not only knights who were grouped in the tactical unit known as the *constabularia*. A. L. Poole has noted, in the administrative records of the late twelfth century, a number of references to *constabulariae* of foot, often under the command of a knight; and it seems that some of the dwindling body of fighting knights were employed 'not in divisions by themselves, but as officers in command of con-siderable bodies of men-at-arms'. A century later the records reveal that men who led bodies comparable to the modern platoon, company, and battalion were paid in accordance with their rank; and the existence of these vintenars, centenars, and millenars can be traced throughout the rest of the middle ages.

Service on foot was also of the highest value in siege warfare, which fills so great a part of the military annals of this period. The attack and defence of strong places required knights to dispense with their horses, while the contribution of men who neither possessed a horse nor fought on one was even greater than on the battlefield. Unskilled labour was needed to fill ditches and to level the ground in preparation for the assault or to dig trenches to facilitate a sap or mine; skilled labour con-structed hurdles, scaling ladders, assault towers, and various forms of siege artillery.

A strong place could be reduced by blockade or by attack, and usually by a combination of the two. In the eleventh century, when towers and enclosing stockades were often built in wood, fire was one of the besieger's most powerful weapons;

but when it became common to construct stone defences, the problem of the attacker was to surmount the walls, or to open a breach in them, or by tunnelling beneath them to bring them down.

The first of these objectives might be achieved by simple escalade or by the construction of a mobile wooden tower, which could be moved to the wall, and from which a picked storming party could gain a footing on the ramparts. Three such towers had been used by the Crusaders who took Jeru/ salem in 1099. Even if such a tower could not be brought alongside the walls, it could be built up to overtop them, and used by archers to keep them clear of defenders. A breach might be made by battering or picking, but these were slow and hazardous operations; for even if the detachment swinging the ram were covered by a penthouse, they were vulnerable to weighty and inflammatory objects dropped from above. A more effective means of weakening walls and bringing sections of them down was by hurling heavy missiles at them, and as the twelfth century advanced there was a marked improvement in the construction of the necessary machines. There were various instruments which the writers of the day never clearly describe, but which they usually call *petrariae,* or even more vaguely *machinae jaculatoriae.* They were built mainly of timber and rope. Those operated by the principle of tension were stretched like great crossbows and discharged javelin/like missiles at the defenders (Fig. 41). Ropes were also twisted in such a way that the torsion swung the free end of a beam through a wide arc and from that free end missiles could be hurled at a not too dis/ tant target. The application of counterpoise could produce the same result. A pivoted beam could be swung violently through a vertical plane by a heavy weight attached to one end. If a sling were attached to the other end a stone could be hurled at or high over a castle wall. Machines such as these, variously called a *tribrok* or *trébuchet,* were freely used at the end of the twelfth century, and effectively battered at the walls of Acre in 1191.

Provided that soil and terrain were suitable, one of the most

effective siege devices was the mine. Here again skilled men were needed, and just as in the east the miners of Aleppo were often mentioned in sieges, so the English kings repeatedly summoned miners from the Forest of Dean. The method used was to dig into the foundations of a tower or important stretch of wall and to shore up the foundations with wood. The besieged at this point were usually called upon to surrender (no besieger wanted the expense of rebuilding a captured castle) and they might even be shown the mine. If they refused, the

FIG. 41. Crossbows

supports were fired, and if the mine had been well prepared, the masonry collapsed. The repairs to the corner of the great tower at Rochester still bear witness to the success of King John's miners in 1214, and an elaborate mine was begun but never completed at Dover castle two years later. In siege operations on a grand scale nearly all known means might be employed. When Henry III attacked the castle of Fawkes de Breauté at Bedford in 1224, siege engines were used against the outer wall, wooden towers were built from which the garrison might be harried, while the inner works and the great tower itself were successfully mined. The efforts needed to reduce this single castle are a reminder that in this form of warfare the means of defence were stronger than those of attack. Even when reasonably effective cannon were available in the fifteenth century, Rouen or Melun could hold out for six months against the army of Henry V.

The armies of feudal England were to an ever-decreasing extent armies of feudal horsemen. Mercenary troops and foot-soldiers took part in nearly all important field operations; the needs of siege operations brought into being technical experts—*ingeniatores* and *balistarii*—responsible for the building and operation of mangonels and trébuchets (Fig. 42). The naming

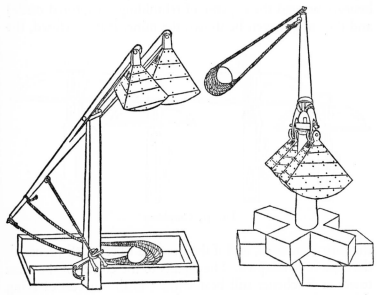

FIG. 42. Diagram of a trébuchet (*left*) loaded, before release, and (*right*) on the point of hurling the missile

of such specialists in the records is a reminder that there was more variety in a medieval army than is conveyed in the bald descriptive phrase so often adopted by the chroniclers: *milites peditesque*. Not only did horse and foot exhibit a growing variety of equipment; but there might also be found carters and pioneers, men like the *fossatores* who cut a road through the woods of North Wales for Edward I's advance, the carpenters and masons who were assembled to build his castles, the smiths and the armourers, even the interpreters and musicians.

PLATE 12

a. Attacking a town with scaling ladders

b. Attacking a town. Siege artillery old and new: one of the earliest cannons, between a crossbow and a trébuchet

3. From Edward I to Edward III (1272–1337)

The seventy years which followed the opening of Edward I's Welsh wars saw striking developments both in military organization and in tactics. Both led to the same culmination—those English victories which astonished Europe in the opening stages of the Hundred Years War. The history of these changes has been elucidated and their importance emphasized by the work of J. E. Morris, Tout, Mackay Mackenzie, Prince, J. G. Edwards, and N. B. Lewis. No more skilled and fruitful researches have ever been undertaken in the field of medieval military history.

Edward I had at his disposal the same main sources from which his predecessors had recruited their armies, but in some respects their value had changed. The terms of Magna Carta did not allow the employment of foreign mercenaries in England, and the feudal host had not only shrunk in numbers, but it fell short of meeting the king's military needs by an even greater margin than it had a century earlier. For the implementation of his policies in Wales and Scotland Edward needed forces which would serve for lengthy periods, through the winter if need be, in which discipline could be enforced, and which could be organized into a coherent order of battle with due hierarchy and subordination of command.

Pay was the key to this situation. As Edward himself soon appreciated, deficiencies in numbers, discipline, organization, quality, and duration of service could be made good by the greater use of paid troops. In 1282, for example, he called out the feudal army, but the records also show that £17,000 was paid out to cavalry alone. Some of the money went to feudal tenants and their followers who were taken into pay after they had served for forty days at their own expense, and the rest to men who served not because of their tenure, but as volunteers, or on grounds of public obligation. There were occasions during the reign, when all mounted troops were paid throughout the campaign. In 1297 Edward had 800 in Flanders, and the earl of Surrey another 750 on the Scottish border. Infantry,

whether enrolled as volunteers from South Wales or selected by commissioners of array under the terms of the Statute of Winchester, always served for pay. They were not kept in the field for long, and during a protracted campaign contingents relieved each other in succession. As the detailed administrative records of the period show, the numbers with the army might vary from week to week, and on occasions they could reach a high figure. In the Scottish campaign of 1297 there were at one time 21,000 foot in the field, while the army which won the battle of Falkirk in the following year included 12,500 foot, of whom all but 2,000 were Welsh.

There was another method of enrolling troops for wages which was to become more important than any other and which was to provide the basis for military organization in England during the later middle ages. The prevalence of warfare in the later thirteenth century resulted in the appearance of subordinate leaders who were virtually professional soldiers. They were usually landed men, often lesser tenantsinchief, who in campaign after campaign brought retinues to the muster and were taken into the king's pay. J.E.Morris was able to infer from the military records of 1277 that some of these captains must have made a contract with the king to raise squadrons of an agreed strength for an agreed period, and in fact the earliest known text of such a contract (discovered since Morris's day by Dr. N. B. Lewis) dates from 1287. Many of the earliest contracts may have been made orally, and they seem not to have become numerous in written form until the reign of Edward III. From the campaign of 1341, however, they become a normal means of raising troops for service in the field, and remained so until the end of the Hundred Years War, and beyond. The indentured contracts between the Crown and the captain were drawn up in duplicate, so that each party had an identical copy sealed by the other. The exact strength and composition of the company to be raised, the place and period of its service, its rates of pay, the conditions covering compensation for loss of equipment and for the payment of bonuses, these and other related matters were usually specified in detail in the contract.

The captain might solve his recruiting problem by making
in his turn similar contracts with individuals who raised a
part of the troop. As is well known, such contracts were used
by English magnates throughout the later middle ages to
retain the service of dependants in return for pay; but agreements of this kind were normally made for life, while royal indentures for military service were rarely made for more than a
year, and usually for less. In the realm of organization it was
certainly 'the most significant development in the history of the
English army in the late Middle Ages'.

The Edwardian period saw some important developments
in the types of soldier used in war. Usually the mounted
troops were still either knights equipped in the most elaborate
armour of the day and mounted on a trained war-horse
which might be worth as much as £100 (the number of
such men in all England did not exceed a few hundreds) or the
less fully equipped sergeants on horses valued at £10 or less.
In the years following the English defeat at Bannockburn the
Scots often harried the northern counties. The leaders who
opposed them found that heavily armed or dismounted troops
were too slow to bring the raiders to action, and as a result increasing use was made of bodies of light horsemen, known as
'hobelars'. Except when used for such special purposes, however, they never became an essential part of English medieval
armies. Among the shire levies who came on foot, the bow and
spear remained the principal weapons; but in this period significant changes were taking place in the effectiveness of the
bow as a weapon and in the skill of the men who used it. Foot-
soldiers in England, and more especially the southern Welsh,
had always used a short, light bow. The generation on either
side of 1300 must have seen the appearance of a longer bow,
of greater range and hitting power, which a growing number of
Englishmen learnt how to draw. The military operations of
the period show the importance of this change. Meanwhile the
exigencies of border warfare resulted in the horsing of archers,
who did not fight mounted but rode in order to pursue the
enemy and to bring him to battle. Unlike the hobelars, they be-

came a normal part of the English armies. In the campaign of 1334, not only were all ranks paid from the outset, but nearly all the archers in the retinues of the magnates were mounted. During the Hundred Years War a normally organized retinue included men-at-arms and mounted archers in equal numbers. It will be seen that both dismounted to fight.

In the realm of operations the period under discussion saw the evolution of a coherent military practice which used in a single tactical scheme the destructive power of archery, the de-fensive solidity of dismounted men-at-arms and, when neces-sary, the offensive power of mounted troops. Just as the key to the contemporary administrative problem had been the systematic use of pay, so that to the tactical problem was the intelligent employment of archery. In the warfare of this period English commanders discovered first, the virtues of archery in attack to break up a defensive infantry formation and second, its power in defence when based on an array of knights and men-at-arms on foot.

Once again a beginning was made in the Welsh wars. At Orewin Bridge in 1282 and again at Maes Moydog in 1295 the Welsh prepared to stand their ground in a defensive posi-tion. The English advanced against them, however, in a for-mation in which archers were interspersed with cavalry. The arrows inflicted sufficient loss on the Welsh to loosen their co-hesion and to enable the English horsemen to ride them down. Similar tactics were repeated against the Scots at Falkirk in 1298. For his operations against Wallace Edward commanded some 2,500 horse and 12,500 foot. The Scots were drawn up in four large and compact divisions—called 'schiltrons'—of spearmen who fought on foot. Between the schiltrons were their supporting archers, and to the rear a body of horse. The English, also in four main divisions, one of which was held in reserve, rode to the attack. Some of the young knights were eager to get to grips with the enemy and were in no mood to accept restraint or to spend time in working out a plan of attack. When the bishop of Durham, Anthony Bek, who had seen much service in Edward's wars, advised them to wait until the

king could bring up his division, he was contemptuously told to stick to his Mass. The mounted attack which followed easily dispersed the Scottish horsemen and archers, but against the schiltrons' outstretched spears it threw itself in vain. Nothing more was accomplished until the king ordered up the Welsh and English archers. Only when their shooting had torn gaps in the Scottish ranks could the knights again charge home, this time to deliver the *coup de grâce*.

These battles revealed the effectiveness of combined archery and cavalry action against immobile formations of foot-soldiers. Falkirk also showed that there were many Englishmen who had not yet learnt the tactical lesson, and it was this lack of appreciation which contributed sixteen years later to their signal defeat at Bannockburn (Fig. 43). In June 1314 Edward II left Berwick to relieve Stirling castle, one of the few places which remained to him in Scotland, and which Bruce then held closely blockaded. The Scottish leader determined to give the English no means of eluding him and so of reinforcing the castle without fighting a battle. He therefore took up a position only two miles south of Stirling, in wooded country known as the New Park, through which the road passed by which the English were advancing. If they attempted to force their way to Stirling, they would need to cross the Bannock and to deliver a frontal attack uphill. If they sought to outflank the Scots, and to approach Stirling by way of the Carse—the marshy country between Bannock and Forth —they could be kept under observation and would be exposed to an attack from a flank delivered by an enemy who was posted on higher ground.

When the English made contact with the Scots on Sunday, 23rd June, they quickly explored both possibilities. The earls of Gloucester and Hereford led the vanguard across the Bannock and straight against the Scottish position; but when resisted they quickly withdrew, and Henry Bohun, kinsman of the earl of Hereford, was slain by Bruce himself, mounted on 'ane gray palfray litell and joly'. Meanwhile Clifford and Beaumont had led 300 horsemen away to the right of the Scottish

position, and along the route towards Stirling castle which lay through the Carse. They were challenged by the earl of Moray at the head of some 500 Scots on foot but, unsupported by archers, they could not break into the ranks of Moray's men; and when Moray ordered an advance, the English fled in confusion.

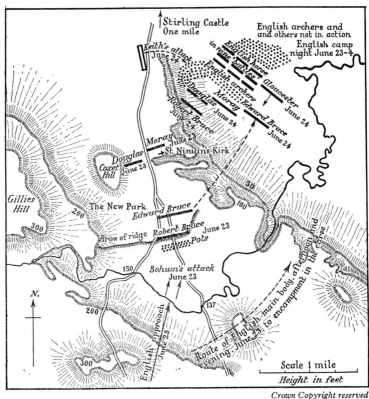

FIG. 43. The Battle of Bannockburn

As a result of these two unsuccessful encounters, the English decided to outflank the Scottish position and to reach Stirling by way of the Carse. They began the crossing of the Bannock on that same day and passed what may have been a wakeful, cheerless night amid the pools and marshes which encumbered part of the ground. In the morning the Scottish spearmen ad⁄

vanced down the slope on foot towards the English. They were
attacked by the English cavalry; but as these had little room in
which to manœuvre, they went into battle without order and
in some confusion. The Scots withstood the first attack of the
horsemen, and having destroyed their impetus, moved relent/
lessly against them. The result was the utter defeat of the
English.

After the experience of Falkirk it was to be expected that the
English archers would have been pitted against the schiltrons,
but it is evident from all accounts that they took little part in the
battle. Some were in action at the northern end of the line
against the Scottish left, but these were ridden down by the
light horse under Keith's command. The bulk of the archers
seem never to have been brought into the fight at all.

It has been seen that in the years after Bannockburn English
leaders in the north were forced to appreciate the uses of
mobility, and that as a result hobelars and mounted archers be/
came prominent in the records. In the same period a tactical
combination was evolved to destroy the advance of the Scot/
tish spearmen. The charge of cavalry was abandoned; if horse/
men were retained at all it was only to cover the flanks or to lead
the pursuit. The enemy's attack was received by dismounted
men/at/arms, drawn up so as to exploit the advantages of mass
and density. Such simple defensive means had been practised
throughout the middle ages, but, in the years between Ban/
nockburn and Crécy, there was a decisive difference. Archers,
drawn up on the flanks of the battle line, were used to inflict
maximum damage on the advancing enemy before he could
come to grips. As early as 1322 Andrew Harcla, fighting for
Edward II, had used archers and men/at/arms on foot when
disputing the passage of the river Ure with Thomas of Lan/
caster and the earl of Hereford. Ten years later, Edward Balliol,
invading Scotland to press his claim to the throne, defeated an
opposing force on Dupplin moor. He stood on the defensive,
and the shooting of his archers from the flank enabled his dis/
mounted centre to win the day. In 1333 Edward III practised
the same tactics with greater elaboration. A Scottish force at/

tempted to compel him to raise the siege of Berwick, and he re-ceived its attack on the slopes of Halidon hill. On this occasion the English were drawn up in three divisions of dismounted troopers, and each of these divisions had its archers on either flank. The archers seem not to have been drawn up exactly in line with the men-at-arms, but, from their point of junction with them, to have been slightly inclined towards the enemy. It is very near the formation of Crécy, and, as at Crécy, it brought a decisive English victory.

The means had been devised to overthrow the schiltrons. If the Scottish spearmen stood firm, they were decimated by archery until the English assault was delivered; at Falkirk in 1298 it was a mounted charge, at Neville's Cross in 1346 an advance on foot. If the Scots attacked, they were received by dismounted knights and troopers flanked by archers, whether on Halidon hill in 1333 or on Homildon hill in 1402. By these early years of Edward III, the essential military conditions of success in the Hundred Years War, both in tactics and in organization, had already been prepared.

4. The Hundred Years War

When Edward III sent his defiance to the king of France in 1337 he initiated a series of conflicts which were not to end until, in 1453, the English had been expelled from all France but Calais. His principal aim was to cast off his feudal obligation in respect of Guienne and to hold that province, not in fee as a vassal of the French king, but in full sovereignty. In future years the fortunes of politics and war enabled him to extend that claim to the whole continental possessions of his Norman and Angevin ancestors, while Henry V was to aspire to succeed to the entire kingdom of France. Although hostilities during the Hundred Years War were often interrupted, and sometimes for years on end, these consistently acquisitive aims of the English kings help to identify it as a single episode in the history of medieval warfare, as do the tactics and organization of the English armies. Something has already been said of

their genesis, and they were to remain essentially unchanged throughout the war.

After expensive and unsuccessful attempts to develop an attack on France from the north-east in alliance with heavily subsidized Flemish and German magnates, Edward in 1346 landed in Normandy with an army, some 15,000 strong, raised in England and Wales by indenture and commissions of array. Edward seems to have had no greater strategic objective than to lead a raid through northern France. His problems began in his attempts to cross the Seine and the Somme. King Philip had organized measures of defence which included not only the muster of a field army just outside Paris, but the destruction of bridges and the use of communal militia to defend the river crossings. For a few days it was doubtful whether the English would be able to find a way across the Somme before the French brought them to battle, and they carried the ford at Blanque Taque with only a few hours to spare. But once he had regained some freedom of action by crossing the river, Edward turned to fight. He chose a defensive position a few miles out of Abbeville and north of the forest of Crécy (Fig. 44). He arrayed his men on a slope with the flanks of his battle-line covered by natural obstacles. In the main line of battle the young Prince of Wales commanded on the right, the earl of Arundel on the left. In the centre of each of these divisions was a solid array of dismounted men-at-arms, with archers on either wing. In the rear and higher up the slope was a reserve under the king's own command.

When the French marched out from Abbeville on 26th August they were not aware that the English had decided to stand their ground. The news came to Philip only during the afternoon, and for many good reasons he accepted advice that he should not attack on that day. His troops had not only been on the road for some hours, but they were still extended on a loosely organized line of march, so that some hours must inevitably elapse before they could be drawn up for battle. But the ardour of the French knights could not be restrained. In the age of chivalry the knights' eagerness for spirited action and regard

for their personal honour and reputation could run counter to higher military considerations, and on the day of Crécy the orders of the royal commander were unheeded. The knights in the vanguard went into action before many of the French were in sight of the enemy, and they rode down their own crossbow, men in order to do so. As they bore down on the invader's line

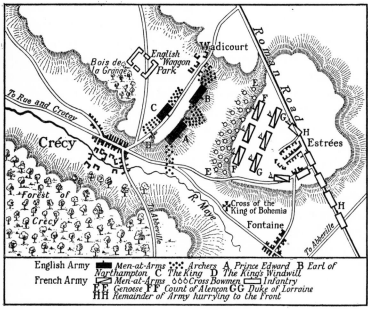

FIG. 44. The Battle of Crécy

they were taken in the flank by the English archers, whose arrows inflicted heavy casualties on men and horses. Those who reached the men-at-arms gave a good account of them, selves; but their attack was inevitably much reduced in weight and numbers, and they were never properly supported. The French seem to have mounted assaults as and when a body of sufficient strength arrived within striking distance of the enemy. English observers counted some fifteen such attacks, delivered at irregular intervals between late afternoon and the early hours of darkness. Edward's army was not dislodged

from its position; and such were the crippling losses which its arms and formation enabled it to inflict that, without the necessity for a general advance, it destroyed the heart of the French army and gained one of the most complete victories in the annals of English warfare.

So great a success gained for Edward only Calais, but when

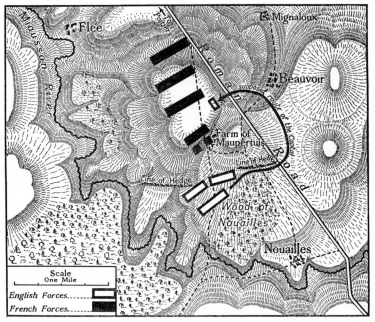

FIG. 45. The Battle of Poitiers

the war was resumed ten years later a victory of similar magnitude gave him for a time his main objective in fighting the war. In the spring of 1356 the Black Prince led a raid from Bordeaux into the Loire valley. A French army under King John's command took the field against him, and as Edward withdrew to the south, much impeded by the spoils of war, the two armies blundered into each other near Poitiers (Fig. 45). Because of the wide discrepancies between the evidence of contemporaries, the reconstruction of the ensuing battle presents difficulties which have never been satisfactorily resolved. It is not even

certain whether the Black Prince welcomed battle or would have preferred to avoid it; but its main outlines are clear enough.

The English men-at-arms and archers, all on foot, awaited attack in a position of which the defensive strength was increased by the hedgerows and broken ground. The French king, in more effective control of his army than his father had been at Crécy, dismounted the main part of it. Contemporaries tell us that French leaders had been impressed by the successes of the English fighting on foot, and paid them the compliment of imitation. As Oman has wisely remarked, they did not perceive that English methods were effective only when used in defence and strongly supported by missile weapons. At Poitiers John made no significant use of his crossbowmen, and his plan was based on attack. He organized his army in four divisions, one mounted and three on foot, which were set to make frontal assaults in succession, with the horsemen leading. The cavalry were impeded by the ground and shot down by the archers; but the dauphin's division on foot were not so vulnerable and they closed with the English men-at-arms all along the line. The hand-to-hand struggle was hard-fought, but after immense efforts on both sides the French were driven back in retreat before their succeeding divisions entered the battle. The next, led by the duke of Orleans, seems to have been unnerved by the dauphin's withdrawal, and never came into the battle at all. Everything therefore depended on the last and largest formation, led by King John in person. His advance represented so serious a threat to the now weary English that Edward felt the necessity for a major effort. He brought up his small reserve, and ordered his whole force to advance against the French. At the same time he sent a Gascon leader, the captal de Buch, to work his way round to the enemy's left flank, and it was in fact the surprise attack delivered by this small mounted force which decided in Edward's favour the final desperate mêlée. The victory was decisive. The number of French men-at-arms killed exceeded 2,000; King John and many of his greatest subjects were taken prisoner.

This success, and the possession of the French king, gave the English the strongest possible position from which to negotiate; and after a further invading march by Edward in the winter of 1359-60 from Calais to Rheims, and then to the neighbour/ hood of Paris, the French made acceptable concessions. The whole duchy of Aquitaine was granted in full sovereignty, together with Calais, Ponthieu, and the county of Guines. John throughout was treated like a king in the luxury of his captivity and the magnitude of his ransom.

When Edward died in 1377 nearly all these acquisitions had been lost. English rule lacked a firm basis. The French popula/ tion might submit passively for a time, but they could never finally accept an authority which they increasingly regarded as alien. French counter/attacks were therefore assured of popular sympathy and support. There were as well subsidiary reasons for the English failure of a more purely military kind. Their skill in battle lay in the defensive. Unless they were attacked, as they were at Crécy and Poitiers, or as the Black Prince's army was at Najera in Spain (1367), they had no way of carrying the fight to the enemy. During the 1370's French forces, often led by du Guesclin, refused to offer battle and so deprived the English of their main tactical weapon. Furthermore, their strength in archery and military organization was balanced by a weakness in siegecraft. Even after his sweeping success at Crécy Edward III had taken nearly a year to reduce Calais. In the later years of his reign English military policy was increasingly based on 'chevauchées', long marauding marches devoid of siege or battle. Historians have not yet finally interpreted the precise purpose and value of these raids. To Oman, as to French scholars, they appear to be entirely aimless and lacking in real military value, contributions to the sum of human misery but failing to apply military means to secure political ends. This verdict has more recently been challenged. The raids have been seen as part of a long/term military plan, designed to provoke the enemy into offering battle and, if he refused, to weaken him materially and to destroy his will to continue the war. They have been seen, too, as part of an ambitious plan for striking at

the heart of the enemy's territory from a number of points on his borders. It has been noted that the campaign of Crécy took place at the same time as the earl of Derby's offensive in Guienne, and that while the Black Prince conducted the raid which was to culminate at Poitiers, Henry of Lancaster was on the march in Brittany, and the two nearly joined forces on the Loire. It is another aspect of medieval military history which awaits investigation.

When Henry V renewed the war on a major scale in 1415 he did so at first in the manner of his great-grandfather seventy years earlier. Like him he landed in Normandy and, after reducing Harfleur by siege operations in which artillery played an important part, he began a march through northern France towards Calais. Like Edward he had difficulty in crossing the Somme, and was pursued by a French army, which on this occasion placed itself across his path at Agincourt (Fig. 46). The battle which followed was in some ways similar to Poitiers. The English adopted a defensive formation, their flanks covered by woodland, although on this occasion they were compelled to make the first move forward in order to bring the French within bowshot. Again the French made an unsuccessful mounted attack, and then sent in two successive divisions on foot. The first of these pressed the English hard, so that the archers were compelled to enter the mêlée with sword, axe, and even mallet. There was further hard fighting when this first French line was pushed back upon the second; and at the end of the day Henry so feared a final challenge from the enemy's mounted reserve that he gave the order to kill the prisoners. But victory remained with the English.

The state of French politics at this time gave Henry the opportunity to aspire to the French crown, and he determined to provide himself with a secure territorial base in France. He therefore embarked on a conquest of Normandy by methods very different from those followed by Edward III and his sons. Between 1417 and 1420 there were no more brilliant battles but a methodical acquisition of territory by reducing and occupying the castles and walled towns from which it was held.

The assassination of the duke of Burgundy and the ensuing Treaty of Troyes gave him the succession to the French crown; but as the dauphin and his supporters did not accept the treaty, Henry continued to extend his power to the south and south-east of Paris. It was an illness contracted at the six months' siege of Meaux which brought about his early death in 1422. By 1428 the attack on the dauphin had been carried to the

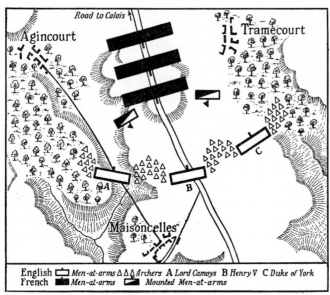

FIG. 46. The Battle of Agincourt

Loire, and in October of that year a small English force, wholly insufficient for the task, began the siege of Orleans. Six months later, when English resources were stretched to the limit, Joan of Arc appeared and French morale was miraculously transformed. Orleans was relieved; the English were expelled from their other strongholds on the Loire and the dauphin was crowned at Rheims.

The conquests of Henry and Bedford had been won by a series of patient and remorseless sieges. During the twenty years following the relief of Orleans the English were driven back

by the same means. The period saw a number of battles in which the English displayed all their old military virtues, especially the archers. At Verneuil (1424) those left in the rear to guard the baggage beat off by their sole efforts an attack by French cavalry which had outflanked the English line. Not content with this success the archers then joined the main battle between the men-at-arms as they had done at Poitiers and Agincourt and by their intervention gained the day for the English. At Rouvray five years later it was the archers who beat off the attack on the supply train which was marching to provision the English camp before Orleans. But the weakness in attack remained, and the power of their defensive was re- duced by the growing efficiency of artillery in the field. At Formigny (1450) the archers were provoked into a sally from their defensive position in order to seek relief from the harassing fire of two guns, and it was the failure of this move which ultimately helped to throw the English, drawn up defensively, into confusion and defeat. At Castillon (1453) Talbot's force was decimated by gunnery as it tried to force its way through to the relief of that fortress. And it was the French siege artillery, expertly handled by the brothers Bureau, which helped to drive the English from all their French possessions, saving only Calais.

5. Epilogue 1450–1600

By 1450 the English were no longer the supreme exponents of the art of war in Europe, and for the next two centuries they failed to keep abreast of continental developments. It was as if England had made her contribution in the fourteenth century, and then had nothing more to give. Elsewhere in Europe the Swiss had learnt to mount irresistible attacks by the manœuvre of serried masses of pikemen. Commanders had once more found effective tactical employment for heavy cavalry, could use artillery in the open field as well as in siege operations, and armed an increasing proportion of their infantry with fire- arms instead of crossbows. There were times when English governments showed appreciation of continental methods. As

the Wars of the Roses drew to a close foreign mercenaries were seen in England, while for his continental campaigns Henry VIII hired Burgundian cavalry and German *landsknechts*. In England itself, however, down to the end of the Tudor period and beyond, there was no true heavy cavalry. When English horsemen were again in action in significant numbers—and at Pinkie in 1547 one-quarter of Somerset's army was mounted—they were nearly all light-armed 'demi-lances'. The government showed a growing interest in the manufacture and employment of artillery, but seem to have used more of it in ships and coastal forts than in the field army. The infantry no longer stood on the defensive as consistently as during the Hundred Years War. They moved into action at Flodden and were intended to do so at Pinkie, but never with the superb order and massive weight of the Swiss. Nor were many of them armed with pikes. The shorter bill remained the principal weapon of the English foot-soldier, while the bow was used and valued down to the last years of Elizabeth.

The design and efficiency of firearms developed very slowly, and the introduction of gunpowder was far from creating even the mildest of revolutions in medieval warfare. As early as 1327 the Scots had found the English equipped with certain 'crakys of war', and six years later Edward III used 'gonnes' at the siege of Berwick. This chronicler's evidence is confirmed by administrative records, for the Chamber accounts and the Issue Rolls show that in the years 1333-5 sulphur and saltpetre were purchased on the king's behalf. It looks as if the age which saw the wider use of the indentured retinue, together with the development of the longbow and of the tactical importance of archery saw also the earliest use in English warfare of gun-powder as a propellent. In 1345 Edward III ordered the manu-facture of *ribaldi* before he crossed to France. These were small cannon of a kind certainly used in the siege of Calais and almost certainly on the field of Crécy. A generation later guns were not only part of the equipment normally stored in the Tower but had been added to the armament of most important English fortresses. Between 1382 and 1387 Randolph Hatton,

the keeper of the Tower wardrobe, 'spent nearly £1800 on the purchase of artillery and ammunition'. In these years 'he bought eighty-seven cannon of four gun-founders'. It is in this last quarter of the fourteenth century that large pieces of ordnance and small hand-guns first appear in the records (Figs. 47, 48).

There are many signs that artillery was slowly developed

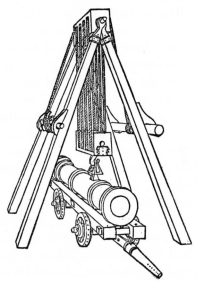

FIG. 47. A large cannon loaded upon its carriage

during the fourteenth century, but none that English military operations were decisively affected by it. In the time of Henry V, however, his reduction of Harfleur and the other Norman strongholds showed that gunnery had become an important addition to the siege-train, although a determined garrison could still make a siege a long and arduous operation. In the field English gunners made still slighter progress. More than a century after Crécy, at battles like Towton, Barnet, and Tewkes-bury, cannon had little effect, and it is only in the Tudor age that they are found being employed in the field in greater numbers and with greater confidence. In the use of firearms by the infantry the English were even more hesitant. Their vic-

tories in France had made the archer and the longbow into objects of national pride, and they were reluctant to abandon them. Even in Elizabeth's reign there was a lively literary controversy on the respective merits of bow and arquebus. Barnaby Rich could urge that the bow was superior in range, accuracy, and rate of discharge, and that it was less affected by wet weather. But the future lay with powder and shot, and by 1600 the bow was no longer officially considered as serious

FIG. 48. *Left* Hooped cannon and *right* Bronze cannon

equipment. At Pinkie (1547) no more than one-twentieth of the English foot were equipped with the arquebus. By the end of Elizabeth's reign it was normal for one half of an infantry company to carry pikes or halberds, and the other half calivers or muskets.

After the end of the fighting in France, English warfare lost much of its professional skill. The necessity of holding a conquest had created the need for permanent garrisons, and the frequent military operations had been carried on by troops raised by contract. The maintenance of the military establishment was ensured by a system of inspection. The captain of a troop was required to muster his men periodically for review by an official, in order to ensure that he was observing the terms of his contract and was drawing no more pay for his men than his entitlement. There were many men who soldiered for long

periods in France during the fifteenth century and who saw much action there. In the generation of the Wars of the Roses (1455–85) the magnates' households contained experienced soldiers, while others were bound to support their lords in their quarrels. With the weakening of the aristocracy, both as the result of heavy casualties in the Civil Wars and of the accession of Henry VII, the professional fighting men diminished in numbers. The Crown resumed its traditional position as the sole power which might lawfully authorize the raising of an army, and there were left to it the traditional sources of recruit' ment of the middle ages. All men between the ages of fifteen and sixty were liable to serve and, as in the days of Henry II, the more prosperous members of the community were required to maintain equipment in the king's service. The Act of 4 and 5 Philip and Mary divided them, according to their means, as Henry II had done in his Assize of Arms three and a half centuries earlier. The Tudors kept no standing force except for small bodies like the Gentlemen'at'Arms; they raised field forces only when a state of war required it. Then they relied on volunteers, or on the normal machinery of commissions of array and (too often, as some critics thought) on the conscription of criminals and vagabonds. The officials who operated the machinery were the Lords'Lieutenant and the Justices, but, as in the later middle ages, the Crown still made contracts with individual captains. These Tudor armies, raised as occasion demanded and equipped with obsolescent weapons, were less effective instruments for war than their forerunners of the four' teenth century.

Tactical plans, too, lacked the old coherence and sharpness. Perhaps for this reason the battles of this final period were not well recorded, and it is not possible to reconstruct them with the clarity of a Crécy or an Agincourt. Two of the greatest engage' ments of the Wars of the Roses were literally obscured from observers by the weather: Towton (1461) was fought in a snowstorm and Barnet (1471) in an April fog. At Barnet, whither Edward had marched out from London to challenge the southward advance of the Lancastrians, the division on the

left of each army outflanked its immediate opponents, and the
Lancastrian centre was ultimately demoralized by an attack
from the rear delivered by a detachment of its own troops as they
blundered back on to the battlefield after pursuing some of the
enemy. These battles were fought on foot with archers flanking
the division of men-at-arms and billmen. After a preliminary
exchange of missiles the two sides came into close combat until
the day was decided by numbers, morale, or accident. At
Tewkesbury in 1471 the armies faced each other in such a
formation. The Lancastrians, commanded by the duke of
Somerset, occupied a defensive position with the slope in their
favour. But Somerset led his left wing down the slope in an
attack on Edward IV's troops. The Yorkists held firm, and
then carried the fight forward as Somerset's men fell back towards their former position. In this way Edward's men were
able to fight their way into the enemy's lines, so establishing an
advantage which proved decisive.

At Flodden and Pinkie there was better planning but the
same imperfect command over amateur troops (Fig. 49). In 1513
the king of Scotland crossed the border while Henry VIII was
campaigning in France. Using his fine train of artillery he took
Norham castle. When he learnt that the earl of Surrey was in
the field against him, James established his army in a defensive
position on Flodden Edge, and there awaited attack. Surrey
saw clearly enough the danger of a frontal assault, and by means
of a wide outflanking march he threatened the Scots from the
rear. It was a bold plan, since it involved the division of his force,
the use by either part of a different route, and a march of many
hours before action could be joined. The Scots were thus compelled to take up a new position, and although the invaders
still had the advantage of higher ground, they moved down to
attack the English. There were many pikemen in the Scottish
ranks, while the mass of the English were armed with the
traditional bill. There was some archery and gunfire as the two
armies approached each other, but these were preliminaries,
and the battle was decided hand to hand. Each army was
divided into a number of contingents, and each had its successes

in different parts of the field. But wherever the push of the Scottish pike was resisted, the English bills were more effective in the subsequent close fighting, while the victorious contingents of the English, unlike those of the Scots, intervened else

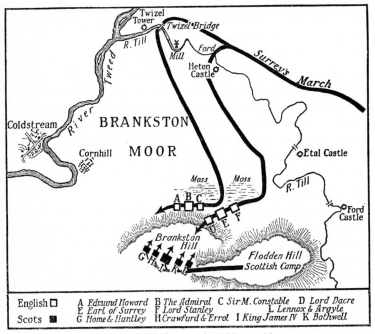

English □	A Edmund Howard	B The Admiral	C Sir M. Constable	D Lord Dacre
	E Earl of Surrey	F Lord Stanley		L Lennox & Argyle
Scots ▓	G Home & Huntley	H Crawfurd & Errol	I King James IV	K Bothwell

FIG. 49. The Battle of Flodden Field

where in the field with telling effect in the later stages of the battle. At Pinkie, too, the Scots attacked on foot. On this occasion, however, their advance was checked by cavalry attacks and by welldirected artillery fire.

English warfare was slowly moving away from the methods and equipment of the middle ages; but although in Elizabeth's days English soldiers were often on the march in Ireland and the Low Countries, great actions and great changes were not to be seen until the days of Prince Rupert, Cromwell, and the New Model Army.

WORKS FOR REFERENCE

BURNE, A. H. *The Crécy War* (London, 1955).

CHEW, H. M. *The English Ecclesiastical Tenants-in-Chief and Knight Service* (Oxford, 1932).

CRUICKSHANK, C. G. *Elizabeth's Army* (Oxford, 1946).

FALLS, C. *Elizabeth's Irish Wars* (London, 1950).

FOWLER, G. H. 'Munitions in 1224', in *Transactions of the Bedfordshire Historical Records Soc.*, v (1920).

GLOVER, R. 'English warfare in 1066', in *Eng. Hist. Rev.*, lxvii (1952), pp. 1–18.

LEWIS, N. B. 'The Organization of the Indentured Retinue in Fourteenth-Century England', in *Trans. R. Hist. Soc.*, 4th ser., xxvii (1945), pp. 29–39.

LOT, F. *L'Art militaire et les armées au moyen-âge.* 2 vols. (Paris, 1946).

MACKENZIE, W. MACKAY. *The Medieval Castle in Scotland* (London, 1927).

MORRIS, J. E. *The Welsh Wars of Edward I* (Oxford, 1901); *Bannockburn* (Cambridge 1914); 'The Archers of Crécy', in *Eng. Hist. Rev.*, xii (1897), pp. 427–36; 'Mounted Infantry in Medieval Warfare', in *Trans. R. Hist. Soc.*, 3rd ser., viii (1914).

NEWHALL, R. A. *The Conquest of Normandy* (Cambridge, Mass., 1923); *Muster and Review* (Cambridge, Mass., 1940).

OMAN, SIR CHARLES. *A History of the Art of War in the Middle Ages.* 2 vols. 2nd ed. (London, 1924); *A History of the Art of War in the sixteenth century* (London, 1937).

POOLE, A. L. *Obligations of Society in the XII and XIII centuries* (Oxford, 1946).

POWICKE, SIR MAURICE. *The Loss of Normandy* (Manchester, 1913).

PRESTWICH, J. O. 'War and Finance in the Anglo-Norman State', in *Trans. R. Hist. Soc.*, 5th ser. iv (1954), pp. 19–43.

PRINCE, A. E. 'The Army and Navy', in *The English Governments at Work, 1327–1336*, i, pp. 332–93, ed. J. F. Willard and W. A. Morris (Cambridge, Mass., 1940).

SANDERS, I. J., *Feudal Military Service in England* (Oxford, 1956).

TOUT, T. F. 'Firearms in England in the Fourteenth Century', in *Collected Papers*, ii, pp. 233–75.

See also Works for Reference appended to Chapter III (Military Architecture), above.

V. SHIPPING

1. *Introduction*

Cheryshe marchandyse, kepe thamyralte
That we bee maysteres of the narowe see.
(Libelle of Englyshe Polycye (1436) ll. 6–7)

SHIPS have always had to play a dual role for the inhabitants of this island. They are an indispensable
means of communication, carrying the necessities of
life and industry, and they are also essential to protect
the merchants as they go about their business and to defend
the coast from attack and invasion.

Already in the early years of the first century A.D. there was
a large and growing trade between Britain and the Continent;
wheat, cattle, skins, and metals were exported and a trading
settlement on the site of London handled goods from Gaul and
Italy, wine and pottery and luxury articles. Again, as soon
as there is any documentary evidence for the Anglo-Saxon
period there is record of a wide range of imports and exports
linking England with the Low Countries, Scandinavia,
France, and the German Empire, and a treaty between Offa
and Charlemagne in 796 gave mutual protection to their
traders. For at least seventy years before the Norman Conquest
England was in continuous relationship with the Continent
through trade, and a treaty made between England and Norway in 991 gave protection from the Vikings to any English
trader and his ship found in the ports of Germany, the Low
Countries, and France. The years after the Conquest were years
of economic expansion, marked by the growth of first the wool
and then the cloth trade, and although much of this commerce
was in the hands of foreigners, and it was only gradually that
the English merchants achieved a predominant position, there

was never a time when there was not a considerable number of native merchants entrusting their wares to English ships and sailors. Traders sailed to Iceland, to the Baltic, to Spain, Portugal, and occasionally to the Mediterranean. The bulk of the ships engaged in the wine trade with Gascony were English, and the capacity of all ships was estimated in the number of casks of Bordeaux wine that they could carry, a ton in two casks occupying sixty cubic feet of space. The typical ship of medieval England was the trader, the round cog, with its ample cargo space, suitable for carrying bulky goods over the Bay of Biscay and the Narrow Seas.

Across this steady commercial interest in ships there cuts the need for defence and war, for a permanent force of swift, well-armed ships to serve the king. The shipwright is naturally extremely conservative, and it was in almost every case the needs of war which led to the changes in ship design which marked the stages by which the decked and fully rigged three- and four-masted sailing ship of the sixteenth century evolved from the single-sailed open ship of the ninth century. Experiments adopted for warfare were quickly followed in building trading vessels, because the inadequacy of the fighting force obscured differences of function and placed upon merchant-men both the necessity of self-defence, and also the obligation of operating with the royal ships in times of national crisis. Medieval ships had to be dual purpose ships, and it was not until the seventeenth century that a real distinction was made between men-of-war and merchantmen.

2. The Pre-Conquest Period

The problem of defence was first faced by the Romans in the third and fourth centuries, when the raids of the Saxon pirates became a menace, and the *Classis Britannica* which had operated in the Channel from the first century was reorganized under the *Comes Litoris Saxonici* and based on twelve forts built on the coast between the Wash and the Isle of Wight. This organization completely collapsed with the withdrawal of the Romans

from Britain, but the problem it was designed to meet recurred when the Saxons themselves had to face the incursions of the Vikings in the ninth century.

From the point of view of the evolution of ships Europe is divided into two areas, the Mediterranean or southern region, and the Atlantic or northern region. The characteristic feature of the southern ships is that they were carvel built, constructed, that is to say, of strakes or planks laid edge to edge on a pre‑ viously constructed frame, whereas the northern ships were clinker built, with strakes overlapping and a framework fitted after the planking had been assembled. The Roman ships of the *Classis Britannica* would have been carvel‑built galleys. Parts of a river barge of this construction, dated to the third century A.D., was found in London in 1910, but Roman methods had no lasting influence, and there is no evidence of their use after the Roman withdrawal.

Three types of primitive native vessels were also in use dur‑ ing the Roman period and for some time later, namely the skin‑ covered coracles and curraghs and the dug‑out canoes. The coracle, a short, rounded vessel, is the oldest type, but was a river craft, and it was the sea‑going, boat‑shaped curragh, still in use in Ireland, which was the more important. From the evidence of classical writers the curragh was in common use in Britain in the period immediately before and after the beginning of the Christ‑ ian era. Caesar in Spain in 49 B.C. ordered his soldiers 'to make boats of the kind that his knowledge of Britain . . . had taught him. First the keels and ribs were made of light timber, then the rest of the hull of the boats was wrought with wickerwork, and covered with hides.'[1] These were the boats extensively used from the fourth to the ninth centuries by the Irish and Scots in their piratical raids, for which these light, fast boats were eminently suitable, for their trade, and also, surprisingly, for the adventurous ocean voyages made by their saints. St. Bren‑ dan, for example, in the sixth century made ' a very light vessel, with wickerwork sides and ribs . . . and covered it with cow hide, tanned in oak bark, tarring its joints: and they put on

[1] *De Bello Civili*, I, cap. liv.

board provisions for forty days, with butter enough to dress the hides for covering the boat',[1] and in this he sailed forty days north, probably to Iceland, and home by way of the Shetlands and Brittany. For his second voyage, on the advice of his foster-mother, the saint built a wooden boat; and it was the introduction of planked boats, capable of carrying heavier cargo, which led to the abandonment of curraghs, except by fishermen of the remoter west and north-west coasts.

The planked boat developed from the third type of primitive native vessel—the dug-out canoe. There is evidence that vessels of this type were in use over a very long period—possibly from as early as 2,000 B.C.—and that well-developed forms were certainly in use prior to the Roman conquest. One found at Llangorse in Breconshire (Pl. 13a), which was just over 15 feet long, had a rounded stern with a well cut seat for the paddler and a beaked prow, while the much bigger boat from Brigg in Lincolnshire was 48 feet 6 inches long with a rounded bow and a square stern, closed by a board fitted into grooves and caulked with moss. Inside the bottom of the Brigg canoe solid ridges were left to strengthen the hull which foreshadow the framework of a plank-built boat. Such dug-outs were very shallow, and in time they were deepened by fastening boards to the sides, until gradually the old dug-out was reduced to a broad basal plank which served as a keel, while the sides were built up of separate planks. Two boats found at North Ferriby in east Yorkshire were constructed with three bottom planks and probably three more on each side, set edge to edge and sewn by ties of twisted yew, and strengthened by transverse bars of ash, passing through cleats left standing on the inner face of the planks. The dating of these boats is not certain, but they were probably not earlier than 150 B.C. (Fig. 50).

Primitive boats found at Als in Denmark, dated to about 300 B.C., and at Nydam in Schleswig (Fig. 51) dated to the third century A.D., show a closer affinity to the later Viking long boat. The Als boat was 40 feet and the Nydam boat 76 or 77 feet long; both were clinker built, with cleats left on the

[1] *Acta S. Brendani*, ed. Moran (1872), p. 9.

inner face, like those on the Ferriby boats, by means of which the planks were lashed to the transverse frames. The later boat, however, shows considerable advances in construction:

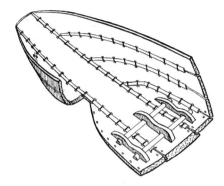

FIG. 50. Section of boat found at
North Ferriby

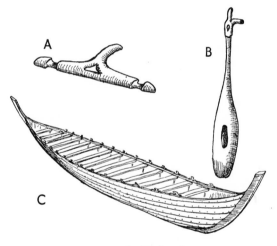

FIG. 51. The Nydam boat
A. Rowlock. B. Rudder. C. Reconstruction of boat

it gains additional strength from the fact that the planks were nailed as well as lashed, it was double-ended, with high stem and stern posts, which decreased the resistance to the water, while fourteen rowlocks on each side show that oars had replaced paddles, adding greatly to the swiftness of the boat.

There was a single paddle-shaped rudder and no sail. It was in boats such as this that the Saxons must have crossed the North Sea to settle in England. The great open rowing boat for thirty-eight oarsmen found in a burial mound at Sutton Hoo in Suffolk in 1939 (Pl. 13*b*), which can be dated to about 655 A.D., was similar in construction. Like the Nydam boat, the strakes are broad and few, but an advance is shown in that whereas the older boat was built of single planks equal in length to the ship, in the Sutton Hoo ship the strakes are made up of several shorter lengths riveted at the overlapping joints.

The fully developed Viking ships of the ninth and tenth centuries differ from the Nydam and Sutton Hoo boats chiefly in the addition of a mast carrying a single square sail. The Gokstad ship, which is one of the finest examples, is 78 feet long. The five wide planks of the Nydam ship are now replaced by sixteen narrower ones, and each strake has only a single cleat. The oars—sixteen a side—worked through oar holes cut in the third plank below the gunwale and fitted with shutters to keep the water out. These boats were gaily painted, often in yellow and black; they had coloured or striped sails, gilded and coloured shields hanging along the gunwales, and a gilded and carved stem post at stern and bow. They had only light decks, and, although an awning might be erected when in harbour, the crews normally slept and ate on shore. The Gokstad ship was typical of the smaller type of Viking ship; warships often had from twenty to thirty pairs of oars.

The building of the bigger type of vessel was no doubt stimulated by King Alfred's shipbuilding. In 897, to meet the attacks of the Vikings at sea, he 'commanded long ships to be built... which were well nigh twice as long as the others; some had sixty oars, some more; they were both swifter and steadier and also higher than the others; they were shapen neither as the Frisian nor as the Danish, but as it seemed to himself that they might be most useful'.[1] Still bigger ships followed, though there is some doubt whether they can ever have been quite as large as Cnut's reputed long ship, which was said to have had

[1] Anglo-Saxon Chronicle, *sub anno*.

sixty pairs of oars, making the over-all length of the vessel from 250 to 300 feet. Olaf Trygvason's *Long Serpent*, built in A.D. 999 and then described as the largest and finest vessel ever constructed, had thirty-four pairs of oars.

Although the primitive types of native craft continued in local use, the Viking ship, with its superior strength and speed, gave the pattern from which the typical medieval ship was developed, and its clinker construction remained characteristic of northern ships until the sixteenth century. The origin of the medieval system of providing ships for purposes of defence can also be traced to the tenth and eleventh centuries.

In times of grave national emergency there existed always the obligation on the whole country of providing ships in its defence, a duty which originally rested on inland as well as coastal districts, but which usually was interpreted as the royal right of placing an embargo on all shipping and of impressing ships and crews as required. Side by side with this emergency fleet, which corresponded to the ancient fyrd, or nation in arms, on land, there was need for a nucleus of well-equipped ships which would provide a semi-permanent force which could be called upon at short notice. On the efficiency of this nucleus depended in fact the successful keeping of the seas, but its provision presented an economic problem which was not satisfactorily solved during the middle ages.

The Saxon kings first followed Alfred's policy of maintaining royal ships. Athelstan in 939 had sufficient ships to send a fleet to help his ally the king of France, and the provision of ships was organized on a national scale by Æthelred in 1008-9, when the whole country was divided into districts of 310 hides, each of which was to provide a warship of about sixty oars. The cost of keeping such a fleet in commission, however, was enormous: it has been estimated that the wages of the crews of only sixteen warships of average size must have cost between £3,000 and £4,000 a year. Cnut, who came to England with a fleet of forty vessels, later reduced his standing fleet to sixteen, and his successor, Harthacnut, met the most serious trouble in his reign when he attempted to raise taxes to pay the crews of his

PLATE 13

a. Dug-out canoe from Llangorse, Breconshire.
Probably first century A.D.

b. The Sutton Hoo ship. About 655 A.D.

PLATE 14

Ships from the Bayeux tapestry. Late eleventh century

sixty-two ships. In 1049 Edward the Confessor introduced a new system. Instead of attempting to maintain a small fleet himself he planned to obtain the same result—namely a force of well-manned ships available at short notice—by offering certain of the Channel ports privileges in return for the obligation of providing a specified number of ships when required. Common obligations and privileges in time bound this group of ports together as the Cinque Port Confederation, and, as such, Sandwich, Dover, Hythe, Romney and Hastings, Winchelsea and Rye and their smaller member ports played an important part in the thirteenth and fourteenth centuries, alongside a varying number of royal ships and impressed merchant-men.

3. *The Norman Conquest to 1400*

The ships used by the English and Normans at the Conquest (Pl. 14) differed little from the Gokstad ship, except that there was some tendency to an increase in depth and the sheer, or upward slope of the ship's lines to the stern and bow was accentuated. Already in Alfred's time a distinction was noted between the Danish and Frisian boats, and there is no doubt that the latter were the slower, broader trading vessels which played an increasingly important part in the more settled conditions after the end of the period of Viking invasions. Although overseas trade was still in the twelfth and thirteenth centuries largely in the hands of foreigners, and English ships were used mainly for coastal trade, individuals were penetrating either as traders, pilgrims, or pirates into the Mediterranean, while the Bay of Biscay was known as the 'sea of the English'.

The trading ships were becoming shorter and rounder and they were increasingly dependent on sails, the area of which could be varied by tying up the canvas in a bundle with the aid of reef points, or by adding or removing an extra piece known as a bonnet at the bottom of the sail. It was the conversion of the rowing ship with an auxiliary sail to the sailing ship with auxiliary oars which led to an important modification in the design of the hull. The earlier ships were steered by

means of a rudder lashed to the side of the ship—whence the term star (or steering) board—but in a sailing ship, if the boat heels over in a wind the side rudder is lifted from the water and becomes useless. The difficulty was remedied by the introduc-tion of a stern rudder hung centrally on the stern post. The first certain evidence of this is found on the seal of Ipswich, dated about 1200 (Pl. 15*a*), but quarter-rudders continued in com-mon use for at least another hundred years. When stern rudders became general the old double-ended Viking type of boat, with similar high curved posts at bow and stern was superseded by boats in which the stern post was straightened to accommodate the rudder.

The loss of Normandy in the thirteenth century brought the problem of defence, which had not been acute in the twelfth century, to the fore again, and was a stimulus to naval activity. Attempts to maintain a royal navy were revived, the Cinque Port Confederation reached the peak of its power, and the general use of all available ships in time of war led to important changes in ship design.

The Norman kings did not keep up a royal fleet: England controlled the northern and western coasts of France, and the only serious threat to shipping was from pirates. Against piratical raids, and for transport purposes, the service of the Cinque Ports of fifty-seven ships for fifteen days a year at their own costs and for longer periods at the king's charges was adequate, although Henry II found it convenient to keep his own private galley or *esnecca* in readiness at Southampton for carrying himself, his family, or his guests across the Channel.

The first occasion when there was need for a fleet of larger size was for transport for the crusade of Richard I in 1189. This fleet, which numbered upwards of a hundred vessels, pur-chased and hired from all the ports of England, Normandy, and Poitou, sailed as a unit under officers described by Roger of Hoveden (Rolls Series, iii. 36) as *ductores et constabularios totius navigii*, who were probably military leaders and navigators and wardens of the fleet. All masters of ships were to show obedi-ence to these leaders, and at night a lantern was hung from the

mast of the king's ship to keep the fleet together 'as a hen gathers her chickens'.[1] For the discipline of the fleet ordinances were drawn up dealing with cases of bloodshed, violence, and theft on board ship. Although the fleet was disbanded when its pur׳ pose was served, the experience of keeping so large a force to׳ gether for a long period, and the knowledge of Mediterranean shipping gained as a result of the expedition, were important for the future.

As soon as the Channel ports fell into enemy hands on the loss of Normandy the need arose for a permanent naval force, and this need continued throughout the thirteenth century and during the Hundred Years War. King John took immediate steps to meet the emergency and in 1205 he had fifty׳one royal galleys stationed in ports in England and Ireland. From then on there was usually a small force of royal ships: in 1242 four swift barges were built for the king's use, and in 1295 twenty galleys, costing between £200 and £280 each, were ordered from ports between Newcastle and Plymouth. In 1317 Edward II bought five galleys from Genoa, and in 1336 galleys were hired from the same source, while in 1373 an eighty׳oared barge *Paul* was built for Edward III at London.

These royal galleys were long swift boats, the length might be five times that of the beam, and they depended still upon oars rather than sails. The *esnecca* owned by Henry II carried a crew of sixty compared with a normal complement of twenty׳three to man a trading ship, while the galley to be built in London in 1295 was to have 140 oars. Except in name, they did not closely resemble Mediterranean galleys; they were, like the Viking ships, clinker built, and the single mast carried a square sail instead of the lateen or triangular fore׳and׳aft sail of the galley proper. Some of the king's ships were roomy enough to serve also as cargo ships, and were sometimes hired out to merchant׳ men. In 1232, for example, John Blancboilly had custody of the king's great ship, known as the *Queen*, for life, with all her anchor cables and tackle, to trade where he pleased for fifty

---

[1] Ambroise, *L'Estoire de la Guerre Sainte*, ed. Gaston Paris, ll. 1235-49; *Itinerarium Regis Ricardi*, Rolls Series, p. 179.

marks a year, in return for keeping the boat in good condition.

It was no use building ships unless measures were taken to
keep them well equipped and in repair, and to King John also
belongs the credit of initiating an organization in which are
seen the origins of the later Board of Admiralty. John's fleet
was in charge of three chief keepers of ports, or keepers of the
galleys, who had the duty not only of looking after the royal
ships, building and repairing them, but also of impressing
additional ships and crews and issuing instructions generally
in conjunction with the local sheriffs and bailiffs. William
of Wrotham, the chief of the three keepers, was often called
Keeper of the King's Ships, the first use of a title which was still
used for officers in charge of building royal ships in the fifteenth
century.

Side by side with the royal ships, and more important because usually more numerous and more easily available, were
the Cinque Port ships, also a permanent force held in readiness
for emergency. The thirteenth century gave the portsmen their
opportunity; the loss of Normandy enhanced their strategic
importance and this was at once given recognition by the confirmation of their individual liberties in 1205. Their ship service,
instead of being confined to transport and patrol duties, took on
a new importance; they served as an integral part of the fleet in
naval expeditions against Wales, Scotland, and France. It was
in the royal interest to encourage closer association between the
various Ports. Hitherto the bargains for service had been made
with each Port separately, but in the thirteenth century their
liberties were confirmed to them on several occasions in joint
charters. They were given immunity from all external courts,
and administrative unity under a Warden, who combined the
functions of sheriff with the special ones of Keeper of the Coast,
Constable of Dover, and judge of their court of Shepway.
Edward I took this organization a step farther when he linked
the Cinque Port unit to the royal and impressed ships under a
single command by appointing first a Captain of the Sailors of
the Realm and then in 1297 an Admiral of the Sea of the King

of England. Both titles were combined when Gervase Alard of
Winchelsea was made Captain and Admiral of the Fleet of the
Cinque Ports and of all other ports from the port of Dover by
the sea coast westward as far as Cornwall and the whole of
Cornwall, an authority which probably united that of commander at sea and administrator. The effect of the royal policy
on the Cinque Ports was to put power in their hands which
they exercised as much in their own interest as in that of the
king. They were ready to take advantage of the fact that circumstances made their help indispensable and to use the threat of
desertion as a weapon to secure pardon if their independence
carried them too far. In the civil wars of the thirteenth century
they were a decisive influence, but their allegiance to one side
or the other was always uncertain.

The fact was, that in spite of the existence of a nucleus of royal
ships, in spite of the closer organization of the Cinque Ports,
and in the fourteenth century of the authority placed in the
hands of the Admiral and the development of maritime law,
the system of keeping the seas was inadequate. The force available was neither sufficient in number, nor regular enough in
service, nor well-enough disciplined to be really effective.

The royal ships were too few in number to be of any great
importance: the Cinque Port ships were manned by men, often
called the king's pirates, who were not particular about where
they took their profit, who were as ready to fight personal
enemies among their own countrymen as the foreign foe, and
who did not stop at murder. Woe betide the crew of a ship
driven by storm on to the coast, for the law that it was no wreck
if a man, or even the cat that all merchantmen must carry for
the protection of their cargo, escaped alive, only encouraged
the secret slaughter of unhappy survivors. Personal quarrels
might grow into inter-town feuds. The Cinque Ports carried
on a running feud with the men of Yarmouth, a rather less
serious one with Poole and the western ports, and a dispute
with Bayonne, which was first mentioned in 1237, was not
finally settled until 1277. In 1293 a private quarrel between
men of the Ports and Norman sailors resulted in a battle at sea

which provided Philip IV with the excuse for seizing the English possessions in France. This state of affairs was in part the outcome of the methods by which hostilities were carried on. Formal engagements and pitched battles at sea were exceptional; it was a case of every man for himself and guerrilla tactics. When war was declared, as for example in 1243, the masters of all ships were licensed and encouraged to annoy the king's enemies by land and by sea wherever they were able. Pirates were often pardoned for their misdeeds if they agreed to equip their ships in the king's service and became official privateers. By traditional law all prizes taken at sea were the property of the king, but in practice encouragement was given to those who would enlist in his service by giving the master and crew a considerable share. In addition to enemy ships, those of neutrals carrying enemy goods were fair game, while the unscrupulous easily disposed of letters of safe conduct by throwing them overboard. It was not until 1414 that the breach of safe conduct was made treason and that keepers of safe conducts were appointed in the ports. In the thirteenth century the use of banners of arms to distinguish port, nationality, and ownership became general, but even so mistakes might be made, especially when the news of the making of a truce or of fresh alliances was slow to spread to men at sea. Disputes about rightful or wrongful attack were naturally numerous, and because the legal means of securing redress were inadequate it was the practice to issue letters of Marque, authorizing the injured party to take reprisals. The earliest of these dates from 1295 and they became extremely numerous and were an obvious source of excuse for piratical exploits.

At the same time, although the High Court of Admiralty was only established at the end of the fourteenth century, there was a growing body of maritime law and custom used by merchants, in contrast to the rough-and-ready justice carried out by seamen. The earliest maritime code, the so-called Laws of Oléron, probably dates from the twelfth century and was accepted in England in the fourteenth century. It stresses the importance of the crew—probably because the science of

navigation was so rudimentary—and helps to explain the difficulty of the admirals in imposing effective discipline over men
accustomed to have so much voice in the management of their
ships. It was, for example, necessary for the master to consult
the crew before sailing; if he failed to do so he was held responsible if the ship was lost by storm. If the master was involved in a dispute with a mariner it was to be decided by the
vote of the rest of the crew, and if the master did not abide by their
decision, but dismissed the man and engaged a less competent
one, he was again held responsible for any damage arising thereby. In case of storm, when the question of jettisoning some of the
cargo and tackle was considered, the crew must be consulted and
the agreement of a third of them secured. In time of war crews
were employed for a wage, but often in merchant ships they
received a share of the profits, or were allowed a certain amount
of free space in which to carry cargo for trade on their own
account.

Even if the permanent nucleus of the maritime force available
for the defence of the kingdom had been well disciplined, it
would have been inadequate in size for the needs of fourteenth-
century warfare. The fifty-seven ships of the Cinque Ports
were to be manned at the rate of twenty-one men and a boy, but
a crew of that size was only competent to handle a ship of under
sixty tons. By the middle of the fourteenth century ships of at
least a hundred tons, with crews of sixty-five men or more, were
usual; in fact at the battle of Sluys in 1340 the French ships
averaged crews of eighty. The summons in 1302 of half the
number of ships due from the Ports, but with the complement
of men for their full service, is an indication of changing conditions. Further, the service of the Ports at their own costs was
limited to fifteen days a year, a length of time probably fixed
when cross-channel transport was their principal duty, and too
short a time for a campaign of any significance. Just as on land
the terms of service of the old feudal levy made it a less convenient body than a paid army, so at sea the same cause led to
the Cinque Port fleet being outdated. Geographical changes
and the silting-up of their harbours accelerated the decline of

the Ports, and after the fourteenth century their fleet had little importance.

The Hundred Years War was the period in which the greatest reliance was placed on the ordinary merchant ships to meet the emergencies of war. Year after year embargoes were placed upon all movements of ships, and their crews were im٫ pressed for national service. The effect on trade was serious. From 1347 onwards there were frequent complaints from the Commons: ships were arrested and forced to discharge their cargoes before reaching their proper destination, the arrest was made long before it was needed and the ships were then held idle. Those not arrested could not follow their trade because all the available crews had been impressed for the royal service. Even the ships of foreigners were liable to impressment if they happened to be found in harbour. The payment of three٫ farthings a ton for the hire of impressed merchantmen was in٫ adequate, and there was little to encourage merchants.

There was also the old trouble of meeting the expense of maintaining a fleet. Edward I had first exploited commerce and found in the wine and wool trade a source of revenue, and in the reign of Edward III special customs were imposed to provide funds for keeping the seas and especially for the pro٫ vision of armed convoys to protect the wine fleet from Gascony. In 1347 a custom was levied of 2s. on every sack of wool ex٫ ported and tun of wine imported, and of 6d. in the pound on all other merchandise exported or imported. Merchants had adopted the convoy system in their own interest, electing one of their number as commander for the voyage, to whom obedience must be shown; now the king took advantage of the prac٫ tice for his own purposes. Ships in the wine fleet served both as merchantmen and men٫of٫war, they carried armed soldiers as well as seamen, and it was their duty not only to protect their cargoes but to take the offensive, destroying galleys and ships of the enemy at sea. In 1353 vessels refusing to join the convoy were liable to forfeiture, and if while at sea any separated them٫ selves causing loss to the others, the deserters were required to make satisfaction according to the size and value of their ships.

The use of merchant ships in warfare and the need for all to go armed in self-defence led to important changes in the design of ships in order to give attackers superior height in dealing with an enemy. As early as 1190 northern long ships had dis- covered when operating against Saracens in the Mediterranean that it was hard to grapple with a *dromon*, for the enemy could pour brimstone and burning pitch over their heads. In the middle ages similar tactics to those used in land warfare were adopted at sea. Sailors did not fight, and the master of a ship remained solely responsible for the navigation, but each ship carried a large number of soldiers armed with crossbows. At the battle of L'Espagnols-sur-Mer in 1350, fought off Win- chelsea, the king himself, the Prince of Wales, and other great nobles and their retinues were distributed in the various ships. They were entertained while awaiting battle by their minstrels, who played a new German dance, and by Sir John Chandos, who sang to them at the king's request. When the enemy were sighted the trumpets were sounded and a frontal attack was launched. The objective was for each ship to select an oppo- nent and either to sink her by ramming or, having grappled her, to disable her by cutting down her sails, killing as many of the crew as possible and then boarding her to finish off the de- fenders in hand-to-hand fighting. In this battle

if the King's ship had not been large and stout she would have been sunk, for she met the great Spanish ship with such force that it was like the crash of a tempest. And with the shock, the turret on the mast of the King's ship caught that of the Spaniard, so that it broke his mast. . . . The King's ship received such a shock that she let in water.

Grappling another enemy the king led an attack which suc- cessfully boarded her, whereupon he abandoned his sinking ship and used his capture for the remainder of the battle. An- other ship—the *Salle du Roi*—grappled so large a Spaniard that she was carried away by the enemy under full sail, and only escaped through the valour of a valet, Hankin, who leapt on to the Spaniard and cut down the sail and the shrouds support- ing the mast.[1]

[1] Froissart, translated in D. Hughes, *Illustrations of Chaucer's England* (1919), pp. 124 seq.

In addition to crossbows the offensive was carried on by a variety of projectiles, stones 'as large as loaves' to sink the ship, soft soap and *tribuli* or three-pronged bits of iron to make movement on deck difficult, quicklime to blind the defenders, and darts and lances to damage the rigging. For the effective use of these weapons superior height was essential, and the seals of the port towns, which are the chief source of information about ships of this period, show that from at least 1238 superstruc- tures were being built fore and aft for this purpose.

At first these castles were very flimsy affairs erected inside the boats, and were probably only put up temporarily when the ship was equipped for battle (Pl. 16). By the end of the thirteenth century they were becoming permanent, much larger erections, built over and incorporating the stem posts (Pl. 15*b*). In the older ships there had been no cabins on board, the only shelter was from awnings, and if there were important passengers on board carpenters had to be brought to make shelters for them. Now the lower part of the castles, boarded in, were made into cabins, and as they developed the castles grew in length as well as in height and projected farther out over the ends of the ship. Fighting tops, or platforms, were also frequently fixed to the masts. Those on the galley built at Newcastle in 1295 were surrounded with a wooden breastwork and had a door in the side to admit the defenders. They were gaily painted in bright colours and decorated with lions in yellow. The defenders in the tops were armed with bows, stones, and lances: in 1340 the French solved the problem of keeping them supplied with am- munition by lashing small boats to the masts to carry a stock of stones. There were dangers in carrying heavy projectiles to such a height, and in 1416 the Lord West was accidentally killed by the fall of a stone being hauled up to the fighting top of his ship.

Towards the end of the fourteenth century it was becoming obvious that the frequent interruptions to trade resulting from impressment in war were having a disastrous effect on ship- ping. The sale of ships had been forbidden in 1340 and the ex- port of wood suitable for boat-building was also prohibited, while in 1381 and 1382 Navigation Acts made it illegal to

PLATE 15

a. The Seal of Ipswich showing a sailing ship with stern rudder.
1200 A.D.

b. Seal of Winchelsea showing castles, quarter rudder, anchor
cable and windlass. Early fourteenth century

PLATE 16

A sea fight showing the use of temporary castles. From a manuscript in the
Fitzwilliam Museum, Cambridge (Marley Add. MS. I, f. 86ᵣ).
About 1270 A.D.

charter foreign ships for trade if English ships were available. These acts foreshadow a changed attitude: the medieval policy was to encourage foreign merchants and shippers of goods in order to secure an abundant supply and to keep prices low: in future English merchants and shipowners were to be given protection and the control of the country's trade. This changed attitude was bound up with the gradual recognition of the fact that commercial prosperity and national security depended upon the command of the seas and the building up of a strong naval force.

4. The Later Middle Ages

Compared with the slow evolution of ship design between 1100 and 1400 the fifteenth century was an age of extraordinarily rapid advance. Northern ships had carried one mast and a single square sail since the ninth century; then, between 1410 and 1419, ships began to be built with two masts; and after 1450 three (Pl. 17) and soon four masts with five, six, or eight sails were in use (Pl. 18). The development was closely connected with an increase in the size of ships. At the end of the thirteenth century ships of 150 tons were usual, those of over 200 tons were exceptional, whereas by 1370 the average was from 250 to 300 tons. A ship larger than this cannot be handled satisfactorily with a single sail, and the increase in the size of ships during the fifteenth century to 400, 600, or even 1,000 tons led inevitably to the use of more canvas.

This development in rig and size came through Mediterranean influence, and it is curious that it had been delayed so long. Crusaders in the twelfth century saw big Mediterranean vessels, such as the three-masted *dromon*, described by Richard of Devizes (*sub anno* 1191) as 'a ship than which, except for Noah's ark, none greater was ever heard of', and although three masts were probably exceptional at that date, two-masted ships were common. The first mention of the two- or three-masted Genoese trading galleys visiting an English port occurs in 1281,

and Venetian galleys were trading regularly with Southampton from 1319. During the Hundred Years War both English
and French used Mediterranean galleys and a number captured from the enemy were added to the fleet of Henry V.
English shipwrights must therefore have been familiar with
Mediterranean ships for a long time, but it apparently required royal initiative to change the traditional northern boat.

The lead was almost certainly given by Henry V, who built
up the royal navy until it exceeded in strength that of any of his
predecessors. Unfortunately there are few accurate pictures of
ships at this vital period in their evolution, and for our knowledge of his fleet of thirty-seven ships we are in the main dependent on inventories, in which ships marked 'of the Tower'
belonged to the royal navy. In 1419 Henry had a large ship in
building at Bayonne, where he would have had the advantage
of shipwrights well acquainted with Mediterranean ships, but
the four ships he built between 1414 and 1420 were constructed at Southampton. The remains of one of these—the *Grace
Dieu*—built in 1418, have been identified in an old wreck in the
Hamble. Her size confirms the suggestion that the king was
giving the lead in building the larger ships which necessitated
more sail, for her length was about 130 feet and her beam 48
feet. She carried two masts and a bowsprit and her equipment
included six sails and eleven bonnets, some of which were
probably spares.

There is some dispute as to whether the foremast or the
mizzenmast was the first to be introduced; the earliest record—
1410-12—refers only to one big mast and one small mast, and
the latter might have been either on the forecastle or the after
castle. On the whole the evidence suggests the priority of the
mizzenmast, but in any case by the middle of the century ships
had main and foremasts, carrying square sails, and also mizzen-
masts with a lateen sail, and to these the bonaventure mizzen
was added in big ships before 1500. At the same time topsails
were sometimes added to the mainmast above the fighting top, a
device which led to difficulty in a storm, as it was not until 1587
that provision was made for striking the topmasts. Bowsprits

PLATE 17

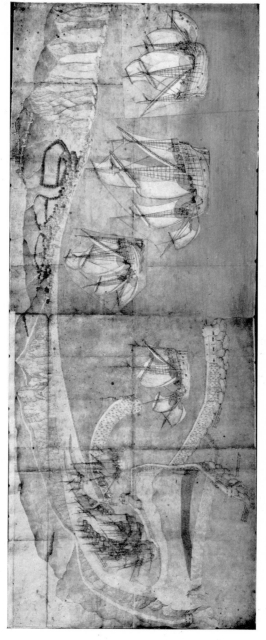

Three-masted ships in Dover Harbour. From a manuscript in the British Museum (MS. Cott. Augustus I. i. ff. 22–23) 1543

PLATE 18

A four masted war-ship. From a manuscript in the British Museum
(MS. Cott. Augustus I. ii, f. 70). Early sixteenth century

are known from the end of the thirteenth century, but they were used at first only as a spar from which a bowline could be fixed to hold the fore-edge of the mainsail forward, and a spritsail occurs for the first time only in 1416. While the foresail increased the driving power of the ship, the sprit- and mizzensails helped to hold her to her course, and with this improved rig it was now possible for ships to sail in varying winds and to windward.

The lead given by Henry V was lost under his successor, for in the early years of Henry VI his navy was dispersed and sold, partly to meet the advances which had been made to William Soper, merchant of Southampton, who had been Keeper and Governor of the King's Ships. William Soper was a typical representative of the rising class of great merchants. The importance of alien shipping was declining, and the trade carried in English ships to and from Southampton, for example, was to increase tenfold between 1463 and 1519. The great merchants took the initiative in patrolling the seas against pirates in the weakness of the government and the absence of a royal fleet. The keeping of the seas was put out to contract, and in 1440 Sir John Sparke was commissioned to guard the sea from February to November with eight merchantmen. The merchants were also taking the lead in ship-building: John Taverner, merchant of Hull, 'with the Divine assistance and the help of divers of the King's subjects' built a great carrack, like those of Venice and Genoa, probably a three-master, while William Cannynges of Bristol owned a fleet of ten vessels totalling 3,000 tons.

The reigns of the first Tudors represent an age of transition in shipping. The personal interest shown by both Henry VII and Henry VIII in ship-building, overseas trade, and naval warfare stimulated advance and experiment, and the developments of the next 200 years were founded upon the results of their policy. On the other hand, the old persisted side by side with the new, and there was no sudden break with tradition. Both kings returned to the plan of Henry V in maintaining a nucleus of royal ships. To the small fleet of four ships which he

inherited Henry VII added four new ones in addition to one prize and one which was bought. The *Regent*, of 1,000 tons, built on the Kentish Rother in 1487, was modelled on French ships, and this and the *Sovereign* of 800 tons, built in 1488, had four masts, but the *Regent* had in addition a topgallant on the mainmast, giving eight instead of seven sails. The *Sweepstake* and the *Mary Fortune*, on the other hand, had three masts, and six sails remained the most common rig until the eighteenth century. Henry VIII went farther, and added at least eighty-five ships to the royal navy. Some of these were captures, some purchases, but about forty-six were new-built, and in these he experimented in new types of construction. His most famous ship, the *Henry Grace a Dieu* (Pl. 19), was built in emulation of the *Great Michael*, 'a very monstrous great ship' built by James IV of Scotland in 1506. In design she was, like Henry VII's new ships, a carrack, a type introduced to England from Spain and Italy by way of Bayonne, with a very overhanging fore-castle having an inverted V-shaped opening below. This was a cumbersome type of vessel, soon to become obsolete, but Henry also built sailing-ships of new design which were swift and manageable enough to operate with galleys and were to supersede them. The earliest of these, such as the *Great Galley*, of 700 tons, built in 1513, combined the features of a four-masted clinker-built sailing-ship with some of those of a true Mediterranean galley; thus, instead of the projecting forecastle of the carrack she had a low-lying beak, while in addition to sails there were sixty oars a side. The *Anne Gallant* and the *Grand Mistress* (Pl. 20), built in 1545, carried the experiment farther. They were comparatively light, long ships of 450 tons, and seem to have been modelled on a Venetian original, with flush decks and castles greatly reduced in height. They had four masts, and oars, when used, were only auxiliary to sails. Royal ship-builders probably also introduced carvel construction in place of the traditional clinker-build of northern ships, which was finally only used for local fishing-boats. The stages by which this change was made are not documented, but carvel construction is known to have been used by Henry VIII for his

PLATE 19

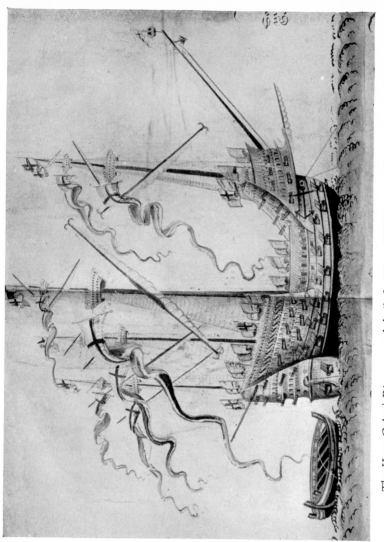

The *Henry Grâce à Dieu*, a carrack built for Henry VIII in 1514. From a manuscript at Magdalene College, Cambridge

PLATE 20

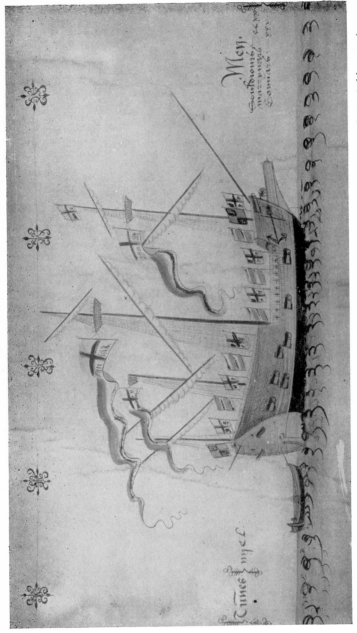

The *Grand Mistress*, built for Henry VIII in 1545. From a manuscript in the British Museum (MS. Add. 22047)

men-of-war, in which greater strength of hull was needed in order to carry guns.

Guns were used at sea from the end of the fourteenth century, but the range and striking power of the first breech-loaded guns, made of bars of iron, welded and hooped round, was insignificant. In the inventories of the early fifteenth century royal ships are listed equipped with three guns each, but they were only useful for damaging rigging and killing men, and were not intended to sink ships. Reliance for defence and attack was still placed in the bow, and the *Grace Dieu* of Henry VII, which was fitted with 21 guns, had also 140 bows, 12 crossbows, 810 sheaves of arrows each containing 24 arrows, 24 spears, 140 billhooks (for cutting the rigging), 37 darts, 14 hammers, and 21 axes. The guns were placed on the deck of the aftercastle, projecting over the ship's sides, or in the waist of the ship, with the spaces between them filled by painted shields.

All this was changed when Henry VIII introduced the use of brass muzzle-loaded guns cast in one piece and bored. These weighed up to three or four thousand pounds as compared with the old 340-pound iron gun, and were capable of firing a shot heavy enough to sink a ship. The results of this development were far-reaching. First the weight of the new guns made it necessary to place them lower in the ship, and the use of carvel construction made it possible to cut port-holes in the hull without weakening it. As guns became the principal weapon there was then no longer a strategic necessity for the great superstructures giving the attackers superior height, and boats were built with flush decks. Guns also made the use of galleys in warfare obsolete since there was no protection for the oarsmen in the hull. Finally, whereas naval tactics had for centuries been based on the direct frontal attack, the objective now became a manoeuvre to give the attacker a position from which to launch a broadside attack. The full effect of the introduction of guns on ship design and on sea warfare was not felt until the seventeenth century, but once cast guns fired from port-holes had been introduced, the most important advances had been made.

It was again Henry VIII who gave the navy the administrative organization it had lacked in the middle ages. Admirals
had been appointed regularly to the command of the fleet from
the reign of Edward I, but during the fourteenth century the
command was usually divided, and one admiral had charge of
the fleet of the ports northward and eastward of the Thames and
the other of the southern and western ships. Towards the end
of the century appointments of a single admiral became more
common, and from 1406 there was always an Admiral of England, with lieutenants in command of sections of the fleet,
but the admiral was usually a nobleman without experience of
practical seamanship. Under Henry VIII the admiral, now
with the title of High or Lord Admiral, bearing a whistle as
the insignia of office, was again in personal command. At the
same time his jurisdiction was extended and defined. Admirals
had had power to hear disputes in the ships under their command from an early date, and the High Court of Admiralty,
with power to determine all causes arising at sea, was established in the second half of the fourteenth century. Its records,
however, only date from 1515, and it is to this period that the
real development of its jurisdiction belongs.

The efforts made at different times before the sixteenth
century to build up an effective permanent nucleus to the fleet
failed because of the lack of means to ensure that the ships built
were kept in good repair, equipped, and provisioned. John
achieved this for a short time with his Keepers of the Ships, but
it was not until 1546 that the organization was evolved which
was to become the future Board of Admiralty. The building of
larger ships accentuated the need for a more effective control.
Henry VII built a dry dock at Portsmouth in 1496 which
took forty-six weeks to complete, and under Henry VIII the
dockyards there and at Woolwich and Deptford were enlarged and new storehouses were provided at Deptford and
Erith. It was partly to ensure their efficient use that administrative officers were needed. In 1546 letters patent were issued
creating four life offices under the authority of the King in
Council and the immediate supervision of the Lieutenant of

the Admiral. One of them, who bore the ancient title of Clerk
or Keeper of the Ships, was responsible for their actual building, the Treasurer of Marine Causes received and disbursed the
funds and kept the accounts, a surveyor saw that the boats,
wharfs, and storehouses were in repair, and a Comptroller had
a general responsibility for seeing that all the work was done
efficiently and economically. Although modifications in this
organization were made after the death of Henry VIII, this
machinery remained in essentials to become the Board of
Admiralty in the seventeenth century.

At the same time, in spite of the great advances made in the
efficient ordering of the fleet there were still no regular crews.
Sailors were impressed for service as required, and the shortage
was such that in 1545 every available sailor was taken for the
king's service and only women were left to man the fishing
boats. Similarly, in spite of the great increase in the number of
ships built and maintained by the king, the medieval system of
impressing ships for national service was not abandoned. The
fleet mustered against the French in 1545 consisted of 56 royal
ships, 25 hired galleys, 60 privateers, and 40 merchantmen.

Henry VII, perhaps more than Henry VIII, realized the
importance of the merchant navy; he encouraged merchants to
build ships by offering a bounty to those who built vessels of
140 tons and over, and he protected English trade by commercial treaties. In his Navigation Acts he returned to the
policy first attempted in the reign of Richard II. The Act of
1485, on account of 'the grete mynishing and decaye' of English
shipping, forbade the import of wine from Guienne or Gascony except in English, Irish, or Welsh ships. In 1489 the prohibition was extended to cover the import of woad as well as
wine, and in future no foreign ships were to be used by English
merchants for the import or export trade if English ones were
available in harbour.

The use of bigger ships was to open up new possibilities of
ocean voyages and new markets for trade. The medieval ships
required a large crew in proportion to their size, and in a long
voyage a disproportionate amount of cargo-space was taken up

in food for the crew. It was a vicious circle: without big ships it was unprofitable to enter upon distant trade, yet there was no incentive to build for a trade which had not been opened up. The fact that Henry VII built larger ships and was willing to venture them in voyages to more distant markets was an in-centive to the merchants and sailors. Here again the king was in advance of his age, and provided a link between the medi-eval and the modern economy.

Henry began to look westward for new markets: he was in-terested in the theories propounded to him by John Cabot, who came to England from Venice, widely read on the subject of the Atlantic, and in 1496 he issued letters patent to Cabot and his sons to sail east, west, and north to find, annex, and occupy lands not hitherto known to Christians. For his second voyage in 1498 the king himself contributed a ship and gave authority for the impressment of other ships and helped merchants of London and Bristol with loans to find cargoes. The first ex-pedition of Cabot probably reached Newfoundland, the re-sults of the second are not known; but the king continued to support enterprises of this kind. The Company of Adven-turers into Newfoundland was founded in 1506, and in 1509, at the end of his life, Henry helped to equip Sebastian Cabot's voyage in search of a north-west passage to the Indies. In these early voyages of exploration the English usually relied on foreign navigators, and it was not until the middle of the six-teenth century that they themselves became competent in this field. Generally speaking the English were backward in the art of navigation. For example, although the compass needle on a windrose card was known, and had been in general use in the Mediterranean from the fourteenth century, in the north many ships in the fifteenth century continued to be equipped only with the primitive needle rubbed with a loadstone and floating in water. Charts were crude and inaccurate and masters sailed more by practical experience and observation than by scien-tific theory. The old trade routes and European markets were still important, but the interest shown by the first Tudors in Atlantic exploration, together with the evolution of ships

capable of long sea voyages, foreshadowed the Elizabethan age with its concern with the markets of the New World.

The early Tudor kings had the vision to recognize the country's need of ships for both war and trade and to realize that the two interests must serve each other. In the middle ages the necessities of war were met at the expense of commercial interests, by the sixteenth century it had begun to be seen that success in both fields depended upon a differentiation of func' tion and the building'up of a fleet designed and reserved for purposes of defence.

WORKS FOR REFERENCE

General Works

ANDERSON, R., and ANDERSON, R. C. *The Sailing Ship, Six Thousand Years of History* (London, 1926).

BRINDLEY, H. H. *Impressions and Casts of Seals, Coins, Tokens and Medals and other Works of Art in the Seal Room of the National Maritime Museum* (London, 1938).

CLOWES, G. S. *Sailing Ships, their History and Development as illustrated by the Collection of Ship Models in the Science Museum*: Part I, *Historical Notes*, 4th ed. (London, 1932).

CLOWES, WILLIAM LAIRD, and others. *The Royal Navy: a History*, i (London, 1897).

HAKLUYT, RICHARD. *Principal Navigations, Voyages, Traffiques, and Discoveries of the English Nation.* 10 vols. (London, 1927).

LEWIS, MICHAEL. *The Navy of Britain* (London, 1948).

Mariner's Mirror. Quarterly Journal of the Society for Nautical Research (London, 1915 onwards); *see below* for special articles.

NICOLAS, SIR NICHOLAS HARRIS. *A History of the Royal Navy* (2 vols. London, 1847).

PERRIN, W. G. *British Flags: their Early History and Development at sea* (Cambridge, 1922).

Commerce

CUNNINGHAM, W. *The Growth of English Industry and Commerce: the Middle Ages.* 4th ed. (Cambridge, 1905).

POSTAN, M. M. and RICH, E. E. (eds.). *Cambridge Economic History*, ii (Cam' bridge, 1952).

RUDDOCK, A. A. *Italian Merchants and Shipping in Southampton, 1270–1660* (South' ampton Record Society, 1951).

SALZMAN, L. F. *English Trade in the Middle Ages* (Oxford, 1931).

UNWIN, G. (ed.). *Finance and Trade under Edward III* (Manchester, 1918).

Maritime Law

MARSDEN, R. G. *Documents relating to the Law and Custom of the Sea*, i (Navy Records Society, London, 1915).

STUDER, P. *The Oak Book of Southampton*, ii, 'Laws of Oleron' (Southampton Record Society, 1911).

Before 1066

ATKINSON, DONALD. 'The Classis Britannica', in *Essays Presented to James Tait* (Manchester, 1933).

BRØGGER, A. W., and SHETELIG, H. *The Viking Ships, their Ancestry and Evolution* (Norway, 1951).

FOX, CYRIL. 'A Dug-out Canoe from South Wales: with Notes on the Chronology, Typology, and Distribution of Monoxylous Craft in England and Wales' (*Antiquaries Jnl.* vi. 1926).

HORNELL, JAMES. *British Coracles and Irish Curraghs* (London, 1938); *Water Transport: Origin and Early Evolution* (Cambridge, 1946).

Sutton Hoo Ship Burial (British Museum, 1947).

WRIGHT, E. V., and WRIGHT, C. W. 'Prehistoric Boats from North Ferriby, East Yorkshire', in *Proceedings of the Prehistoric Society*, N.S. xiii (1947).

1066–1400

ANDERSON, R. C. 'English Galleys in 1295', in *Mariner's Mirror*, xiv (1928); 'The Bursledon Ship', ibid. xx (1934).

BRINDLEY, H. H. 'Medieval Ships in painted Glass and Seals', ibid. i, ii, iii (1915–17).

BROOKS, F. W. *The English Naval Forces, 1199–1272* (London, 1932).

JOHNSON, C. 'The London Galleys', in *Antiquaries Jnl.* vii (1927).

MOORE, SIR ALAN. 'A Barge of Edward I', in *Mariner's Mirror*, vi (1920).

MURRAY, K. M. E. *Constitutional History of the Cinque Ports* (Manchester, 1935).

WHITWELL, R. J., and JOHNSON, C. 'The Newcastle Galley', in *Archaeologia Aeliana*, 4th ser. ii (1926).

1400–1547

ANDERSON, R. C. 'Early Two-masted and Three-masted Ships in England', in *Mariner's Mirror*, xiv (1928).

BURWASH, H. D. *English Merchant Shipping, 1460–1540* (Toronto, 1947).

CORBETT, J. S. *Drake and the Tudor Navy*: Introduction, i (London, 1898).

DILLON, VISCOUNT, and ST. JOHN HOPE, W. H. *Pageant of the Birth, Life, and Death of Richard Beauchamp Earl of Warwick* (London, 1914).

GOLDINGHAM, C. S. 'The Navy under Henry VII', in *Eng. Hist. Rev.* xxxiii (1918).

MURRAY, SIR OSWYN. 'The Admiralty', in *Mariner's Mirror*, xxiii (1937).

OPPENHEIM, M. *A History of the Administration of the Royal Navy, 1509–1660* (London, 1896); 'Accounts and Inventories of Henry VII' (*Navy Records Society*, vii. 1896).

SPONT, A. 'Letters and Papers relating to war with France', 1512–1513. (*Navy Records Society*, x (London, 1897).

TAYLOR, E. G. R. *Tudor Geography, 1485–1582* (London, 1930).

WARNER, SIR G. (ed.). *The Libelle of Englyshe Polycye, 1436* (Oxford, 1926).

WILLIAMSON, J. A. *The Ocean in English History* (Oxford, 1941); *Maritime Enterprise, 1485–1558* (Oxford, 1913); *The Voyages of John and Sebastian Cabot* (Historical Association pamphlet, no. 106, 1937); *The Voyages of the Cabots and the English Discovery of North America* (1929); *Sir John Hawkins: The Time and the Man* (Oxford, 1927), Book 3, chap. 1.

VI. COMMUNICATIONS

THE system of communications established by the government of the Roman province of Britain was planned with the end of providing arterial roads for the passage of armies and the purposes of trade. Direct routes to every part of the province radiated from London, its commercial capital. With the end of Roman rule this road-system fell slowly into decay, although Roman roads were so well built that in many parts of the country the neglect of centuries could not altogether mask their lines. These roads aided the Anglo-Saxons in their penetration of the country, and long stretches of Roman road were used through Saxon and on into medieval times. Watling Street cut through the forest of Mercia on its north-westerly course between London and the Severn. In Saxon times Lichfield grew up near the point where this road is crossed by the so-called Ricknield Street, which provided a through route between Cirencester and Doncaster. The Bowes–Brough road over Stainmore and the road from Penrith north to Carlisle were likewise guides through difficult country, and were never allowed to disappear. The survival of Lincoln and Leicester into Saxon times and their development into county towns has caused the Roman road between them to be made into a modern motor road, but travellers between Lincoln and Leicester in the middle ages rarely used it, preferring the longer way by Grantham and Melton Mowbray, or going by way of Belvoir castle and priory. The disappearance of the Roman town of Silchester as an inhabited site destroyed the Roman road-system of the centre of southern England. All over England new settlements drew traffic from the old lines. Few county towns of the midlands have a continuous history from Roman into modern times. Chester was still waste in 893 when an army of Danish raiders took refuge within its walls. Oxford

and Northampton, the two places which recur most often in medieval itineraries, were foundations of the Saxon age.

The conception of through-roads for long-distance traffic was lost with the departure of the Romans and only slowly recovered. The road north from London became known as *Earninga stræt*, Ermine Street, the road which led to the ford over the river Cam which gave its name to Armingford Hundred in Cambridgeshire. The road north-west from London became known as *Wæclinga stræt*, Watling Street, because it led to the settlement of the obscure tribe called the Wæclingas around the Roman town of Verulamium.[1] The establishment of boroughs as minting places had before the Norman Conquest laid down lines of local travel and it would be rash to assume that the earl of Mercia or of Northumbria wishing to visit the court of the West Saxon king set out on an uncharted journey. But the idea that roads should run to one centre of trade and government from all parts of the land was never recovered in the Saxon age. Although the laws of Edward the Confessor, written down in the early Norman period, have reached the conception of the king's peace prevailing over the four great through-roads of the kingdom, it is noted that two of these roads are drawn through the length of the kingdom and the others across its breadth. Of these roads Watling Street and Ermine Street have been mentioned. The Fosse Way established a line between Exeter and Lincoln and the Icknield Way is a prehistoric trackway running beneath what the Anglo-Saxons called 'the eaves of the Chilterns'.

The Saxon kings clearly regarded roads less as through-routes than as the means of communication between market and market. The laws of Edward the Confessor contrast with the four great roads 'the ways from cities to cities, from boroughs to boroughs, by which men go to markets or about their other affairs'. Such roads were described as royal roads and the king was concerned to keep them open. The laws of Henry I of about 1118 lay down the width of a royal way. Two

[1] *The Place-Names of Bedfordshire and Huntingdonshire* (English Place-Name Society, iii. 1926, pp. 2–7).

wagons must be able to pass each other, two oxherds to make their goads just touch across the width of the road, and sixteen armed knights to ride abreast. The same laws define a royal way as a road which is always open, which no one can shut or turn from its course, which leads to a city or borough or castle or royal port. The penalty of *strætbreche* was a hundred shillings and the laws define the offence: 'if anyone breaks the way by closing it or turning it or digging it up.'

Already before the Norman Conquest the king's writ was penetrating the shires of southern and central England. The Conquest secured the establishment of a highly centralized government under a king concerned to bring the whole land under his direct control. From the beginning of the reign of the first Norman king a stream of royal writs began to flow from the court to every quarter of the land. By the thirteenth century this stream had become a flood. The king's obligation to keep in touch with Normandy meant a new importance for the Channel ports and the roads leading to them. The work of castle-building which was carried on at speed in every shire through the Conqueror's reign meant much carting of timber along the roads. Traffic was further increased by the carting of stone for the new cathedral and parish churches everywhere in building before the end of the eleventh century. The road from Westminster to Winchester by way of Staines bridge, Guildford, Alton, and Alresford must have been frequently ridden by the court when the royal treasure lay at Winchester. After the Exchequer was established at Westminster in Henry I's reign the Winchester treasury was still maintained for the convenience of a king with responsibilities both in England and in France.

The twelfth century saw Westminster become the effective centre of the financial and judicial administration of the land. Henry I and II still moved between England and Normandy and in England from Westminster across the southern counties to the marches of Wales and in the midlands in accordance with the demands of policy or their desire to hunt a particular forest. Their barons were summoned to the king sometimes at

one of the ancient centres, Westminster, Winchester, or Gloucester, or to Northampton, or to one of the hunting-lodges, such
as Brampton in Huntingdonshire, Clarendon in Wiltshire, or
Woodstock in Oxfordshire. Irrespective of the king's personal
calls upon his subjects' time their financial or judicial business
at the Exchequer drew them regularly to Westminster from
every shire. From Henry I's reign royal justices were visiting
the shire courts at frequent intervals—sporadic visitations were
being made even from an earlier date. From 1166 onwards an
increasing volume of judicial business was called to Westminster. Each sheriff with his clerks and servants made the
journey from his shire to Westminster twice a year on financial
business alone. Every plea which came before the Westminster
court necessitated the appearance of many people there; messengers from the sheriff, if he himself evaded the journey, the
parties and the jurors, or one or two people to explain the
reason why each individual was unable to obey the summons
to appear before the court.

The actual lines that this volume of travel followed from
distant parts to Westminster are not often indicated in the
thirteenth century. It is not safe to assume that travellers always
used the shortest routes. They were more concerned with safety
than speed and preferred to follow short distances between
places of habitation rather than a straight road through empty
country. For this reason the direct Roman road south from
Lincoln along the top of the Lincoln Edge fell into decay in
the middle ages (it has now been made up and provides the
shortest road to the south), and in the thirteenth century
travellers followed the road below the Edge where springs
thrown out by a belt of impervious clay had given rise to a
string of populous villages already before the Norman Conquest. The earliest itineraries are those which can be compiled
from the dating clauses of royal writs and charters, and the first
royal itinerary which can be studied in detail is that of King
John. Unlike his predecessors John was not prepared to leave
any part of his kingdom unvisited, even the harsh far north, but
he did not of necessity follow the roads which his subjects

would take to Westminster, for he constantly turned aside from
the direct road to hunt from a forest lodge.

A good example of John's activities in England is afforded
by his itinerary for the months between 26 November 1200 and
12 March 1201. On 26 November writs were issued both
from Lincoln and Sleaford. The Roman road between these
points was still in use during the middle ages. On 28 November he was at Geddington; on 29 November at Northampton;
on 3 December he had passed through Abingdon and reached
Bedwyn in Wiltshire. In December he was hunting the forests
of Wiltshire, Dorset, Hampshire, and Oxfordshire, and fewer
writs were issued, but on 4 and 6 December he was at Ludger-
shall. On 10 December he was at Cranbourne; on 13 December at Canford and at Christchurch; on 17 December at
Marlborough; on 20 and 21 December at Freemantle; on 23
December at Farnham; on 25 and 26 December at Guildford,
and on 26 December he had reached Reading. From 28 December 1200 to 1 January 1201 he was at Woodstock; on 3 January
at Silverstone; on 6, 7, and 8 January at Geddington; on 9 January at Bourne, and on 12 and 13 January at Lincoln. On 13
January he began his journey to the far north, riding that day to
Stow, a manor of the bishop of Lincoln, then in his hand. On
14 January he was at Stow; on 18 January at Louth, another
bishop's manor, where he still was on 20 January. On 23
January he was at Great Coates near Grimsby, and on 25
January he crossed the Humber, probably at Immingham. He
stayed the night at Cottingham and went on to Beverley the
next day. From Beverley he followed the road to Driffield, 27
and 28 January; Pickering, 1 February; Scarborough, 2 and 3
February; Egton, 4 February; Guisborough, 5 February;
Stockton, 6 February; Durham, 7 and 8 February; Newcastle,
9 and 10 February; Mitford, 11 February; Alnwick, 12
February; and Bamborough, 13–15 February. He then turned
south by way of Rothbury and Hexham, where he was on 19
February. By 21 February he had reached Carlisle. He did not
take the Roman road south to Penrith, but turned south-east by
way of Kirkoswald to Morton Tinmouth, Ravensworth,

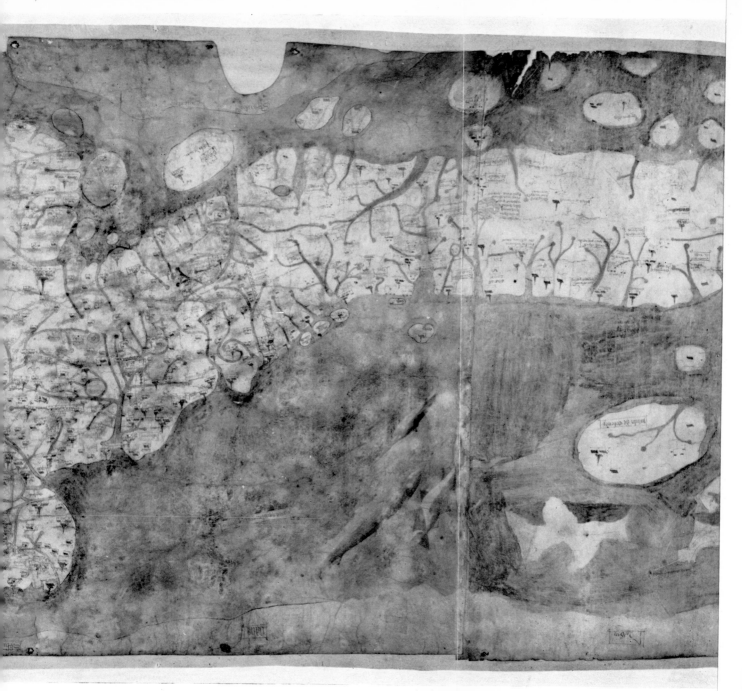

The Gough map of Britain in the Bodleian Library, Oxford

Northallerton, and York. He was at York for the first two days of March, but on 4 March he was at Brotherton for the passage of the Aire. He went by way of Conisbrough, Clipstone, and Bolsover to Nottingham, where he spent 10–12 March. In a little over two months of incessant travel he had shown himself in every part of England along a line from the Channel coast to the farthest north.

King John, like most English travellers for many generations, must have ridden his immense journeys. His heavy trappings went in long carts, which moved more slowly than horsemen. There is little evidence that men complained of bad roads and slow travel in the thirteenth century. They set out on long jour/neys with far less preparation than would be made today. When everyone must go by road it was probably not difficult to find company for travel. The king's great men were con/stantly on the move from one to another of their houses. Many lesser men also held estates in more than one shire. The freemen of every shire were bound to attend the court of the hundred or wapentake within which they lived and the court of their shire. Markets and fairs drew both free and unfree from their homes. Between the distant estates of great men humble messengers and carriers of goods were constantly passing. It seems certain that dwellers in remote parishes of thirteenth/century England were much more mobile than their descendants some four hundred years later.

There survives in the Bodleian Library a map of Britain which, from the hand in which the place/names are written, appears to come from the early fourteenth century. It is known as the Gough map (Pl. 21) from the name of the man who be/queathed it to the Library. Although the maker of the map recorded the names of many places in Scotland he did not venture to indicate the lines of any Scottish roads. It may be that he inserted the line of a road only when he felt competent to note the distance between the places marked along it. He did not draw the line of the Northampton–Southampton road, but he put in Middleton Stoney, a village which has always marked a stage upon this road. He did not draw in the road which runs

north-west down the Eden valley, though he drew and named
Pendragon, now a ruined and isolated castle beside it. But he
drew and indicated mileages upon a much more remarkable
cross road which runs from Doncaster through Wakefield,
Bradford, Skipton, and Settle to Kirkby Lonsdale, where one
branch diverges to Kendal and the other continues by Shap to
Penrith. As well as a considerable number of cross-country
roads he inserted five distinct through-roads from London to
distant parts.

One through-road is drawn from London by way of King-
ston, Guildford, Farnham, Alton, Alresford, Winchester,
Salisbury, Honiton, Exeter, Okehampton, and on to some
indeterminate point in west Cornwall. Another runs from
London through Brentford, Colnbrook, Maidenhead, Reading, Hungerford, Marlborough, and Chippenham to Bristol.
A third runs from London through Uxbridge, High Wy-
combe, and Tetsworth to Oxford and thence through Witney to
Gloucester. From Gloucester the line goes on by Newent, Hereford, and Hay to Brecon. Much road-making has been done in
Wales from the sixteenth century onwards and the modern
road to St. Davids no longer follows the medieval line. A fourth
road is marked between London and the north-west, passing
through Barnet, St. Albans, Dunstable, Stony Stratford,
Daventry, Coventry, Coleshill, Lichfield, Stone, Newcastle-
under-Lyme, Preston, Lancaster, Kendal, Shap, and Penrith
to Carlisle. The draughtsman's own habits of travel may be
indicated by the fact that the fifth line of road, the great north
road, makes Carlisle its goal rather than Newcastle. It is
marked running from London through Waltham Cross,
Ware, Royston, and Huntingdon. Thence the map shows it
passing through a property of the Knights of the Temple called
Ogerston to Wansford Bridge. The modern line of the north
road runs to the east of the old line in order to avoid the heavy
clay round Ogerston. From Wansford Bridge the road runs
through Stamford, Grantham, Newark, Tuxford, Blyth,
Doncaster, Pontefract, Wetherby, and Boroughbridge.
Thence it went on to Leeming Bar, Gilling near Richmond,

Bowes, over Stainmore, by Brough, Appleby, and Penrith, where it joined the main road from Preston to run on to Carlisle.

Between places connected by a line of road the draughtsman inserted the mileage. The figure he gives is always less, and sometimes materially less, than the actual distance. When under Charles II John Ogilby in his *Britannia* published the first detailed survey of the main roads of England he gave two separate figures for the mileage between point and point, representing what he calls 'computed' miles and measured miles. These computed miles more often than not agree with the distances recorded in the Gough map. It is evident that the computed miles of Ogilby and the mileages of the Gough map represent traditional distances handed down from traveller to traveller from a remote past. This continuity would prove, if proof were needed, that no revolutionary change had taken place in the lines of English roads between the heart of the middle ages and the seventeenth century.

The information preserved by the Gough map is supplemented by the itineraries recorded in a manuscript of about 1400–5 which once belonged to the Premonstratensian abbey of Titchfield and has been published by Professor Dickins.[1] The author was concerned to provide guidance for a traveller visiting from Titchfield abbey other Premonstratensian houses in England. Instead of London the centre is Titchfield on Southampton Water, and the purpose of the work may very well have been to help foreign visitors of the order, who would almost certainly land in England near Titchfield. The Premonstratensian houses were spread widely over England. The map which illustrates Professor Dickins's paper shows a road going by way of Havant, Chichester, Arundel, Bramber, and Lewes to Mayfield, whence one way goes to Bayham and another on into Kent. Part of this road is marked on the Gough map, where it leads on to the Cinque Ports. The rise of the seaside towns in modern days has drawn the main road from the medieval line after Arundel. A short stretch of road goes from

---

[1] *Proceedings of the Leeds Philosophical Society*, iv, pt. vi (1938), pp. 349–61.

Titchfield to Durford, a few miles to the east of Petersfield. The third line from Titchfield joins the familiar road from Win- chester to London at Alton; from London one way branches off to Beeleigh in Essex and Leiston in Suffolk and another to Newmarket. One road branches off thence to Langley in Nor- folk while another goes to Thetford, Dereham, and Wendling. The fourth road from Titchfield goes to Winchester, whence one road branches slightly to the north-west by way of Ink- pen, Hungerford, Lambourne, Faringdon, Burford, and Stow-on-the-Wold to Halesowen, and another branch runs on from Winchester to Oxford, and thence by way of Ded- dington, Banbury, Southam, Coventry, Lichfield, Newcastle- under-Lyme, Holmes Chapel, Warrington, Wigan, Preston, to Cockersand. Another main line of this central road goes on from Oxford to Brackley, where it branches again; one line with offshoots running to the Northamptonshire, Leicester- shire, and Lincolnshire houses and the other running on to Nottingham on the way to Dale, Beauchief, and Welbeck abbeys. North of Nottingham the road known in the twelfth century as 'the great way of Blyth' was taken, and through Blyth to Doncaster. From Doncaster one way goes on by Went- bridge, York, Tollerton, Northallerton, Darlington, Chester- le-Street, Newcastle-upon-Tyne, and Morpeth to Alnwick, while another branch goes in a slightly more westerly direction to reach Coverham, Easby, Shap, and Blanchland abbeys. The abbey of Torre in Devon was the most westerly house of the order and was reached by way of Salisbury, Shaftesbury, Sherborne, Yeovil, Crewkerne, Chard, Stockland, Honiton, and Exeter.

It is significant that the compiler of the Gough map, whose object was practical, is at pains to mark what he conceived to be the courses of a large number of rivers, which he names. In the remoter parts of the land the known course of a river still had its value as a guide to travellers. Elsewhere, rivers have a more definite economic value as a means of transport for heavy loads. The rivers which converge on the Humber estuary were largely used for this purpose. The Severn provided an

occasional means for the passage of goods for the rich country through which it ran, and the course of the Thames had been improved as early as the eleventh century for the carriage of goods to Oxford. The Romans had been conscious of the limitations of river transport and had gone some way to correct them in eastern England. From the Witham at Lincoln to the Trent at Torksey they extended and straightened the river Till into a canal, so that a passage by water could be taken from the Wash to the Humber and up the Ouse to York. South of Lincoln the Romans made a much more elaborate water communication running fifty-six miles from the Witham down to join the Nene on the east side of Peterborough. The Car Dyke, as this work is called, may have been used for some part of its course into the post-Roman times since a load of dressed Barnack stone, described as 'obviously intended for a church', has been found in its bed.[1] Nevertheless both these waterways must have been out of use for some generations before the Norman Conquest. Henry I recut the Foss Dyke in 1121, but the Car Dyke was not put in order again. In some parts it is now only a mark in a ploughed field.

Such an elaborate water communication as the Car Dyke was never attempted by any medieval king. But it was possible in the middle ages to go for the greater part of the way between Cambridge and York by water. In 1319 Edward II invited the scholars of the King's Hall, Cambridge, to spend Christmas with him at York. The older scholars made the journey by road on horseback in five days. It was evidently thought that the younger ones were hardly strong enough for the journey and they were in consequence taken by boat from Cambridge to Spalding. From Spalding they rode on horseback to Boston, their luggage following them in carts. At Boston they took boat again and went the rest of the way by water. They were three days late for the Christmas feast for which they had been bidden. This miscalculation may suggest that such a journey was exceptional. Even when ample supplies of carts and horses

[1] C. W. Phillips, 'The Present State of Archaeology in Lincolnshire', *Archaeological Jnl.* xci. 1934, pp. 117–23.

to draw them could be found it was often thought worth while to make the last stage of the journey from London to York by water. When the Exchequer was moved from London to York for the Easter session of 1322 the twenty-three carts, each drawn by five horses, and the company of Exchequer officials, their clerks and servants, all riding on horseback, made the journey by road from Westminster by way of Ware, Royston, Caxton, Huntingdon, Ogerston, Wansford Bridge, Stam-ford, Grantham, and Lincoln to Torksey. From Torksey some of the horsemen went on ahead by road, while the wine casks into which the rolls and other Exchequer properties had been packed were loaded on to 'four good strong small ships' to go by water to York. The party set out on Monday, 5 April, and reached Torksey on Tuesday, 13 April, not without having to hire extra horses every day. On the Wednesday the convoy sailed to Burton Stather, but it was held up there from Wed-nesday night until Friday by storms and contrary winds. On Saturday, 17 April, the company landed at York in time for rest and refreshment before the opening of the Exchequer session on the following Monday.[1]

Despite the occasional convenience of making the journey to York by water it is probable that the medieval traveller was more conscious of rivers as obstructions to his passage by road than grateful for the possibility of being carried along them. Bridges over the Trent, Thames, and Severn were infrequent. In 1350 the monks of Worcester complained of the burden of hospitality thrown upon them by the absence of any bridge, save at Worcester, between Gloucester and Bridgnorth. Wor-cester bridge was repaired in 1088 and the bridge at Bridgnorth existed in the early tenth century. Edward the Elder bridged the Trent at Nottingham in 920, but it was not until the twelfth century that a bridge was built over the Trent at Newark by Bishop Alexander of Lincoln with the permission of Henry I, who stipulated that the work should not hurt his borough of Nottingham or his city of Lincoln. At the end of the middle

---

[1] Dorothy M. Broome, 'Exchequer Migrations to York in the Thirteenth and Fourteenth Centuries' (*Essays presented to T. F. Tout* (1925), pp. 293-8).

ages there was still no bridge between Nottingham and Newark or lower down the Trent. London bridge is mentioned in-
cidentally in the reign of Edgar when a widow was drowned
there for practising pin-sticking magic. The bridge over the
Thames between Caversham and Reading is mentioned in
1219; William I crossed the Thames by Wallingford bridge
in 1066; and Grandpont at Oxford (now known as Folly
bridge), vital to the road from the midlands to Southampton
Water, was built before 1094. Henley bridge was probably
built later than 1190, since the abbot of Abingdon paid the
ferryman of Sonning a yearly fee to ferry him over the river
there. Maidenhead bridge is of the fourteenth century. The
prosperity of Wallingford was vitally affected when the new
bridge over the Thames was built at Abingdon in 1416, for
it took the Gloucestershire traffic through Abingdon instead
of Wallingford. The town of Wilton suffered in the same
way when Harnham bridge was built over the Avon to serve
the new town of Salisbury, for Harnham bridge took the
London-to-Exeter traffic.

From the evidence which can be collected about the use of
roads and waterways in medieval England the conclusion
grows that for all but the heaviest transport they served men
well enough. In times of danger, such as the Wars of the Roses,
when the rapid transmission of accurate news was vital to safety,
horsemen succeeded in covering long distances at a remarkably
high average speed. In 1437 the news of the murder of James I
of Scotland on 21 February at Perth had reached London in
time for Cardinal Beaufort to compose a suitable letter and dis-
patch it to the Pope on 28 February. The messenger must have
covered the 440 miles between Perth and London at an average
speed of over forty miles a day.[1] But such speeds were exceptional, and there is little evidence that Englishmen allowed
their daily business to make excessive demands on man or
horse. William of Worcester at the end of the fifteenth century

---

[1] C. A. J. Armstrong, 'Some examples of the Distribution and Speed of News
in England at the Time of the Wars of the Roses' (*Studies in Medieval History presented to F. M. Powicke* (1948), pp. 444-5).

thought it worth while to record that John, the clerk of Ware, rode from Ware to St. Michael's Mount in ten days and back again in the same time. The distance is roughly 610 miles and his average was not much above thirty miles a day. Com munications which enable men of all ranks of society to move freely and constantly from place to place without audible discomfort, and at the same time allow of speed where speed is demanded, can fairly be described as a satisfactory system.[1]

[1] I could not have written this paper without the help of my husband, who has made a lifelong study of English roads; see his paper, 'The Road System of Medieval England' (*Econ. Hist. Rev.* vii. 1936, no. 1, pp. 1-21).

VII. TOWNS AND TRADE

IN those first disordered centuries of the middle ages, when the Teutonic invaders were occupying the land and settling down, the towns of Roman Britain, last strongholds of resistance, were slowly dying. Their imposing amphi-theatres, their temples, forums and public baths, and their centrally heated houses crumbled gradually into ruin, uncared for—if, indeed, they had not actually suffered destruction in the tumults of the times. Their metalled streets, dividing them up as by a symmetrical grid, fell into disuse and were blocked and obscured by fallen masonry. Yet they were not everywhere wholly abandoned. If the new-comers were primarily farmers, caring little for the amenities of city life, and if their standard of housing was a low one, nevertheless they were not unaware of the advantages of a stout protective wall and of a convenient site for trade, and they were very ready to use the old Roman towns—for which they reserved the dignified title of 'city' (*civitas*)—as defensive points, as ports, and as centres of govern-ment. At least by the end of the sixth century, if not earlier, Kentish kings had made their court within the Roman walls of Canterbury, where in the middle of the fifth century Saxon warriors had built themselves squalid dwellings on an open site near the great theatre. Winchester became a centre of the West Saxons, and when our first clear picture of Saxon Eng-land emerges in the pages of Bede, London is described as 'the metropolis of the East Saxons' and 'a mart of many people coming by land and sea'.

The first Christian missionaries who came from the Con-tinent to preach to the pagan invaders made their headquarters in ancient cities such as these, building there as soon as possible a church, and establishing there the seat of a bishopric. So we are told that Augustine 'resided at Canterbury', where with

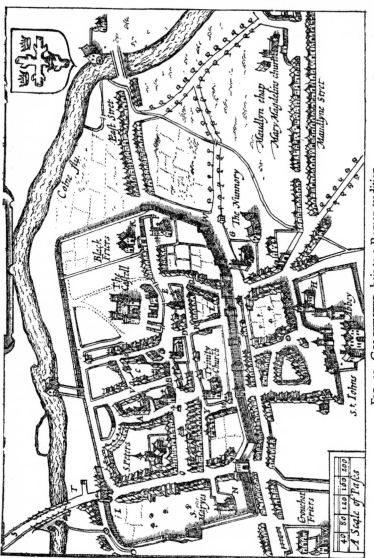

FIG. 52. COLCHESTER, heir to a Roman tradition

the king's assistance he 'restored a church which he was in-
formed had been built by the ancient Roman Christians' and
'built also a monastery not far from the city to the east'. London
quickly became an episcopal see, with its church of St. Paul
on the highest ground in the city. In the north Paulinus made
the centre of his diocese in the capital of Northumbria at York,
once Roman 'Eboracum', where King Edwin built for him
a church, first of timber and then of stone. And when he set out
on a missionary expedition into the province of Lindsey he
made his way to the old Roman city of Lindum, now Lincoln,
where he converted the 'prefect' and his family and built 'a
stone church of beautiful workmanship'.

Thus under the patronage of kings and bishops some semblance of urban civilization revived on the site of many an
ancient city. The circuit of the Roman walls, surviving often
in its entirety through medieval times, as it survives today in
part at Colchester, Lincoln, Chester, and elsewhere, became
the framework of a new and very different city. And though the
Roman street plan as a whole became blurred and obscured,
yet the lines of the two main roads crossing at right angles, linking the north gate with the south and the east gate with the
west, were commonly perpetuated, becoming the main streets
of the medieval and of the modern town, as for instance at
Leicester and Colchester (Fig. 52).

The Romans bequeathed to the medieval town-builders not
only admirable sites, substantial fortifications, and the rudi-
ments of a serviceable town plan, but also excellent communications by land along metalled roads made to last for centuries,
as indeed they did. At least five roads radiated from Winchester.
Three roads from the three principal Channel ports converged

Note to Fig. 52. The medieval walls follow throughout the line of the Roman
walls, and at many points along their course the actual Roman walls still stand,
rising sometimes almost to their original height. The principle north, south, and
east gates (I), (N), (K), are on the sites of Roman gates, as is the west, or Balkerne,
gate (seen in the centre of the west wall) with its impressive remains of the three
original Roman archways; here the road from London formerly entered. The walls
of the Norman keep ('the Castell') were built round the raised platform on which
the Temple of Claudius once stood in the middle of the Forum.

at Canterbury, whence Watling Street provided a direct route to London and on, by Verulamium, across the midlands to the borders of Wales. Lincoln was linked with York to the north and London to the south by Ermine Street, while south-west from the city the Fosse Way struck across country to Leicester, Cirencester, Bath (once 'Aquae Sulis'), and on to Exeter. On these and other main arteries traffic persisted, so that a tradition emerged in late Saxon times of the four great highways on which travellers enjoyed the king's special peace.

The widespread establishment of monasteries, as all England was converted to Christianity in the seventh and eighth centuries, was a potent influence in the growth of England's towns and trade. Often, as at Canterbury and Winchester, they were planted in urban surroundings. Then the communities, lay and religious, which they maintained merely enhanced the importance of some ancient city, as did the presence of a bishop and his household. But sometimes they were planted out in the open country at a point where there were as yet few if any inhabitants, and then, here and there, in a favourable environment, they formed a centre of attraction round which a new town slowly developed. So it was with St. Albans. When King Offa had made search for the body of the martyred soldier Alban, he founded a monastery for the preservation of the relics on a hill near the abandoned Roman city of Verulamium. Before long Watling Street was diverted to pass by the abbey precincts, and round them a new town grew, resort of many pilgrims, while Verulamium continued to crumble into ruin, or was used as a quarry by the builders of the new 'St. Albans'. Similarly the towns of East Anglia owe much to the munificent piety of the family of East Anglia's first Christian king, Redwald. His son Sigeberht founded not only the bishopric at Dunwich, with a school attached, but also a monastery, nucleus of the future Bury St. Edmunds, to which he himself retired as a monk, while his granddaughter Ætheldreda founded the abbey round which in a later age grew Ely, as, farther north, Whitby developed round that founded by Hilda.

Richly endowed by pious benefactors with landed property for their support, the monasteries, like the bishoprics, became centres for the administration of wide estates. To them there came each year produce in kind, to be consumed on the premises or sold on the market, and revenues in cash, to be spent for the benefit of the community and its guests, high and low—on food and drink and clothing, on the fabric, on books and parchment, on the improvement of the property. To some extent, indeed, these religious houses were self-sufficient, especially in their early years. Their need for food was largely met in the first few centuries of their existence by the annual quotas sent up as 'food farms' by manors on their estates. Their need for building materials also was often supplied off the property itself. English, like continental monasteries and other great households would endeavour to make provision for essentials, such as lead for roofing, by acquiring rights in land from which they could be obtained. In 835, for instance, the archbishop of Canterbury was annually receiving renders of lead worth 300 shillings from Wirksworth in Derbyshire. But from the first some consumer goods were bought for cash; not merely luxuries such as spices, eastern textiles, and works of art, but necessaries such as clothing, which at a very early date the monks were travelling some distance to purchase. Thus the monasteries became centres of consumption, attracting craftsmen and merchants and promoting trade and the development of a market. Monastery and market grew side by side, with a little urban community busily engaged in servicing the monastery, supplying its wants, and dealing in the produce of its estates.

As the needs of wealthy households, royal, episcopal, and monastic, stimulated trade both within England and with lands abroad, ancient cities like London and York again became active ports visited by foreign merchants such as the Frisians, who in the eighth century handled much of Europe's northern commerce. English merchants, with English pilgrims and churchmen, journeyed to the Continent, crossing France to Spain, Italy, and the Mediterranean. Silver dishes of

Byzantium, books, jewellery, glassware, silks, wines, and spices came into England from oversea. By the eighth century at least cloaks of fine English wool were being marketed on the Continent, as they had been in Roman days, supplementing the age-old traffic in slaves from the barbarian north to the more civilized south. They were at one time the subject of diplomatic exchanges between Offa and Charlemagne, who wrote that his subjects were complaining about them and asking that they should be made in the manner customary of old. From early in the seventh century Saxon kings were minting coins to meet the needs of trade, and tolls on ships entering the ports were a valued source of income.

The peaceful development of urban communities, of which the seventh and eighth centuries thus gave good promise, was rudely interrupted in the ninth century by the depredations of the Viking pirates, that brought havoc and destruction to many of England's infant towns. In East Anglia the monasteries and the tiny urban settlements round them fell an easy prey to the first attacks. Ely was utterly destroyed (870). Whitby was sacked (867); the bones of its foundress, evacuated inland for safety, were in due course carried as far as Glastonbury, if William of Malmesbury is to be believed. Sigeberht's monastery in Suffolk also perished, and when in a peaceful interval it was re-established (903), the body of King Edmund, slain by the Vikings, was brought there and a new abbey church of St. Edmund began to rise, only to be plundered in the fresh Norse incursions of a century later (1010), when the body of the saint was hastily taken to London for safety. So, too, Winchester, York, London, and many other cities suffered time and again from the fury of the Norsemen.

When peace came at last, as the Norse immigrants who followed in the wake of the raiders settled on the land, and all England became part of the maritime empire of Cnut, paramount power in Europe, progress was resumed. The monastic communities, founded often entirely anew, grew in wealth and consequence, as did the urban communities round them, often under the patronage of Cnut himself. Lands and privileges

PLATE 22

a. Gloucester: an early fourteenth-century sketch added to Geoffrey of Monmouth's History. Note castle, cathedral of St. Peter's, and various city churches

b. Pilgrimage to the shrine of Bury St. Edmunds

PLATE 23

London in the fifteenth century showing the Tower of London with London Bridge, &c. behind. The Duke of Orleans, captured at Agincourt and held prisoner in England for twenty-five years, is seen writing within, also at a window, and in the courtyard sending a letter

Ref. Poems of Charles Duke of Orleans. B.M. Roy 16. F ii, executed probably in England

were again bestowed upon them. By the time of the Norman Conquest the abbey of Bury St. Edmunds possessed three hundred manors and an income of over £600, nearly as great as that of Canterbury priory. The fame of its shrine attracted not only gifts but hosts of pilgrims (Pl. 22 b), while a concourse of tradespeople gathered around to minister to the needs of both pilgrims and monks: 'eighty less five bakers, brewers, tailors, washerwomen, shoemakers, robemakers, cooks, porters, *dispensatores.*' 'All these', wrote the Domesday commissioners, 'wait daily upon the Saint, the Abbot, and the Brethren.' There was money in plenty to be spent at Bury, and employment for many in the spending of it, not least in the erection of the new stone buildings, of which the great gateway still remains. Ely, wholly refounded in the late tenth century, was even more richly endowed than Bury by the end of the Saxon period. With an annual income of £800 or more, it was farming lands in more than a hundred villages scattered over six counties, while in addition some 1,200 landholders great and small in more than two hundred villages were dependent upon it. At St. Albans, too, a great work of reconstruction and refounding began in the late tenth century. Plans were made for rebuilding, and a vast store of stones and bricks was collected for the purpose from the old Roman city of Verulamium, just as the brethren of Ely were fetching stone from the deserted site of Grantchester. As the abbey grew in wealth and reputation, attracting gifts of landed property until it enjoyed a comfortable income about a third of that of Ely, so too the urban community developed around it, fostered by the last Saxon abbots. Abbot Wulsin, for instance, established a market place, encouraged people to settle in the town by offers of money and building materials, and built three churches for the townspeople outside the abbey precincts. Abbot Leofstan repaired Watling Street and the bridges upon it, for the safety of travellers and pilgrims.

The defences that from the first were important, particularly in the debatable land between Saxons and Britons or between one Saxon kingdom and another, became increasingly so when

the Viking raiders appeared. Through the ninth and tenth centuries towns were first and foremost places of refuge. The building and repair of walls, the digging of ditches, and the throwing up of embankments were matters of immediate and pressing concern. Old towns were put into a state of defence; new towns were founded, to be strongholds at strategic points in what had been open country. Such, apparently, were Ox-ford and Wallingford. This was an era of town-planning com-parable to that which Britain had known under Roman rule. In many places, as at York, Chester, and Manchester, ancient Roman walls, crumbling into ruin, were patched up. Behind them the English put up a stout resistance, and when at times they were overwhelmed, the defences were often further strengthened by the enemy occupying force, as at York, and they became strongholds of the invaders. So the chronicler tells how at Exeter the Danes 'came into the fortress, where they could not be got at'. If the English succeeded in recapturing them, their first concern was to see to the repair of the walls, as did Alfred when he regained London. So stout were London's defences thereafter that all attempts to subdue it by force were in vain. 'Praise be to God it standeth yet', wrote the Saxon chronicler when London, assaulted again and again, stood firm. Monasteries and cathedrals, if they survived the first shock of the invasions, and had sufficient resources, put up their own fortifications. Thus inside Winchester a wall was built round the cathedral precincts which seems to have protected the epis-copal community when the rest of the city was ravaged and pillaged in 860.

The new defensive points were often hurriedly thrown up, like that 'fort within the fen, where sat a few churls, which was hastily wrought'. At first they consisted of little more than an enclosure surrounded by ditch, earthen bank, and wooden palisade, to be replaced by a stone wall as time and occasion served. Sometimes the site of an old pre-Roman hill fort was used; sometimes a Danish encampment; sometimes a wholly new earthwork was begun. Gradually, as the resistance of the English strengthened, the defence of the territory they held was

systematically organized, with *burhs*, or defensible centres, at
strategic points, permanently garrisoned and maintained by
the surrounding country. Alfred, 'builder of fortresses', compelled his reluctant subjects to labour at this task, as he con-
scripted them for service in the national army. So important
were the *burhs* in his scheme of national defence that he reserved
one third of the army to do garrison duty in them, while one
third was out in the field and one third on leave, attending to
the essential job of tilling the land. His son and his daughter
continued the work, strengthening old strongholds and establishing new ones. At Witham, where Edward the Elder sent
his men to build an earthwork on the Roman road from
Colchester to London in 912, there may still be seen remains of
the outer ditch surrounding an oval enclosure of some twenty-
six acres, with a scarped inner citadel of some ten acres. At
Warwick and Stafford the earthworks erected by his sister
survived to dictate the lines of the later medieval walls (Fig. 53).

The boroughs founded by Alfred and his successors were
often designed not merely as garrison towns, to be held in times
of national emergency, but as centres for permanent civilian
occupation. To this end the area within the walls was laid out
in regular building plots. Settlers arrived, attracted by the prospect of personal freedom and highly favourable tenancies; as
'burgesses' they might hold their plots for a fixed money rent,
free of services other than those personal services for which the
borough as a whole was responsible, and they might freely sell
or mortgage them. Signs of such deliberate planning may perhaps be detected at Oxford in the grid-like pattern of the
streets that were once within the walls; almost all of them meet
at right angles. Sometimes the borough tenements were taken
up by craftsmen and others coming to ply their trade in places
often, like Oxford, as advantageously situated for commercial
as for strategic purposes. Sometimes they were taken up by
churchmen, noblemen, or owners of small country estates, like
the thanes of north Berkshire and Oxfordshire who had town
houses in Oxford, or those of south Oxfordshire who had town
houses in Wallingford. By the end of the Saxon period they

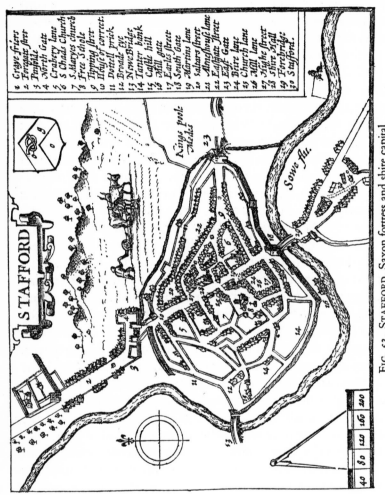

STAFFORD

Kings poole Medus

Sowe flu.

FIG. 53. STAFFORD, Saxon fortress and shire capital

were evidently a popular form of investment, acquired often
for profit rather than as residences for their owners. The archbishop of Canterbury, for instance, had six houses in Wallingford, and the bishop of Lichfield fourteen in Stafford.

As the borough was part of the planned scheme of national
defence, so too it became part of the framework of government.
By the late Saxon period all England, except the land north of
the Tees, was divided into administrative districts called shires,
each with its central fortified capital, on the pattern long
familiar in Wessex. In the west midlands Saxon fortresses like
Warwick and Stafford became the shire towns of new counties
carved out round them. In the east midlands, in regions re-
conquered from the Danes, the districts occupied by the various
Danish armies became shires, while in each the Danish army
headquarters, perpetuated as a borough by the Saxons, became
the shire capital and gave its name to the whole, as did Derby,
Nottingham, Leicester, Cambridge, Huntingdon, Northampton, and Bedford. Whether the shire was a new artificial creation like these in the midlands, or an ancient territorial division
like Kent or Suffolk, everywhere the place chosen to be the shire
capital acquired a new significance and a new importance, for
it was not only a military and administrative but also a judicial
centre, seat of the shire court, presided over by the king's representative, even if it had also its own town court. A steady
stream of correspondence passed between the central government and the shire court, where the king's chief executive
officer in the shire—the *sheriff*—collected the profits of justice
due to the king, as he collected all other payments due to him,
besides supervising the administration of the royal lands.

The last century of Anglo-Saxon England saw a remarkable
development of towns not merely as centres of administration,
justice, and defence but as markets and centres of commerce.
Within England a lively exchange was carried on. Though
every town had its fields and pastures outside the walls and
orchards and gardens within them, few lived wholly on their

Note to Fig. 53. The medieval walls follow the line of the early Saxon defences.
Note irregular oval shape of town, and contrast Colchester (Fig. 52).

produce. The great households, lay and religious, established
in them might and did draw their supplies partly from their
own extensive estates, but there was a brisk demand for food
bought on the market, whether from the countrywomen with
their hampers of butter and cheese, eggs and chickens; from the
butchers, often established with permanent shops of their own;
or from the fishermen, who seemed unable to keep pace with the
demand. In Ælfric's *Colloquy,* a Latin lesson book in the
form of a dialogue compiled for English schoolboys about
A.D. 1000, the fisherman, asked where he sells his fish, says: 'In
the city.' And when asked who buys it he replies: 'The citizens.
I cannot catch as much as I could sell.' Many an east-coast town
like Beccles, which at the time of the Domesday survey paid
rent to the monks of Bury of 60,000 herrings annually, must
have lived by distributing fish far into the interior, supplementing with the harvest of the North Sea that of the fresh-water
fisheries and eelponds. Even places in the heart of England like
Oxford expected to be supplied with salt herrings. Salt was
even more necessary than fish, and if some households secured
what they needed—for the dairy, the salting tub, and the table
—by acquiring saltpans on the coast or at inland saltsprings,
many more bought the salt carried into all parts of the country
from these specialized producing centres. Domesday tells not
only of the salthouses held at the Cheshire wiches (Nantwich,
Middlewich, and Northwich) by distant landowners, but also
of the carts, drawn by two or four horses, the packhorses, and
the men with loads on their backs, coming in from other
counties and departing with their loads of salt to sell. Iron, like
salt, was distributed all over the country from specialized producing centres such as Gloucestershire, where Pucklechurch
paid its rent in 90 blooms of iron and Gloucester city rendered
each year to the king 30 dickers of iron and 100 rods suitable for
making bolts for his ships.

At the same time English merchants were busy seeking on
the Continent those luxury wares which England, amply supplied with all ordinary needs, could not herself provide. The
merchant of Ælfric's *Colloquy* stoutly maintains that he is

useful to the king, the nobles, the rich, and all the people. Asked what he does for his living, he gives a vivid description of sailing with his wares overseas, buying precious things not to be had in England, and returning home with them, at the risk of shipwreck and death, to sell at a profit for the maintenance of himself, his wife, and children. Asked what he brings back he replies: 'Purple and silk, precious gems and gold, rare garments and spices, wine and oil, ivory and brass, copper and tin, sulphur and glass, and suchlike things.' Thus Englishmen participated in the age-old traffic between east and west, and it is matter for no surprise that we hear of them at this time journeying across the Alps with their northern wares—slaves, horses, hunting-dogs, furs and silver, linen and woollen cloth, weapons of war—to the busy international marts of north Italy. Here, early in the eleventh century, they grew so restive at the interference of the local customs officers, who took toll on goods coming over the Alpine passes, that discussions were held between the kings of England and Lombardy and a friendly agreement was reached: the English were to compound for all their dues by a three-yearly payment of two fine greyhounds with gilded and embossed collars, 50 lb. of pure silver, 2 shields, 2 swords, and 2 lances, with 2 fur coats and 2 lb. of silver for the official in charge.

Merchants from foreign lands, too, were frequently to be seen in English harbours. The men of Rouen, with wine, were well known in London, as were men from other parts of France and the Empire. Irish merchants were often in Chester and Danish merchants in York. The commercial links between England and Scandinavia were quite as close as those between England and the lands across the Channel, strengthened and maintained as they were by the many Norse settlers in this country. And as the Vikings pushed out westward beyond Iceland to Greenland and the New World, or south to the Bay of Biscay and the Mediterranean, England found herself no longer on the outer fringe of the world, but in the midst of a network of lively trade routes.

The conquest of England by William of Normandy gave a

momentary check to the growth of her towns, while pro-
foundly affecting their future development. Even where towns
had not actually been laid waste, townsmen were in many cases
ruined and poverty-stricken as a result of the revolution. In late
Saxon times many towns had, like Oxford and Lincoln, spilt
over into the suburbs outside the fortifications. Lincoln had
overflowed its wall southwards across the river and on the
eastern and western hillsides, and of the thousand or so houses
to be found at Oxford perhaps about a third were outside the
walls. But when the Domesday commissioners made their re-
turns they reported 478 houses at Oxford so 'wasted and destroyed' that they could not pay their taxes, and another 24 of
the 225 that were responsible for repairing the town wall so
dilapidated that this service could not be secured from them;
while at York, out of 1,476 houses, 540 could pay nothing and
400 very little. Sometimes houses were deliberately demolished
and whole areas cleared to make room for one of the new Norman castles that became so conspicuous a feature in any town
of consequence, dominating it and keeping in awe the subject
inhabitants with its garrison and constable in charge. At Lincoln 166 houses were destroyed in the south-west corner of the
upper city, inside the walls, 'on account of the castle'. This
was splendidly placed, commanding the steep ascent from the
river. Ditches were dug around the area, cutting into the line of
the old Roman wall; earth banks were thrown up, burying the
Roman west gate, and the west street was diverted farther north.
At Oxford a temporary castle was erected outside the west gate;
the courtyard round it, partly inside and partly outside the
walls, was protected by its own moat, and the west street diverted to run to the south of it. In every county town William
saw personally to the building of such a castle. If at first most
of them consisted only of an inner mound and outer bailey
with ditch, earthen bank, and wooden palisade, before long
wood was replaced by masonry. In Colchester, as may still be
seen, Roman remains were turned to good account and late in
the eleventh century a massive keep rose, resting on Roman
vaults.

Many French immigrants now took up their quarters in
English towns, not only as members of castle garrisons but also
as civilians. Often they formed for a while separate communities, with their own language, customs, and courts of justice,
specially favoured over the conquered English in matters of
taxation. At Norwich the 'new borough' founded by French
settlers to the west of the Norman castle, with forty-one burgesses at the time of Domesday, came in course of time quite
to supplant the 'old borough' round Tombland to the east of
the castle as the centre of the city's life. At Shrewsbury the
English complained that they had to pay as much in taxation
as the whole town paid before the Conquest, although fifty
houses were waste, the castle occupied the site of fifty-one
more, the French burgesses held a number which once paid
and now no longer did, and the earl had given fifty-nine burgesses, whose predecessors used to pay, to his newly founded
abbey.

Nowhere was the vigour and vitality of the Norman conquerors more in evidence than in the stone buildings, planned
on the grand scale, which soon began to give a new and impressive dignity to towns which had hitherto been mostly of
wattle and daub, timber and thatch, even if, where stone was
plentiful as at Oxford, they had sometimes boasted at least a
stone-faced wall and a rude stone church. Churchmen were
early in the field. They were no respecters of ancient buildings.
Even before the castle mounds were crowned with their keeps
of stone, Norman prelates and priors were sweeping away
every vestige of the Saxon buildings they found on their arrival,
clearing and enclosing sites as extensive as those taken for the
castles, and pushing on boldly with the erection of edifices even
more splendid than those with which they were familiar in
Normandy. 'You do not know which to admire more, the
beauty or the speed', wrote William of Malmesbury of Lan-
franc's new cathedral at Canterbury, built in the first ten years
that he was archbishop there to replace the old cathedral,
burnt down in 1067. At Winchester in 1079 Bishop Walkelin began a wholly new cathedral to the west of the existing

one, and on the day after it had been consecrated, in 1093, in the presence of almost all the bishops and abbots of England, his men 'began to pull down the old minster, and before the end of the year they had demolished the whole of it, except one apse and the high altar'. At St. Albans Abbot Paul of Caen, as forceful in execution as he was bold in conception, swept away every trace of the former buildings and, using the great store of bricks and stone laboriously collected by his predecessors, built a new monastery with the magnificent church which still stands as a monument to him today, as it stood, almost complete, at his death in 1093. When Remigius, rewarded with a bishopric for his handsome contribution to the Conqueror's invading force, moved his see from Dorchester (Oxon) to the more illustrious city of Lincoln, he 'bought lands in the highest parts of the city, near the castle with its strong towers', and there replaced the 'old church' with a majestic modern one (*ecclesia moderna*). So, too, when the see of Thetford was moved to the greater city of Norwich, Bishop Herbert de Losinga acquired, by purchase or exchange, an extensive site close to the castle, demolished houses big and small, together with the principal church of the old borough, enclosed the whole with a strong wall, and within it established a monastery and built a cathedral church. Henceforward the townsmen of Norwich, like many elsewhere, had in their midst two rich and powerful alien communities, military and religious, centred on the castle and on the cathedral, each under its own rule and secure behind its own fortifications. With neither of them were they to live at peace. The story of almost every medieval town is punctuated by disputes, often sanguinary, between town and cloister or between town and castle.

The first century after the Norman Conquest saw an immense work of building in stone in England's towns. The massive castle keeps on mounds often artificially raised, the battlemented walls, and the towers of churches and cathedrals surmounted by their timber spires, were the most prominent features of the landscape, as we may see them silhouetted against

the sky in the charming illustrations added later to Geoffrey of Monmouth's history (Pl. 22*a*).

Great as were Lincoln, York, Norwich, and Winchester at this time, London was probably as great as all of them put together. A vivid picture of it as it was in the reign of Henry II has come down to us in the contemporary description written by William FitzStephen at the opening of his life of that eminent Londoner, Thomas Becket. London then boasted not only three castles—the White Tower at its east end with two others at its west end—and the great cathedral church of St. Paul's, but also 'thirteen greater conventual churches and a hundred and twenty-six lesser parish churches' inside and outside the walls. Upstream to the west the royal palace of Westminster rose above the river, 'two miles from the city, and joined thereto by a populous suburb'. London was already a centre of social life for the whole land. Almost all the bishops, abbots, and magnates of the realm owned houses there, 'lordly habitations, whither they repair and wherein they make lavish outlay when summoned to the city to councils and assemblies or when drawn thither by their own affairs'. The city was celebrated for its social occasions, its fashionable dinners, parties, weddings, and church services, and for its excellent entertainment of visitors. It was renowned also for its schools, its law courts, its charities, its water supply and drains. Among the special amenities 'appropriate to a city and appertaining to the art of city life' was the restaurant on the north bank. The Londoner caught unawares by visitors, with no fresh food in the house, would 'hasten to the river bank', there to dine out with his guests, finding all he could possibly wish for on the menu, whether he was rich or poor, and able to take his choice 'at any hour of day or night' of roast, fried, or boiled meat, many kinds of fish, game, and poultry, and delicacies such as sturgeon, guinea fowl, or 'Ionian francolin'. In London, indeed, were to be found all the pleasures of urban society combined with many of the delights of country life. Outside the walls were sports grounds and pleasant suburban houses whose gardens, touching each other, were planted with trees.

Beyond were meadows and pastures intersected with streams; fertile cornfields, mills, and a great forest with wild beasts of the chase.

But FitzStephen was writing the biography of an arch-bishop who was the son of a London mercer, and he did not forget the commercial activity on which the prosperity of the city was largely based. So he tells of the markets where livestock and country produce could be sold, and necessities such as cart-horses and agricultural implements bought, and, much more important, of the international trade of the port of London, into which, he writes with pardonable exaggeration, goods were brought by 'merchants from every nation under heaven'.

From this time on it is the vigorous trading communities in England's towns that claim more and more attention as they become an increasingly assertive element in urban life, chal-lenging the dominance of castle and convent, and claiming an equal if not a greater share in the control of the city's affairs. The twelfth and thirteenth centuries, a period of peace and relative stability despite a momentary setback during the civil war of Stephen's reign, witnessed a quickening of economic activity in England, as on the Continent, which has seldom been paralleled. The long centuries of invasion had come to an end. Swords could be turned into ploughshares. The country knight could become the country gentleman. Peasants could reap what they had sown, and, if they were thrifty, accumulate a comfortable surplus. Ships could ply to and fro on their peaceful occasions, and a lively and regular exchange could be maintained between one region and another, little hampered by export or import dues. Great landowners, sensible of a growing demand at home and abroad as population increased, and able to sell on a rising market, turned to improving their land and stepping up output, producing cash crops for sale and growing rich on the proceeds. Very revealing are accounts such as those of the bishop of Ely's estates. While some corn continued to be brought from the Ely manors to make bread for the bishop's table or the monastic refectory, more came into the town for sale

in the open market, either in small quantities or in bulk, to merchants of substance who carried it far afield, often by sea from the port of Lynn. Land was reclaimed by the bishop from forest and fen, stocked with beasts or sown with corn, and the bishop's revenues from sales of farm produce grew rapidly, increasing some fivefold between Domesday and the reign of Edward I, until his total net income (a large part of which came from agrarian profits) reached about £2,500, trebling between 1170 and 1300. From the Lancashire vaccaries of the earl of Lincoln, with over 2,000 head of cattle, butter and cheese were sold, and beasts were driven over the Pennines into the markets of Bolton and Pontefract, either for stock or to be slaughtered for meat and hides and tallow. Ipswich was doing a thriving trade in the export of bacon and cheese, and the prior of Canterbury was making a handsome profit on the cheeses from some of his Kentish manors, as well as from their corn, some of which was being exported from Kentish ports in the early thirteenth century.

If corn, meat, hides, and dairy produce found a ready sale in England and abroad, still more in demand was fine-quality English wool, which fetched higher prices than any other in Europe and became indispensable to the rapidly growing industrial cities of Flanders, living almost wholly by textile manufacture. Without it, looms of Ypres and Ghent and many another clothmaking town would have lain idle; with it, Flanders could support an ever-increasing population. Sheep-farming on a commercial scale, with close attention to breeding, was embarked on by high and low. Ely market did a thriving business in the sale of wool from the abbey's manors, which even at the time of Domesday stocked over 13,000 sheep, and merchants of Lynn eagerly bought up the clip of this and other east-Anglian monasteries. In the Cotswolds the nuns at Minchinhampton had 1,700 sheep grazing on the common early in the twelfth century, and year by year packhorses laden with the convent's fine-quality wool, as well as its cheese, went off towards Cirencester to be sold. The earl of Lincoln grew rich by the huge flocks he kept in Lincolnshire, Yorkshire, and

elsewhere, while the monks of the new Cistercian order, settling in remote Yorkshire dales or in the valleys of Wales, transformed what had been empty wastes into vast sheep runs. They turned arable land too into pasture, evicting the former cultivators, and sold their wool upon long-term contracts, living off the advances given by the merchants. Humble villagers vied with their lords in the number of sheep that they put out to graze. If they were not themselves within easy reach of a market they could still be sure of a sale for their wool. Estate officers, carrying their employers' clip to market, regularly collected also the wool of the peasants from all over the countryside. Exporters' agents, too, riding round the great houses, lay or religious, to gather in the wool for which they had signed advance contracts, would also call at the small farms to buy up their wool, though often the big houses had themselves contracted to deliver not only their own clip but a certain quantity from the neighbourhood. In good years towards the end of the thirteenth century, when the sheep-shearing was done and all was collected, the wool of some eight million fleeces left England's ports for the Continent.

Though such great quantities of wool went down to the ports for shipment abroad, some was made up on English looms, not only on those of peasant households or village weavers supplying the needs of their own neighbourhood but also on those of urban craftsmen congregated together in the towns and working, like those of Flanders, for a national and even an international market. The first surviving Pipe Roll of the royal Exchequer (1130) reveals substantial groups of such weavers, paying considerable sums to the Crown for permission to have their own gilds. The London gild paid £16, those of Winchester, Lincoln, and Oxford £8, and that of Huntingdon £2. A little later a weavers' gild at York was paying £10 annually and one at Nottingham £2. Similar gilds no doubt existed elsewhere in towns where they had no need of royal sanction. The town craftsman's looms were sometimes narrow like those of the countryman, and his cloth was sometimes rough and cheap, as was the coarse burel of Oxford and Win-

chester sold in quantities for clothing the poor. But often they
were broad double looms of complex mechanism, at which
two weavers sat side by side, weaving broadcloths some two
yards wide and twenty-six yards long. Some of these weavers'
cloths, when fulled, dyed, and finished, were among the finest
produced anywhere in Europe in the thirteenth century, and
the manufacturers who organized their production, buying the
raw wool, putting it out to spinners, weavers, and fullers, dyeing and shearing it on their own premises, and finally marketing it at home or abroad, brought wealth and prestige to their
towns. Scarlet of Lincoln was among the most highly priced
cloths in a tariff of tolls at Venice in 1265, and both this and
Stamford and Beverley cloths of many colours were much in
demand for royal and noble households in England and oversea throughout the thirteenth century. Henry III made presents of English scarlet to his wife's French relations, to the king
and queen of Norway, and to the sultan of Damascus, and
'cloths of scarlet and other cloths from Stamford, Beverley,
York, Lincoln, Northampton, and Louth' were among the
cargo of a Spanish merchantman plundered off the Norfolk
coast in 1271. Fine light English worsteds were also in brisk
demand as summer wear, particularly for members of religious
orders like the Knights of St. John of Jerusalem.

English minerals were being exploited as never before in the
two centuries following the Conquest. Iron-mining regions
such as Sussex, the Forest of Dean, and Cleveland supplied not
only the increasing amounts of iron needed by local smiths all
over the country for making up into agricultural implements
such as ploughshares, spades, harrows, sickles, but also great
quantities of military stores mass-produced on the spot. From
the forges of St. Briavels, for instance, came spades, pickaxes,
and other mining tools for the Irish expedition of Henry II,
50,000 horse-shoes for Richard I's crusade to the Holy Land,
and constant consignments of arrows. England's iron, however,
was scarcely sufficient for her own needs, and by the late thirteenth century at any rate she was importing from Spain.

The tin mines or 'stannaries' (*minaria stanni*) of Devon and

Cornwall were still, as they had been for many centuries, one of
the principal sources of supply for Europe. Under the supervision of a Warden appointed by the Crown in 1198 production was vigorously stepped up. In the course of the next
century it multiplied some tenfold, and increasing quantities
were exported, either in ingots of tin assayed, stamped, taxed,
and sold in certain 'stannary towns' especially designated for
the purpose, like Bodmin, or as manufactured pewter.

Even more highly valued was lead, which roofed many an
abbey and castle in England and abroad, and provided
gutters, rainpipes, fresh-water pipes, and basins for the in-
tricate water systems installed in the towns and in the greater
country houses, lay and religious. About a century after the
Conquest an energetic prior of Canterbury acquired land
near the city containing springs, and installed the elaborate
water system, complete with lead pipes, basins, and taps,
which may still be traced from a contemporary diagram.
Soon afterwards the abbey of Bury St. Edmunds brought its
water supply two miles underground by lead pipes. For some
time English plumbers had been in request on the Continent,
as when Coutances cathedral was struck by lightning in 1091
and the bishop 'sent to England and called to him Brismet the
plumber' to see to the leading of the roof, and English lead
was used in the building of many of the great Cistercian
abbeys of the twelfth century. In royal accounts we can read
of the carts laden with lead that made their way laboriously
over the moors from the mines on the borders of Yorkshire
and Cumberland; 100 cartloads were once shipped from
Newcastle-upon-Tyne to Rouen for the roofing of Clairvaux,
and 241 cartloads from York to Rouen. From the Derbyshire
mines lead was carted to Boston or Lynn and thence shipped
to the Continent or around the coast—to London, to Southampton for the roofing of Winchester, to Topsham for the
roofing of Exeter. The mines of Mendip were a profitable
source of income to the bishop of Bath, to whom they were
granted by Richard I. But the king kept in his own hands the
famous silver-bearing lead mines of Devon, which supplied

a considerable part of the needs of the Mint in days when the
current coin of the realm was of silver. And as the need of
ready money grew with the expanding economy of the realm
and the increasing expenses of government, production in
these silver mines was increased by every possible means, by
opening up new workings, by directing labour compulsorily
into the mines, and by improving equipment. Under Edward I,
as the result of a considerable outlay on extensive drainage
schemes, output was doubled. Here miners toiled by candle-
light underground, digging ore for piecework wages, while
weekly rates were paid to the women who washed it, to the
smelters, to the blowers of the bellows, to the smiths, to the
silver refiners, to the clerk, and to the labourers who pierced a
way through the rock. And on Saturday, when the workers
had received their weekly pay, they went off to the nearest
market town to spend it, strictly forbidden to linger there
after the ninth hour on Sunday. So little towns like Tavistock
did a flourishing business in bread, meat, fish, and other
goods.

England's coal mines also were being vigorously developed
at least from the late twelfth century, and in the following
century considerable quantities of coal were being exported,
chiefly from Newcastle-upon-Tyne.

Thus England's exports through the twelfth and thirteenth
centuries, while no doubt greatly increased in volume, were in
kind much what they had been in Roman days. As in colonial
countries today they consisted primarily of food and raw
materials, though with the beginnings of a trade in manufactured textiles. 'From England', it was written in a Bruges
book of about 1200, 'come wool, hides, lead, tin, coal, and
cheese.' The list would have been much the same towards the
end of that century, with wool far and away at the top, so much
so that parliament, discussing how the government's financial
difficulties could best be met, resolved upon a tax on wool exports, since wool was 'half the wealth of the whole land'. By
that time it was supplying not only the clothmakers of Flanders
but also those of Italy, where Florence, with the help of English

wool, was producing a cloth as fine as that of the North. Indeed, so much wool was being shipped abroad that England was even importing some from Spain and Germany for the needs of her own cloth manufacturers.

Enriched by her production of first-rate wool, England was able to import increasing quantities of those goods which her own land was less well able to supply. From Gascony, part of the realm of the English sovereign since 1152, came wine in such abundance and of such good quality that few Englishmen now attempted to produce the very inferior vintages their own land could yield. On the quays of Bordeaux ships were each year laden for English ports—from Newcastle in the north to Bristol and Chester in the west—with up to 20,000 tuns containing four million gallons of wine from growers in and around Bordeaux and far up-country along the river valleys which there converged. Back in exchange went English corn, cheese, and herrings to feed the Gascons, who devoted themselves more and more to the cultivation of the vine. With Norway England carried on a busy trade, exchanging cloth and corn, of which Norway was in constant need, for fish, whale oil, and softwoods, made up into boards, rafters, masts, shafts, and other goods. Thence, too, and from the Baltic area came other products of the vast forests that still covered much of northern Europe—pitch, tar, potash, and many varieties of costly furs such as sable, marten, ermine and, above all, squirrel, to be made up by English skinners into the fur linings which were an indispensable adjunct to the robe of a lady or gentleman of quality. From Flanders came fine cloth of many colours, woven often out of English wool. From southern Spain and Portugal came olive oil, soap, fine leather of Cordova, figs, dates, raisins and almonds, sugar, and occasionally oranges and lemons, as yet an expensive luxury. Mediterranean fruits came also from Italy, but Italy had more exotic wares than this to supply— silks, cloth of gold, sweet wines of the Levant, and currants of Greece, together with all the riches of Asia, ranging from pepper, cinnamon, cloves, ginger, and other spices in bewildering variety, to rubies and emeralds; ivory and sandalwood;

cotton and muslin; monkeys and parrots, and a quantity of costly trifles for the delectation of the wealthy. Such oriental luxuries had from time immemorial made their way across Europe to England; but in the late thirteenth century the Italians, who virtually monopolized the trade, with their factories scattered over the Levant and the Black Sea and even as far afield as China, opened a direct sea route from the Mediterranean to northern Europe. Henceforward galleys of Venice and carracks of Genoa came regularly into the Channel ports, particularly into Southampton, Sandwich, and London.

By this time England was importing not only luxuries but also necessaries such as fish and timber and raw materials for her own growing industries, particularly dyestuffs for her cloth-makers. The first national customs duty of which we have clear evidence was that on woad, which at the time of Richard I brought a substantial sum into the Exchequer. This dye, universally used for dyeing in blue, in compounds of blue such as violet or green, and in black, was produced in vast quantities by the woad growers of Picardy and marketed in Amiens and neighbouring towns, whence it was shipped down the Somme to England. The brilliant scarlet *kermes* (or 'grain') was brought from Spain and Portugal, and the best-quality alum necessary for use with it came from the Mediterranean, especially from Asia Minor. *Brasil*, a cheaper red dye much used, and mentioned in Northampton's dyeing regulations of the mid-thirteenth century, was derived from a tropical redwood tree, and came from Ceylon and the East Indies. These and many other imported raw materials appear in lists of tolls charged at English harbours and at the gates of inland cities in the thirteenth century.

The English themselves took an active part in these exchanges. In every port of any consequence there was a substantial body of English merchants engaged primarily, though seldom wholly, in overseas trade, and among them were some of the most notable citizens of their time William of Doncaster, for instance, thrice mayor of Chester, merchant, ship-owner, army contractor, and government official, was much

concerned with the import of Gascon wines, traded frequently with Ireland, and exported wool from Chester and elsewhere, sending it in 1309 across country to Ipswich and thence to Flanders. He also managed lead mines in North Wales, whence he supplied lead for the roofing of Chester castle. A Shrewsbury merchant, Laurence of Ludlow, 'mercator notis-simus' as the chronicler calls him, was a yet more outstanding figure and one of the leading wool merchants of his day, as his father had been before him. The spacious and elegant country house which he bought and enlarged for himself at Stokesay, one of the finest medieval English houses still extant, speaks eloquently of the high standard of life enjoyed by the success-ful business man in England at the end of the thirteenth century.

But a very large share of England's trade was at this time in the hands of foreigners, some of whom enjoyed privileges as great or greater than those of the English themselves. Drapers of Flanders and northern France were marketing their cloth in London and throughout the land. Gascon vintners were im-porting the bulk of England's wine supplies and were even allowed to sell retail as well as wholesale all over the country, stoutly though their liberties were contested by English vintners, particularly those of London. Woad merchants from Amiens, Corbie, and Nesle were doing a thriving business in London, where, united in a trading association or 'Hanse', they freed themselves from the restrictions customarily imposed on the alien by an amicable arrangement with the City in 1237. Whereas formerly their woad had all to be sold on the quay within forty days of its arrival, and to burgesses of London, now they could stow it in warehouses, sell it to anyone they pleased, take it to any part of the country, and stay as long as they liked. In return for these privileges they paid £50 annually to the City and a lump sum of £100 down towards London's new water supply. Very similar agreements were negotiated elsewhere as at Norwich in 1286, and the Picards travelled freely all over the realm, selling their woad even in remote parts of Cumberland. Many had permanent depots in England, and some married

English wives, settled down, and were admitted as burgesses in the towns where they lived. Far more exclusive were the merchants of the north German cities, from Cologne eastwards to Hamburg, Lübeck, and beyond. These cities were now leagued together and rapidly rising to a position of premier importance in the commerce of northern Europe, where they threatened altogether to eclipse the Norwegians and the Flemings, as they planted their fortified outposts in Bergen and Bruges. In London, where they boasted privileges going back at least to the year 1000, members of the 'Hanse of the Germans' lived apart, as in a foreign 'concession' of modern times, in their own communal settlement known as the Steelyard. This occupied one of the best positions on the north bank of the river, close to London Bridge. Here were their wharves where their ships berthed, and behind them their warehouses, offices, dwelling houses, and communal dining hall, with taverns and beer gardens, the whole enclosed by a high wall. The settlement was governed by their own aldermen and councillors and strict discipline was maintained over the young bachelor representatives of the German firms. Each had a suit of armour for use in case of need. Once the gates had been shut in the evening they might not emerge, nor might they ever fence or play tennis with the English, or consort with English women. Marriage was forbidden to them while stationed abroad. Similar settlements of the German Hanse were to be found in a number of east-coast ports, such as Lynn and Boston.

Pre-eminent among all the foreign merchants were the representatives of the wealthy Italian companies of Florence, Lucca, Siena, and elsewhere, whose influence in England was reaching its zenith in the late thirteenth century. Profiting by their position as collectors of the papal taxes they travelled through the land, buying up wool as they went, shipping it abroad, and paying the pope out of the proceeds. In this way they gained such an ascendancy in the wool trade that even the Flemings came to be largely dependent upon them for supplies. And if all foreign merchants were useful to kings of England for the money that could be borrowed from them, it was these Italians,

with their branches all over the world from London to China, who were the bankers *par excellence* and could be depended upon to provide money whenever and wherever it was needed.

The increasing volume of business handled by merchants, English and foreign, as a vigorous exchange was carried on both within England and with lands abroad, meant the rapid growth of ports and inland market towns. A favourable site for trade had from earliest times been one of the determining factors influencing urban development; now it became far and away the most important. Towns which were of little, if any, consequence at the time of Domesday leapt into the front rank, though London remained immeasurably the greatest. All round the coast of England old seaports sprang into fresh life and new ones emerged. Newcastle, named after the castle founded there by Henry I, prospered by exporting coal, lead, hides, and a little wool, and quickly forged links with Nor/ way which have lasted to the present day. Hull, a town of sea/ men and merchants scarcely heard of in Saxon days, outport of York and Beverley, was drawing to itself the trade of the great waterways that converged on the estuary of the Humber, shipping thence wool, hides, lead, and small amounts of cloth. Boston, created by Breton followers of the Conqueror, linked closely by the river Witham with the city of Lincoln, reached the height of its fame as the wool trade rose towards its zenith late in the thirteenth century; more wool was then shipped from its port than from any other in England, London not excepted. Lynn developed rapidly as the natural outlet for the wool of fenland abbeys like Ramsey, Crowland, and, above all, Ely. Yarmouth, outport for Norwich, grew rich by exporting Norfolk worsteds, but became even more famous for its annual herring fair, principal mart for the North Sea fisheries on the English side. Ipswich exported the bacon and cheese of Suffolk, with some corn and wool, and English cloth. Southampton entered upon two centuries of considerable prosperity in the late thirteenth century with the first arrival in the English Channel of the Italian ships, which found there a convenient port of call on their way to

and from the much greater marts of the Low Countries. In
Southampton Water they loaded large quantities of the wool
that was destined to be shipped direct to Italy by way of the
Straits of Gibraltar, instead of being sent, as hitherto, by sea
to Flanders and thence overland across the Alps. All these
ports had business connexions far into the heart of England,
by cart, packhorse, or river barge, and through them merchants English and foreign distributed their varied imports.
From Newcastle, for instance, woad, alum, ginger, and
pepper were sold to the Lake District; from Lynn men of
Amiens sent woad to Stamford and far into the midlands to
Leicester and many small towns in Northamptonshire.

Most remarkable, perhaps, was the expansion of the port of
Bristol, which in due course became third city of the realm, outdistanced only by London and York, and which owed its rise
wholly to its unparalleled advantages for trade. 'Bristow', as
Speed wrote later, 'is not so ancient as it is fair and wel seated.'
Close enough to the estuary of the Severn to attract much of
the trade of the fruitful valleys that there converged, it was yet
sufficiently withdrawn up the narrow Avon gorge to be safe
from the attacks of pirates and the storms of the open sea, while
the high tides, caused by the contraction of the Severn
where the Avon joins it, floated ships swiftly up the gorge into
its sheltered harbour. There, at the junction of the Avon and
the Frome, almost completely encircled by these two rivers
as by a natural moat, was the original nucleus of the city, with
its central market cross where the two main roads met. The
castle built by the Norman conquerors on the narrow neck
of land between the two rivers completed its defences, closing
in the one point of access by land, 'like a stopper in a bottle'.
But even before the castle was finished Bristol was expanding
in every direction beyond the first circle of the city walls. Already known in late Saxon days as a convenient port for
Ireland, its position close to the inner Viking route from Scandinavia by the Hebrides and the Irish Sea to the Bay of Biscay
made for close contacts both with Norway and with the west
coasts of France. Early in the twelfth century, when trade with

Norway was flourishing, we know that Norwegians were accustomed to winter in Bristol, and William of Malmesbury then described the city as being one of the richest in the country on account of its commerce, and as one of the best defended on account of its situation. Before long the political union of England and Gascony so stimulated trade with Bordeaux that more and more ships laden with wine docked each year at the wharves of Bristol. Most striking was the growth of the city across the bridge over the Avon, on the land of the Templars and the manor of Bedminster (Fig. 54). Here was developing the busy industrial and commercial suburb of Redcliffe, filled with the houses of craftsmen and merchants, dwarfing alto-gether the original nucleus of the city. So rapidly was the city's overseas trade expanding that early in the thirteenth century an immense programme of public works was under-taken by the community for the improvement of its port. At a cost of £5,000 an entirely new harbour was created by cutting a new channel for the Frome across St. Augustine's marsh, and it was here that Bristol's ocean-going ships were henceforth built and loaded, while the smaller boats engaged in local and coasting traffic continued to dock at the 'Welsh Back' on the Avon. The new suburb between the two quays, inhabited largely by seamen, was then walled in. The works were completed by the construction of a new stone bridge over the Avon, which involved damming the river and tempor-arily diverting it, and by the walling-in of the wide suburb of Redcliffe. The men of Redcliffe, to their chagrin, were made

---

Note to Fig. 54. The central market cross appears close to All Saints' (N), and the gates of the original town, almost circular in shape, at the churches of St. Leonard (K), St. Nicholas (S), and St. John (G), where the gateway still stands, running through the church tower beneath the spire. The new suburb by the Marsh and that south of the Avon are shown enclosed by their thirteenth-century walls. In the suburb by the marsh can be seen part of the original channel of the Frome. Ocean-going ships docked at 'the Kay', where the Frome had been deepened and widened when the new cut to the Avon was made. This map, derived from that drawn by John Smith in 1568, is less accurate than many of those in Speed; it underestimates considerably the extent of the suburb south of the Avon, and fails to show how the castle and its defences closed the gap between the rivers.

The Armes of ÿ City

FIG. 54. BRISTOL, a commercial and industrial city

responsible for the building of their own wall, but the rest of
the work was a co-operative effort financed by citizens on both
sides of the bridge.

Meanwhile inland towns also, with good communications
by land and water, were doing a brisk business as markets for
local produce and as centres of distribution for the rarer goods
brought from overseas or from distant parts of England. In
many there had existed from time immemorial an appointed
'market place', often under the shadow of a church or round
a market cross where, protected by the 'peace of the church',
dealings could be openly transacted before witnesses, and
where standard weights and measures, tested and approved,
could be made available to buyers and sellers. At Canterbury
there was a market place (*venalis locus*) at least by the eighth
century, and certain Saxon kings attempted, though without
success, to confine all buying and selling to such recognized
market towns, which were entitled 'ports' whether or no they
were on the sea or on a navigable river. Now markets grew and
multiplied. By the late thirteenth century towns which had
once had but a single market place boasted a number of specialized ones, each often with its own market cross. Lincoln had
its separate markets for corn, meat, fish, poultry, cloth, and
skins; Ipswich for butter, wool, and timber. All over the
country, too, new markets appeared where none had been before, often in small and hitherto insignificant places, sponsored
by enterprising lords of the manor very sensible of the benefits
which they might bring to themselves as well as to the whole
neighbourhood. The holding of a weekly market was a valuable source of income, since rents could be charged for stalls as
well as for the shops of the craftsmen the market would attract,
and tolls could be taken on goods brought in for sale, on the
services of brokers arranging bargains, and on the use of the
standard weights and measures provided. If only for this
reason the Crown tended to regard it as a royal prerogative,
though one which could be transferred, for a consideration, to
a subject. Hence those wishing to set up a new market, or even
to establish their right to an old one, secured their position by

purchasing a royal grant. No less than 3,000 such grants were obtained in the course of the thirteenth century, so eagerly was the right coveted, and law courts were often called upon to decide whether a newly created or projected market should be allowed or whether it was so near to an old-established one as to be harmful to it. Edward I, always alert lest any potential source of revenue should escape him, challenged many holders of markets to show by what right they held them. Some urged ancient usage, and others urged a charter from one of his predecessors, but many were fined for holding without warrant. By the early fourteenth century, except in the most sparsely populated areas, there was scarcely a peasant in the land who was not within reach of a market where he could dispose each week of his surplus produce and buy what he needed, walking there and back the same day.

The creation of new markets was matched by the creation of new fairs. Held more occasionally than the weekly market, and continuing for longer than a single day, the fair was intended to attract dealers from far afield. The more successful of them became international marts, famed throughout Europe. Like the market, the fair was a highly prized source of profit and one which sovereigns were prepared to bestow for a suitable payment. That astute man of business Bishop Walkelin of Winchester obtained from William Rufus the grant of a three days' fair on St. Giles' Hill, the proceeds of which helped him to complete his magnificent cathedral and convent buildings. After his death his fair continued to prosper. While it was in progress—and its duration was extended to fourteen and then to twenty-four days—all other buying and selling was forbidden not only in Winchester and within a radius of many miles round it but also, at one time, in the port of Southampton, and the keys of the city gates were handed over to the bishop's officers. Here, in the thirteenth century, foregathered merchants, bankers, and money-changers from all parts of Europe—men of Ypres and Douai with their luxury woollens, goldsmiths of London, men of Dinant with bronze and copper ware, men of Gothland with wax and furs, Spaniards, Portu-

guese, Irish, Normans, and men of Provence. The abbots of
Ramsey declared they would rather lose several manors than
their fair of St. Ives, so handsome an income did they derive
from it. 'Your robes buy at St. Ives', wrote Bishop Grosseteste,
advising the youthful countess of Lincoln, left early a widow,
how best to manage her affairs. And it was here and at the fairs
of Boston, Stamford, Northampton, and Winchester that
Henry III's agents laid in each year their main stocks of fine
coloured woollen cloth, English and Flemish, to make robes
for the royal family, with soft squirrel pelts, grey and white, by
tens of thousands for the lining of them, besides wines for the
royal cellars, and spices—pepper, cinnamon, ginger, mace,
cloves, and much more besides—for the royal kitchens.

The two centuries after the Norman Conquest that saw the
proliferation of markets and fairs and the expansion of many
old towns, sprawling out into suburbs beyond the walls, saw
also the foundation of new towns, designed from the first as
places whose inhabitants could devote themselves primarily, if
not exclusively, to trade or a craft rather than to agriculture.
The creation of new towns, once a public enterprise undertaken
for purposes mainly strategic and administrative, was now
principally the work of private landowners—great feudal lords,
lay and religious. Their achievement was notable. Even if they
were not invariably successful in choosing sites with good
commercial possibilities, even if some of their foundations
grew slowly or not at all and few developed into towns of any
great size, yet all over England today there are to be found
little market towns, planned as systematically as any Roman
city or Saxon borough, which witness to their energy and
initiative.

In turbulent frontier districts such as the marches of Wales
the laying out of towns went hand in hand with the building of
castles, as Norman barons occupied the valleys thrusting up
into the Welsh mountains. But elsewhere, after the Norman
period, new towns were being founded all over England with
scarcely a thought to their fortification unless they were on the

coast. Frequently the site selected was carved out of a manor, on
the outskirts of an existing village. So Maurice Paynell, lord of
the manor of Leeds, sensing perhaps the possibilities of the
Aire crossing, laid out his little borough with its sixty burgages along Bridge Street or 'Briggate' in 1207, away from the
ancient parish church and the peasants' cottages of the then
agricultural community of Leeds. More spectacular was the
venture of Bishop Poore of Salisbury a few years later. Desiring
to move his cathedral and palace from the windswept hill on
which his Norman predecessor had placed them, in uncom-
fortable proximity to the royal castle of Sarum, and wishing to
attach to them a town of his own which would attract craftsmen and merchants from far and wide, he chose with unerring
insight that incomparable site in his manor of Milford where
Salisbury now stands, at the meeting point of three river valleys, a choice so felicitous that his upstart city of 'New Sarum'
grew and prospered exceedingly, drawing to itself more and
more business, while its venerable neighbours, 'Old Sarum'
and Wilton, the county capital, faded into insignificance
(Fig. 55).

Whether planned on the grand scale like Salisbury or as a
single street like Leeds, the new towns of the late twelfth and
thirteenth centuries all conformed in certain important respects
to the accepted pattern approved by contemporary town
planners, and town planning was then an art with its recognized experts; such were the experts called in by Edward I
when he wrote to London from Bordeaux asking for four men
to be sent out to him 'who best know how to divide, order and
arrange a new town (*une novele vile*) in the manner most bene-
ficial for us and the merchants'. Streets, if there were more than
one, were laid out chess-board fashion, as regularly as in any
Roman city, and the principal ones were broad as well as
straight. An open square was left for the market place or, in the
smaller towns, the main shopping street was made so wide that
there was ample space down the centre for the market stalls,
space that was often built over later with a market hall and even
a row of permanent shops. Building plots were marked out,

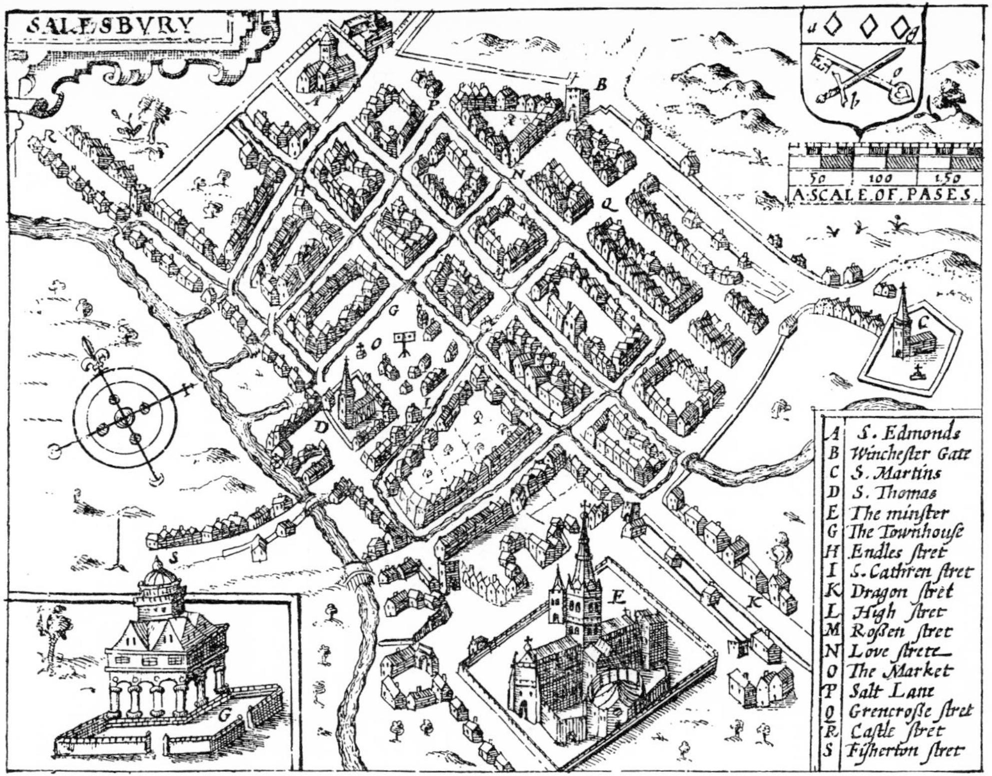

SALISBVRY

A SCALE OF PASES

A S. Edmonds
B Winchster Gat
C S. Martins
D S. Thomas
E The minster
G The Townhoufe
H Endles ftret
I S. Cathren ftret
K Dragon ftret
L High ftret
M Raften ftret
N Love ftret
O The Market
P Salt Lane
Q Grencrofte ftret
R Caftle ftret
S Fifherton ftret

Fig. 55. SALISBURY, a new town of the thirteenth century

each with a broad frontage (some 40 to 60 feet) allowing for
a house not very different from one of the smaller manor houses,
with a hall in the middle, one or two rooms on each side, of two
storeys high, perhaps, and a central gateway leading through
into a courtyard, garden, and outbuildings behind. Sometimes a small portion of arable land outside the built-up area
was allocated to each plot. Settlers were attracted by the
promise of personal freedom and highly favourable tenancies.
The holding was offered at a uniform money rent, free of any
services or dues; even more important, the tenant was at liberty
to sell, mortgage, sublet, or divide it, and to bequeath it by
will. Sometimes complete exemption from rent was given for
the first few years. Thus householders in the new towns enjoyed the privileged tenure long familiar in ancient Saxon
boroughs. Holding by 'burgage tenure' they were themselves
called 'burgesses' and their town a 'borough', however small
it might be. Only gradually, when the summoning of burgesses to Parliament with the knights of the shire became a
regular practice, did the term 'borough' come to be restricted
to the larger towns which were asked to send representatives,
and could afford to do so, while the smaller ones became
merely 'market' or 'merchant' towns.

Typical of many such small market-towns was Stratford-on-
Avon, founded in the reign of Richard I by John de Coutances,
bishop of Worcester, in his manor of Stratford. There at the
crossing of the Avon he laid out his borough, offering uniform building plots of 12½ by 3 perches (about 206 by 50 feet)
to be held as burgages for a rent of 1s. a year, payable quarterly.
For it he procured the grant of a weekly Thursday market.
Three streets ran parallel to the river and three at right angles to
it, the principal one leading down to the bridge. Within half a
century a thriving little borough had grown up with some 250

Note to Fig. 55. Note the regular chess-board planning, with watercourses down
each street, and the open market place with market cross (o), pillory, Council
House or 'Townhouse' (G), and parish church of St. Thomas (D), founded in 1240.
St. Martin's, the old church of the manor of Milford, is shown outside the city (C).
Note gateways between the city and the precincts of the cathedral (E).

householders, each holding the whole or a part of a burgage, or more than one, alongside the ancient village where villein tenants still did labour services, which by this time was appro-priately called 'Old Stratford'. Immigrants had come from almost all the villages and hamlets in the fertile region around within a radius of some 6½ miles, and some even from farther afield. There were at least three separate markets, each with its cross; a bridge with a bridge keeper; ovens, smithies, and several mills, including one for fulling cloth. The burgesses were a diverse throng of traders and artisans, such as were to be found in most small market towns: smiths, carpenters, wheel-wrights, coopers, tilers; leather workers like tanners, shoe-makers, glovers; cloth workers such as weavers, fullers, dyers, and tailors; millers, bakers, cooks, butchers, and mercers; besides a doctor, a piper, a woman minstrel, and some lesser clergy. By the late thirteenth century three annual fairs had been established and the tradesfolk had their gild with its Fraternity of the Holy Cross, its 'hospital' for the sick and aged, its school, its gildhall, and its own chapel, quite distinct from the ancient parish church half a mile away. Stratford-on-Avon had become the prosperous little market town that it still remained, enjoying a happy mediocrity, when William Shakespeare, son of one of its glovers, was born there.

While most of these new towns were founded by private in-dividuals, the State was not wholly inactive. Military needs prompted Richard I to lay out his little town of Portsmouth with its burgage tenements, market and fair, and royal docks from which his troops could set sail for France, just as King John selected the site of Liverpool as a suitable spot for the dis-patch of expeditions to Ireland and there issued a proclamation offering burgages, with holdings in the fields, at a rent of 1s. a year 'with all the liberties and free customs which any free borough has'. More striking were the projects of Edward I, conceived and executed in a manner at once more methodical and more magnificent than that of his predecessors. They con-cerned principally his foreign dominions, Gascony and Wales, though in England he greatly assisted the inhabitants

of Winchelsea to rebuild their town after its total destruction
by inundation, sending down his planning experts to lay out
a new town on a wooded site above the estuary.

In addition to benefits such as burgage tenure, a regular
market and fair, and perhaps a gild of traders in the town,
these urban communities, whether large or small, old or new,
enjoyed the boon of a law specially suited to their needs, ad-
ministered in their own borough courts, which were often of
great antiquity. Already in Saxon days there existed a small
body of special 'merchant law'. With the post-Conquest expansion of trade this grew until by the end of the thirteenth
century, if not earlier, a whole treatise could be compiled on the
Lex Mercatoria, such as that which was enrolled in Bristol's
Little Red Book for the guidance of its citizens. This law applied,
it is there written, to all pleas, except pleas of land, 'in cities,
fairs, seaports, market towns, and boroughs', unless the dis-
putants openly expressed a preference for the Common Law.
Its advantages were many for a trading community. Not least
was the swift and sure redress it provided in cases of debt. The
merchant stranger eager to depart, no less than the resident
merchant, could promptly recover what was owing to him;
for instead of the tedious and lengthy adjournments customary
elsewhere, the court 'of the dusty-foot' ('*piepoudre*'), administer-
ing the law merchant, could be adjourned not only from one
market to the next, or from high tide one day to high tide the
next, but from one hour to the next. At the third adjourn-
ment, if the defendant still failed to appear, judgement could
be given for the plaintiff, whereas elsewhere the non-appearance
of the defendant often meant the failure of the suit. A case
opened at 8 a.m. could thus be determined by midday. The
goods of the defendant, already distrained on, could then at
once be seized and valued, and sufficient of them handed over
to the plaintiff to satisfy his claim, with the proviso that they
were not yet absolutely his but might be redeemed within a
year and a day.

But the peculiar customs and privileges that had come to be
associated with mercantile communities did not always go un-

challenged. At the very time that the wealth and influence of the merchants was increasing, so too were the claims of kings and feudal lords. After the Norman Conquest some towns came for the first time under the control of a feudal lord. Whereas in Saxon days most boroughs had been directly subject to the Crown, which had played so important a part in their creation, Norman kings transferred their rights in some of them to great magnates of the realm. Thus Leicester, Warwick, and Chester were 'mediatized', each coming under the authority of a powerful earl who was not merely custodian of the castle as deputy for the king but also lord of the town, holding it of the king. Similarly Bath was granted to the bishop of Wells, while Henry I gave Reading to his newly founded abbey there as one of its endowments. New burdens were now often imposed upon the townsmen. At Leicester the earl converted part of the burgesses' arable land outside the walls into his own demesne, enclosed for his own cattle some of the best meadowland where they were accustomed to pasture their own beasts, expected them to assist in cutting his corn, and insisted that they must use his mills and ovens. At Reading the abbot moved the site of the market, deprived the burgesses of their merchant gild, summoned them to answer pleas elsewhere than in their gildhall, and extorted from them customs and services hitherto unknown. But nowhere were the rigours of feudal control more keenly felt than in those boroughs which had grown up from the first under the shadow of a great religious house. The men of Reading and of Malmesbury, resisting the demands of their abbots, could cite the customs and liberties their boroughs had enjoyed 'when in the hands of the king'; not so the men of St. Albans or Bury St. Edmunds, where the abbots tightened their grip, exploiting every conceivable source of profit, even to claiming a monopoly of the use of wind and water. Even those boroughs—and they were the great majority—which remained directly subject to the king, had often to bear new burdens as active Norman sheriffs with increased powers, responsible for the revenues due to the king, exacted the utmost possible. Indeed, the very pre-

sence of these alien officials was often an irritant. Everywhere, too, the powers of the town courts were threatened by the growth of royal justice. As the king's courts assumed ever wider powers, burgesses found themselves more and more often called upon to attend them. Merchants of Bristol living in High Street might be summoned to the shire town of Gloucester, those across the river in Redcliffe Street to the Somersetshire capital of Ilchester. And where powers of royal justice had been conferred on a subject, burgesses might have to appear before a feudal lord in matters not normally under his jurisdiction.

Hence the twelfth and thirteenth centuries saw not only the foundation of new boroughs, endowed from the first by written charters with certain liberties, but also attempts by townsfolk in many ancient boroughs to secure the definition and confirmation, and sometimes the extension, of liberties which they had long enjoyed. By the end of John's reign more than 100 charters had been obtained from kings of England and more than 200 from private lords—some comprehensive in scope, some concerned merely with one particular privilege; some recognizing existing customs, some introducing novelties. They were to be purchased almost for the asking from needy kings like Richard I or John. The charter granted by John before he was king (1188) 'to his burgesses of Bristol', still carefully preserved as one of the city's most treasured possessions, confirms to them 'all their liberties and free customs, as well, freely and entirely, or more so, as ever they had them', including the liberty to 'hold in free burgage', to have 'all their reasonable gilds', to grind their corn 'wheresoever they will', and never to have to plead in any court outside the walls of the town, except concerning lands held outside it. Even before this some towns had bought (as did Lincoln in 1130) the coveted privilege of collecting themselves all the dues owing to the Crown and paying in at the royal treasury through their own agent a fixed sum, the '*firma burgi*', thus freeing the borough from the interference of the sheriff in their financial affairs. Nor were great barons unwilling to grant charters for ready cash, especially at the time of the Crusades,

though often they sold privileges only one by one or for short periods. Leicester achieved its freedom piecemeal, the earl reserving his rights of mill and oven into the late fourteenth century. More reluctant were the lords spiritual, who kept jealous hold upon their rights, so that throughout the last centuries of the middle ages the townsmen waged a constant struggle, breaking out at times into open revolt and compelling the granting of charters, only, perhaps, to have them later revoked as 'contrary to God and the Church'.

The full privileges of the chartered borough were reserved to those admitted as 'freemen', whose names were enrolled in 'Freemen's Registers' such as those still surviving at Norwich and York, after they had taken a solemn oath and paid the customary fee. Each town had its own rules as to whom it would admit. Outside their ranks was a host of humbler folk—servants, labourers, hired workers of all sorts such as those weavers and fullers who were not their own masters but who toiled at the loom or trod cloth in the trough for piece-work wages, and men of villein birth dwelling in the borough, with or without licence from their lords, hoping perhaps to be enfranchised when they had spent the customary year and a day there and had proved themselves 'loyal men' and solvent citizens.

Government everywhere was in the hands of 'the more substantial men'. Ipswich had no sooner received its charter in 1200 than a general assembly of burgesses met in the churchyard of St. Mary Tower, chose the chief officers for the year—bailiffs and coroners—and decided that a body of twelve sworn 'Portmen' should be appointed to assist them, 'just as there are in other boroughs of England', 'to govern and maintain the borough and its liberties, to render its judgements and to ordain and do what should be done for the state and honour of the town'. The twelve were elected by a select group of townsmen nominated for the purpose by the officers. Two months later the ordinances they had devised were solemnly read out to the whole community gathered together again in the churchyard, to receive their unanimous consent. After another month's interval the common seal, newly made, was exhibited, with a

ship on one side and a church on the other—perhaps the very
one to be seen today in the British Museum; officers were
elected to govern the merchant gild; and it was agreed that the
laws and free customs of the town should be written in a roll to
be called the Domesday, and the statutes of the merchant gild
in another roll, 'as is customary in cities and boroughs where
there is a gild merchant'. So Ipswich set up the government
which continued to order its affairs for many centuries. Other
towns too had their oligarchical ruling bodies, chosen in diverse
ways from among 'the better people', and presided over sometimes by a mayor and sometimes by the alderman of the merchant gild; at Leicester the two were virtually indistinguishable.

Behind, in the background, was the shadowy body of 'the
whole commonalty', which continued to make its voice heard
from time to time, invading the council room 'in a great mul-
titude' (*in multitudine copiosa*), shouting its approval or dis-
approval when some question of popular moment was under
discussion, such as the assessing of a borough rate, and sharing
in the election of the borough officers. But more and more the
'assent of the whole community' was taken for granted or obtained from a limited number of specially invited people, until
at Leicester, for example, not only were the unfranchised forbidden to attend the common hall meetings (1466) but even
the burgesses themselves were excluded (1489) except for a
body of forty-eight of the 'most wise and sad' commoners chosen
by the mayor and the Four and Twenty. Since the Four and
Twenty alone could fill vacancies in their own number,
Leicester was from this time on a closed corporation. So too
were many other boroughs.

Rank in the medieval city was determined by wealth, and
great wealth carried with it great responsibility. A man rich
enough to be described as 'of the degree of a bailiff' or 'of the
degree of a mayor' had before him much arduous toil in the
service of his town. He would be expected to serve on its
council, in due course to take office, first, perhaps, as bailiff and
later as mayor, solemnly sworn to keep the peace of the town, to
chastise evildoers, to defend and keep all widows and orphans,

to do everyone right, poor as well as rich, and to maintain the franchises and free customs of the town and all its 'laudable ordinances' (Fig. 56). The mayor of Bristol, for example, was bound to keep his court each weekday from 8 to 11 a.m. and, except on Saturday afternoons and the eve of festivals, from 2 to 5 p.m. On Wednesdays and Saturdays he was expected to go round to the brewers' houses with his ale-taster to see that the ale being served to the people was good and of true measure. It was also his duty to make sure that there were sufficient stocks of wheat in the town, that firewood was readily available, and that coal-merchants were not supplying sacks of short weight. Many were the ceremonies he must attend, from processions and services on certain anniversaries to mayoral receptions like that on All Saints' Day, with drinks and 'spiced cakebread', or that on St. Nicholas Day, with music and games of dice. He must be ready to receive the St. Katharine's players at his door and give them drinks and reward them for their plays, and now and again there was royalty to be welcomed and vast preparations to be made for the brilliant pageants shown at various points along the royal route. Well indeed did he deserve his salary of £20, paid quarterly (the same as that of the mayor of York), and, at Christmas, those 12 yards of 'skarlet' valued at £8, with 8 marks for his fur, 5 for his wine, and 5 for his minstrels.

The functions of the town's government were multitudi-nous, so closely ordered was the life of the townsmen. In its court were enrolled contracts, conveyances, wills, and ap-prenticeship indentures. It undertook the guardianship of orphans; in some cases it appointed churchwardens and audited their accounts. Poor relief, health, and education were very much its concern; schools, hospitals, and old people's homes were often under borough control even if endowed by individuals. It made provision for a public water supply, perhaps fixing a special rate for heavy users like brewers and fishmongers. It controlled the building and repair of houses; prohibited noxious factories like the Southwark lime-kilns; restricted to special areas noisy or unsavoury trades like those

FIG. 56. Swearing-in of a new Mayor of Bristol

The retiring mayor hands the bible to the new mayor; both
mayors are dressed in scarlet gowns and scarlet cloaks lined with
grey squirrel. The sheriff and members of the council stand by.
Below, the town clerk reads out the oath and next to him is the
sword-bearer with the mayor's sword and hat of office. These,
like the sergeants and other city officials, are dressed in particoloured robes of murrey and dark blue striped with red. On the
table is a money bag, an inkstand and pencase, a parchment roll,
and the case in which the bible was kept. Outside the bar are the
commons looking on. Above the dais may be seen in the
windows the Cross of St. George, the royal arms of England,
and the arms of the city of Bristol. This picture appears as a
frontispiece to Part IV of *The Maire of Bristowe is Kalendar*, compiled by Robert Ricart, who was elected town clerk of Bristol
in 1479.

of smiths, tanners, and butchers; took steps to abate the coal-smoke nuisance, to prevent river pollution, and to check those who obstructed the roadway or let their big dogs out not on a lead. It paved the streets, and insisted that each man should clean the pavement in front of his house; it inspected private latrines and erected public ones with water sluices. Above all it strove to check dishonest dealing; to keep the peace, appointing watchmen and constables and forbidding the carrying of swords, daggers, or long knives; and to ensure that food, 'good and cheap', was within reach of everyone (Pl. 24*b*). Food shops, especially those of the fishmongers, were regularly inspected; restaurants were forbidden to sell warmed-up meat dishes. The retail prices of necessaries such as bread and ale, and, in case of a scarcity, other goods too, were closely controlled, lest anyone should make an unreasonable profit. Forestalling and regrating were strictly prohibited, all dealings had to be in public, and market hours were regulated. Tavern hours, too, were fixed; closing time was when the curfew sounded, and none might open on Sundays till after Mass. A town bell rang out the hours and, on occasion, summoned the burgesses together in an emergency, and a town clock was often set up in its own clock tower in the late fourteenth or fifteenth century, such as that which still stands at St. Albans.

Further, the town government controlled all the crafts in the town, insisting that ordinances made by the craftsmen for the conduct of their business, whether concerning prices, wages, standards, or conditions of admission, should be submitted for its approval and enrolled in the town books, and that the wardens of each craft, answerable for their enforcement, should be presented to it. It also decreed the order in which the crafts should go in procession, and the plays for which each should be responsible. Only the 'fraternities' of the crafts escaped its supervision. Religious in origin, their ordinances were subject to the approval not of the secular but of the spiritual authorities. Under the protection of the Church they held their meetings, passed resolutions, collected subscriptions, set up their 'benefit clubs' to assist members and their families in sickness or any

PLATE 24

b. Enforcement of civic ordinances: initial letter of Bristol Charter of 1347 showing transgressors being put into confinement (above), and baker convicted of selling short-weight bread being drawn on a hurdle through the streets (below)

Ref. Charter of Edward III to Bristol, 24 April 1347, in the possession of the Corporation

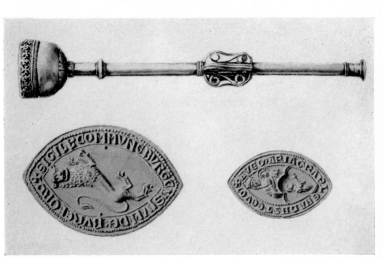

a. Civic insignia of Burford

PLATE 25

a. Town Hall, Leominster

b. Dyeing cloth

other adversity, made provision for funerals, with the appropriate number of candles, and appointed priests to say masses
for their souls and to keep a light ever burning before the altar
of their chosen patron saint, sometimes building on to their
parish church a chapel of their own.

Much money was lavished by the townsmen on their parish
churches, which were frequently enlarged or rebuilt in the
latest style of the day. So, too, was the town hall or 'Council
House', where the mayor held his court (Pl. 25*a*). Indeed the
upkeep of public buildings was an ever heavier charge upon
the public purse. If there were no town walls there was probably at least a town ditch, with gatehouses over the principal
entrances; a prison with a jailer, and a pillory; at least one
market place with its official 'weigh-house'; there were usually
bridges also and, in seaports, a custom house, cranes, wharves
and quays, expensively bound with freestone, where ocean-
going ships could load and unload.

The later middle ages saw a striking transformation in
England's oversea trade. The export trade in minerals, farm
produce, and above all fine wool, which reached its zenith in
the late thirteenth or early fourteenth century, when in some
years over 30,000 sacks of wool left England, dwindled to a
mere trickle, while in its place the export of manufactured
English woollens increased more and more until in early
Tudor times English ships were laden with little else than cloth,
with small quantities of wool, hides, lead, and miscellaneous
goods making up the remainder of the cargoes. When from
the end of the thirteenth century wool became subject to increasingly onerous export dues, the foreign manufacturer
was placed at a disadvantage through the increased cost of
his raw material. Englishmen, long skilled in the making
of fine cloth, with cheap and abundant supplies of wool and
plenty of water power to drive the mechanical mills that
greatly reduced the labour of fulling, were not slow to profit
by their opportunities. Early in the fourteenth century they
captured the home market. Imports of Flemish cloth, once

so much in demand, now virtually ceased. In the second half
of the century they were seriously competing on the Continent.
Exports of English cloth grew from 4,000 to 40,000 cloths a
year; English ships laden with cloth were pushing into the
Baltic and Scandinavia together with those of the German
Hanse, as well as to Gascony, Spain, Portugal, and even to the
Low Countries, while Italian ships took English cloth to the
Mediterranean. English wool exports shrank to some 9,000
sacks a year. Never again was Flanders to recover its lead.
England's exports of raw wool continued to decline and her
exports of cloth to grow, though more slowly, and not without
a considerable setback in the mid-fifteenth century. When at
last she was free from civil strife and constant warfare on the
Continent a further remarkable advance took place. Some
4,000 sacks of wool were still exported each year, but cloth
exports continued to expand, reaching a climax towards the
end of Henry VIII's reign at some 120,000 cloths a year.
England's export trade, transformed in character, was worth
perhaps twice what it had been in the late thirteenth century.

Within England the immense expansion of 'the noble art of
clothmaking', which for so long was to remain her premier industry and a matter of vital concern to her people, resulted in
the development of many villages into prosperous little industrial towns, more particularly in valleys where water power was
to be had for driving fulling-mills. In the countryside industry
could grow unfettered by the regulations by which it was tied
and bound in the cities where once it had flourished, unham-
pered by the constant drain of taxation, of contributions towards
gilds, pageants, and plays. Wages and hours were alike uncontrolled, and there was an abundance of labour, part-time as
well as full-time, both among smallholders whose manorial
services had never been heavy and among those who, with the
general abandonment of demesne farming, had gained freedom
from them. So Maurice Paynell's little borough of Leeds,
which at first seemed stillborn, at last began to grow in the late
fifteenth and early sixteenth centuries. Its rent roll increased;
fulling-mills sprang up along the river, with tenter-grounds

close by and on 'Tenterhill' for the stretching of the cloth; new houses were built on what had been waste; and Leeds became a lively clothing town, with a busy market by the bridge for the cloth of its own people and for that of the surrounding villages. During the sixteenth century its clothiers, who employed many, far and wide, were building streets of new houses, and endowing Leeds with a second church, a school, and an alms-house; early in the seventeenth century they obtained a royal charter of incorporation for their town. Near by Bradford, Wakefield, and Halifax were similarly developing, 'standing all by clothing' as Leland described them in his Itinerary (1535–43). So, too, elsewhere, particularly in Suffolk and Essex and in the west of England, many rural communities blossomed out into small industrial towns. In Devon, for example, Tiverton, which for three centuries had remained in obscurity after the foundation of the borough, became the scene of great activity, with its fulling-mills, its newly built streets full of craftsmen, and its merchants and clothiers, vying with one another in the munificence of their benefactions as one enlarged and beauti-fied the parish church, proudly displaying his ships and merchant mark upon it (1517), besides building an alms-house, while another built a second almshouse, and yet another, in days when church-building had gone out of fashion, founded the school famous as Blundell's (1599). While these and a host of other 'pretty clothing towns' sprang to life, ancient cloth-making cities like Lincoln, Stamford, and Beverley, once noted throughout Europe, shrank into insignificance. Lincoln, with numbers of its houses empty, untenanted, and crumbling into ruin, became 'little better than a common market town'. Leland, visiting Beverley, could find little worthy of record save relics of the past like the exquisite Percy tombs; once there had been 'good cloth-making at Beverley, but that is now much decayed'.

The long struggle between the kings of England and France sounded the death-knell of free trade in more ways than one. The imposition of export duties on wool, loans on the security of the customs, loans in kind like the forced loan on wool of

1294, the granting of export monopolies, and at times the com/
plete prohibition of wool export to bring pressure to bear on
Flanders, all led to the canalizing of the wool trade compulsor/
ily through one or more fixed points, or 'staples', at which it
could be closely controlled. After various experiments with
one or more home or foreign staples a single staple was fixed at
England's newly conquered port of Calais; there it remained
from the time of Richard II until the loss of Calais in 1558. To
Calais alone might wool be shipped, except for very poor
quality wool and that destined for Italy, which might be sent
direct by sea through the Straits of Gibraltar. All merchants
shipping to Calais were bound to belong to the 'Fellowship of
the Merchants of the Staple of Calais'. This body, wholly
English, enjoying a monopoly of the wool trade to lands north
of the Alps, made regulations for the trade, held its own
courts in Calais, organized a close inspection of all wool sold
there, and negotiated on behalf of its members with the king
or with foreign rulers. Yet more, it was an important organ of
Crown finance. Not only did it lend large sums to the king
but it became entirely responsible for collecting the wool
customs, for paying the wages of the Calais garrison and
maintaining its fortifications, and for meeting the expenses of
convoying the wool fleets. Among its members in the late fif/
teenth century were London merchants like the Celys, whose
letters, vividly revealing their business as well as their private
lives, show us, as do those of the Stonor family, all the pro/
cesses of the trade from the purchase of wool from Cotswold
farmers or wool dealers like John Fortey of Northleach to its
sale at Calais (Pl. 26a and Fig. 57).

But however much the Merchants of the Staple might boast
that their fellowship was 'the most worshipful company of
merchants subject to a king that any prince christened hath
had', the future lay not with them but with the rival Fellow/
ship of the Merchant Adventurers, which was concerned not
with the old, much regulated and much diminished trade in
raw wool but with the newer, ever expanding trade in manu/
factured cloth, some half of which was in the hands of the

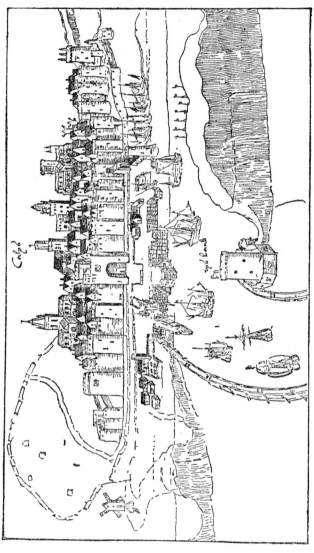

FIG. 57. Calais Town and Harbour from a sixteenth-century drawing

English themselves. The Adventurers, unlike the Staplers going regularly to and fro to Calais, voyaged far afield wherever
they could find an opening—to Prussia, Norway, Iceland,
Ireland, France, Spain, Portugal, the Low Countries, and
even into the Mediterranean. By the late fifteenth century there
were merchants described as 'Adventurers' in most of the
ports concerned with the shipping of English woollens, and
at least in the three chief cities of the realm—Bristol, York, and
London—they were associated together in their own local
Fellowships of Adventurers. In York there may still be seen
their fine timbered hall (Pl. 26a), and there, as at Bristol, there
still exists a Society of Merchant Adventurers, proudly, and
not without justification, tracing its lineage back half a millennium. But far more important, though boasting no hall of
its own, was the London Fellowship, for London was en-
grossing more and more of the export of English cloth, in
whatever part of England it had been manufactured, as the
sale of the cloth came increasingly to be concentrated in the
great international marts of the Low Countries. Its members,
drawn together by their common interest in the shipping of
cloth, were already members of one or other of the wealthy
livery companies in which all who aspired to be merchants of
London were enrolled, and in the hall of one of the most
venerable of these companies, that of the Mercers, they held
their meetings. There they discussed their common problems,
kept their common funds, received foreign emissaries, and
dispatched letters, written by the Mercers' clerk, to the Governor of the Adventurers in the Low Countries. The governor
himself was often a mercer, as was William Caxton, who
later abandoned venturing in cloth for the newer business of
the printing of books. So powerful were the Adventurers of
London that they compelled all who sold cloth in the Low
Countries to contribute to their Fellowship, dictating even to
the Yorkshiremen, and virtually arrogating to themselves the
title of Merchant Adventurers of England.

To an intelligent foreign observer, familiar with the mighty
sovereign cities of Italy, there seemed 'scarcely any towns of

PLATE 26

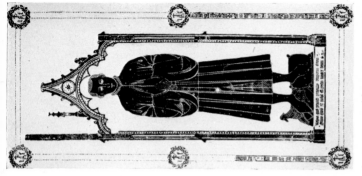

b. A Cotswold wool dealer: John Fortey of Northleach (died 1458)

Ref. Brass in Northleach church

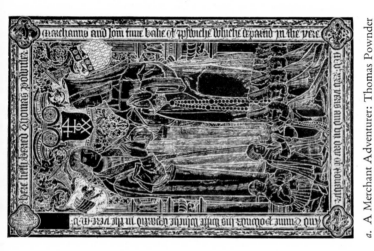

a. A Merchant Adventurer: Thomas Pownder of Ipswich (died 1525) with his wife Emma, their two sons, and their six daughters. Note merchant mark in the centre, and arms of the Merchant Adventurers to the right

Ref. Brass of Flemish workmanship originally in St. Mary Quay, Ipswich, now in Ipswich Museum

importance' in England at the opening of the sixteenth century, apart from London, 'except Bristol and York', and even these were now declining from their former grandeur, outdistanced altogether by London. But if foreign visitors found England at this time incorrigibly rural and lacking in great cities, despite its industrial development, they were all agreed that London, with its superb port, could stand comparison with any city in Christendom. London, indeed, was unique, for no other city in Europe was at once the political and the commercial capital of a realm of comparable size and wealth. The Italian observer was of opinion that London's population was no smaller than that of Florence or Rome, that its citizens were as highly esteemed as were gentlemen in Venice, that its Lord Mayor was of quite as much consequence as the Doge, and that the fifty-two goldsmiths' shops in a street close to St. Paul's were so rich and full of gold and silver vessels, great and small, that in all the shops in Milan, Rome, Venice, and Florence put together there would not be found so many of such magnificence. The Lord Mayor's Banquet, given then as now on the day that he took office 'to all the principal people in London as well as to foreigners of distinction, a thousand or more in all', left him duly impressed. It was at another civic dinner given by the Lord Mayor in honour of the Scottish ambassadors negotiating, in 1501, the marriage of an English princess with a Scottish king, that the Scottish poet William Dunbar was moved to immortalize London in verse as 'soveraign of cities, seemliest in sight, of high renoun, riches and royaltie'. Extolling the river 'where many a ship doth rest with top-royall'; the Bridge with its pillars white; and the Tower with its formidable artillery, he concluded, as befitted the occasion, with praise of the Londoners, more especially the merchants, their lovely wives and daughters, and the Lord Mayor himself:

> Strong be thy wallis that about thee standis;
>   Wise be the people that within thee dwellis;
> Fresh is thy ryver with his lusty strandis;
>   Blith be thy chirches, wele sownyng be thy bellis;

Rich be thy merchauntis in substaunce that excellis;
Fair be their wives, right lovesom, white and small;
Clere be thy virgyns, lusty under kellis:
London, thou art the flour of Cities all.

Thy famous Maire, by pryncely governaunce,
With sword of justice thee ruleth prudently.
No Lord of Parys, Venyce, or Floraunce
In dignitye or honour goeth to hym nigh.
He is exampler, loode-ster, and guye;[1]
Principall patrone and rose orygynalle,
Above all Maires as maister most worthy:
London, thou art the flour of Cities all.

[1] guide.

WORKS FOR REFERENCE

BALLARD, A. (ed.) *British Borough Charters, 1042–1217* (1913).

BATESON, M. (ed.) *Borough Customs*, Selden Society (2 vols., 1904–6).

CARUS-WILSON, E. M. *Medieval Merchant Venturers* (1954).

CONSITT, F. *The London Weavers' Company* (1933).

CUNNINGHAM, W. *Growth of English Industry and Commerce*, i. Early and Middle Ages (5th ed., 1927).

GREEN, A. S. *Town Life in the Fifteenth Century* (2 vols., 1894).

GROSS, C. *The Gild Merchant* (2 vols., 1890).

HARRIS, M. D. *Life in an Old English Town* (1898); (ed.) *The Coventry Leet Book* (1907–13).

HILL, J. W. F. *Medieval Lincoln* (1948).

LOBEL, M. D. *The Borough of Bury St. Edmunds* (1935).

POWER, E. *The Wool Trade in English Medieval History* (1941); *Medieval People*, chaps. v and vi (1924); and M. POSTAN (eds.), *Studies in English Trade in the Fifteenth Century* (1933).

RILEY, H. T. *Memorials of London* (1868).

RUDDOCK, A. A. *Italian Merchants and Shipping in Southampton, 1270–1600* (1951).

SALTER, H. E. *Medieval Oxford* (1936).

SALUSBURY, G. T. *Street Life in Medieval England* (1939).

SALZMAN, L. F. *English Trade in the Middle Ages* (1931); *English Industries of the Middle Ages* (new ed., 1923).

SMITH, J. TOULMIN. *English Gilds* (1870).

TAIT, J. *The Medieval English Borough* (1936).

THRUPP, S. *The Bakers of London* (1933); *The Merchant Class of Medieval London* (1948).

The Little Red Book of Bristol, ed. F. B. BICKLEY (2 vols., 1900).

Ricart, The Maire of Bristowe is Kalendar, ed. L. TOULMIN SMITH (1872).

Cambridge Economic History of Europe, ii. Trade and Industry in the Middle Ages (ed. M. M. POSTAN and E. E. RICH (1952)).

The Libelle of Englyshe Polycye, ed. G. WARNER (1926).

Records of the Borough of Leicester, ed. M. BATESON (2 vols., 1899, 1901).

Records of the Borough of Northampton, ed. C. A. MARKHAM (2 vols., 1898).

The Records of Norwich, ed. W. HUDSON and J. C. TINGEY (2 vols., 1906–10).

Records of Nottingham, ed. W. H. STEVENSON (1882).

York Memorandum Book, ed. M. SELLERS, Surtees Society (2 vols., 1912–15).

The York Mercers and Merchant Adventurers, ed. M. SELLERS, Surtees Society (1918).

VIII. COINAGE

---

1. *The Anglo-Saxon Period*

THE most primitive form of trade, the direct exchange of one commodity for another, had at the beginning of the fifth century long been supplanted in this country by purchase through the medium of coinage. Immediately before the Belgic invasions there seems to have been a local currency of iron bars in the west, and a speculum ('tin') coinage derived from Massiliot archetypes in the south-east. The latter was supplemented by a few gold staters, not all of continental minting, the types of which were derived from Gallic imitations of Macedonian originals. These gave way to a large native coinage of gold and silver which turned more and more to Roman Gaul for inspiration. The Romans usually imported their coinage, but the usurper Carausius struck at Bitterne, Richborough, and London. The last mint continued striking after his death, and enjoyed a transitory revival under Magnus Maximus. During the fifth century the currency of Britain consisted mainly of silver and bronze coins of the later emperors; the former are found in large hoards in Mendip and the neighbouring country. In the sixth century any coinage there was consisted of increasingly mutilated Roman coins, perhaps a few barbarous imitations, and later a few Merovingian gold pieces that were to inspire the first English coinage.

The development of a native coinage subsequent to this long period without currency in Britain seems to have taken place quite late in the seventh century increasing intercourse with the Continent and brought to England Merovingian craftsmen, and one, Eusebius by name, struck at Canterbury the gold coin bearing the name of the mint 'Dorovernis

Civitas' which is illustrated in Pl. 27, *a*. The name of Abbo, hardly the Abbo who worked at Châlons and Limoges at the end of the sixth century, appears on a coin of ruder workman-ship which was in an important hoard found at Crondall in Hampshire in 1828. In this find were two Anglo-Saxon gold chains with jewelled ornaments, and 101 gold coins of which some 73 were English imitations of Roman and Merovingian gold issues. In Pl. 27 may be seen a triens, or thrymsa as it is called in the laws, of Roman (*c*) and of Merovingian type (*e*); *b* and *d* in the same Plate show the parent types on a solidus of Magnus Maximus and a Merovingian triens; the reverse de-sign of *d* was copied from gold coins of Tiberius II (578–82). The legends are almost always blundered and may combine Roman and Runic scripts. The names of several mints have been read into them, but none is more than plausible, with the possible exception of London. The legend of Pl. 27, *e*, may include the name of Eadbald of Kent, and an older piece of heavier solidus type seems to read in part CIOLH and has been given to Ceol of Wessex. The weight of the thrymsa averages about 20 grains.

It was not long before this currency of gold was supplemented by, or gradually reduced to, a silver coinage. At the time of the Anglo-Saxon invasions both the invading and the conquered peoples had for many years been accustomed to use silver as the chief medium of currency. They had been influenced in the adoption of gold by the rising power of the Merovingians in the sixth and seventh centuries, but their sources of gold were soon exhausted. The types show so little degeneration, and the debasement is so rapid that it was at one time thought that the new silver directly imitated continental gold issues. Enough electrum survives, however, to show that the new silver repre-sents a dramatic debasement and not a supersession of the thrymsa. Although the silver was in turn to suffer tempo-rary debasement, we may attribute to the last years of the seventh century England's final adoption of the northern Euro-pean silver standard. For the next seven hundred years all attempts to introduce a gold coinage were to be abortive, and

several at least of the very few gold pieces struck are not coins
in the strict sense of the word.

The new silver coins are known as 'sceats', though this
name belongs more properly to Roman coins found in the
soil by the Saxon invaders. The earliest are of thrymsa weight,
but in certain series there is a marked falling away, notably in
Northumbria and London, where it is accompanied by debasement. At the very end of the series, perhaps under Kentish
influence, some attempt was made to restore pristine standards.
The whole question of chronology, however, still awaits de-
finitive resolution, and many attributions can be arrived at
only on the basis of style. Pl. 27, *f* to *j*, trace the evolution o
a bird from a profile head, and *k* to *o* are some of the unin-
scribed types. Coin *p* has a runic inscription PADA, and is
usually associated with Penda's son Peada (655–7), but even
this identification is improbable, while other legends seem to
supply names of princes or moneyers quite unknown to history.

The Northumbrian sceats, often completely lacking in
silver due to local scarcity, are known to numismatists as
stycas, though this was probably the invader's name for the
smallest Roman copper coins found in the ground of the
Saxon conquest. Pl. 27, *q* to *t*, show stycas of Ecgfrith,
Aldfrith, Eadberht, and Alchred, and *w* what is perhaps the
first coin struck by a northern primate, a York styca of Archbishop Ecgberht. There are still pronounced affinities with
southern sceats, especially in the reverse types, but the Mercian
supremacy left Northumbria a backwater and led to the
crystallization of the styca into a single type. These later issues
were struck in almost pure copper, and did not circulate outside Northumbria. Pl. 27, *u*, *v*, and *y*, illustrate examples
attributed to a doubtful Eardulf, to King Eanred, and Archbishop Wigmund. The fact that they were current at a time of
Civil Wars explains their presence in large numbers in
hoards, especially in the neighbourhood of York. Pl. 27, *x*, is
an exceptional issue, probably more to impress than to meet a
monetary need, a unique gold solidus struck by Archbishop

PLATE 27

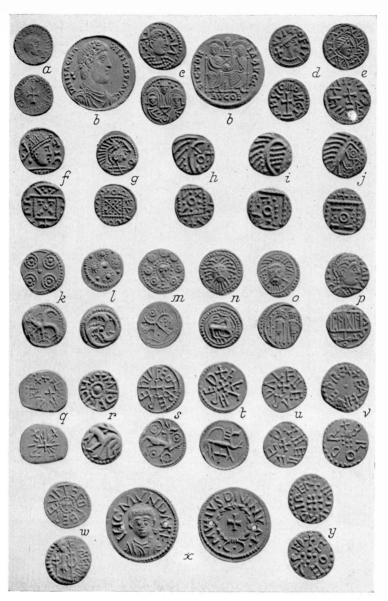

Anglo-Saxon coins. Thrymsa, Sceat, and Styca coinages

PLATE 28

Anglo-Saxon coins. Kings of Mercia

Wigmund in imitation of an issue of Louis the Pious. Particular importance attaches to the fact that the prelate should
have substituted the hieratic full-face portrait for the imperial
profile of the original.

Towards the close of the eighth century there was a large
circulation of Arab coins in Europe; the Scandinavian and
north German countries were still true to their preference for
silver currency, and consequently the large hoards of Arab
coins found in the Baltic regions are always composed of silver
dirhems; in southern and western Europe, however, the gold
dinar was prevalent. In the British Museum there is a most interesting coin (see Pl. 28, *a*) which imitates closely an Arab
dinar of the year 774 but bears on the reverse the title OFFA
REX inserted upside down in the Arabic inscription. That
the title of Offa was worked in the die and not counterstruck on
the coin is sufficient proof that the dinar was copied in this
country; in addition, the errors in the Arabic legends prove that
the dies were not made by Arab workmen. It is interesting to
note that three similar dinars are known of the same date which
have the same errors but have no Roman inscription added;
these also are doubtless either Frankish or Anglo-Saxon copies.
Marseilles was the port of landing for Eastern trade, and the intercourse between the Carolingian emperors and the Abassid
caliphs was marked by frequent embassies. It was through
France that the dinar was known to England.

It must have been a few years before the copying of Arab
dinars occurred that a very important change took place in
the coinage of this country. This was the substitution of the
heavier, broader, and thinner penny for the sceat. The new
penny did not pretend to compete with the new denier introduced by the House of Heristal—at least as far as weight was
concerned—but the consistent purity of its silver soon put it
into a class by itself. Obviously the new coin owed much to the
denier—standardized by Charlemagne early in the last decade
of the eighth century—and it is significant that Offa should have
struck his first pence at Canterbury, probably some years before the slaughter at Otford in 774. Coins of this first issue

represent a compromise, being in effect full-weight sceats struck on broader flans (Pl. 28, *b* to *l*). The dependence on old types is still very close (cf. the reverses of *e* and *h*), and some designs, especially the serpent wreaths, spirals, and the boss-and-pellet pattern (Pl. 28, *b*, *c*, *e*), may be compared with illustrated manuscripts of contemporary Anglo-Saxon and Irish work. The high sense of artistic composition and the skill of the die-engraving are remarkable; the execution of the portrait is curious rather than artistic, but shows more life than most English coin-portraits before 1503, when Alexander of Bruchsal engraved the dies of Henry VII. By no means all the pennies of Offa display this artistic merit, some (see, for example, the obverse of *e* in Pl. 28) are of the poorest execution. The name of the moneyer, the officer responsible for the coin, now forms the reverse legend; at a later period the name of the mint is added. This precaution against forgery was, later at least, very ineffectual.

At the very end of his reign, Offa once more raised the weight of his coins, and these now weighed as much as 22 grains. The flans were proportionately broader, and one or two experiments produced a standard obverse type with the legend in three lines (Pl. 28, *j*). The break with the sceat was final, and the penny had come to stay. Under Alfred's immediate successors its weight rose as high as 27 grains, and it did not fall below 22½ grains—in theory at least—until the fourteenth century. Thereafter decay was rapid, until under the early Tudors it was a bare 12 grains. It is noteworthy that Offa's principal mint remained at Canterbury, and the Kentish moneyers inspired much of his monetary policy and even influenced the limited coinage of his East Anglian tributary Æthelberht. Of Otford it may well be said that:

> Cantia capta ferum victorem fecit et artes
> Intulit agrestis. . . .

At this period, with the introduction of the penny, we see for the first time the privilege of coinage being exercised by the archbishops of Canterbury. In what circumstances and in

whose archbishopric the privilege was granted is, as at York, uncertain; the earliest name found on coins is Jænberht, the contemporary of Offa, and on all his coins the name of Offa appears as king (see Pl. 28, *i*). It is interesting to find at the same time coins of Eadberht, bishop of London (Pl. 28, *g*). Jænberht died in 790–1 and was succeeded by Æthilheard, who struck coins under both Offa and Cœnwulf (Pl. 28, *j. k*).

A coinage of Cynethrith, the wife of Offa (Pl. 28, *f*), must have been struck during Offa's life and may perhaps be regarded as a complimentary issue. Cœnwulf, the successor of Offa, struck pennies of various types and made use of the mint of Canterbury (Pl. 28, *l*, has the tribrach, or pall, of Canterbury); in his reign the coinage falls into a conventional style which continues under Ceolwulf, Beornwulf, Ludican, and Wiglaf. Wiglaf (Pl. 28, *m*) was defeated at Ellandune and deposed by Ecgberht of Wessex, who struck coins at London and adopted the title King of the Mercians.

As we have seen, the penny originated in Kent, doubtless because that kingdom had close ties with the Continent. Possibly the earliest is one with the name of King Ecgberht (Pl. 29, *a*), though it has been suggested that a coin usually attributed to his contemporary Æthelberht of East Anglia (Pl. 29, *f*) may belong to his predecessor Æthelberht II of Kent. No coins are known of Alhmund, but between 796 and 798 Eadberht Praen struck imitations of Offa's last type (Pl. 29, *b*). A king Eadwald (Pl. 29, *g*) is only doubtfully Kentish though his coins are generally, but not very convincingly, attributed to the period before the succession of Cœnwulf's puppet Cuthred, whose coins are typically Mercian (Pl. 29, *c*). His title 'Rex Cant[iae]' was revived by the usurper Beldred or Baldred (*c.* 820–5), the last of the 'kings' of Kent (Pl. 29, *d*).

Under Offa may be detected the beginnings of a locally struck coinage in East Anglia. There is an interesting group of coins which bear the Mercian king's name but which are of rude workmanship, and which occasionally embody in their design the monogram A that is a feature of the coins of later

independent kings (cf. Pl. 29, *i*). It is not without significance that Mercian coins of this group cease with Æthelstan's achievement of autonomy in *c.* 825, and it has been surmised that the new dynasty took over a branch mint established by Offa or Cœnwulf at Thetford.

The year 825 marks an epoch in the history of the coinage no less than in political history. After the battle of Ellandune Ecgberht became master of the whole of England south of the Humber; but this did not bring to an end the coinages of all the tributary states. Wiglaf of Mercia was allowed to resume coinage after a temporary deposition, but had to confine striking to London. A coin of Burgred is shown in Pl. 29, *h*; his coins are the last struck by an independent Mercian king; in 874 he was driven out by the Danes, who set up the puppet king Ceolwulf II. The East Anglian kings, of whom little is known, continued a coinage till the death of (St.) Edmund (Pl. 29, *i*, is a penny of Edmund), and his death was followed by an issue of memorial pennies (Pl. 31, *c*). Kent was more definitely merged into the kingdom of Wessex; the Kentish title was held by the king of Wessex or his heir, and the independent coinage ceased. The archbishopric of Canterbury was at this time held by Wulfred, whose coins are the earliest that bear a tonsured bust and the first to use the monogram of Dorobernia as the reverse type (see Pl. 29, *j*). The officers of the Canterbury mint, at which doubtless were struck the issues both of the kings of Kent and of the archbishops of Canterbury, seem to have adopted a temporizing policy before the battle of Ellandune, while the future position of the kings and archbishops remained uncertain, for we find a curious double series of coins on which no royal or episcopal title appears; some have a diademed bust in profile (Pl. 29, *k*), others a facing bust with tonsure, both bearing on obverse the moneyer's name and on reverse 'Dorobernia Civitas'; the moneyers are known to us as moneyers of Baldred and Wulfred. The probable explanation of these coins is that the royal and episcopal moneyers in the uncertainty of the political position thus continued their work at the mint, without binding themselves to a particular

PLATE 29

Anglo-Saxon coins. Kings of Kent and Archbishops of Canterbury

PLATE 30

Anglo-Saxon coins. Kings of Wessex

cause or overlord. Wulfred for a time wavered in allegiance
between Baldred and Ecgberht, but did not, like his predecessor, put the name of an overlord on his coins. His successor,
Ceolnoth (833–70), also exercised the privilege of coining (see
l in Pl. 29) and in the same plate are pennies of Archbishop
Æthelred (870–89) and Plegmund (890–914).

The supremacy of Wessex, which dates from the battle of
Ellandune (825), produced the first large scale series of coins
of the kings of Wessex. The earliest were probably struck at
Canterbury, the mint of the defeated Kentish kings, for some of
the coins of Ecgberht bear the Dorobernia monogram on the
reverse. A coin reading 'Londonia Civitas' (Pl. 30, *a*) must
have been struck at the Mercian mint after the expulsion of
Wiglaf in 829. Another reverse legend found on coins of Ecgberht, 'S[an]C[tu]S Andreas', may no doubt be interpreted
as St. Andrew of Rochester (Pl. 30, *b*). Ecgberht sometimes
adopted on his coins the titles 'Rex M[erciorum]' (see Pl. 30, *a*)
and 'Rex Saxoniorum'. His successor Æthelwulf added 'Oc-
cidentalium' to Saxonum or Saxoniorum (both forms are
found in the latinity of the die-engraver; see Pl. 30, *c*). He also
took the monogram of Cantiae as an obverse design, thus
assuming the title 'Rex Cantiae', in conjunction with the
Dorobernia monogram on the reverse. It is not, however, possible to assign these Kentish coins to the period of his Kentish
title during the lifetime of his father, for no similar coins are
known of his younger brother Athelstan, who followed him
as sub-king of Kent. Probably the crown of Kent did not
carry with it the privilege of striking coins. Ecgberht had at
least three mints, Canterbury, London, and Winchester, and
Alfred appears to have added three more, Exeter, Gloucester,
and Oxford. Coins uniting his name with the Lincoln monogram are Danish imitations. The practice of monogram signature had up to the present only been found on coins from the
two Kentish mints where it was introduced by Archbishop
Wulfred, who derived the style from the coins of the Carolingian kings. Its revival and common use in the reign of Alfred
comes again from the same original source, and seems to have

been no less popular with the Viking invaders, who imitated both the Carolingian prototypes and the English adaptation. Unfortunately there is not as yet the material necessary for dating the majority of Alfred's issues, and it is not possible to establish the date of the introduction of the London mono/gram. To judge from the number of Viking imitations, the obol or halfpenny was another innovation extremely popular with the Great Army, and to Alfred must go the credit of being the first English king to strike a round halfpenny. He also struck a large silver coin inscribed ELIM$\overline{\text{O}}$, possibly a multiple of the slightly heavier Carolingian denier, for the payment of part at least of the 'elimosinae' which he sent to Rome and Jerusalem.

2. *The Danish Invasions*

At the end of the eighth century the Viking settlements on the coast of Ireland began, and from these settlements came the earliest raids on the English coasts. A hoard of English pennies was found in 1874 at Delgany near Wicklow which comprised issues of kings of Mercia and Kent, of archbishops of Canter/bury, and a few of Ecgberht of Wessex, together with a few of the anonymous Canterbury pennies attributed above to a date *c.* 820; this hoard of coins must have formed part of the plunder carried back by the Vikings to their Irish homes after a raid such as that on Sheppey which took place in 834. The first definite settlement in Thanet seems to have come in 850-1, after the defeat of Rorik at Ockley. In 867-8 the Great Army, marching from East Anglia, defeated and killed the North/umbrian kings Osberht and Ælla, but before this the so-called styca currency had come to an end. The army then went south to Nottingham, but after sustaining siege by Burgred, who was supported by Æthelwulf and Alfred, withdrew to the north. In 870 the Vikings again invaded East Anglia and murdered (St.) Edmund, who, we have already seen, was commemorated on an issue of coins after his death (Pl. 31, *c*). After Ashdown in the following year Halfdan alone of the

leaders escaped to Reading; in 874 he had returned to Mercia and, deposing Burgred, set up the puppet king Ceolwulf II (see *b* in Pl. 31). It was probably a later Halfdan, however, who struck the most interesting coin (Pl. 31, *a*) with the London monogram as its reverse type and on the obverse a crude version of Alfred's adaptation of the reverse of a solidus of Magnus Maximus. In 875–6 Halfdan marched north and seized the southern half of Northumbria, including York, leaving the northern part under its own kings as tributaries. The remainder of the army, under Guthrum, continued the attack on Wessex, and, after his decisive defeat at Æthandune and the partition of the Wessex and Mercian kingdoms by which he held possession of the part north of the Thames and east of Watling street, he settled there in 880 under the name of Athelstan II. In East Anglia the memorial coinage of St. Edmund is followed or accompanied by a coinage of Guthrum-Athelstan, and to the Danes or to the disordered conditions consequent upon their invasions may be attributed the many blundered imitations of St. Edmund, Alfred, and Plegmund. This is followed by a coinage of Lincoln dedicated to St. Martin, and rather later a very large and apparently prolonged issue of St. Peter at York (Pl. 31, *d*).

Halfdan was expelled from Northumbria in 877 and, after an interval of six years, a new king, Guthred or Cnut, was set up at York and reigned from 883 to 894. To him have been assigned both pennies and halfpennies entitled 'Cnut Rex' and bearing on the reverse the mint signature 'Ebraice Civitas' (Pl. 31, *e*). Some of the coins bear the Scriptural legends 'Dns Ds Re' (Dominus Deus Rex) or 'Mirabilia Fecit' in place of the mint-name. One penny is known which couples the title of Alfred on the one side with that of 'Cnut' on the other, but it is hardly safe to read in this coin evidence of an acknowledgement by Cnut of Alfred as overlord, for its barbarous workmanship classes it rather with the many blundered imitations of the time; a close parallel for such a 'muling' of types may be found in a penny that combines the St. Edmund legend with an obverse of Alfred, and another bears

T

the St. Edmund legend on the obverse and the signature of the mint of York on the reverse. Moreover, recent work would put the Cnut coins after *c.* 895 and perhaps as late as *c.* 900. Siefred, who followed Guthred at York in 894 and brought an army south to help Hasting in his attacks on Wessex in 893–6, struck coins similar to those of 'Cnut' and used the same varieties of legend on the reverse (Pl. 31, *f*). Closely connected with the Cnut and Siefred coinages is a penny which bears the name 'Alwaldus' and the reverse legend 'Dns Ds REX' (see *g* in Pl. 31); it has been attributed to Æthelweald who made an attempt to seize the throne on the death of Alfred and was acknowledged king by the Danes in Northumbria and East Anglia; this coin was found in the Cuerdale hoard, and the attribution is therefore possible in point of date. A coin, illustrated in Pl. 31, *h*, which bears the title 'Sitric Comes' and on the reverse the name of the moneyer Gundibert and the mint 'Sceldfor' (Shelford in Nottingham-shire?), was also in the Cuerdale hoard, but its attribution is uncertain; in type it resembles the Oxford pennies of Alfred.

It is chiefly from the hoard of coins which was found at Cuerdale in Lancashire in 1840 that we derive our knowledge of the Viking issues; the hoard contained nearly 7,000 coins, including as many as 900 of Alfred and only 51 of Edward the Elder, whence the deposit may be dated shortly after the death of Alfred. In addition to the Danish issues already described, there were a few oriental and more than 1,000 French, German and Italian coins, mostly of the Carolingian emperors, the latest being of Berengar. The coins of 'Cnut' numbered over 2,500, of Siefred nearly 250, and those of St. Edmund over 1,800; there were in the hoard more than fifty pennies of Archbishop Plegmund, and only one each of Ceolnoth and Æthered. It was therefore essentially a Viking hoard, and thoroughly illustrative of the currency of the Danelaw at the very end of the ninth century. The constant incursions of the Vikings into France are illustrated not only by the large number of Frankish pieces in the hoard but by the number of pennies of Cnut which reproduce the name of the mint of Quentovic.

PLATE 31

Coins of the Danish invasions

Closely allied to these are coins of Frankish style with a mint-name Cunetti which would seem to have been struck not so very far from York, possibly at Chester-le-Street. Most Viking coins struck in England in the ninth century have a Frankish appearance, and many of the moneyers of the St. Edmund coinage have Frankish names.

At the beginning of the tenth century the arrival of Norwegians and Danes from Ireland introduced a new factor into the already stormy politics of Northumbria, and even now there is fundamental disagreement among historians as to the exact identities of various names that dominate the stage in rapid and baffling succession. Coins with the legend 'Raienalt' have been attributed to Regnald I (919–21) and to Regnald II (942–3), but cannot well be later than *c.* 825. In appearance these pieces (Pl. 31, *m*) resemble early tenth-century anonymous issues of York, and Regnald I is a possibility seriously to be considered. Sihtric Caoch (921–7) struck coins of two types. One was quite Danish (Pl. 31, *i*), the other a curious blending of Christian and pagan motifs. Anlaf Guthfrithsson's coins fall into three main classes. His famous 'raven' type (Pl. 31, *l*) may perhaps be associated with a transient occupation of York in 937, but his imitation of Sihtric (Pl. 31, *k*) must fall between 940 and 942 if it is not an issue of Anlaf Sihtricsson. During his occupation of the Danelaw in 941 he employed English types with obverse dies that were patently cut by English workmen. In 942 there began a disputed succession between Regnald II, Guthfrithsson, and Anlaf Sihtricsson, and their types included coins of very English appearance such as Pl. 31, *i*. Both were expelled, but English rule was twice interrupted by Eric Blothox, in 948 and again in 952–4. His coins reproduced one type of Sihtric's (Pl. 31, *n*) and the standard English type of his day. The latter continued an issue by Anlaf Sihtricsson (who now spelt his name Onlof) between 948 and 952 when he ruled at York with the tacit approval of the English, who obviously considered the local man the lesser of two evils. Economically York was fast becoming a part of England, and there can be little doubt that the final

annexation of 954 was welcomed by the commercial classes in Northumbria.

Before returning to the coinages of the kings of Wessex a coin deserves mention which is known to us from one specimen only, now in the British Museum (Pl. 30, *i*). It is of the common English type of this period but bears the title 'Howael Rex' and the name of the moneyer Gillys. The date of the coin, *tempore* Edmund, assigns it without doubt to Howel Dda, who is best known for his code of laws; he was king of South Wales for about thirty-five years and died in 948 or 950. He was one of the kings who did homage to Athelstan in the north in 926, and is said to have been among the kings defeated at Brunanburgh. The coin seems, from its resemblance to pennies of Edmund, to have been struck towards the close of Howel's reign, after the death of Athelstan. The coin was struck by a Chester moneyer, and is the only piece known that can be attributed to a Welsh prince.

The progress of culture which became possible once more after the peace of Wedmore had a marked influence on the coinage of Edward the Elder. The pennies of his reign owe their elegance not only to the greater care with which they were struck and to the better finish with which the dies were engraved, but to an entirely new development of artistic composition in the workmanship of the die-engravers. The portrait, when it appears, though still of a conventional form which fails to attain the lively realism of the portrait of Offa, is more carefully engraved and ceases to be a mere outline drawing. But the chief feature of this reign is the original work shown in the elaborate and carefully executed designs which appear on some Mercian coins; floral designs especially (see Pl. 30, *f*) are most artistically treated, and other new designs, such as the Hand of Providence and representations of buildings, are a welcome relief from the cross-and-pellet patterns which were previously the limits of the engraver's imagination. The church towers which appear on some coins (see Pl. 30, *g*) were once supposed to be a type commemorative of the burgs that were erected by Edward and Æthelflaed in their successful warfare

against the Danes. This artistic level is not long maintained; the coins of Athelstan, with a few exceptions, revert to the small cross as the central design with the names of mint and moneyer forming a circular inscription, or the arrangement of the moneyer's name in two or three lines across the field of the coin, but good style is shown in the neatness of the engraver's work and the striking of the coins is still very carefully done; a portrait occurs on only a few types, but it shows in some cases an improvement on that of Edward; a jewelled crown, instead of the Roman diadem, is for the first time depicted (see Pl. 30, b). Numismatists generally have attached far too much significance to the letter of the edicts of the Council of Greatley in 928. It is true that they are the earliest surviving ordinances in which mention is made of the mints, but their provisions applied to part only of the country and were varied even before Athelstan's death. They did, however, establish once and for all the concept of the burgh mint providing for the monetary needs of the vicinity but subject to strict royal control. So far we know of at least thirty mints operating under Athelstan, and at Chester there were at least thirty moneyers. It is probable that no coins have survived from many little mints where there was only one moneyer, and it must also be borne in mind that it was not until the reign of Edgar that the name of the mint became an essential of the legend. By 975 there were some forty-five mints at work, and the eleventh-century coinage suggests a doubling of the total under Æthelred II. It is likely, though, that some of the 'new' mints had opened on a smaller scale in the preceding century.

The correct interpretation of the legends on Anglo-Saxon coins presents certain difficulties. The dies were cut by men who if not illiterate were only human, and when cutting letters in reverse it was natural to make mistakes. Occasionally whole legends are retrograde, and often the workmen misspelt or blundered a name. Little distinction was made between M, N, and H, and W, P, and VV express the same consonant. The obverse legend gives the name of the king followed by the Latin title REX. Occasionally Alfred adds ANGLORUM or

even SAXONUM, and the later types of Athelstan TO BRI for 'totius Britanniae'. From Edgar onwards the standard title is REX ANGLORUM. On the reverse appears the name of the moneyer. On tenth-century coins this is followed by a contrac- tion of the Latin *monetarius*—usually MO—with or without an abbreviated form of the name of the mint. From Æthelred's last type onwards the general practice is to omit the *monetarius* contraction and to precede the by now essential mint-name by ON. The reverse of Pl. 30, *h*, for example, a coin of Athelstan, reads AMELRIC MO VVINCI (Amelric the moneyer, Win- chester'), while that of Pl. 30, *n*, a coin of Harold II, reads WVLFGEAT ON GLE ('Wulfgeat at Gloucester').

We have also to be prepared for unfamiliar forms of the mint-name EO for Eoferwick for York, LEG for Leigeceas- ter for Chester, and GIOTHA a lost 'borough' in the west country. Pl. 30, *j* has usually been attributed to York by reading the reverse legend, partly retrograde, as DEORVLF M ON EO, but 'ON' is not found as early as Edwig. From other coins we know that Deorulf was a Chester moneyer, and a recent hoard leaves no room for doubt that the coin should be read DEORULFMONEO and given to Chester on stylistic and prosopographical grounds. Pl. 30, *k* is an early Æthelred II penny of the Stamford moneyer Wulfstan, *l* a Cnut penny of the York moneyer Frithcol, and *n* an Edward the Confessor penny of the London moneyer Wulfred.

The very large and frequent hoards of Æthelred's pennies that have been found in Scandinavia prove that the payments to the Danes must, in some cases at least, have been conveyed in coin to Denmark; the very large collection of these coins in the museum at Stockholm is evidence of the great extent of their exportation. The pennies of Æthelred were commonly imitated for the currencies of the Danish kings of Denmark and Ireland. From this period the king's likeness, which was hitherto only occasionally used, is always placed on the obverse of the coins. There is one exception, a curious issue of the latter part of Æthelred's reign, on which the *Agnus Dei* on the obverse is joined with the Dove on the reverse; the coins bear the names

of Mercian mints, and one cut halfpenny of this issue is
known.

The later Anglo-Saxon coins call for little comment. The
portrait forms the obverse design and the reverse is usually, but
not always, a cross variously ornamented. The chief object
seems to have been a clear differentiation of the types, and there
does not appear to be adequate reason for attempting to attach
a political significance to the Hand of Providence on coins of
Æthelred (Pl. 30, *k*), to the use of the word 'Pax' on coins of
Edward the Confessor and Harold II (Pl. 30, *n*), or to other
particular devices; they are probably religious rather than
political in their origin. On some coins of Cnut and the
Confessor the king is shown wearing a helmet with high peak
such as may be seen on the Bayeux Tapestry (Pl. 30, *l*). The
type of Edward the Confessor shown in Pl. 30, *m*, is the last
instance of direct copying from a Roman model—in this case
a gold coin of the second half of the fourth century—but the
reverse, with a martlet in each angle of the cross, seems
entirely original.

3. *From the Norman Conquest to the Middle of the Fourteenth Century*

The coinage of William the Conqueror is illustrative of his
political principle of adopting the native institutions and
adapting them, when necessary, to suit his purpose. Therefore
we find after the Norman Conquest a continuance of the de-
nomination, standard, value, and design of the Anglo-Saxon
coinage; two of the eight types issued by the Conqueror are
illustrated in Pl. 32, *a*, *b*. The number of mints in operation in
both the Conqueror's and the Confessor's reigns is approximately seventy, and many of the same moneyers continued in
office after the Conquest. Mention of moneyers occurs occasionally in Domesday, whence we learn that the office was one of
importance and that the men who held it were men of substance. From the same source we learn that the moneyers made
a payment when the type of the coinage was changed (*quando*

moneta vertebatur), from which we may conclude that the periodical change of type was a source of revenue to the king, though probably its primary object was a control similar to the later Trial of the Pyx (see below, p. 285), a tax being collected on delivery of the new dies. Assaying was certainly understood at this time, for payments in Domesday are sometimes 'blanched', i.e. assayed and compensated. In France the privilege of coin-age was made a considerable source of profit to the feudal lords by means of its debasement; in Normandy William had in-stituted a triennial hearth-tax in place of this source of revenue, but it had led to failure owing to his better coins being driven out by the more debased deniers of the neighbouring feudal states. The dies for the coinage throughout the country were, with few exceptions, made at London, where, Domesday tells us, the moneyers made their payments on receipt of their new dies. The pennies of William Rufus do not bear any marks of difference from those of his father, but it is possible, on the cumulative evidence of the grouping of types by the hoards in which they have been found, the 'muling' of types (i.e. the combination of the obverse die of one type with the reverse of another), the overstriking of coins (coins are not infrequently found which were restruck with a pair of dies of a later type than those which originally struck the coin), and from the forms of lettering employed on the coins, to arrange in their order the thirteen types which bear the name of William, and, by a proportionate distribution, to assign the first eight to the Conqueror and the remaining five to Rufus; the second of the five types of William II is illustrated in Pl. 32, *c*. The style of the coins shows a great deterioration under Rufus which is progressive throughout the reign.

The Coronation Charter of Henry I removed the *Monetagium*, which was probably identical with the payments *de moneta* mentioned above: 'Monetagium commune quod capiebatur per civitates et comitatus, quod non fuit tempore regis Ead-wardi, hoc ne amodo sit, omnino defendo.' His ordinance *de moneta falsa et cambiatoribus* fixed the penalty of mutilation for forgery and forbade the moneyers to exercise their rights of ex-

change outside their own *comitatus* and any but the moneyers
to hold exchange; this charter is assigned to 1100–1 or 1103.
Nevertheless, forgery or debasement by the moneyers was rife in
his reign, and the Anglo-Saxon Chronicle records that in the
year 1125 Bishop Roger of Salisbury summoned all the moneyers to Winchester and had them all mutilated in accordance
with the king's instructions, 'and that was all with great justice',
says the chronicler, 'because they had foredone all the land with
their great quantity of false money'; the Winton Annals say
that all the moneyers of England except three of Winchester
were mutilated, and the Margam Annals give the number
mutilated as ninety-four. A more curious monetary difficulty
is noted in the summary of Henry's character by William of
Malmesbury; curious, too, is the homoeopathic remedy which
was applied: 'Cum nummos fractos, licet boni argenti, a ven-
ditoribus non recipi audisset, omnes vel frangi vel incidi prae-
cepit.' This seems to mean that the traders made a practice of
incising or snicking the coins for the purpose of testing their
quality and that pennies so disfigured were being refused for
ordinary circulation; Henry, to meet the difficulty, ordered all
coins to be snicked at the mints before issue. The evidence of the
coins agrees with this interpretation; such an incision is found
in all the coins of Henry I from his seventh to his twelfth type in-
clusive (see *d* in Pl. 32, which shows the snick through the N of
'Henricus' and between A and L of the mint-name Wall[ing-
ford]), the order being, presumably withdrawn under the re-
organization following the examination and punishment of the
moneyers in 1125. It is interesting at this period to observe the
proportion of the types to the length of the reign; Edward the
Confessor issued ten or eleven types in twenty-four years,
Henry fifteen types in thirty-five years; this rather points to the
conclusion that each issue had a regular currency of three
years, the type, however, being varied upon an accession. Two
types of Henry I, his twelfth and fifteenth, are shown in
Pl. 32, *d, e*.

The civil wars of the reign of Stephen produced a great
variety of interesting coins, though some are as yet of uncertain

attribution. The normal issues of the king do not require special comment, but their rarity gives them a special value for collec٭ tors; his first and last types only are, by the discovery of hoards in Hertfordshire and Hampshire, known to us in any number. A coin of the first type is illustrated in Pl. 32, *f.* The Angevin party had a coinage struck at mints in the west of England in the name of Matildis Imperatrix or Comitissa (Pl. 32, *i,* struck at Oxford), and, after her retirement in favour of her son, in the name of Henricus or Henricus Rex. A series of coins, on which the type is identical with Stephen's first issue but the king's name is replaced by the inscription 'P(or W?)ereric' or 'P(or W?)ereric M', may perhaps be explained as a temporary issue of the period of the king's captivity (1141), the engravers, who presumably prepared the dies at London, having clumsily en٭ deavoured to introduce the name of the Empress (Empereriz) Matilda in place of that of Stephen. To the same period seem to belong pennies having on the obverse two full٭length figures, male and female, holding between them a long sceptre, with the king's title as inscription but ornaments in place of a reverse legend (Pl. 32, *g*); the two figures are probably Queen Matilda and Stephen, signifying the attempt of Matilda to support her husband's cause during his captivity. Coins of Eustace Fitz٭ John (Pl. 32, *k, l*) and Robert de Stuteville (Pl. 32, *j*), two northern barons of whom little is known, of Henry, bishop of Winchester and brother of the king (Pl. 32, *h*) and of Brian FitzCount (?), who took an active part on the Ang vin side and was three times besieged in his castle at Wallingford, show either a freedom in granting the privilege of coining or its fre٭ quent usurpation during these troublous times.

In the reign of Henry II the periodical changing of types was abandoned, perhaps with a view to decreasing forgery, and the first type of his reign continued to be struck until 1180 (Pl. 32, *m*). The money was then in a wretched condition through the incompetence of the moneyers; and the king decided to issue a new type and to obtain the services of a foreigner, Philip Ay٭ mery of Tours, to supervise the new coinage; the foreigner is said to have quickly fallen a victim to the profitable abuses that

PLATE 32

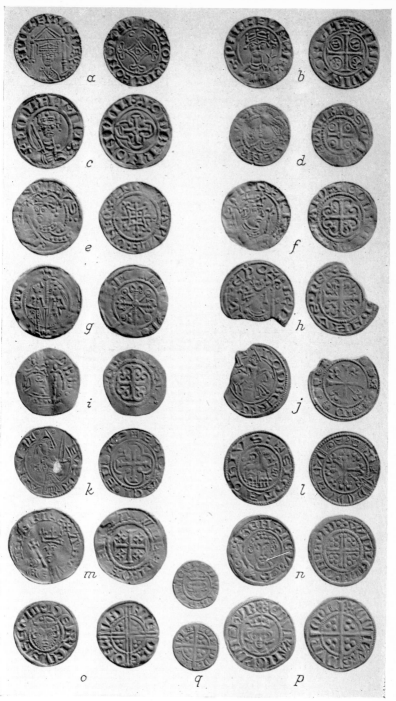

English coins

were still rife among the moneyers and to have been dismissed from the country for conniving with them. The various abuses that were practised on the coinage were too profitable to be amenable to the most severe penalties, and, though there seems to have been some further action taken against the moneyers in 1205, the abuses continued. In 1247 Henry III, in the hope of putting an end to the clipping of the coins, made another change in the type. In the meantime the type of 1180, which is commonly known as the Short-cross type (Pl. 32, *n*), had remained unchanged through the reigns of Richard and John, who omitted even to replace the name Henricus by their own names on the pennies issued during their reigns. The new coinage of 1247 was somewhat similar to that of the previous issue, but on the reverse the voided cross was continued to the edge of the coin, and an order was issued that no coin should pass current on which the ends of the cross were not visible (see Pl. 32, *o*).

From the death of Plegmund (914) and Wulfhere (900?) the archbishops ceased to place their names on their coins, and we are therefore unable to distinguish in the issues of the Canterbury and York mints the royal from the ecclesiastical pennies, except in certain cases where a moneyer is known from the Pipe Rolls or other sources to have been employed in the king's or the archbishop's service; but in the reign of Edward I and in subsequent reigns a quatrefoil in the centre of the reverse differentiates the coins of the archbishop of York. The palatinate bishops of Durham had, from some early date which we cannot determine, the right of coinage; the earliest Durham coin at present known is of the last type of William I. In the foundation charter of the abbey of Reading (1125) Henry I granted to the abbey a mint and a moneyer at Reading, which was soon exchanged for the use of one of the moneyers at the London mint. But a grant of greater importance to the student of coins is that to the abbot of St. Edmund's; charters of renewal only are extant and the date of the original grant is not known, but, apart from the memorial coinage at the end of the ninth century, the earliest coins attributed to the mint of Bury St. Edmunds are of the Con-

fessor's reign. The coinage of the abbey of St. Edmund is of value in determining the chronological arrangement of coins of the twelfth and thirteenth centuries owing to the limitation of the grant to one moneyer and to the use of one pair of dies which had apparently to be returned before a new pair was obtained. The coinage of the bishops of Durham is even more valuable as a guide to the classification of groups of coins; from about the end of the thirteenth century, except during the reigns of Richard II and Henry IV and V, it was customary for the bishops to place on their coins personal symbols which are therefore absent from coins struck at periods when the temporalities of the see were in the hands of the king's receiver through the suspension or death of the bishop.

These ecclesiastical issues have been the chief means of arriving at a classification of the long series of pennies bearing the name of Edward, which were substituted in 1279 for the 'Long-cross' pennies and continued to the end of the reign of Edward III without any change except a very slight variety of style; they remained, in respect of type, unchanged till the reign of Henry VII. The crowned head of the king is the obverse design and the reverse a long cross with three pellets in each angle. Pl. 32, *p*, shows one of these pennies bearing at the beginning of the inscription on both sides the cross moline of Anthony Bek (1283–1311); his successor, Kellawe, used a crozier as his badge, and Beaumont a lion rampant.

With the introduction of the new coinage of Edward I the custom of placing the moneyer's name on the coin disappears, but there is a curious survival in the occurrence on some pennies struck in and shortly after 1280 of the name Robert de Hadley. The name of the mint is omitted, but from documentary evidence we know Robert de Hadley to have been the moneyer of Bury St. Edmunds. There was a mint at Berwick in use by the English kings at this time; most of the dies were made locally and consequently the coins are of somewhat barbarous workmanship.

The striking of halfpennies at the end of the ninth and for most of the tenth centuries has already been noticed, but after

Edgar only the penny was struck, and small change was provided by shearing the coins into halves and quarters, cutting
being facilitated by the inclusion of a plain or voided cross in
the reverse design. There is documentary evidence of an order
to strike halfpence under Henry III, and almost conclusive
evidence in the chroniclers for the existence of round halfpence
as early as the reign of Henry I. None of the Henry III pieces
are known, and the solitary example reported of the Henry I
piece has not convinced all numismatists. In 1279, however,
farthings were struck (Pl. 32, q), and halfpence followed a few
months later, in 1280.

The coins of Edward I can only be distinguished from those
of his son and grandson by arranging the coins upon a close
scrutiny of their style and lettering and applying to the series
thus formed the evidence available from the ecclesiastical coinages mentioned above and the documentary evidence drawn
from Exchequer accounts and other sources.

The appendix to the chronicle of John de Oxenedes gives a
long account of a trial of the money which was held in the
thirty-second year of the reign of Henry III. A mandamus was
issued to the mayor and citizens of London to summon twelve
'de discretioribus et legalioribus hominibus' and twelve good
goldsmiths to present themselves before the barons of the Exchequer at Westminster, and there to examine both the old and
the new coinage and to propose measures for its improvement.
An assay by fire was accordingly made both of the old money
(i.e. the 1180 issue of 'short-cross' pennies) and of the new
money (i.e. the 1247 issue of 'long-cross' pennies); the new
money was found to be up to standard but the short-cross
pennies were below standard. For future use it was decided to
keep two proof-pieces, one of pure silver and the other of
standard silver, in the treasury at Westminster, and similar
proof-pieces were sent to each of the mints. An order follows
for the appointment of officers of mints other than London
and Canterbury, the mints numbering sixteen, excluding
Durham and Bury St. Edmunds; a few years later the pro-
vincial mints were closed, only the mints of London, Canter-

bury, Durham, and Bury St. Edmunds remaining in operation. About the year 1300 the mints of Chester, Newcastle,
Kingston-upon-Hull, and Exeter were opened for a short
time; Bristol was working towards the beginning and the end
of the reign of Edward I, and Calais in 1363-4.

4. *The Coinage of the English Possessions in France*

The coins issued for circulation in the English possessions in
France, though properly regarded from the numismatic point
of view as belonging to the French series, have considerable
interest as illustrating the history of this country in its relations
with France from the middle of the twelfth century to the
middle of the fifteenth. The issues of the Calais mint are not
included in this section; Calais was regarded as an English
mint and issued English coins under indentures identical with
those for the mints in England; it was often under the same
Master as the mint of London.

The earliest of the coins are deniers and obols struck by
Henry II for Aquitaine, which came to him by his marriage
with Eleanor; they are of a simple form, inscribed on one side
'Henricus (or Enricus) Rex' and on the other 'Aquitanie'. In
1168 he ceded the province to his son Richard, who continued
the coinage in his own name without the title Rex until his
father's death, when he resigned Aquitaine to Eleanor; after
his accession he struck similar coins for Poitou and a rare denier
of Issoudun (Exolduni) which must have been struck after the
treaty of 1196. After the death of Eleanor (1204) the French
king confiscated John's possessions, and neither he nor Henry
III is known to have struck coins for French circulation. In
1252 Henry III ceded such rights as he had in France to his son
Edward, who struck during this period deniers and obols
of lion type with the title 'Edwardus Filius Henrici Regis
Angliae'. A coinage without name of mint struck by Edward
for Ponthieu (*Moneta Potivi*), which fell to Eleanor of Castille
in 1279 and was confirmed by the treaty of Amiens, and some

coins struck at Abbeville were followed by a coinage for Guienne (1268–93), part of which bears the mark of Bordeaux.

The interest of these early issues is purely historical; the spas-
modic issues of coins by the English kings show the varying
security of the tenure of their French possessions, and the coins
of Richard and Edward struck before their accession to the
English throne illustrate the principle of ceding the French
territories to the heir apparent which culminated in the creation
of the principality of Aquitaine in favour of the Black Prince.
In the reign of Edward III the Anglo-Gallic coins assume a
much wider interest. The adoption of a gold coinage and the
addition of the groat to the silver series are important innova-
tions in this coinage, both of which, if we overlook the abortive
attempt of Henry III to introduce gold, preceded similar in-
novations in the English currency. There is also at this time a
great artistic interest in the study of the Anglo-Gallic gold
coins. The artistic imagination of the engravers is given ample
scope in this series; it is not, as in the English coinage, limited
by the political or financial necessity of adhering so long as
possible to a single type. The *écu*, *léopard*, and *guiennois* of
Edward III, and the *pavillon* and *hardi* of the Black Prince, are
fine examples of the application of Gothic art to the limited
medium at the disposal of the die-engraver. The short-lived
English florin series and the earliest nobles are, as we shall see
later, not inferior to these; but as no new designs were introduced for a century and a quarter, the noble with its half and
quarter, which were the only gold currency of this country, very
quickly assumed the spiritless style that differentiates the work
of the copyist from that of the original artist.

It is not possible to assign a date to the first gold coinage of
Edward—the gold florin struck for Aquitaine—but it was
certainly struck before 1337. It is one of the many close imitations of the famous *Fiorino d'oro* which was first struck at
Florence in 1252; on the obverse is the *fiore*, or lily, and on the
reverse the standing figure and the name of S. Iohannes Bap-
tista. The obverse is inscribed 'Dux Aquitanie'; the name of
Edward does not appear (Pl. 33, *a*). The *écu* or *chaise d'or*,

imitated not long after 1337 from the coinage of the king of France, where it first appeared in 1336, represented the king enthroned holding a sword and the shield of France. This was soon superseded by a coin of original design, named, from its obverse type, the *léopard*, which continued till after the treaty of Brétigny, when Edward gave up the use of the title 'Rex Franciae'. Between 1360 and 1362 was struck for Guienne a new coin of the same value as the *léopard*, which was the first gold coin to be marked with mint initials; the letters of Bor-deaux, Limoges, Poitiers, Rochelle, and Figeac are found. The king is represented on the *guiennois* standing in full armour under a portal of Gothic style; a specimen from the Rochelle mint is illustrated (Pl. 33, *b*). The reverse legends of these coins are liturgical: 'Christus vincit, Christus regnat, Christus imperat' appears on both *écu* and *léopard*; 'Gloria in excelsis deo et in terra pax hominibus' on the *guiennois* has a special refer-ence to the peace following the treaty of Brétigny. The florin had a currency value of three shillings; the *écu*, *léopard*, and *guiennois* were equivalent to the half-noble, or 3*s*. 4*d*.

The alliance of Edward III with Flanders and Brabant in 1339 was the source of the introduction of the groat into the Anglo-Gallic coinage. The gros of the Lion type was the 'mon-noye commune, bonne et loyale, qui aura son cours dans les deux pays' under the treaty of the same year between the count of Flanders and the duke of Brabant, and the same coin was included in the French coinage of Edward III, presumably at the same time. He also struck a *gros tournois* which was the original type of groat introduced into the French coinage by Louis IX in 1266. A sterling, copied from the English penny but having a crown in place of the three pellets in each angle of the cross on the reverse, was struck for Aquitaine. After 1360 a half-length figure of the king was placed on the obverse of the groat and sterling, and the 'Gloria in excelsis' legend took the place of 'Benedictum sit Nomen Domini' on the groat.

A very extensive coinage was issued by the Black Prince during the few years of his tenure of the principality (1362–72). During the first year he continued the issue at Bordeaux of

léopards and *guiennois* of the type previously issued by his father. Pl. 33, *d*, shows a *léopard* struck by the Black Prince at Bordeaux. After July 1363, when he arrived in France, he struck the *écu* or *chaise d'or* at Bordeaux, Limoges, and Rochelle. In the following year he is said to have turned his attention to the coinage after returning from his tour of the principality, and to have issued the new gold coin called the *pavillon* or 'royal'; the prince is represented seated under a Gothic pavilion, robed, and wearing a wreath of roses, his right arm resting on a shield and holding a sword; his feet rest on two leopards couchant, and in the field are four feathers, two at either side of the prince; the reverse, which has feathers inserted in the highly ornamental design, bears the legend 'Dominus adiutor et protector meus et in ipso speravit cor meum' (Pl. 33, *c*). The mint-marks of Bordeaux, Limoges, Poitiers, and Rochelle are found on the *pavillon*. Another gold coin was issued after the prince's return from his Spanish expedition in 1368 called the *hardi d'or*, of much simpler design; the obverse has a three-quarter figure of the prince facing, holding a sword, the reverse a floriate cross with leopard and lis in alternate angles and the inscription 'Auxilium meum a Domino'; it was issued at Bordeaux, Limoges, and Rochelle (Pl. 33, *e*, struck at Limoges). In silver there were regular issues of gros and sterlings, the sterling being superseded by a *hardi d'argent*, with three-quarter-length figure, at the same time as the *hardi d'or* was introduced. In billon, or base metal, he struck doubles and deniers. The style adopted by the Black Prince on his coins was 'Edwardus Primogenitus Regis Angliae Princeps Aquitaniae'.

Henry of Lancaster in 1347 was granted the town of Bergerac with the right of coinage; between 1347 and 1352 he struck gros and demi-gros with the title 'Henricus Comes Lancastriae Dominus Bragairacii', and after 1352, as 'Dux Lancastriae' demi-gros and sterlings. On his death in 1361 Bergerac reverted to the Crown, and in the following year became part of the principality of the Black Prince, who granted it in 1370, with rights of coinage, to John of Gaunt.

In addition to the right of coinage at Bergerac, John of Gaunt was granted by Edward III coinage at Bayonne and Guiche in 1377, and at Bayonne and D'Ax by Richard II in 1380. In 1390 he became duke of Aquitaine with privilege of coining. Nevertheless, we have no coins bearing his name, but it is possible that a Bordeaux double and denier bearing the title 'Edwardus Rex Angliae' and a denier of D'Ax reading 'Dux Aquitaniae' without a name were struck by him under the grant of 1377.

Richard II and Henry IV continued the gold and silver issues of the *hardi* type and a billon *denier* similar to those of the Black Prince. In the latter reign the planta genista takes the place of the fleur-de-lys on the silver coin.

At the accession of Henry V the scene of English activity in France is removed from Aquitaine in consequence of the strife for the French throne. Henry's offer to forgo his claim to the crown of France in virtue of certain concessions was rejected and, war being declared, he landed at Harfleur in 1415 but gained nothing beyond the moral effect of the victory of Agincourt. In 1417 he took Caen, and there issued a curious and very rare demi-gros of French type. After the capture of Rouen (January 1419), he established a mint there and struck the *gros d'argent* and *mouton d'or*. The *mouton*, or *agneau*, was a type introduced into the French coinage in 1311; on the obverse is the Paschal Lamb with banner and the legend 'Agnus dei qui tollis peccata mundi miserere nobis', the king's title in abbreviated form being below the lamb. The reverse has the usual ornate design with floriate cross and the legend 'Christus vincit', &c. In the following April another mint was opened at St. Lô. By the treaty of Troyes (May 1420) Henry acquired the regency during the lifetime of Charles and the succession at his death, and in the following month he issued an order for the inscription 'Henricus Francorum Rex' on his coins to be changed to 'H Rex Anglie et Heres Francie'. In November 1421, to remedy the loss consequent upon his fine coinage being undervalued in comparison with the poorer coins issued by the dauphin, a new coinage was ordered. The new gold coin was

the *salute*, which represents on the obverse the Annunciation with the crowned shield of England and France quarterly between the Angel and the Virgin; on the reverse it has a plain cross between a lis and a leopard, with the letter H below, and the 'Christus vincit' legend (Pl. 33,*f*).

On the death of Charles in October 1422, Henry VI became, in virtue of the treaty of Troyes, *de facto* king of France. He issued an extensive French coinage which was no longer a currency struck by an English king for feudal possessions in France, or, as in the reign of Henry V, in virtue of tenure by force of conquest, but the French coinage struck by the king of France.

5. The Introduction of Gold

With a very few but significant exceptions such as the gold dinar of Offa, the gold solidus of Archbishop Wigmund of York, and gold pence of Edward the Elder, Æthelred II, and Edward the Confessor, the coinage of this country had been confined to silver from the beginning of the eighth century. The tendency towards the adoption of a gold currency, which was the outcome of the increase of trade in the thirteenth century and which produced in Italy the florin in 1252 and the sequin in 1284, made its appearance also in England in the attempt of Henry III to bring a gold penny into circulation. This coin (Pl. 34, *a*) was struck, under an order of the year 1257, of the weight of two sterlings, or silver pennies, of pure gold, and was proclaimed in the same year at the value of 20 pence, raised later to 24 pence. It is of neat and careful workmanship and of admirable design; on the obverse is a figure of the king enthroned holding sceptre and orb; on the reverse, as on the silver pennies of the same period, a long cross voided, but with the addition of a rose between the three pellets in each angle. It was very unfavourably received by the public, and a protest from the city of London resulted in the withdrawal of the obligation to accept it in payment. Its issue seems to have been discontinued about 1270; the unpopularity of the coin was probably due to the low ratio which the gold held to the silver coinage.

No further attempt was made to establish a gold coinage until the end of the year 1343, when an indenture was issued ordering the first English gold coinage of Edward III, which was put into currency by a proclamation of January 1344. This was the famous florin series, consisting of a florin, or two-*léopard* piece, a *léopard*, or half-florin, and a helm, or quarter-florin, weighing 108, 54, and 27 grains and current for 6, 3, and $1\frac{1}{2}$ shillings respectively; the standard gold of which they were made was 23 carats $3\frac{1}{2}$ grains fine. The use of the name florin was inappropriate: its value was double that of the continental florin, and the florin type was not adopted on any of the three coins. In type the florin was somewhat similar to the *pavillon* of the Black Prince; on the obverse the king is represented in royal robes seated under a Gothic canopy; the *léopard*, or half-florin, and the helm, or quarter, take their names from their obverse designs, the one a crowned leopard with a banner bearing the arms of England and France fastened to its neck, the other a crested helm; the obverse fields of the florin and quarter are sown with fleurs-de-lys. The reverse of each has an ornamental design with a floriate cross as its main feature (Pl. 34, *b, c, d*). Scriptural mottoes are taken as reverse legends: 'Iesus transiens per medium illorum ibat' on the florin is supposed to have reference to the activity of the king's ship at the battle of Sluys; on the half is 'Domine ne in furore tuo arguas me', and on the quarter 'Exaltabitur in gloria'.

These coins are the finest in the English series; they are beautifully designed and most carefully executed. The issue did not, however, obtain a favourable reception; the gold was too highly valued in proportion to the silver; after six months the acceptance of the gold coins was made optional, and they were almost immediately withdrawn and a new gold coinage issued. The noble, with its half and quarter, was proclaimed in August 1344, at the value of 80 pence and weighing $138\frac{6}{13}$ grains, and the weight of the penny was reduced to $20\frac{1}{4}$ grains. The proportion between gold and silver still caused trouble, the gold being now slightly undervalued, in addition to the difficulty of retaining in currency a coinage that was very ex-

tensively imitated on the Continent. After an intermediate step in 1346, the ratio between standard gold and silver was fixed in 1351 at 12 to 1 by reducing the noble to 120 and the penny to 18 grains. The name of the noble is assumed to refer to its metal, signifying the standard coin of gold as opposed to the sterling of silver. Its design, the king standing in a ship and holding shield and sword, is often supposed to refer to the naval power of Edward and his victory at Sluys. The half-noble is of the same type as the noble; the obverse design of the quarter is a shield of arms. The reverse legends and types are similar to those of the florin series. The noble, half-noble, and quarter-noble of the issue of 1346–51 are illustrated in Pl. 34, *e, f, g*.

In 1351 Edward III was able to carry through a reform that under Edward I had been attempted in vain. This was the introduction of a multiple of the penny, the groat (Pl. 35, *a*), of the value and weight of fourpence. The reverse bore the legend 'Posui Deum Adiutorem Meum' and the name of the mint, e.g. 'London Civitas', arranged concentrically. Later, 'Civitas London' is the more usual order. As a result of the Treaty of Brétigny, the French title was omitted from 1360 until 1369.

The mint of Calais was at this time in active operation, coining both gold and silver, as an English mint. The Calais nobles and half-nobles of the earlier issues are distinguished from those of the London mint by the use of the letter C in place of the king's initial in the centre of the reverse, and on later coins by a flag at the stern of the ship on the obverse. The mark of differentiation on the quarter-nobles is not known; the silver coins bear on the reverse the inscription 'Villa Calisie'.

In 1411 Parliament ordered a reduction in the weight of the coins, the noble from 120 to 108 grains and the penny from 18 to 15 grains, 'because of the great scarcity of money at this time within the realm of England, and because of other mischiefs and causes manifest'; the other causes are not now manifest, but probably the removal of English coins and importation of foreign coins of poorer quality is implied, as this had in recent years been a matter of grave concern to Parliament. It appears that the king's revenues were considerably increased both by

the reduction of weight in the coinage and by the seizure of forfeited money, presumably foreign coins and imitations that
were not legal tender. With this exception the coinage remained
unchanged in value, quality, and design from the time of
Edward III until Edward IV came to the throne. In the reign
of Henry VI the issues are for the first time clearly marked by
the insertion of certain marks of difference such as roses, pinecones, leaves, annulets, and mascles between the words of the
inscriptions, and in later reigns the initial cross of the legends is
superseded by a similar differentiating mark; but it is not at
present possible to assign a definite period of duration to a particular mark. The mark in place of the initial cross is sometimes called the mintmark, but only occasionally denotes the
place of issue. Edwardian pence of the Durham mint, for example, can often be distinguished even from the obverse by the
use of a cross moline in place of the usual cross *patée*. As early as
Edward III the form of the cross indicates the particular issue,
while a narrower dating was achieved by the socalled privymark, a deliberate fault in a particular letter, or even a misspelling. Under Edward III, too, the initial cross is replaced for the
first time by a noncruciform symbol such as a crown. Consequently there is much to be said for the use of the term 'initial
mark' in preference to 'mintmark', but it should always be remembered that it was a public mark distinguishing coins of an
issue. At least until the Tudor period individual responsibility at the quarterly Trial of the Pyx was established by the
privymark, many of which have still to be deciphered.

In 1464 the weight of the silver coins was reduced, the penny
being struck at 12 instead of 15 grains; the gold coins were not
reduced in weight but were increased proportionately in value,
the noble being proclaimed at the value of 100 instead of 80
pence. In the following year a new gold coin, called the 'rose
noble or ryal', was issued, weighing 120 grains and having
a value of ten shillings, and another, called the angel, of the
weight of 80 grains, took the value of the old noble of 80 pence.
The ryal issue continued the types and legends of the noble
issue, but on the reverse a rose upon a radiate sun was imposed

PLATE 35

a

c

b

b

c

d

English coins. Groat, rose noble or royal, angel, and sovereign

upon the centre of the floriate cross, and on the obverse of the
ryal and half-ryal a rose was placed on the side of the ship and
a banner bearing the king's initial set in the stern (Pl. 35, *b*).
For the angel a new type was introduced, from which it took its
name, the archangel transfixing the dragon; on the reverse is a
ship which has a cross set in front of the mast with a shield of
arms below it and the king's initial and a rose at either side (Pl.
35, *c*); 'Per Crucem Tuam Salva Nos Christe Redemptor' is
used in slightly abbreviated form as the reverse legend of this
coin. There was a very large output of the new coinage, and
to meet the increase of work mints were opened at Bristol,
Coventry, Norwich, and York for the coining of both gold and
silver; the gold coins of these mints are differentiated by an initial
placed on or below the side of the ship; a Bristol ryal is shown
in Pl. 35, *b*. The extensive recoinage was soon effected and the
extra mints closed down.

During the short period of his restoration (1470–1) Henry
VI struck a very large coinage of the light standard introduced
by Edward IV; in gold he struck angels and half-angels only,
the issue of the ryal having been previously discontinued by
Edward IV. The type of the angel remained the same but for
the substitution of the letter H and a fleur-de-lys for Edward's E
and rose on the reverse. The ryal coinage was revived by Henry
VII with a new reverse design which covers the field with an
exquisitely moulded Tudor rose bearing in its centre a shield
with the arms of France (Pl. 36, *a*).

The reign of Henry VII brought two important changes in
the coinage. The first, which took place quite early in the reign,
was the issue of the sovereign, a gold coin weighing 240 grains
and having a current value of twenty shillings. It was a large,
thin coin, about 1½ inches in diameter (Pl. 35, *d*). The king is
seated on a throne of elaborate design which fills the field of the
obverse; the reverse type is the same which he adopted for the
ryal (Pl.36, *a*), but usually the work is more crowded, a fleured
tressure being added round the rose, and lions and fleurs inserted in the small intervening spaces. The coin, in spite of the
somewhat restless effect produced by the massing of detailed

ornamentation on the reverse, is a wonderful creation of Tudor art; the composition of the throned figure, adapted most skilfully to the circular field, and the powerful handling of perspective to defeat the limitations of the shallow relief which was necessary in the engraving of dies for striking so thin a flan, show a complete mastery of technique combined with the highest artistic inspiration.

The other noteworthy change in the coinage during this reign was the removal from the groats and half-groats of the conventional bust which was used with very slight change from the time of their introduction by Edward III to the end of the fifteenth century. In the years 1503–4 a new type of groat was issued (Pl.36, *b*); the inner legend which contained the name of the mint was removed, the scriptural legend 'Posui Deum', &c., being retained; in the field a shield of arms was imposed upon the centre of the long cross which divided the legend into four parts. A new portrait in profile was engraved for this coinage by a foreigner, Alexander of Bruchsal. A piece of twelve pence, 144 grains in weight, of the same design as the new groat, is known, but no record exists of such a coinage and these may have been struck only as trial pieces. The type of the penny was also changed in this reign, probably in 1489 when the sovereign was introduced; on the obverse a seated figure takes the place of the king's bust, and the new reverse type, a shield on a long cross, was the design which was adopted fifteen years later for the new groat coinage.

The early coins of Henry VIII were similar to the latest of the previous reign. In the groat series he even used the portrait of Henry VII, though he changed the numeral in the title; his own portrait was first engraved in profile (Pl. 36, *c*) in 1526 and changed to a facing portrait (Pl. 36, *d*) in 1542. In 1526 a warrant was issued to Wolsey appointing him the king's agent with full powers for the purpose of the coinage; this irregular system was regularized in 1530 by a warrant to the new chancellor, Sir Thomas More, and the usual indentures with the master-workers of the mint. The warrant to Wolsey ordered him to carry into effect the king's design of reducing his money

PLATE 36

English coins. Ryal, groats, half-crown, george noble, shilling, gold crown, silver half-crown

to the standard of foreign coins. 'Owing', a proclamation of the
same year informs us, 'to the enhancement of value abroad,
money was carried out of this realm by secret means.' Wolsey,
acting on the advice of a committee of goldsmiths, ordered a
new standard of gold of 22 carats fine gold alloyed with 2 carats
sterling silver (known as crown gold) to be introduced, of
which a crown of 5s. was struck and its half, bearing a double
rose crowned on the observe and a crowned shield on the reverse (the half-crown is shown in Pl. 36, e); this coin superseded
a crown of 4s. 6d., called the 'crown of the rose', which had
been issued three months previously. The sovereign, valued at
22s. 6d., the angel (7s. 6d.), ryal (11s. 3d.), and a new coin called
the 'George noble' (Pl. 36, f) of the value of 6s. 8d. were still
struck of the old standard gold. The silver coinage remained at
the old standard of 11 oz. 2 dwt. fine. The Reformation gave
the king mastery not only of doctrine but of the old archiepiscopal mints of Canterbury and York and of the episcopal
mint of Durham. Wolsey, it must be admitted, had abused
his privileges—though doubtless with royal connivance at the
time. At York he had struck not only the permitted half-groat,
penny, and halfpenny but also groats, a strictly royal prerogative. Had he lived, this technical treason would have figured
in his indictment, and the prejudice of the time is shown by
the fact that the draft indictment of 1529 makes great play of
the fact that the cardinal's hat was the archiepiscopal mark
(Pl. 36, e).

The issue of crown gold, though its object seems to have
been to prevent the coinage being removed from the country,
was the beginning of the debasement for which the reign of
Henry VIII is notorious. The gold of the sovereign and angel
series was reduced to 23 carats in 1542, 22 carats in 1545, and
20 carats (including crown gold) in 1546; the silver went to
10 oz. fine in 1542, 9 oz. in 1544, 6 oz. in 1545, and 4 oz. in
1546. In the following reign, though the debased coinage continued, there was evidently an intention to reform it, for we find
Henry's name on all the early coins issued by Edward, and his
portrait also on the early groats; further, the inscription, 'Redde

cuique quod suum est', which may be interpreted (in conjunction with the use of Henry's name) 'Give the devil his due', is
found on base silver coins struck at a mint which was opened at
Durham House, Strand, for about a year in 1548–9. The restoration of the coinage was a long and difficult business, and for a
time coinages of two standards were being issued together.
Edward's last issue consisted of a sovereign of thirty shillings
and angel of ten shillings of standard gold, a sovereign of twenty
shillings and crown of five shillings of 22 carat gold, and a
crown, half-crown, shilling, and sixpence of silver of 11 oz.
1 dwt. fine. The shilling (*g*) and the gold crown (*h*) and silver
half-crown (*i*) of Edward VI are illustrated in Pl. 36. The use
of both standard and crown gold continued to the time of the
Commonwealth, when the angel, which was the last surviving
coin of old standard gold and had a peculiar connexion with
royalty through its use in the ceremony of touching for the king's
evil, disappeared from the coinage. Twenty-two carat gold has
remained ever since as the standard for the gold coinage. The
restoration of the silver to the old standard of 11 oz. 2 dwt. was
completed by Elizabeth, to whom is also due the less fortunate
distinction of having taken, by the introduction of the screw
press, the first step towards the elimination of art by modern
machinery.

WORKS FOR REFERENCE

Three standard works, to some extent complementary, are:

BROOKE, G. C. *English Coins*, 2nd ed., with supplement (1950).

CRAIG, SIR JOHN. *The Mint* (1953).

OMAN, SIR CHARLES. *The Coinage of England* (1931).

It would be a work of supererogation to reproduce their excellent bibliographies,
but mention should perhaps be made of one or two continental works that have
been unaccountably overlooked:

HILDEBRAND, B. E. *Anglosachsiska Mynt i Svenska Kongliga Myntkabinettet*, 1st ed.
(Stockholm, 1846). Contains valuable material omitted from the 1881 edition.

NORDMAN, C. A. *Anglo-Saxon Coins found in Finland* (Helsinki, 1921).

The standard journals are:

The British Numismatic Journal (1904–).

The Numismatic Chronicle (1836–).

Much of fundamental importance appears in these annual publications, and the student of Anglo-Saxon coinage in particular will need to refer to recent numbers. Continental numismatic journals often contain papers of English significance, notably:

Nordisk Numismatisk Årsskrift (1936–)

There is a very full but uncritical bibliography of Danish hoards of the Viking period in:

Aarbøger for Nordisk Oldkyndighed og Historie (1942).

It will be understood that the literature is unusually scattered, but recent work is generally noticed in the American periodical:

Numismatic Literature (1947–).

Papers read before the different numismatic societies are briefly summarized in

Seaby's Coin and Medal Bulletin (1947–);

Spink's Numismatic Circular (1897–);

usually within a few weeks of their being given.

IX. CIVIL COSTUME

THE study of dress is of value to the historian or to the reader if it helps him to visualize the people of a past age. Dress is, from one point of view, a protection against the weather, from another, a concession to modesty, but the differences and developments of dress, which will be described here, indicate the social rank, the occupation or profession, and, less clearly, the nationality of the wearer.

So few actual clothes have survived since the middle ages that the illustrations are mainly confined to reproductions of illuminated manuscripts and sculpture. In both fields there are obvious stylizations and mannerisms—faithful portraiture developed slowly, and it is extremely hard to determine exactly what a particular person wore. In literature there are similar conventions and archaisms, and since three languages, Latin, French, and Middle English, are involved, the terminology—quite apart from the risk of mistranslations—is most obscure. Specialized glossaries cover French fairly well, as will be seen from the bibliography, but an adequate scholarly dictionary of English medieval costume-terms is badly needed.

This lack of definitions is most apparent when dress materials are considered. Animal skins in the middle ages were used for the fur lining of dresses and of course for footwear, but the normal materials were textiles, primarily linen and wool, and to a lesser extent silk and cotton when their use spread westwards and northwards in Europe. Trade and importation may account for the multiplicity of names for materials which as textiles were really very much alike.

The primitive forms of dress are few. First there is the oblong piece of material with a slit for the wearer's head; it covers the shoulders and is open at the sides. When seamed and given sleeves it becomes the smock, shirt, or tabard. Then the front is made open and it forms the coat. Secondly, the large piece of

PLATE 37

a. Harold and Stigand. From the Bayeux tapestry

b. Domus incenditur. From the Bayeux tapestry

PLATE 38

a. Effigy of Richard I, at Fontevrault (from C. A. Stothard)

b. Effigy of Queen Eleanor, at Fontevrault (from C. A. Stothard)

material may be wrapped as a toga or plaid about the whole body; worn on the shoulders it is a mantle, cape, or scarf, worn about the waist it is a skirt. The smaller skirt is an apron, and when the lower corners are drawn between the legs and fastened again to the waistband the breech-clout is formed, and so the breeches. The head, the hands, and the feet have their own specialized coverings.

It is fortunate that Bishop Odo's cathedral at Bayeux kept the long strip embroidered with William the Conqueror's exploits, since all similar work has perished including the hangings at Ely cathedral, probably seen by Bishop Odo, in which Byrhtnoth's widow commemorated the battle of Maldon. At this date sculpture of the human figure was undeveloped, and the Durham school of illumination subordinated details of dress to the interlace pattern. The basic dress for men in the Bayeux tapestry is a shirt and breeches, which the manual worker would tuck into his waistband. Soldiers and middle-class people wore a tunic as well, and to this the nobles and kings added a mantle with a clasp at the throat. Banded stockings, which were probably puttee-like wrappings, and low shoes completed the dress (Pl. 37a). Only two women are depicted (Pl. 37b); they seem to have worn a shift, a loose dress with hanging sleeves, and a kerchief wound about head and neck. The Virtues slaying Discord in the St. Albans Prudentius are the manuscript counterparts to the Bayeux tapestry; there are no clear variations between Norman and Saxon civilian dress, and indeed the changes since the tenth-century Benedictional of St. Æthelwold are slight.

From the beginning of the twelfth century English luxury of dress slowly but perceptibly increased. The tunic became a robe, women's sleeves trailed to the ground, and inner garments were elaborately pleated or else embroidered. Sculptural representations in England are few (the trousered figures on the door pillars at Kilpeck and Shobdon merit special study), and it is best to turn to France. On the enamel plaque at Le Mans (Fig. 72) Geoffrey of Anjou wears a green knee-length tunic over a pleated blue robe, both with bands of gold embroidery

and rosettes; over all, his blue mantle is lined with vair, shown heraldically, and a gold lion is embroidered on his peaked blue cap; he has green stockings and blue shoes with pointed toes. This plaque shows the continuation of what William of Malmesbury had said of William Rufus's time (Rolls Series, ii, p. 369) when first flowing hair, luxury of dress, and the use of shoes with pointed toes were introduced. The pointed toes of the shoes (*pigaciae*), stuffed with tow and curling like rams' horns, are described by Ordericus Vitalis (*lib.* viii. c. 10).

The royal effigies at Fontevrault mark the next stage. Richard I (Pl. 38*a*) wears a mantle, sleeved gown or tabard, under-robe, and broad-toed boots, all embroidered at seams and hems. The effigy of Queen Eleanor (Pl. 38*b*) is draped in an elaborate mantle held by a cord across the shoulders, her gown (*bliaut*) fits more tightly and may have been open at the sides to show the shift (*chainse*) within. The unusual fashion of knot-ting the end of the sleeves is shown as worn by Rebekah in the Munich psalter (Pl. 39*a*).

The sculptured figures at the north portal of Chartres cathe-dral show the most elaborate dresses in this Romanesque-Byzantine style: and while no bracelets, necklaces, or ear-rings were worn, women's jewellery included rich girdles, clasps (*fermails*) for mantles and the neck-slit (*amigaut*) of gowns, and other brooches (*nowches*). Indoors, mantle and *bliaut* might be taken off (Pl. 39*b*), and men wore fewer garments. Breeches con-tinued as underclothes and their wearing by the religious orders was not forgotten by Walter Map (*De nugis curialium*). So also at Bury St. Edmunds when Abbot Sampson was about to ex-communicate those who had taken part in riotous sports in the graveyard on the day after Christmas, all the men stripped themselves and, naked save for their drawers, prostrated them-selves before the door of the church.

The thirteenth-century developments in costume are not at first obvious. In general, upper-class dress seems to have been simplified, and lacked decoration; outer garments have fewer pleats and folds, materials may be thicker, following perhaps the progress in weaving, and are not embroidered. Yet Matthew

PLATE 39

b. Woman with two bethrothed

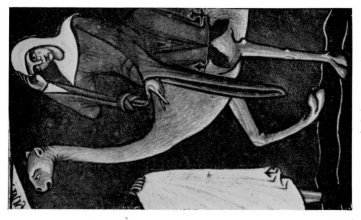

a. Rebekah on camel

PLATE 40

a. Guthlac leaves his companions

b. Pega steps into a boat

Paris describes the Londoners of 1236 as 'decked in silken vest-ments, and wrapped in mantles woven with gold'. The life of St. Guthlac gives good examples; when Guthlac leaves his companions (Pl. 40a) they are in chain-mail, but he wears a three quarter-length mantle with no clasp, a belted kirtle hardly reaching to his knees, and puttee stockings. His sister Pega (Pl. 40b) steps into a boat wearing a full gown which shows the pleated sleeves and wrist-bands of her shift. She has a kerchief wound over her head and round her neck.

Monumental sculpture is still stylized; amongst the effigies of English kings and queens there is nothing to compare in detail with the late thirteenth-century founders' statues of Naum-burg cathedral, though Eleanor of Castile (Westminster abbey) in a conventionalized dress has assumed a characteristic thirteenth-century pose with one hand holding the cords of her mantle.

The French romances are a great boon to the historian of costume who finds little in King Horn or Layamon's *Brut*. As the *Dit du Mercier* has been printed by F. W. Fairholt as an English-costume document, the plea of close connexion between Norman-French and English justifies quotations from *L'Escoufle*, in which dress is constantly described. Aelis, the heroine, rose naked from her bed, and put on 'over a white chemise, pleated with more than a fathom of material', a *bliaut*, 'furred with vair, and trimmed with ermine, and on her head instead of a wimple she had a little circlet of gold braid'; the saffron-tinted wimple, already an elderly woman's wear, would have hidden her neck and throat. When she escaped by night in her chemise and *cote*, without stopping 'to tire her hair', she took off her silk *bliaut*, and for riding wore a *cote* and *coterel* of Flemish cloth and a cape over all. Later, when sleeping in the open in hot weather, she left off *chape* and *jupe* and was in her unlaced *cors* and chemise. By the fireside after dinner she was wearing a sleeveless *peliçon* when the count of St. Gilles, the master of the house, stripped off his clothes to scratch himself, retaining only his drawers (*braies*), but later took a winter sur-coat to keep himself warm. Coat and surcoat were men's as well

as women's garments, breeches were still undergarments (not to be seen in Pl. 41a). Shirts were quite elaborate (Pl. 41b).

While at the end of the thirteenth century women were about to abandon veils and kerchiefs, men, who had previously been bareheaded, adopted first a round hat and then a hood pulled on over the head and fitting tightly round the face and neck (Pl.41b). Hats (*capellae*) or, more properly, garlands of peacock's feathers, are recorded in 1211 and 1274. A good idea of men's dress may be had from the household accounts of Bogo de Clare (1284–6);[1] these give robe and tabard, with a cloak, together with furs and hoods as the dress for the more important people, and distinguish the *roba integra* and the *roba partita*; the actual word 'robe' often means a suit, that is, the supertunic, cloak, and cape. Children's clothes are listed in the household accounts of Henry, son of Edward I (1268–74).[2] The boys had linen shirts, robes of shorn cloth, hose of brown cloth, gloves with the king's arms embroidered on the thumbs, and caps with peacock feathers; the girls' robes were furred, but not particularized except that they were decorated with many buttons and silk loops.

The fourteenth century was a century of changes which began long before the reign of Richard II and his marriage to Anne of Bohemia, though these sovereigns have been held to be originators of new fashions. While most of the men's garments became shorter and fitted more closely, women's dress was also tight-fitting, buttons, lacing, and belts combining to give the right effect. Tailoring had advanced a long way, and there is evidence of a greater variety of colours and of fabrics; Italian velvets and Lucca figured silks were travelling northwards. Good illustrations of the dress of all classes are frequent, first in the Tickhill and Gorleston psalters, then Queen Mary's psalter, and finally the Luttrell psalter. The tomb of Sir Roger de Kerdeston (*d.* 1337) at Reepham, Norfolk, is surrounded by a row of 'weepers' in quite a variety of these new dresses.

[1] *Archaeologia*, lxx (1920), pp. 1–56.
[2] *John Rylands Library Bulletin*, vii (1923), p. 384.

PLATE 41

a. Wise man and fool

b. Angels clothing souls

PLATE 42

a. William of Hatfield, Westminster Abbey   *b*. Joan de la Tour, Westminster Abbey

Although its name is not established till the end of the century, the lined doublet (*pourpoint*), buttoned to below the waist and worn with a hip-belt (Pl. 42*a*), is the typical tailored garment for men, and quite unlike anything which had gone before. Possibly these padded and quilted garments were all derived from the *gipoun*, which Chaucer's knight wore under his coat of mail, just as in military dress may be sought the origin of the loose surcoats and *cotehardies*, which could have been worn over armour. Gowns, as affected by Chaucer's squire, were shorter and gay with floral designs. Jackets and paltocks cannot easily be distinguished from doublets. Under the year 1362 the Malmesbury writer of the *Eulogium Histori-arum* (Rolls Series, iii, pp. 230–1) censures not only the effeminate gowns, both wide and short, or ankle-length and closed in front, but another silken garment, *quod vulgo dicitur paltok*, and striped hose made in two parts and bound to the *paltoks* with laces called *harlottes*, an indecent fashion.

Instead of mantles, which except for ceremonial occasions now become rare, men wore in the open air short hooded cloaks (the Green Knight's *capados* was probably a hood with shoulder-pieces), the longer *sclavin*, the *garnache*, or else a sort of gown (the French *houce*) with half-sleeves and distinctive rounded tabs at the throat which is first recorded on a monu-ment at Gresford, Denbigh.

For women, the shape of the body began to be shown:

> A woman wel more fetys is
> In roket than in cotte, y-wis.
> The whyte roket rideled faire.[1]

And though Joan de la Tour's gown (Pl. 42*b*) cannot be given a name, it is not pleated and fits more tightly than a *sorquenie* (sukkenye). One of its features, the *fichets* into which the hands were thrust to keep them warm, is noteworthy, because inside these slits the first pockets were made as an alternative to leather pouches (*gipcières*) attached to the belt. The old wide sleeves were not used as pockets (*pokes*) but were mere strips hanging

---

[1] Chaucer, *Romaunt of the Rose*, ll. 1241–3.

from the elbows:

> And but ʒif it were elbowis adoun to the helis
> Or passing the knee it was not accounted.[1]

The sleeveless gowns (*cotehardies*) were often open at the sides, to judge from the Knight of La Tour Landry's story of the knight's daughter who failed to get a husband because she was blue and shivering in a *cotehardie* undoubled and unfurred (E.E.T.S., 1906, p. 165). The hair was no longer covered completely by a kerchief but plaited in two bosses over the ears.

It was at this stage in the fourteenth century, that the most marked distinctions in national dress began to appear. The Knight of La Tour Landry devotes a chapter (xxv) to ladies who with their 'gret purfiles' and 'slit cotes' aped the English, while their serving-women copied those of high estate. So also he reproves the young squire who came to dinner in a 'cote hardy upon the guyse of Almayne' which was only fit for a minstrel or a pursuivant. Particoloured striping was common, and the slitting and cutting (*dagging*) of the edges of garments into knife- or tongue-like strips became a conspicuous fashion. Chaucer's Parson (§ 27) speaks strongly against

nat only the cost of embroudinge, the degyse endentinge or barringe, oundinge, palinge . . . and semblable wast of clooth in vanitee; but . . . so muche pounsoninge of chisels to maken holes, so muche dagginge of sheres.

Having finished with superfluity, the Parson turns to

the horrible disordinat scantnesse of clothing, as been thise cutted sloppes or hainselins that thurgh hir shortnesse ne covere nat the shameful membres of man, to wikked entente. Allas! somme of hem shewen the boce of hir shap . . . and eek the buttokes of hem faren as it were the hindre part of a she-ape in the fulle of the mone . . . departinge of hir hoses in whyt and reed.

The cloth or linen stockings had grown long as the doublet or paltock grew short, and were laced tightly to its inner lining by points, as is illustrated by the tale of Boucicault in the book of the Knight of La Tour Landry. Another excess was in shoes; not only did Franciscans wear buckled shoes 'for blenynge of her heles' (Piers Plowman's *Crede*, l. 299), but Absolon in Chaucer's *Miller's Tale* (ll. 3318–22):

[1] 'Mum and the Sothesegger', E.E.T.S. (1936), iii, l. 154.

> with Powles window corven on his shoos
> in hoses rede he went fetisly.
> Y-clad he was ful smal and proprely
> al in a kirtel of a light wachet
> ful faire and thikke been the poyntes set.

The toes were piked and stuffed and, while the chaining of their ends to the knees is a sixteenth-century chronicler's fabrication, the *Eulogium Historiarum* (iii, p. 231) says that in 1362 they had shoes with peaks as long as a man's finger which they called *crakowes*; these were judged more like demon's claws than men's adornments, so giving the actual length of what the French called *poulaines*.

Meanwhile, middle-class people such as Chaucer's Reeve still wore the long surcoat tucked up like a friar's, and the Clerk of Oxenford's gown (*courtepy*) was probably long also. The Shipman wore a short gown, the Miller a white coat and blue hood, and the Ploughman's tabard or smock, shaped like a knee-length blouse, put on over the head and tied in with a cord to the waist, can be illustrated from the Luttrell psalter. For Sundays the Wife of Bath had heavy kerchiefs, no doubt imitating hair-bosses, but ordinarily she wore a hat and about her neck a wimple; she had a foot-mantle, later called a safeguard, to cover her legs when she rode astride. Even so, her well-gartered red stockings and her new shoes caught the eye. Her inner garment, favoured also by the wife of Simkin the miller of Trumpington, was a scarlet *gyte* or gown made of the west-country cloth in which she dealt. Alison's dress (in the *Miller's Tale*, ll. 3235–43) fitted tightly,

> a ceynt she werede barred al of silk
> a barmclooth eek as whyt as morne milke
> up-on her lendes ful of many a gore.
> Whyt was hir smok and brouded al bifore
> and eek behinde, on her coler aboute,
> of col-blak silk, with-inne and eek withoute.
> The tapes of hir whyte voluper
> were of the same suyte of her coler
> hir filet brood of silk and set ful hye.

The important points are that her fillet covered her hair, the

colour of which is not mentioned but only that of her eye-
brows, that she wore a big old-fashioned brooch, and carried
a leather purse. Black silk embroidery was clearly a medieval
English fashion, though it is sometimes declared to have been
introduced by Catherine of Aragon.

As might be expected, there are archaisms in *Sir Gawain and
the Green Knight* such as the trailing *bliaut* worn indoors with a
surcoat and a hood hanging on the shoulder; when Sir Gawain
comes to the castle at Christmas time, the kerchief and gorget
of the old lady are described at length, while the young one
showed her bare neck and throat. The writers of sermons were
more up to date, and the preacher blames the pride of the
wretched knave, who should have been content with a white
kirtle and a russet gown, but now must have a fresh doublet
and a costly gown with *bagges* (sleeves) hanging to his knee
(Pl. 45a), and the back pleated under his girdle like the gauf-
fered *rochet* of a priest.

The various types of men's dress at the beginning of the
fifteenth century are described in Adrien Harmand's study of
the costume and armour of Joan of Arc. The duke of Bedford's
velvet gown (Pl. 44) was probably a *houppelande* (upland) as it
seems to have buttoned in front and had fur-lined sleeves and
a belt. The hood on his left shoulder has a dagged edge. His
patron saint, St. George, wears a close surcoat and the blue
mantle, the first dress of the Order of the Garter. A nobleman's
inner garment would have been a tight surcoat or doublet to the
lining of which the long hose were laced; the wearing of men's
hose (*caligae simul junctae*) was one of the charges preferred
against Joan of Arc; women's hose were always separate and
much shorter, needing garters below the knee to keep them
up. The more exotic forms of dress such as the full-pleated
houppelandes, some of them with fringes and collars garnished
with small bells in rows, were perhaps rare in England but are
shown in the frontispiece to Chaucer's *Troilus* in the manuscript at Corpus Christi, Cambridge. In Foxton's *Cosmographia* (Pl. 45a) the allegorical male figures have fashionable
high collars. Women's gowns also had stiff-standing collars,

PLATE 43

a. Joan de la Pole, Chrisall, Essex

b. Countess of Arundell, Arundel, Sussex

c. Joan Etchingham, Etchingham, Sussex

d. Lady Crosby, Gt. St. Helen's, London

WOMEN'S HEAD-DRESSES

PLATE 44

John Duke of Bedford and St. George

and the waistline was much higher than in the fourteenth century. To judge from the inventory of Catherine, widow of Henry V (*d.* 1437),[1] the distinction between gowns lay in the sleeves, 'ryven', 'trompe', 'rounde', as well as 'grete' and 'smale'; these may have been of different material firmly sewn, not lightly stitched as in earlier days.

Social distinctions may be reflected in the head-dresses, many types of which are shown on tomb sculptures and brasses. By 1400 the bosses of plaited hair were replaced by a *tressour*, a horse-shoe-shaped roll of pleated linen and false hair in a net, which may be seen on the alabaster wall tablet of Lady Foljambe at Bakewell; on the brass of Joan de la Pole at Chrisall, Essex (Pl. 43*a*) the hair seems covered by a head-dress of pleated linen. The next development (Pl. 43*b*) was to add above the wig-structure a kerchief supported by wires, so forming a horned head-dress resembling those against which continental preachers inveighed. The most usual English form (Pl. 43*c*) continued to retain the caul or net foundation and let the kerchief rise in a point on each side. The steeple head-dress, a late Burgundian fashion dear to the nineteenth-century illustrators, is unknown in England, and although on English brasses a head-dress sometimes looks like a truncated cone, this is shown by the heads of stone monu- ments (Pl. 43*d*) to be a way of depicting the horns. The roll of hair (*bourrelet*) still covered by the kerchief closes from a U- or V-form until it appears solid. Such a head-dress-wig lies on the bench behind Pygmalion (Pl. 45*b*) as he laces up the front of the gown of the image in the French *Roman de la Rose*.

In the second half of the fifteenth century the excesses of the Burgundian court were not, as is clear from the monuments, adopted in English dress. Doublets and the upper part of sleeves were padded but the shoulders were not drawn out in *mahoitres*. The diary of Jorg von Ehingen (ed. M. Letts, 1929), a knight-errant, who visited England in 1458, pre- serves the portraits of the European kings of his time. Henry VI wears a blue gown with full sleeves and a crimson collar;

[1] *Sussex Arch. Soc. Coll.* xxxvii (1890), p. 173.

James II of Scotland, known by his 'fyrie countenance', has a
short black jacket padded above the waist and shoulders. This
series of portraits show how the felt hat with a wide brim was
replacing the hood. John Russell's *Book of Nurture* (c. 1460,
E.E.T.S., 1868, pp. 176, 181) does not imply the wearing of a
great number of garments: the chamberlain must

> Se that youre souerayne haue clene shurt & breche
> a petycote, a dublett, a longe coote, if he were suche
> his hosyn well brusshed, his sokkes not to seche
> his shon or slyppers as browne as is the waturleche.

The hose would still have been of cloth, cut bias and shaped
to the leg—knitted hose were uncommon even in the sixteenth
century. The shirt and breeches were linen underclothes and
the petycote was a sort of vest under the doublet, to which a
stomacher could be added. In dressing his lord the chamberlain should:

> Furst hold to hym a petycote aboue youre brest & barme
> his dublet than after to put in bothe hys arme,
> his stomachere welle y-chaffed. . . .
> Then drawe on his sokkis & hosyn by the fure
> his shon laced or bokelid, draw them on sure;
> strike his hosyn upwarde his legge ye endure
> then trusse them up strayte to his pleasure
> then lace his dublett euery hoole. . . .

A few years later the household books of John, duke of Norfolk,[1] give details of materials and tailor's charges:

> Delyverd the vijth day of Decembr. anno vjto.K.H.vijmi. to Magnus
> chyld of the brewhows at my Lordis fyndyng, ij yards and iij qtrs. fryse for
> a cote, and ij yardes of fustain for a dowbelett. Item, a yard of canvas for
> the lynyng. Item, a yard and a half of blankett for the same dowbelett. Item,
> iij qtrs of blankett for the lynyng of his hosyn. . . .

While the trains of women's gowns continued to be ample
until the end of the fifteenth century, the sleeves as well as the
body were tight-fitting. The straining of the hair back off the
forehead demanded a new type of head-gear; the horns disappeared except for a fold along the crown of the head ending
in a point over the forehead; the stiff kerchief now stood out at

---

[1] *Roxburghe Club* (1844), p. 512.

PLATE 45

a. Foxton, *Cosmographia: Sexta ymago.* The Moon

A youth in a short gown, half-brown, half-blue with fur trimming and bag sleeves: a gold crescent on his head: girt with a napkin, holding two golden ewers: the sign of the Crab embroidered on his chest and a full moon below

b. Roman de la Rose. Pygmalion and Galatea

PLATE 46

H. Holbein. Sir Thomas More and his family

the back of the head. The real name of this so-called 'butterfly' head-dress is unknown; it is common on incised brasses *c*. 1480, and may, like the Burgundian head-dresses still worn by the sisters at the Hospices de Beaune, have been fixed by pins. Lappets sometimes hang down over the ears.

As so many of the monumental effigies represent widows, and the younger women (their daughters) are depicted less clearly, it is hard to say when the medieval sideless *cotte* dis-appeared, since Englishwomen did not take over the simplified Italian Renaissance style or indulge in the cutting, slashing, ribboning, and exuberance of the German. The square or horizontal neck opening is a marked feature, but at the begin-ning of the sixteenth century the types of dress can be listed rather than described in detail. The apparel devised for Mary, the sister of Henry VIII, at her marriage with Louis XII of France in 1514 includes kirtles of the French and after the English fashion, gowns of the French fashion, after 'myllayn' (Milan) fashion (these mostly lined with cloth of gold) and after the English fashion (these all with wide or else 'strait' sleeves). The hood alone at the turn of the century was still characteristically English; worn over a stiff caul, it now framed the face in four sides of a hexagon, forming the so-called 'gable' hood which is associated with the portraits of early Tudor ladies.

If reliance is placed, as it must be, on portraits and monu-ments, men's costume was predominantly German in style. The flat cap with its turned-up brim cut here and there and ornamented with a brooch, the pleated shirt with narrow em-broidery at the collar, the doublet with low neck, exaggerated shoulders, and chest often slit in long slashes, the short gown, with a roll-over collar and full sleeves, the blunt-toed shoes also slashed, all these are the German-style dress of Charles V adopted by Henry VIII or by Francis I. Only the excessive puffs and ribbon-panes (slashes) and the knee-length trailing breeches distinguish the *lanzknecht* from the English or French soldier.

In the More family group (Pl. 46) Henry Patenson in the

background shows how the middle classes took up the fashion. The ladies in the same group all wear dresses in a style which, if Holbein's influence was really so extensive, seems to have remained fixed almost till 1540. The basic garment is a kirtle with a stomacher laced in front; the square neck-opening is modestly filled with a partlet or neckerchief, or a shirt; the full sleeves, sometimes cut (paned) longitudinally, are attached to the bodice; over all is worn a gown with full sleeves and cuffs turned back to reveal a fur lining. The 'gable' hood over the elaborately folded coif is beginning to vary; Cecilia Heron and Anne Cresacre wear a tight linen coif rounded over the forehead, and on top of this a hood with earpieces and a kerchief falling behind, somewhat like the Elizabethan 'French hood'. For the early Tudor period it is not easy to find good illustrations of lower-class or country dress; rather than rely on the group of pictures at Hampton Court and elsewhere representing the Field of the Cloth of Gold, it is better to turn to Foxe's *Book of Martyrs*, in which the woodcuts give some general impression of what ordinary citizens and country people were wearing. The men mostly had loose coats with waist-belts, tight cloth hose, and boots rather than shoes. Women wore gowns, petticoats, and kerchieves about head and neck. London citizens, both men and women, are distinguished by flat woollen caps. At the stake the men are shown to be wearing shirts and the women shifts.

Ecclesiastical and liturgical dress may be briefly mentioned. Vestments at the beginning of the period correspond roughly to ceremonial dress, the chasuble and cope to the robe and cloak, the alb, rochet, and dalmatic to the surcoat and tabard, the cassock to the gown, and the surplice to the *chainse*. Later the copes, which open out to a semicircle, the chasubles, and dalmatics came to be decorated with orphreys and apparels, embroidered in the *opus anglicanum* techniques for which England was famous throughout Europe. Other ecclesiastical garments were the white amice tied over the shoulders, the almuce or fur cape, the stole, the maniple, as well as the bishop's vestments— the mitre, buskins, and gloves.

Each of the religious orders had its own habit, distinguished by form and colour, always including the cassock (*tunica*) fastened with a cord, over which was worn the cowl (*cucullus*), a loose, wide-sleeved, hooded gown. The dress of the orders of nuns was more elaborate, and corresponds fairly closely to that of fashionable widows at the time when the particular order was founded. The elaboration is especially noticeable in the pleated wimple or *barbe* hiding the neck, and in the various forms of head-dress under the hood.

Academic dress in the middle ages is hard to distinguish from ecclesiastical; caps and gowns did not take their characteristic forms until the sixteenth century; indeed, while the hood has a medieval origin, the cut of the gown and the square cap show their affinity to Germany and the Reformation.

WORKS FOR REFERENCE

CROSSLEY, F. *English Church Monuments, 1150–1550* (1921).

DRUITT, HERBERT. *Costume in Brasses* (1906).

ENLART, CAMILLE. *Manuel d'Archéologie française*, iii, 'Le costume' (1916).

EVANS, JOAN. *Dress in Mediaeval France* (1952).

FAIRHOLT, F. W. *Costume in England*, ed. Viscount Dillon (1896); *Satirical Songs and Poems on Costume* (Percy Soc., 1849).

GARDNER, ARTHUR. *Alabaster Tombs* (1940).

GAY, VICTOR. *Glossaire archéologique* (2 vols., 1883, 1928).

HARMAND, ADRIEN. *Jeanne d'Arc, ses Costumes, son Armure* (1929).

HARTLEY, DOROTHY. *Medieval Costume and Life* (1931).

KELLY, F. H., and SCHWABE, R. *A Short History of Costume and Armour*, i (1931); *Historic Costume 1490–1790* (1929).

LUNDQUIST, EVA R. *La Mode et son Vocabulaire* (1950).

PLANCHE, J. R. *A Cyclopaedia of Costume* (1876).

POST, PAUL. *Die französisch-niederländische Männertracht im Zeitalter der Spätgotik* (1910).

STOTHARD, C. A. *Monumental Effigies* (1817).

STRUTT, JOSEPH. *Dress and Habits of the People of England* (2 vols., 1796–9).

STENTON, SIR FRANK. Editor. *The Bayeux Tapestry* (1957).

X. ARMS AND ARMOUR

ARMS and armour played a prominent part in the history of the middle ages. Not only did they settle the fate of nations and encompass the deaths of kings, but the esteem in which they were held made them the subject of great artistic skill. The profession of arms was the only one open to a gentleman, and although England had a comparatively peaceful internal history compared with other countries on the continent, England's possessions abroad, and especially the Hundred Years War, involved Englishmen in a great deal of fighting.

The subject can be studied for the tactical part which it played in the shaping of history, and more especially in its technical evolution as one of the most sensitive branches of the applied arts. Evidence is provided from a number of sources, all equally valuable. Firstly, from the examination of surviving examples of arms and armour that have come down to us; secondly, from their pictorial and sculptured representations in medieval art; and thirdly, from the particulars of manufacture and possession which are supplied by documents, especially inventories and account rolls.

The pleasure given to the medieval eye by fine arms is well exemplified by the illuminator of manuscripts, who delighted to fill his coloured miniatures with figures armed cap-à-pie in the pages of romances, chronicles, and religious books.

Arms and armour are both of great antiquity. Man is himself a physical weakling and needed from the earliest times some kind of weapon to preserve his life against wild beasts and to hunt them for his food. The ox-goad served as a spear, and the axe was, and still is, as much a domestic as a military instrument. A great impetus was given to the craft by the

discovery of the malleability of metal, firstly bronze and then iron.

The evolution of defensive armour was governed by two opposing considerations; firstly, the endless struggle between the forces of attack and defence, for every new weapon had to be countered by new armour and vice versa; secondly, the contest between the need for mobility and the desire for safety. In Greek, Etruscan, and Roman times the importance of mobility was never lost sight of, and defensive armour was confined to a shield, carried on the left arm, which was a movable defence, a helmet, a cuirass, and greaves on the shins. The introduction of the stirrup to the west during the Dark Ages enabled the horseman for the first time to be armoured from head to foot. He was no longer top-heavy and so loosely seated that he could easily be pushed out of his saddle. A sure seat enabled him to couch his lance under his arm and put the whole impetus of his horse behind his thrust. It led to the armouring of not only the man but of the horse itself.

Throughout the middle ages the queen of weapons was the sword. Its invention in early times came comparatively late, but its value as a thrusting and striking weapon with both point and edge was enhanced by great improvements in the working of metals. The sword introduced to western Europe by the Vikings was the prototype of the medieval sword. They had discovered the virtue of the carbonization of iron into steel. Their blades, which were hammered out from many strips of iron, folded and refolded, often present as a result a patterned surface known as damascening. This must not be confused with the other use of the word, for inlaying with precious metals. There are swords famous in romantic literature which bore proper names, such as Arthur's *Excalibur* and Roland's *Durendal*.

During the greater part of the Dark Ages and the first half of the middle ages the warrior who was rich enough to afford them wore a conical iron helmet and a mail shirt of interlinked riveted iron rings. This armament can be seen in all its splendour of gold enrichment and coloured enamel in the objects found in the grave of an Anglo-Saxon king of the seventh

century recently discovered at Sutton Hoo in Suffolk (Pl. 47*a*). This shirt of mail is the byrnie or 'tangled war-net' referred to by Beowulf. Mail, which takes its name through the French *maille*, the Italian *maglia*, and from the Latin word *macula* which means a dot or spot and hence the mesh of a net, is of unknown antiquity. It has been found on the site of Nineveh, on Roman sites of all dates, and is sculptured with unmistakable clarity upon Trajan's column in Rome. It was not, however, much worn by the Romans, who preferred, as already mentioned, plate or hooped armour of bronze, and later iron.

The construction of a shirt of mail requires very considerable skill and also time, because it is composed of many thousands of separately forged links, each of which had later to be riveted after being linked to others. Recent research has discovered how, by the use of special punches, mail could be put together more quickly than had hitherto seemed possible. Nevertheless, a shirt of mail was a very valuable garment, and at first could be afforded only by chieftains. But mail does not wear out quickly as does a cloth garment, and the supply must have been cumulative. Both horsemen and foot soldiers are shown in mail shirts and conical helmets with nasals (for partial pro-tection of the face) in the Bayeaux Tapestry (or, more cor-rectly, needlework), which commemorates in a long series of scenes the events before and during William I's invasion of England (Pl. 48). The Normans are shown carrying long, kite-shaped shields, and some of the Anglo-Saxons have round shields. The duke himself and his half-brother Odo, bishop of Bayeaux, are among the few to wear mail stockings. They wield lances and swords; and the 'bearded' axe, which had been *par excellence* the weapon of the Vikings, is still prominent (Pl. 47*b*). The fact that the campaign was decided by the death of King Harold, who received an arrow in his eye, is of significance. Archery had not yet reached the high standard of skill of the thirteenth century in England, but this fatality was governed by the stage to which the evolution of defensive armour had then reached. If Harold had been able to wear a visored helmet of the kind used in the fourteenth

PLATE 47

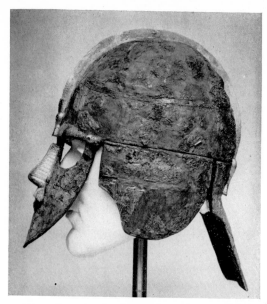

a. Helmet from the ship-burial at Sutton Hoo, of iron overlaid with gold, seventh century. British Museum

b. Viking 'bearded' axe-head, ninth century. British Museum

c. Detail from the Winchester Bible of warrior wearing helmet with nasal, shirt of mail, kite-shaped shield, sword, and lance [topped with a pennon], *c*. 1150. Winchester Cathedral

PLATE 48

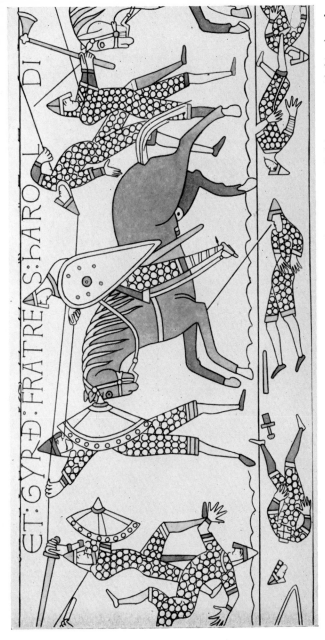

Detail from the Bayeux tapestry of the Battle of Hastings (after C. A. Stothard). Norman mailed horseman with kite-shaped shield charging Englishmen with round shields and axes

century he might well have escaped alive from the battle and rallied England against the invader.

Sometimes the padded garments worn under mail were regarded as sufficient protection in themselves. A contemporary record of the battle of Arsuf (1191) describes the Crusaders as bristling with the arrows which had lodged in their quilted gambesons (wambais) but done no harm to their wearers. In the Assize of Arms of Henry II (1181) it was laid down that the holder of a knight's fee should have a mail shirt, helmet, shield, and lance, and a free burgess a wambais, an iron cap, and a lance.

The kind of armour shown in the Bayeaux Tapestry and the Winchester Bible (Pl. 47c) continued in use for a considerable time, but at the end of the twelfth century one notices certain changes. One is the introduction of the great helm which covered the whole head and face in place of, or in addition to, the open conical helmet. It is represented on the second seal of Richard I (Pl. 49a). Secondly, the long, kite-shaped shield was shortened to a triangular shape with curved sides (Pl. 49b). The mail shirt (hauberk or habergeon) was shortened and the skirt reached no farther than the knee. Pictorial evidence shows that the earlier long hauberk reaching to the calf was worn over an even longer linen garment. From now the position was reversed and a sleeveless surcoat with long skirt was worn over the shortened mail shirt.

With the advent of heraldry, every portion of a knight's or squire's equipment that could be so decorated was made to serve in establishing his identity. The shield was painted with formal heraldic devices, which had previously occurred in a primitive form. Heraldic charges were embroidered on the surcoat of the man and the trapper of the horse, and when, later, crests were introduced they were prominently displayed on the summit of his helm and even on the poll of his charger. About the middle of the thirteenth century there is a further heraldic embellishment in the form of aillettes, which were rectangular pieces of leather laced to the shoulders. It used to be thought that these had a protective intention, and possibly that may

have been a consideration, but they were obviously so loose and unwieldy that one is led to think that their main reason was decorative.

A word of warning is necessary in interpreting the various formulae used for the portrayal of mail in contemporary art. To draw every link on a small scale was impossible, and lines of dots or circles were used, and sometimes a very close depiction is found on monumental brasses or paintings where there was room for it. But a popular short-hand depiction of mail in the thirteenth and fourteenth centuries has in the past been interpreted as mail of another construction called 'banded' mail. This is unsupported by any other evidence, either from finds or written sources, and must be accepted as no more than a facile way of representing ordinary interlinked mail. Mail constructed of links whose ends were merely butted together instead of riveted did not find favour in Europe, and examples are almost always of oriental origin.

In the twelfth and thirteenth centuries the armoured horseman dominated the battlefield and rode down the ill-organized levies of feudal footmen. When the lance was shivered, the horseman had recourse to the sword which hung on his left side and the axe or mace at his saddle-bow. The sword of this period had somewhat longer quillons than its predecessor, the Viking sword, and the pommel, which formed a counterpoise to the weight of the blade and made the weapon easier to wield, was either circular or brazil-nut shaped. The blade was two-edged, with a hollow down the centre of each side, and tapered to a sharp point (Pl. 50). It was frequently inscribed with letters inlaid in metal, gold, silver, or tin, but most frequently copper or brass, and sometimes bore the maker's mark. The earliest of these are names like 'Hitlr' and 'Ulfbehrt'; and later the running wolf of Passau, or a crozier, show how the export of blades spread from centres of manufacture to the rest of Europe.

An alternative to the straight two-edged sword was a curved and single-edged weapon known as a falchion. It was depicted on the thirteenth-century walls of the Painted Chamber at

Westminster, and examples survive from the fourteenth century. A falchion and a small circular fist-shield are shown wielded by the grotesque figures in the margins of the Luttrell psalter (*c.* 1340) (Fig. 58).

Mail had the great advantage of flexibility, but its weight was considerable, and despite the wearing of a padded gambeson or wambais beneath, it could not prevent bruising of the body or broken bones. A violent thrust could break and drive links

FIG. 58. Grotesque figure with curved falchion and fist-shield
c. 1340, from the Luttrell Psalter

into the wound and make it septic. The advantage of plate armour was that it opposed a rigid instead of a flexible surface to a blow.

In the course of the second half of the thirteenth century, small pieces of plate armour were applied to the shoulders, elbows, and knees, probably of moulded leather (*cuir bouilli*). In those days the healing of a broken joint was a difficult matter. It is also probable that some kind of plate protection for the body was worn beneath the mail shirt. This and the surcoat prevent its being seen in pictorial representations of the times, but there are occasional references in manuscripts to *plastrons de fer*, either of leather or iron, and some such defence is discernible in one of the early thirteenth-century effigies in the Temple church (unfortunately badly damaged by fire in 1940), and

on one in Pershore abbey in Worcestershire. The hood of mail was separated from the hauberk to form a coif which reached to the chest and shoulders, and enabled a helmet to be dispensed with. Lighter substitutes for the helm were the brimmed war-hat (*chapel-de-fer*) or a simple steel cap. The sleeves of the mail hauberk were extended to form mittens for the hands, and the great helm, which at first had been flat topped, became dome-like towards the end of the century. This was a great advantage, as it presented a glancing surface to a downright blow (Pl. 53).

The couching of the lance mentioned earlier, and the high, built-up saddles, made possible the recreation of jousting. Mock battles had always been a pastime of a military society. There are early mentions of the 'Troy game', or 'Round Table game'. Tournaments, introduced into England in the twelfth century, are described by Matthew Paris as the *ludus Gallicus*, which clearly shows their French origin. They are not to be confused with the judicial combat or 'wager of battle', for which special arms were sometimes prescribed, when combat-ants fought on foot with clubs and square shields.

If, as we have seen, the early middle ages can bear the title of the 'age of mail', the fourteenth century must be called the 'age of transition', because it saw the passing of the predominance of mail to the predominance of armour of beaten plate. As the skill and knowledge of the armourer improved and he used better material, it became possible to make additions of plate armour, constructed in such a way as to respond to the move-ments of the body (Pl. 53*b*). Body armour of hoops of iron or small plates riveted together were tried. Plates of simple form strapped over the mail (Pl. 51) were used to reinforce the limbs. During the first half of the fourteenth century the fully armed man was weighed down with such a succession of de-fences, not only the padded garments under the mail but plate additions on top, as to render rapid movement impossible and a fall from the saddle in the thick of battle fatal. In the middle of the century experiments were made with lighter materials, such as *cuir bouilli* and even horn, and colour and gilding

PLATE 49

b. Ivory chessman. Middle of the thirteenth century. Showing flat-topped helm, surcoat over mail, and straight-topped shield. Ashmolean Museum

a. Second seal of King Richard I, d. 1199, showing crested helm and mail shirt worn over a flowing undergarment

PLATE 50

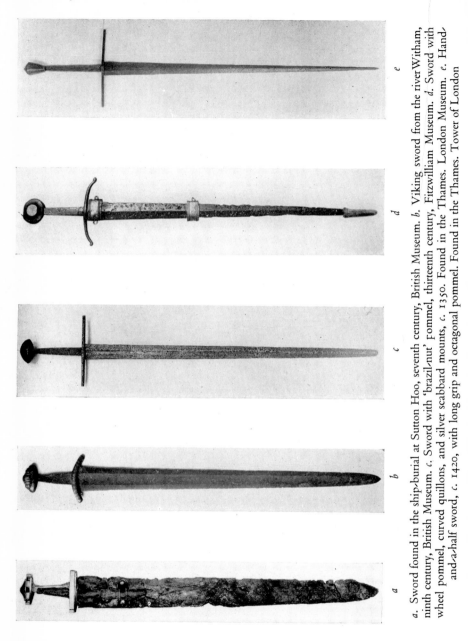

a. Sword found in the ship-burial at Sutton Hoo, seventh century, British Museum. b. Viking sword from the river Witham, ninth century, British Museum. c. Sword with 'brazil-nut' pommel, thirteenth century, Fitzwilliam Museum. d. Sword with wheel pommel, curved quillons, and silver scabbard mounts, c. 1350. Found in the Thames. London Museum. e. Hand-and-a-half sword, c. 1420, with long grip and octagonal pommel. Found in the Thames. Tower of London

were freely used. The flowing surcoat was cut down to what has been called the 'skirted jupon' (Pl. 51). The length of the old garment caused the death of Sir John Chandos in 1370, when he dismounted to fight on foot and became entangled in its skirts. Rowel spurs had replaced the earlier pointed 'prick' form by 1330.

During the course of the fourteenth century, with its many battles, the full carapace of articulated plate armour was evolved, and mail took thereafter a secondary place. This process was greatly assisted by the development of certain centres of the craft, especially the city of Milan, where metal of the finest quality was produced and hammered to the most subtle forms conforming to the human anatomy.

Apart from documentary evidence in which inventories specify armour of Milan and bills mention payments to Italian merchants, we could easily guess that many sculptured effigies and brasses of English knights and squires of the fourteenth century represent the armour made at Milan by comparing them with such examples as exist. The earliest example of any completeness is the harness of one of the Vogts of Matsch in the family armoury at Churburg, a castle on the frontier of Italy and Austria (Pl. 54 *a, b*). The engraved brass decoration of its borders and short cuffed gauntlets are the same as those seen on many English monuments, manuscripts, and wall paintings.

By the second half of the fourteenth century the transition was nearly complete. The fashion for wearing a close, tight-fitting jupon in place of the surcoat prevents us from seeing in English medieval art the breast-plate itself, but a globose appearance of the body, as on the Black Prince's effigy (Pl. 52), makes it quite clear that beneath the jupon there was some solid defence in one piece, such as a breast-plate would imply. This is confirmed when the jupon was discarded in the early years of the next century and a breast-plate with a *fauld*, or skirt of hooped plates or lames was revealed. Mail was still used as protection for the interior joints of armpits and elbows, and the conical bascinet had suspended from it on staples called *vervelles* a

tippet of mail to guard the throat and neck. At the same time the improved, but heavy, great helm was abandoned for use on the battle-field, its place being taken by the pointed, egg-shaped bascinet furnished with a movable visor, sometimes hinged on the brow but usually in England pivoted at the sides. The visor was deliberately drawn out into a sharp point in front to present a glancing surface (Pl. 56). The great helm retained its place in the lists.

It is about this time that we begin to find special forms of armour made for the tournament, as distinct from armour for war, called 'hosting harness'. Some of these pieces are mentioned for the first time in the inventory of Sir Simon Burley (d. 1388). The earliest medieval plate armour of English origin to survive are several great helms of the fourteenth century and early fifteenth century. Whereas pagan times provided valuable evidence of armour buried with its owners in graves, Christianity relegated armour to the insignia hung over the monument of the deceased, which in the majority of cases has long since disappeared. The 'Funeral Achievements', as they were called, of the Black Prince (Pl. 55) provide the best surviving example of an English gentlemen's armour of the third quarter of the fourteenth century. They comprise a helm forged of five pieces riveted together, its crest of a lion standing on a cap of maintenance, a pair of copper-gilt gauntlets with short cuffs and the knuckles decorated with little lions, a shield of light wood coated with canvas and gesso, to which have been applied the quartered arms of the fleur-de-lys of France and the lions of England. The sword is missing, but the scabbard remains. The prince's effigy 'in his arms as he lived', cast in bronze, lies on the tomb chest below.

In place of the loose sword-belt of the thirteenth and early fourteenth centuries we now find a horizontal hip-belt, known as a baldric, often in the form of a band of highly ornamental brooch-like components. There is one addition; the short dagger (misericord), balancing the sword which hung from the left side, was attached to the right hip. Daggers took several forms. Most effigies and brasses show rondel or quillon dag-

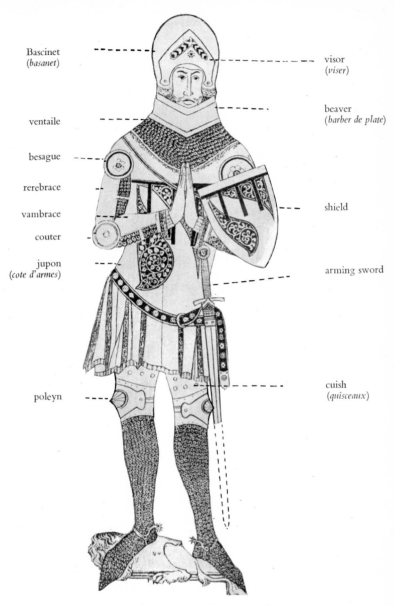

PLATE 51

Bascinet
(*basanet*)

visor
(*viser*)

beaver
(*barber de plate*)

ventaile

besague

rerebrace

vambrace

couter

jupon
(*cote d'armes*)

shield

arming sword

poleyn

cuish
(*quisceaux*)

Figure of the deceased from the brass of Sir Hugh
Hastings, d. 1347, in Elsing Church, Norfolk, showing
mixed armour of mail and plate, with the names of the
different parts

PLATE 52

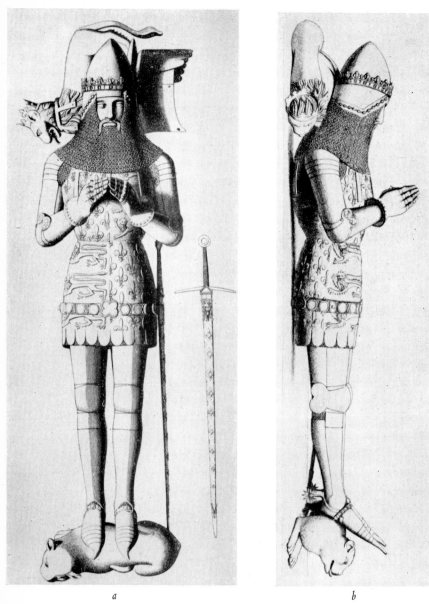

a   *b*

Gilt-bronze effigy of Edward, the Black Prince, d. 1376, on his tomb in Canterbury Cathedral (after Stothard), showing bascinet with mail aventail, tight-fitting jupon, and articulated plate-armour enclosing the limbs

gers, but a very popular form of dagger for all classes in England was the ballock-knife (Fig. 59c), so called from the two lobes

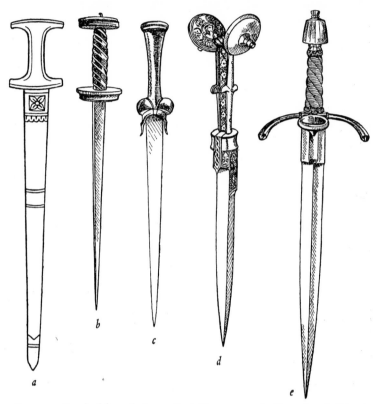

FIG. 59. *a.* Baselard from the brass of a civilian, *c.* 1370, in Shottesbrook Church, Berks. *b.* Rondell dagger, fourteenth to fifteenth century (Guildhall Museum, London). *c.* Ballock dagger, fourteenth to early sixteenth century (Guildhall Museum, London). *d.* Ear-dagger, Hispano-moresque (Armouries, Tower of London). *e.* Left-hand dagger to match a rapier, second half sixteenth century

which protected the hand. It lasted from the fourteenth century to the second quarter of the seventeenth century.

The armour worn between 1360 and 1430 was simple and practical; that for the legs now consisted of plate cuisses for the thighs, poleyns (knees), and greaves made in two pieces hinged together, and laminated sabatons, ending in short points, for the feet. These correspond almost exactly to similar elements for

the arms, notably a laminated rerebrace for the shoulders overlapping the vambrace for the lower arm. This last consisted
of a cannon, or tubular defence for the fore-arm, hinged longitudinally and strapped together like the greaves, a pointed,
cup-like elbow-piece with heart-shaped plates at the sides to
protect the tendons, and a further plate extending part of the
way along the upper arm. It is necessary to mention this in
order to correct some writers who regard the rerebrace as the
armour of the upper arm to the elbow and the vambrace as
that for the fore-arm below the elbow. All elements were
riveted together in such a way that they were flexible, and this
flexibility was further increased by allowing the rivets to
operate in a slot known as the sliding rivet. With the full
development of plate armour not only mail but the shield also
took a less prominent place. Shields disappear from English
effigies and brasses after the middle of the fourteenth century,
and the last instance is that of two effigies of about 1370 at
Dorchester in Dorset. Plate armour had made this defence
redundant.

The horse, with its large and vulnerable body, also shared
in the development of plate armour (Pl. 58). A steel chamfron
was fitted to the front of the head, a laminated crinet on the
neck, a peytral on the breast, and plates were placed over the
flanks; the high peak or cantle of the saddle was also plated.
Sometimes this armour was of leather, painted. The arming of
the horse was called barding. The brilliantly coloured textile
trapper continued in use until the fifteenth century and then
passed to the service of the tournament only.

The introduction of the plate beaver and gorget replaced the
mail aventail or camail round the throat and chin in the first
quarter of the fifteenth century. By this addition the full 'all
white' armour of plate enclosing the wearer from top to toe was
completed (Pl. 57). The apex and pointed visor of the bascinet
became rounded. England is rich in sculptured effigies and
brasses which show the plate armour worn by Englishmen
throughout the fifteenth century. That Englishmen still looked
towards Milan as a source of supply, or at any rate as the leader of

PLATE 53

a. Stone effigy of William Longespée, Earl of Salisbury, d. 1226, in Salisbury Cathedral (after Stothard), showing mail coif and early heraldry on shield

b. Brass of Sir William Fitzralph, *c.* 1323, in Pebmarsh Church, Essex (after Waller). Showing additions of plate armour to the limbs

PLATE 54

a. Italian armour (Milanese), *c.* 1450, from the Castle of Churburg in South Tyrol, and now in the Corporation Museum and Art Gallery, Glasgow

b. Brass of Sir John Barnard, d. 1451, in Isleham Church, Cambs., showing Milanese plate-armour of the time

fashion, is shown by their accurate portrayal of developments which took place there in the second quarter of the fifteenth century. The previous symmetrical appearance of the armoured man gave way to a loading of the left or bridle arm with large plate defences, enveloping reinforcements on the elbows, and increased protection to the shoulders in the form of large pauldrons. Gauntlets were now given mittens instead of separate fingers.

A certain amount of complete armour of Italian make of the middle and second half of the fifteenth century, stamped with the marks of Milanese craftsmen, is still in existence and can be compared with English effigies—for example, the effigy of Richard Beauchamp, earl of Warwick, who died in 1439 but whose monument was not erected until 1453. This shows an exact replica of a fine Milanese harness of the middle years of the century (Pl. 54). It is significant that when the earl of Derby and Thomas Mowbray, duke of Norfolk, prepared for their abortive duel before Richard II in 1398, one sent to Milan and the other to Germany for his armour.

Writers on armour have often described the armour of the fifteenth century as 'Gothic'. This term applies more cor-rectly to the German variety, whose forms and ornamental details reproduced in miniature the architecture of the times (Pl. 58). The toes of sabatons were extended to excessive length, the fauld was shortened, and a pair of pointed plates, known as tassets, hung from it by straps. The breast-plate was often made of two parts, the lower one overlapping the other and rising to a point in the centre; the back-plate was often laminated, the edges of the plates were cusped. Italian armour of the fifteenth century shows smoother and rounder forms, but the gauntlets have pointed cuffs and cusped plates below the knee, which shows distinct Gothic influence. The centres of the German craft were at Nürnberg and Augsburg, and by the last quarter of the century they were producing armour that was in every way equal in quality to the products of Milan. These elegant, graceful coverings of the human form are among the most aesthetically satisfying products of the armourer's craft.

The applied borders of gilt brass were often pierced with tracery, the surfaces broken by fan-like flutings and ripplings which did nothing to weaken the strength of the plates. The essential requirement in the production of armour, namely, practic-ability, was still obeyed. The making of a pair of greaves was no easy task, and the skill with which the subtle lines of shin and calf and ankle were worked are beyond praise.

About the middle of the fifteenth century the bascinet was replaced by the sallet, though it was retained, as the great helm had been, for use in the lists. The sallet in Germany was gener-ally rounded over the brow and produced to a long, pointed tail at the back of the neck (Pls. 56, 58). Corresponding Italian sal-lets or barbutes are generally taller and less elongated, and some frankly copied the Boeotian helmet of classical times. English-men, who had a special liking for this light form of headgear, seemed to prefer a style half-way between the two, as sallets pre-served in English churches testify. The recently evolved Italian close-helmet, called an armet, appears to have been less popu-lar in this country.

For some years after the rejection of the jupon early in the century, armour was usually worn without any textile cover-ing so that the full beauty of the glazed steel could be seen and admired. In the second half of the fifteenth century one notices the wearing of a tabard, a loose garment with short sleeves that bore the warrior's heraldic insignia or badges. During the middle of the century the pole-axe became a favourite weapon for fighting in the ring on foot (*champ-clos*), and surviving examples show how well this weapon lent itself to the elegancies of the Gothic style (Pl. 64*a*). The helmet used for this sport was the bascinet of former times.

Edward III had abandoned the old and inefficient feudal levy in favour of raising troops by contract. Gentlemen of posi-tion, or professional soldiers of small rank but high reputation, enrolled under them men-at-arms, archers, and footmen to serve them on a business basis in the French wars. In the fif-teenth century the English archers, whose importance had been growing since the wars of the thirteenth century, became a

PLATE 55

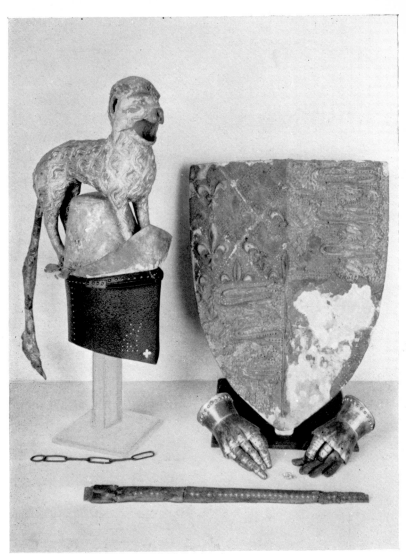

The funeral 'achievements' of Edward, the Black Prince, d. 1376, hung over his monument in Canterbury Cathedral, consisting of helm with crest, shield, gauntlets of copper-gilt, and leather scabbard of his sword

PLATE 56

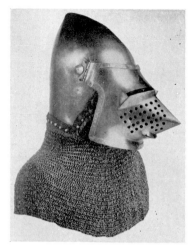

b. Sallet with movable visor, second half of fifteenth century, in Witton-le-Wear Church, Durham

a. Visored bascinet with brass borders and mail aventail, c. 1390, from the Castle of Churburg, now in the Tower of London

c. Armet (early close-helmet) in the Italian style, fifteenth century, in Buckland Church, Berks.

d. English jousting helm known as the 'Brocas helm', c. 1500. Tower of London

PLATE 57

Miniature of St. George and the Dragon from 'King Henry VI's Book of Hours' in the Bodleian Library, showing full plate armour, the bascinet with rounded visor, and plate gorget, *c.* 1420

PLATE 58

German Gothic armour for man and horse, made at Landshut for Pancraz von Freyberg, *c.* 1475, formerly in his castle of Hohenaschau and now in the Wallace Collection

decisive factor in battle. Falkirk and Homilden hill against the Scots, Crécy, Poitiers, and Agincourt against the French, were all won by the disciplined skill of the English archers, who 'shot so wholly together'; but the armoured cavalry still played their part, and each was necessary to the other. The practice of archery on the village green was officially encouraged, and the archer was well paid in time of war. Archers had of necessity to dispense with cumbrous armour, although the looting of the battlefield and the taking of prisoners must often have won them possession of it. The archer wore an open helmet (during the second half of the fifteenth century the sallet), and a short-sleeved mail shirt or brigandine sufficed for the body (Pl. 63). He protected his left wrist from being chafed by the bow-string by wearing a leather or horn wristlet known as a bracer. He defended himself by driving a sharp stake into the ground in front of him, and this, being multiplied, provided a fence to cavalry. He also availed himself of a large wooden, hide-covered shield known as a pavise. Its bottom edge rested on the ground, and it could be stood up by the support of a prop behind. His other weapon was a sword or a maul (a large mallet) with which he joined the mêlée when the shooting was over and both forces had joined in hand-to-hand combat. The sur-name Fletcher, common today, signified the man who 'fledged' the arrow with feathers. These were mostly goose, but peacock was used for show. The shafts were pointed with steel heads, those of Sheffield steel being regarded as the most penetrating. The cross-bow was not much used in England because the trained English archer could shoot so much more quickly with the longbow. Crossbows could be spanned in four ways: first, by muscular strength, the foot being placed on the bow and the string pulled back by hand; secondly, by a lever called a 'goat's foot'; thirdly, by winding an iron ratchet with a handle, called in English a 'rack' and in French *cric* or *cranequin*; and fourthly, by a kind of windlass; although not particularly common in England; this was known in Germany as the *Englische winde*. Its cumbrousness made it more useful for siege work rather than in the field.

As a result of the casualties inflicted on horses by archers, English knights and their French opposites often dismounted and fought together on foot with shortened lances, swords, and axes. The sword became longer than the old single-handed arming sword, and sometimes had a grip long enough to accommodate both hands when necessary. In this form it was used as much for thrusting as for striking when fighting on foot.

There has been considerable dispute whether cannon were used at the battle of Crécy or not. No English text mentions the fact, and it has been suggested that the French texts which refer to it use it as an excuse for their defeat. However that may be, cannon had been used in the field some years earlier, and were also employed in naval engagements. The recovery of Normandy by the French in the second quarter of the fifteenth century was much assisted by the use of cannon (Fig. 60). Cannon led to the invention of the hand-gun, which was at first a tube of very small bore mounted on a wooden stock and ignited by hand. The last battle of the Hundred Years War, at Castillon in 1453, when the great Talbot's army was slaughtered by the French, was largely won by their artillery, and Talbot himself was dispatched with a hand-gun. These, however, were only beginnings, and the full exploitation of artillery had to wait until the next century (Fig. 60).

The turn of the century at 1500 closes an era in the history of arms. Gothic armour gave place to armour of a new fashion evolved under the influence of the Renaissance, and that the old armies of men-at-arms, spearmen, and archers, taking their orders from individual leaders, were replaced by national armies equipped on a national scale. Firearms had passed their nonage and were handled by trained men, and mathematicians were making gunnery into a science. Yet the craft of the armourer continued to supply men of wealth with military evidence of their rank. One must recognize that the workshops of Milan and south Germany produced during the first half of the sixteenth century some of the finest armour, from the technical point of view, ever made. The Emperor Charles V

was a lavish patron, and the dynastic armouries at Madrid and Vienna are the greatest in the world, and the bulk of their con-tents date from this century. Henry VII's decrees against livery and maintenance put an end to private armies in Eng-land, and apart from that in the Royal collections and the later and minor armour of the Civil War, little native armour has survived in this country.

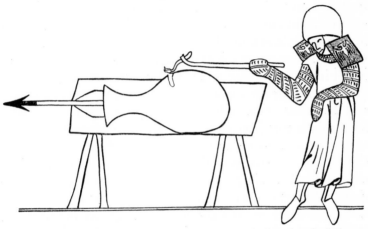

FIG. 60. Early cannon from the manuscript Treatise of Walter de Milemete *De Nobilitatibus, Sapientiis et Prudentiis Regum,* c. 1327, in the library at Christ Church, Oxford (Roxburghe Club, 1913); showing a vase-shaped cannon ejecting a jardin and touched off by a soldier armed like a knight in steel cap, mail shirt and surcoat, and heraldic ailettes

Decoration was brought forward a further stage by the newly found art of etching with acid, an art first devised by the armourers themselves, and also by embossing and damas-cening with gold (Pls. 59b, 62a). Embossing with the hammer which enabled the surface to be enriched with classical scenes and floral ornament in the half-round, was from a military point of view heretical, for it abandoned the principle of the glancing surface. But it was in keeping with the spirit of the age, and enhanced the wearer in the eyes of all. It was eminently suitable for the pageantry and parade that sur-rounded a Renaissance prince.

When Henry VIII (Pl. 59a). came to the throne he had

inherited a rich treasury from his father, and was endowed
with great physical strength and energy for which he found
an outlet in the tournament. The Field of the Cloth of Gold,
which lasted for twenty-eight days and entailed immense preparations, was the biggest tournament ever held. It was natural
that he should not wish to be beholden to his rival monarchs
on the Continent for armour made in Milan, then under
French domination, or from south Germany, then under the
emperor. Although there had been an active Armourers' Guild
in London at least from about 1322, which occupied the site in
Coleman street on which its hall still stands, Henry decided to
have his own workshop and to staff it with men of continental
training. He set up a workshop in his manor at Greenwich,
and the names of the craftsmen employed show that they were
for the most part foreigners. They are often referred to in contemporary documents as the 'Almayns'. None the less, the
Greenwich workshops quickly evolved a national style. It is
characterized by simple outlines and solidity (Pl. 60). Although subject to contemporary changes in form and fashion,
its special characteristics continued throughout the sixteenth
century and only disappeared in the reign of Charles I, when
the days of armour were over.

The structural peculiarities that enable Greenwich-made
armour to be easily recognized are the humpy build of the
pauldrons of lames of equal breadth, the formation of the
elbow-pieces in two parts, and the concave outline of the visor
of the close-helmet (Pl. 62a). In its original form Greenwich
armour can be said to be a compromise between the Milanese
and the German styles. In the second half of the century German influence prevailed, but it retained its own special features
and sturdy character when decadence had set in elsewhere. It
is well represented in the armouries of the Tower of London.
Greenwich workmen were the king's own servants, wore his
livery, and were paid from his privy purse. To have an armour
made at Greenwich required a royal licence, and one must not
think of the Greenwich workshops as a commercial under-
taking, as were some of the great workshops in Germany and

PLATE 59

a

b

c

Drawings from a contemporary book on Henry VIII's army in the British
Museum showing (*a*) King Henry VIII, (*b*) an officer of the king's bodyguard
with pole-axe or 'spear', and (*c*) a hackbut man with match-lock gun, match,
and powder flask

PLATE 60

a. Armour of King Henry VIII made in his own workshops at Greenwich *c*. 1535. Windsor Castle. Reproduced by gracious permission of Her Majesty the Queen

b. Armour of Robert Dudley, Earl of Leicester, made in the Royal workshops at Greenwich *c*. 1585, decorated with the ragged staff, in the Tower of London

PLATE 61

b. Portrait by an unknown artist of Henry Windsor, 5th Baron Windsor, showing him wearing a German armour with etched decoration, dated 1588, belonging to the Earl of Plymouth

a. Portrait of a member of the royal bodyguard known as the 'Gentlemen Pensioners', *c.* 1560, and traditionally called 'Vaughan of Tretower', by an unknown artist, showing him in an armour of Italian make, with morion and halberd, belonging to Major J. R. H. Harley

PLATE 62

a. Close-helmet embossed and richly damascened with gold, part of an armour probably made in Paris, *c.* 1550, later belonging to Henry, Prince of Wales. Tower of London

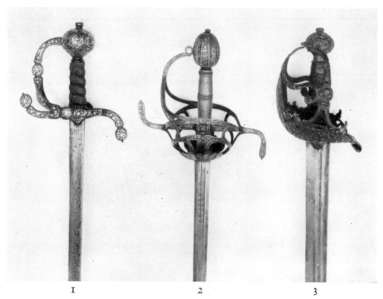

I   2   3

b. 1. Sword-rapier, the hilt encrusted with silver, English, *c.* 1590. Tower of London. 2. Rapier with swept basket-hilt inlaid with gold and silver, *c.* 1620. Tower of London. 3. Cavalry back-sword, the basket-hilt embossed with the arms of Ward, of the time of the Civil War, *c.* 1645. Tower of London

Milan such as those of the Colmans and Missaglias. English, men outside court circles continued to import armour from these countries, as can be seen in the family portraits of the time. The last private armoury of any size to survive in England was that of Wilton House, which contained armour dating from the earl of Pembroke's expedition to St. Quentin (1557), and most of this, though rough, has noticeable Italian features. It was dispersed in 1921 and 1923.

Armour during the sixteenth century tended to follow the forms of civilian dress. The slender lines of the Gothic style gave place to a more rounded outline. Breast-plates became rounded, even globose; the points of cuffs and toes were cut square; laminated tassets took the place of the pointed ones made in one piece that were so marked a feature of the Gothic style. One finds the puffed and slashed costume of the early sixteenth century copied in armour, but during the first third of the sixteenth century German armour is usually distinguished by its surface being broken by straight, parallel flutes (Pl. 65). This fashion does not appear to have been much adopted in England, though one can see signs of it on the monument of John de Vere, earl of Oxford (d. 1539) in the church of Castle Hedingham in Essex, and the chronicler Edward Hall describes Henry as wearing a 'crested' (i.e. fluted) armour on one occasion.

In the middle of the sixteenth century the short round breast developed a central ridge, and then a longer waist until it was prolonged into the 'peascod' fashion of the Elizabethan doub, let (Pl. 61). This long, pointed 'Polichinelle' feature reached its extreme about the year 1585. This was the year when the earl of Leicester led his expedition to Flanders, and there is an example of it in the Middle Temple hall which is believed from the badges on it of the Low Countries to have belonged to him or to one of his companions. One also finds this fashion worn by pikemen who followed Sir Philip Sidney's funeral, as portrayed in Lant's Roll, preserved in the library of Christ Church. At the beginning of the seventeenth century the breast-plate became short again and rather flat and stiff in

appearance. The short laminated tassets which had previously overhung the cuisses were extended so as to displace the latter and reach from the waist to the knee. The style appears at first to have been a French one, but by the end of the sixteenth century it had become universal, and it is one of the character istics of 'cuirassier' armour of the first third of the seventeenth century. The cuirassier was the successor of the lancer and the earlier man at arms. He wore heavy armour with a visored helmet, large pauldrons, full arms, and long tassets to the knee, and carried a sword and a brace of pistols.

Armour for the tournament became highly specialized in the sixteenth century, and was heavier than 'hosting' or field armour, being worn only for such time as the wearer ran his courses. Several English tilting helms have survived (see Pl. 138, chap. xix). The 'tilt' or barrier which divided the combatants as they ran at each other was introduced about 1429 to avoid collisions. Fighting on foot with spears at barriers and the harmless 'tilting at the ring' were other peace ful diversions. King James I disliked all forms of war (though he fancied himself at the last of these pastimes), and the tourn ament came to an end in his reign. Duelling was at first a simple affair of personal combats on foot with broadsword and buckler, but the introduction of the rapier, a long, thrusting sword, was accompanied by the skilled art of fencing, and the weapon was used for parrying as well as thrusting.

In the first quarter of the sixteenth century the Swiss infantry, used as mercenaries, played a prominent part in the wars be tween France and the Empire in north Italy. Their counter parts were the German landsknechts, and numbers of both were hired by Henry VIII for his expeditions abroad. These pro fessional infantrymen wore a light helmet, a globose breast plate with tassets, and carried halberds (a form of pole axe) and pikes, and swords with characteristically recurved quillons (cross pieces). Their costume was of the most exaggerated kind, cut and slashed and plumed (Pl. 66b). Alongside the landsknechts, and growing rapidly in importance, were the

PLATE 63

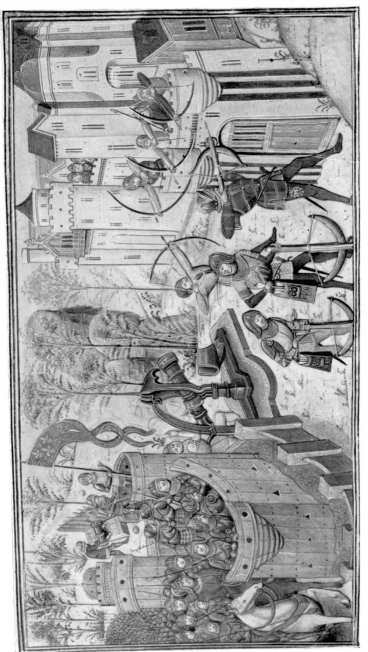

Siege of a town from *Les Chroniques d'Angleterre*, Royal MS. 14 E. iv, in the British Museum, showing archers, crossbowmen, cannon, and men-at-arms, *c.* 1480

PLATE 64

b. Illustration to a manuscript treatise, 'How a man shall be armed at his ease'. Hastings MS., *c.* 1480, in the Pierpont Morgan Library, New York, showing the arming doublet sewn with patches of mail worn beneath the armour

a. Combat in the ring with pole-axes between Sir John Astley and Philip Boyle, Jan. 1441–2, from a manuscript formerly belonging to Lord Hastings and now in the Pierpont Morgan Library, New York

PLATE 65

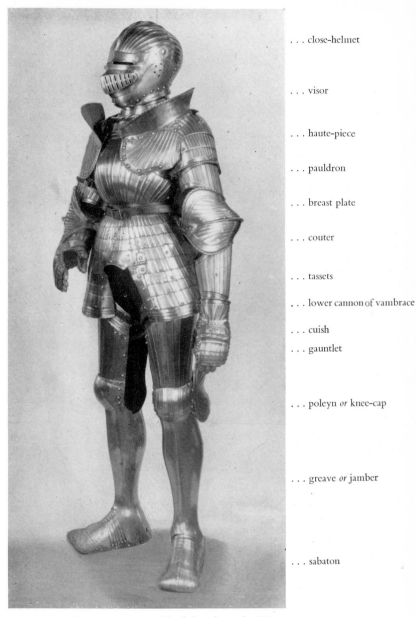

. . . close-helmet

. . . visor

. . . haute-piece

. . . pauldron

. . . breast plate

. . . couter

. . . tassets

. . . lower cannon of vambrace

. . . cuish
. . . gauntlet

. . . poleyn *or* knee-cap

. . . greave *or* jamber

. . . sabaton

German fluted armour, *c.* 1520. The helmet bears the Nürnberg guild-mark. It was already in the Tower of London in
the eighteenth century and may have formed part of Henry
VIII's armoury

PLATE 66

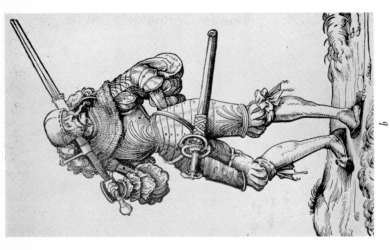

a

b

a. Figure wearing a brigandine of crimson velvet lined with small tinned plates and mail sleeves, fifteenth or early sixteenth century. Tower of London

b. German 'Landsknecht' or professional foot-soldier, wearing mail 'bishop's mantle', carrying a two-handed sword, and also another sword with typical S-shaped quillons; from a contemporary woodcut, time of Henry VIII

hand-gun men or arquebusiers, later to become musketeers (Pl. 59c). They wore little armour in order to be free to manipulate their newfangled weapons. Gradually the musket ousted the English bow, but it took a long time, because in their early days fire-arms were slow, unwieldy, and unreliable, and their effective range was short. In English levies of the sixteenth century one finds a regular proportion of bill-men or pikemen to musketeers; gradually, as the latter were able to give a better account of themselves, the musketeers predominated. But bill-men still formed the main force of the muster at Tilbury in the year of the Armada, and the steadiness of the London pike-men in ordered ranks held the cavalry at Edgehill fifty years later (Fig. 61).

A feature of the armies of the sixteenth century was the light horseman or demi-lancer; he wore a 'corselet', that is, half-armour with an open helmet, generally a burgonet, and his legs covered to above the knee by long boots. He was much more mobile than the man-at-arms, and at this time, when strategy had begun to become as important as tactics, he proved his value. Once more in the battle between safety and mobility, mobility was beginning to get the upper hand. Shakespeare speaks of 'armour that scalds with safety', referring to the discomfort of wearing armour under a hot sun. English-men have never enjoyed, nor enjoy to this day, the wearing of heavy equipment.

As early as the fifteenth century, gentlemen sometimes chose to dispense with plate armour and wore brigandines, that is to say, flexible tunics built up of small tinned plates fixed together on to a leather foundation. These were covered with velvet and often with the heads of the rivets gilt (Pl. 66a). They are fre-quently referred to in the Paston Letters and English inven-tories of the time.

The successor of the brigandine was the jack, a doublet stuffed with tow and reinforced with small plates which were fastened together by a network of cords. The foot-soldier of these times wore a morion (a steel helmet, often with a prominent comb on top and a brim, peaked fore and aft). The

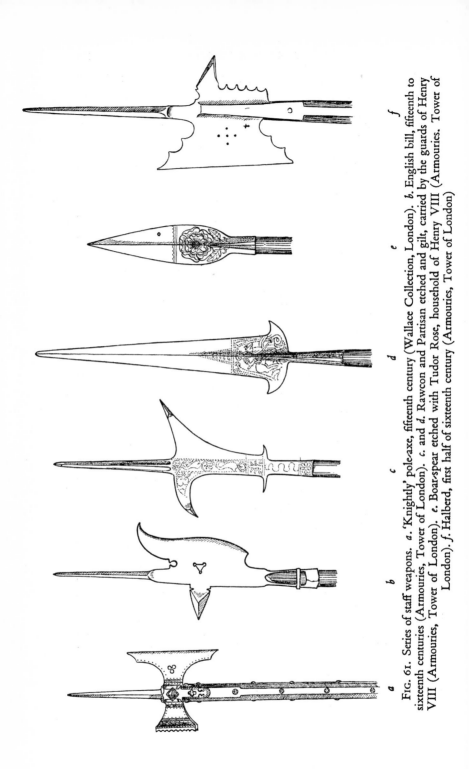

FIG. 61. Series of staff weapons. *a*. 'Knightly' pole-axe, fifteenth century (Wallace Collection, London). *b*. English bill, fifteenth to sixteenth centuries (Armouries, Tower of London). *c*. and *d*. Rawcon and Partisan etched and gilt, carried by the guards of Henry VIII (Armouries, Tower of London). *e*. Boarspear etched with Tudor Rose, household of Henry VIII (Armouries. Tower of London). *f*. Halberd, first half of sixteenth century (Armouries, Tower of London)

PLATE 67

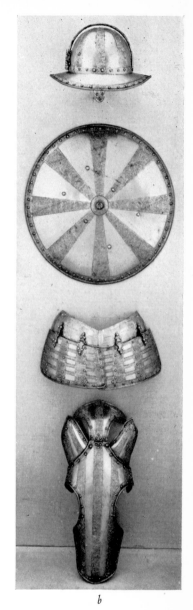

a

b

Armour made for Charles II as a boy at the beginning of the Civil War, 1642, comprising
(a) a cuirassier armour for mounted use, and (b) pot helmet and tassets for use as a pikeman on
foot. Also target and horse's chanfron *en suite*. Tower of London

morion was too top-heavy for the horseman, who wore in its
place a burgonet, that is to say, an open helmet with a peak
over the eyes, hinged cheek-pieces, and an extension protecting
the neck (Pl. 67).

When Crown and Parliament assembled their forces for the
Civil War in 1642, the infantry were composed of pikemen,
still wearing a certain amount of armour, a broad-brimmed pot
helmet, a short breast- with back-plate and tassets; and musketeers wearing little or no armour. 'Cuirassier' armour (Pl. 67)
had been used in the Thirty Years War in Germany, in which
some of the English commanders had served, and it was worn at
the beginning of the war by Essex's bodyguard and Sir Arthur
Haselrig's cavalry, who were nicknamed his 'lobsters' in
consequence. But the three-quarter harness was by now an
anachronism, and cavalry thenceforth limited themselves to
a helmet with a movable guard for the face, often of 'triple
bar' type, and a laminated tail protecting the neck which was
probably derived from Poland, and short breast- and back-
plates. The lance had given way to the petronel (a long pistol
or short carbine), a brace of pistols, and a broadsword (Pl. 62b).

The pistol first came into use about 1520 and was actuated
by a wheel-lock, never a match-lock except in the case of
Henry VIII's pistol-shields preserved in the Tower of London.
A simpler form of mechanical ignition known as the snap-
lance at the end of the century was the precursor of the flint-
lock. Englishmen always seem to have preferred the snap- or
flint-lock, though Germans remained faithful to the wheel-
lock for many years. The wheel-lock had to be wound up by a
key, and was more useful as a sporting weapon than the cheaper
and simpler match-lock, which was carried by the arquebusiers (hackbut-men) and musketeers in war. After the
middle of the seventeenth century armour had virtually disappeared from use, though its prestige was so great that
portrait painters continued to represent their sitters wearing it
for another century. In the Seven Years War, in an emergency,
breast-plates were called for from the Tower to arm the cavalry
in Germany. A century earlier Pappenheim had commented

on how much more confidently the cavalry armed in cuirasses had charged compared with those without. After a long interval armour has come back to us in a new form, several men being encased in one tank and its weight carried by mechanical traction. The battle between defence and attack, between mobility and safety, continues.

WORKS FOR REFERENCE

The literature of arms and armour is very extensive and includes many monographs and countless articles scattered in periodicals, and especially in the *Zeitschrift für historisches Waffenkunde* (1896–1945). W. Böheim's, *Waffenkunde*. (Leipzig 1890) is still the best textbook. There is a long bibliography and glossary at the end of the Wallace Collection's *Catalogue of European Arms and Armour*, part iii (1945).

For the study of existing arms and armour the illustrated *catalogues raisonnés* of public collections and the more important auction sales are the best guides.

The greatest armouries in Europe are those at Vienna and Madrid (Real Armeria). The Musée de l'Armée at Paris comes next. The Metropolitan Museum at New York has a recently formed representative department of arms and armour (useful handbook by S. V. Grancsay).

In England there are the Armouries of the Tower of London, which are the largest and most representative in the country. It was founded in its present form by Henry VIII. The Royal Collection at Windsor Castle derives from the same source. The Wallace Collection has an important section of arms and armour which is distinguished by the quality of its contents, being part of an art collection and not an arsenal. The armour there is almost entirely of continental origin, but contains a fine English helm and a Greenwich harness.

A Short History of Costume and Armour by F. M. Kelly (Batsford, 1931), illus-trated by R. Schwabe, has two good but much compressed chapters on armour. Sir Guy Laking's *Record of European Armour through Seven Centuries* (5 vols., 1920–2), is very fully illustrated, but the text is in parts out of date as a result of more recent research.

J. von Hefner-Alteneck's *Waffen*, 1903 (though dealing mainly with German material), is useful for the middle ages.

John Hewitt's *Ancient Armour and Weapons in Europe* (3 vols., 1855–60), is still helpful for its use of medieval documents and extracts from chronicles.

Mr. F. H. Cripps-Day's privately printed *Fragmenta Armamentaria* contains a special study of the Greenwich School of Armour in England.

The iconography of medieval armour can be studied in books on monumental effigies and brasses, though the armour terms given in the text are often wrong.

C. J. Stothard's *Monumental Effigies of Great Britain* is of importance for the

accuracy and beauty of its engravings. J. S. Crossley's *English Church Monuments* (1921), and Arthur Gardner's *Alabaster Tombs of the pre-Reformation Period* (1940) have many useful photographs. Monumental brasses are served by the early books of Boutell and Haines and the illustrated *List of Rubbing of Brasses* in the Victoria and Albert Museum.

Books reproducing illustrated manuscripts such as Eric Millar's *The Luttrell Psalter* (British Museum, 1932) and M. R. James's *The Romance of Alexander* (Oxford University Press, 1933) are helpful. The Bayeaux Tapestry has been published in the King Penguin series by Sir Eric Maclagan.

For weapons Sir Guy Laking's book mentioned above is the most comprehensive. R. Forrer's *Catalogue of the Schwerzenbach Collection* (1905) (in German) gives a good history of the evolution of the sword. Other weapons have each their own monograph. For fire-arms C. Thierbach's *Die geschichtliche Entwicklung der Handfeuerwaffen.* J. F. Hayward's *European Firearms* (Victoria and Albert Museum, 1955) contains an excellent summary of the subject (1886-99) is still the best textbook for the early history of fire-arms.

XI. HERALDRY

1. *Origins*

(*a*) *Pre-heraldry*

HERALDRY means the business of heralds, and especially that part of it which relates to the use of armorial bearings. Heraldry in this sense, also called armory, is a system of personal and family devices which appeared in western Europe early in the twelfth century and quickly developed patterns and usages of a distinctive kind. There had been other such systems, though less developed ones, and heraldry doubtless inherited something from them, though its most characteristic features were new.

Herodotus (i. 171) says that the Carians were the first to wear crests on their helmets and devices on their shields and that they taught this to the Greeks. Family shield-devices seem to have been used in Athens in the sixth and fifth centuries before Christ. A mosaic in the church of San Vitale, Ravenna (consecrated A.D. 547) shows a warrior attendant on the Emperor Justinian (527–65) bearing a shield charged with the Christian XP emblem (Pl. 68).

Asser's life of Alfred tells us that a raven was woven by the daughters of Ragnar Lothbroc on a banner (called Reafan) which was captured from his sons in 878. There is some evidence for the use of a dragon as an emblem by both Britons and Saxons in the eighth century, and the Bayeux Tapestry (probably *c.* 1080) shows a modelled dragon on a pole held over King Harold at the moment of his death at Hastings (Pl. 69*a*), where William of Normandy carries the banner or gonfanon, charged with a cross and roundels, sent him by the pope (Pl. 69*b*). Some of the knights' shields on the tapestry are painted with dragons, some are plain, and others bear crosses and other markings which may be cognizances but are equally likely to be merely part of the construction of the shield. Wace,

PLATE 68

Mosaic from the church of San Vitale, Ravenna, showing a warrior attendant on the Emperor Justinian

PLATE 69

a. Harold with dragon standard from the Bayeux tapestry

b. William with the Pope's banner from the Bayeux tapestry

writing of the Norman Conquest a hundred years after it, says
that the Normans there showed devices on both their lance
flags and their shields so that they might recognize and not
kill each other. These references, however, seem to be to tribal
or group devices, not to the personal and family emblems of
true heraldry.

(b) The Evidence of Seals

In quite a different context—the sealing of documents with
personal seals to authenticate them—the notion of a purely per
sonal device had come down from a remote, pre classical anti

FIG. 62. Seal of Waleran, count of
Meulan and lord of Worcester,
1141–2; on B.M. Harl. ch. 45. i. 30.
His seal in Paris is similar. Cf. G. H.
White, in *Trans. Roy. Hist. Soc.* 4S,
vol. xiii, pp. 62–67

quity, and developed again about this period as the use of seals
began to spread. Seals, however, were ahead of heraldry and
the earliest seal devices were of other kinds—ancient gems,
non heraldic symbols, or a picture of the seal's owner mounted,
enthroned, or otherwise. Indeed, the first appearance of heraldry
on seals is as an incident in the owner's portrait, the flag at his
lance point, or the shield on his arm showing his heraldic
device. Most of our earliest evidence of heraldry is, in fact, of
this kind.

A device may fairly be called heraldic if we can show that its

FIG. 63. The Checky Coat

1 3 5   2   4   6   7

FIG. 64. Seal of Gilbert de Clare, earl of
Pembroke, 1141–6; from a drawing in B.M.
MS. Landsdowne, 203, fo. 15[b]

The Checky Coat (see Fig. 63)

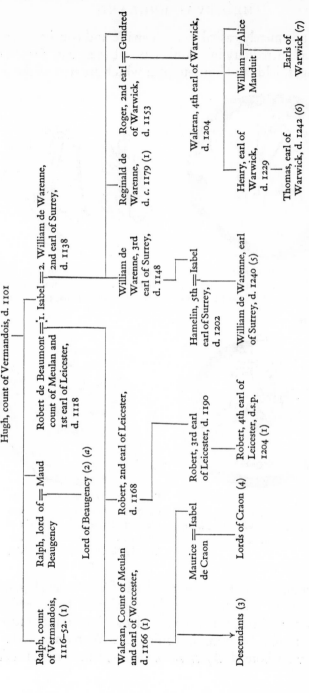

Hugh, count of Vermandois, d. 1101

(1) *Checky* (tinctures unknown; seal evidence only).
(2) *Checky or and azure a fess gules.*
(3) *Checky or and gules.*
(4) *Lozengy or and gules.*
(5) *Checky or and azure.*
(6) *Checky or and azure a bend ermine.*
(7) *Checky or and azure a chevron ermine.*

(a) Anselme, *Histoire généalogique,* iii. 171. For other references see *Complete Peerage,* vol. xii, pt. i, app. J.

use was not merely casual but systematic and consistent and, most of all, hereditary in a family. By all these tests the *checky* lance-flag, shield, and horse-trapper which are seen on the seal

FIG. 65. Seal of Gilbert de Clare, earl of Hertford, 1141–6. P.R.O., Duchy of Lancaster Charter A.157

FIG. 66. Seal of Amadeus III, count of Savoy, 1143; from the *Archives heraldiques suisses*, 1925, p. 11

FIG. 67. Seal of Henry the Lion, duke of Saxony, 1144. Cf. D. L. Galbreath, *Manuel du Blason*, 1942, p. 26

FIG. 68. Seal of Ramon Berengar, marquis of Provence, 1150; from Blancart, *Iconographie des sceaux et bulles . . . des Archives départementales des Bouches-du-Rhône*, 1860, pl. 2

of Waleran, count of Meulan and lord of Worcester (Fig. 62), between 1136 and 1138 can be considered true heraldry. Variations of these arms were used by an important group of families related to him, including the Warennes, earls of Surrey, who bore *checky or and azure*, and the earls of War-

wick, who bore the same with a chevron *ermine* superimposed
(Fig. 63).

FIG. 69. Seal of Ramon Berengar
IV, king of Arragon, 1157; from
Sagarra, *Sigillografia Catalana*, i (1922),
pl. v

FIG. 70. Seal of Welf VI, marquis of Tuscany,
1152; from the *Archives heraldiques suisses*, 1916,
p. 57

A very little later than Waleran's use of the checkers—between 1141 and 1146—the seals of an uncle (Fig. 64) and
nephew (Fig. 65) of the great house of Clare shows their
mounted figures bearing shields charged with chevrons. The

chevrons in the arms of the later Clares were three in number, red on gold, but the earliest examples show six or more.

Within a few years after this heraldry makes first appearances upon a sprinkling of seals right across Europe. What is interpreted as the cross of Savoy has been detected on a seal of Count Amadeus III of Savoy in 1143 (Fig. 66). A seal of Henry the Lion, duke of Saxony and Bavaria, shows a lion in 1144 (Fig. 67), and seals of Ramon Berengar of Provence in 1150

FIG. 71. Seal of Ottokar III, marquis of Styria, 1159; from Anthony von Siegenfeld, *Das Landeswappen der Steiermark*, 1900, p. 142

(Fig. 68), Ramon Berengar IV of Aragon in 1157 (Fig. 69), Welf VI, marquis of Tuscany and prince of Sardinia in 1152 (Fig. 70), and Ottokar III, marquis of Styria in 1159 (Fig. 71), show the first known occurrences of the devices of their several houses.

(c) The Arms of England

A piece of literary evidence takes us back a few years farther still, for the biographer of Geoffrey Plantagenet, count of Anjou, tells us that when he was knighted by his father-in-law Henry I of England upon his marriage in 1127, a shield painted with golden lions was hung about his neck. Geoffrey died in 1151, and there still exists at Le Mans a portrait in enamel made in his lifetime for his tomb there, which shows him with such

a shield of golden lions in a blue field (Fig. 72). These arms were borne by Geoffrey's illegitimate grandson, William Longespee, earl of Salisbury.

It is at first sight surprising not to find the kings of France,

FIG. 72. Geoffrey Plantagenet enamel at
Le Mans, *c.* 1151

England, or Scotland, or the emperor, among these earliest known bearers of arms, but we should not draw too hastily the negative conclusion that, because we find no arms on their seals, therefore they cannot have used any. The crusading chronicle called the *Chronique d'Ernoul* (ed. de Mas Latrie, 1871, p. 157) refers to the existence of arms of the king of England in 1157 but does not describe them. The first king of England

whose great seal shows arms is Richard I. On his first seal of 1189 the shield carried by his mounted figure is charged with a single lion facing to the sinister. On his second great seal of 1198 this changes to the shield of three leopards or lions passant guardant which was ever afterward that of England. Now the great seal of Richard's father Henry II shows no arms at all, but

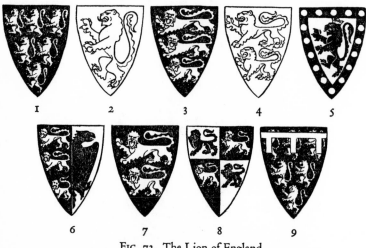

FIG. 73. The Lion of England

the seal of Henry's younger brother, William FitzEmpress (between 1156 and his death in 1163), shows a single lion rampant on both the shield and the horse trapper. Mr. Geoffrey White has pointed out (*Complete Peerage*, xi, app. G, p. 141) that an early seal of William Longespee, earl of Salisbury, natural son of Henry II, also shows this single lion, though his later seal, as mentioned above, shows six. When we add to this that Geoffrey Plantagenet, the father of Henry II, bore the shield of six lions and that *his* father-in-law, Henry I, gave him this, it is hard not to conclude that a lion coat of some kind was used by Henry II, and probably by Henry I before him (Fig. 73).

(d) Originating Causes

The probable conclusion is that heraldry was coming into use and taking formal shape for a generation or more before our

The Lion of England (see Fig. 73)

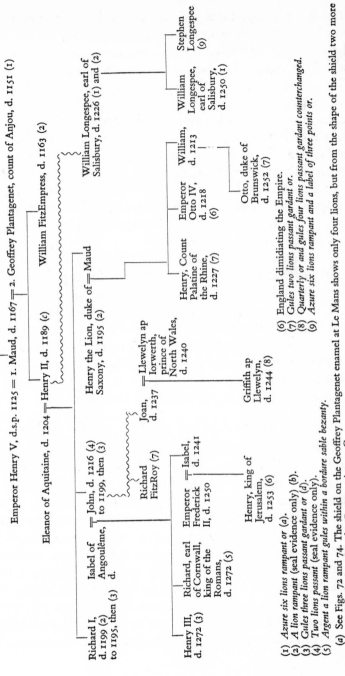

Henry I, d. 1135

Emperor Henry V, d.s.p. 1125 = 1. Maud, d. 1167 = 2. Geoffrey Plantagenet, count of Anjou, d. 1151 (1)

Eleanor of Aquitaine, d. 1204 = Henry II, d. 1189 (c)

William FitzEmpress, d. 1163 (2)

Henry the Lion, duke of = Maud
Saxony, d. 1195 (2)

William Longespee, earl of
Salisbury, d. 1226 (1) and (2)

Isabel of
Angoulême,
d.
= John, d. 1216 (4)
to 1199, then (3)

Joan, = Llewelyn ap
d. 1237   Iorwerth,
prince of
North Wales,
d. 1240

William,
d. 1213

Stephen
Longespee
(9)

William
Longespee,
earl of
Salisbury,
d. 1250 (1)

Richard I,
d. 1199 (2)
to 1195, then (3)

Richard
FitzRoy (7)

Emperor = Isabel,
Frederick   d. 1241
II, d. 1250

Henry, Count
Palatine of
the Rhine,
d. 1227 (7)

Emperor
Otto IV,
d. 1218
(6)

Otto, duke of
Brunswick,
d. 1252 (7)

Henry III,
d. 1272 (3)

Richard, earl
of Cornwall,
king of the
Romans,
d. 1272 (5)

Griffith ap
Llewelyn,
d. 1244 (8)

Henry, king
of Jerusalem,
d. 1253 (6)

(1) *Azure six lions rampant or (a).*
(2) *A lion rampant (seal evidence only) (b).*
(3) *Gules three lions passant gardant or (a).*
(4) *Two lions passant (seal evidence only).*
(5) *Argent a lion rampant gules within a bordure sable bezanty.*

(6) *England dimidiating the Empire.*
(7) *Gules two lions passant gardant or.*
(8) *Quarterly or and gules four lions passant gardant counterchanged.*
(9) *Azure six lions rampant and a label of three points or.*

(a) See Figs. 72 and 74. The shield on the Geoffrey Plantagenet enamel at Le Mans shows only four lions, but from the shape of the shield two more may be inferred. See *Complete Peerage*, xi, app. G.
(b) See Figs. 75 and 77. It is uncertain whether the lion on the shield on the first seal of Richard I represents a single lion or one of two lions combatant. See H. S. London, *Royal Beasts*, p. 12, and the seal of William FitzEmpress shows the lion facing to the sinister (see Fig. 77). Whether he actually bore it so, or whether this is merely an adaptation to the design of the seal is uncertain.
(c) Evidence that Henry II used arms, though it is not known what, is quoted on p. 345.

(d) See Fig. 76.

first clear evidence for it. We have seen that certain elements which went to make it were in existence both long before and at the date of its appearance: the standard to which the leader rallied his men; the shield bearing a device; the personal seal. We can see, too, that in the century which followed the Norman Conquest the forces which wrought out the new, aristocratic, feudal order were at their height. The professional fighters on horseback, the owners of armour, were growing into the 'Chivalry', the closed caste of knights, the new nobility; and as this transformation occurred, what was more natural than that the standards of the leaders and the shields of their companions should grow into a system, ministering at once to their practical needs in war and peace and to the dramatiza' tion of their status and their *ethos*?

The developments in armour which made the individual knight ever less easily discerned save by his cognizance; the Crusade and the tournament which now brought together knights who were strangers yet rivals; the growth of feudalism and the emphasis on the knight's hereditary attachment to his lord and his land; the efflorescence of romantic chivalry and its poetical expression; and the simultaneous culmination of the decorative arts all seem to join together to bring heraldry to birth and thereafter in one century to perfection.

(e) *Heraldry becomes a System: collateral Adoption of Arms*

There is slight but important evidence of a moment in the dawn of heraldry when identical shield-devices were borne by a whole company of knights following one leader—rather as badges were borne in the fifteenth century. Giraldus Cam' brensis relates an incident in Ireland in 1176 (*Expugnatio Hibernica*, Rolls Series, 21, V, p. 335) when Raymond le Gras appeared with a retinue of some thirty kinsmen with shields of one pattern (*clipeis assumptis unius armaturae*). Anna Com' nena (*Alexias*, X, p. 350) tells us how in 1190 during the preparations for the third Crusade an agreement was made between Philip II of France, Henry II of England, and Philip, count of Flanders, that the French should bear red crosses, the

FIG. 74. William Longe-
spee, earl of Salisbury, d.
1226. Effigy in Salisbury
cathedral

FIG. 75. First great seal of Richard I,
1189

FIG. 76. Second great seal of Richard
I, 1198

FIG. 77. Seal of William FitzEmpress,
1156–63; Stenton, *Early Northamptonshire
Charters*, pp. 24–26

English white, and the Flemings green, the Germans having earlier adopted a yellow cross on a white field.

The *Itinerary of Richard I* (Rolls Series, 1, p. 367), describing the king's advance from Ascalon in 1192, speaks of shields adorned, seemingly wholesale, with 'fiery red prowling lions or golden flying dragons, and John Garland in his *Dictionarius*, written after 1218, says that 'the shield-makers [of Paris] serve

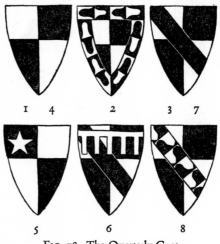

FIG. 78. The Quarterly Coat

the towns throughout France and England, and sell to knights [*militibus*] shields . . . on which are painted lions and fleurs de lys'. As late as 1227 a poet describes the escort of Otto von Lengenbach, carrying with them fifty shields for his knights, all alike charged with his arms. The use of badges in the fifteenth century (p. 357) is in some ways similar to this, but between 1200 and 1250 the normal heraldic principle that every knight's shield-bearing should be distinct became generally established.

There is, indeed, good evidence of its introduction a century earlier. In more than one case similar but slightly differing arms were used in the thirteenth century by groups of families sharing a connexion with an outstanding figure of the twelfth century, whose arms were the basis of theirs. Thus the families of Say, Beauchamp of Bedford, Clavering, Vere, and Lacy all

The Quarterly Coat (see Fig. 78)

Aubrey de Vere

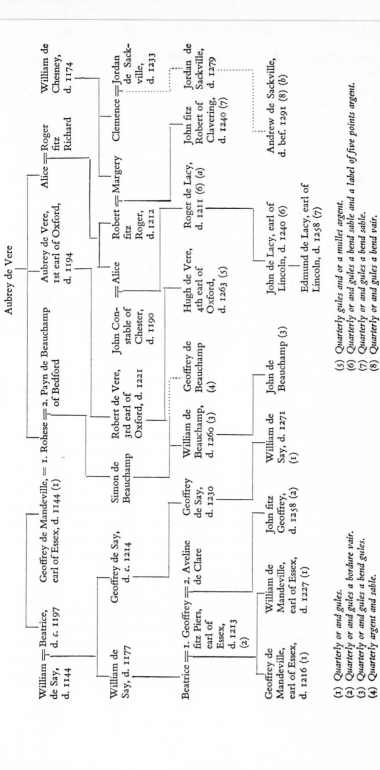

(1) *Quarterly or and gules.*
(2) *Quarterly or and gules a bordure vair.*
(3) *Quarterly or and gules a bend gules.*
(4) *Quarterly argent and sable.*
(5) *Quarterly gules and or a mullet argent.*
(6) *Quarterly or and gules a bend sable and a label of five points argent.*
(7) *Quarterly or and gules a bend sable.*
(8) *Quarterly or and gules a bend vair.*

(a) Also bore *Party per pale gules and sable three garbs or.*
(b) For the pedigree, see *Genealogist's Magazine,* vii. 472, and Farrer, *Honors and Knights' Fees,* i. 212.

used variations of the coat, *Quarterly or and gules*, and were all connected through Geoffrey de Mandeville (*d.* 1144), the rebel earl of Essex, but not otherwise (Fig. 78). The inference that he bore this coat and that variations of it were assigned by him to his kinsmen is difficult to resist.

In the same way the checkered coat, which, as we have seen, was used in its plain form by 1138, was adopted with variations by a group of families—Beaumont, Warenne, Craon, the earls of Warwick—who were linked together through the two marriages of Isabel of Vermandois, who died about 1147. A group of related families with *indented chiefs*—Fitz Randolf, Sandwich, d'Auberville, Butler, Fitz Warin—centres on Ranulf de Glanville, who died in 1190.

This *collateral adoption* of similar arms by distinct families, connected by ties of marriage—and no doubt of friendship—is a phenomenon of the very early days of heraldry and can be distinguished from two later practices: (*a*) the *differencing* of the family coat by younger sons and branches; and (*b*) the adoption (with or without permission) by feudal tenants of arms derived from those of their lord; these are dealt with later (p. 376).

(f) Crests

The display of a three-dimensional heraldic figure on the crest of the helmet is seen as early as 1197 on the seal of Baldwin, count of Flanders (Fig. 79), but did not become usual till the fourteenth century. The adoption round about 1300 of a more pointed form of helm in place of the earlier cylindrical shape may have favoured the development of the crest. By about 1350 the use of a crest had become normal. It was usually either fixed to the helm by a twisted wreath or torse of silk or surrounded by a crest coronet. From the back of the torse or coronet a protective scarf or cloth hung over the back of the helm. The earlier form of this, called the lambrequin, consisted of two tails or scarf-ends; the later, more voluminous form, called the mantling, which came in during the fourteenth century, was conventionally shown as slashed into ribbons. A standardized way of showing the whole 'achieve-

PLATE 70

English arms from the armorial de Gelre in the Royal Library, Brussels

ment' of arms, with the crest, helmet, and mantling sur/
mounting the shield (tilted or straight), with the 'word' or
motto on a scroll above or below, was adopted in the four/
teenth century (Figs. 80 and 81), and this has remained a

FIG. 79. Seal of Baldwin, count of
Flanders, 1197; from the original. Cf.
Demay, *Inventaire des Sceaux de l'Artois et
de la Picardie*, Paris, 1875–7, no. 52

standard form of heraldic device, though the use of shields,
helmets, and crests in war or tournament has long since
ceased. One finds this layout in its earliest form on the seal of
Henry, earl of Lancaster, as early as 1300 (Fig. 82), but it does
not become normal in England much before 1400. On the
Continent it is found as early as *c.* 1375 in the painted records
called Rolls of Arms (Pl. 70), but in England these normally
show the shields only, though achievements are found in some
fifteenth/century examples.

(g) Mottoes

The motto, which in the sixteenth century became an in/
tegral part of the achievement of arms, usually appearing on a
scroll below the shield, seems to have come into heraldry by
more than one channel. Rallying cries in war, often the names
of leaders or standards, go back to the earliest times, and some/
times found their way into heraldry as mottoes. 'Montjoye',

FIG. 80. Sir John Daubeney, 1346; incised slab at Brize Norton, Oxfordshire, showing the figure of the knight wearing his coat of arms, with the conventional group‑ing of shield, surmounted by crested and mantled helm, in front

FIG. 81. Garter Stall Plate of Ralph, Lord Basset, 1390; St. George's Chapel, Windsor

FIG. 82. Seal of Henry, earl of Lancaster, 1300; on the barons' letter to the pope

PLATE 71

Armour and heraldry, middle of thirteenth century (Cambridge MS. Ee. 3. 59): showing for armour, helms, helmets, maces, pommels, surcoats, saddles, housings, the panache and battle-axe

PLATE 72

The sons of Edward III. From a copy by Robert Smirke, R.A., of the fourteenth-century paintings discovered in 1800 in St. Stephen's Chapel, Westminster

which in the eleventh-century *Chanson de Roland* is both the standard and the rallying cry of Charlemagne, passed into heraldry as the motto of the kings of France, but well-authenticated English parallels are hard to find. The scriptural texts and secular tags occasionally found on seals from the thirteenth century were another source, and more direct forerunners still were the words attached to badges or *devises* such as the Garter motto *Hony soyt qui mal y pense* (1348) and the Black Prince's *Ich dien* (1370) linked with his ostrich-feather badge. Certain armorial seals of the late fourteenth century show words on scrolls, and during the fifteenth the usage grew towards its modern form.

(h) Coats of Arms

The loose-fitting linen surcoat worn over armour in the thirteenth century was often plain (Pl. 71), but the drawings illustrating the histories of Matthew Paris (*d.* 1259) show more than one instance of a knight wearing a surcoat with the same device as his shield. Well before 1300 this had become normal. In the fourteenth century the loose surcoat gave place to the close-fitting, sleeveless jupon (Pl. 72), and in the fifteenth this turned into the tabard with wide, hanging sleeves on which the arms were repeated. The term 'coat of arms' (*cote armure*) belongs properly to this armorial coat, but before 1500 had acquired its present generic application to armorial devices as such.

(i) Supporters

From the middle of the thirteenth century dragonlike monsters often appear on armorial seals filling the spaces on the flanks of the shield. In the later fourteenth century beasts or other figures with a clear heraldic meaning succeed to this role, but it is not always easy to say when their purely decorative use gives place to the significant. Significance is best established when the beasts which support the shield are independently known as the owner's badge (Fig. 83), as when two bears support the shield of Thomas Beauchamp, earl of Warwick, on his seal of 1379 (Fig. 84). Indeed, heraldic supporters in their be-

FIG. 83. Fifteenth-century tiles from Tewkesbury abbey with Beauchamp
arms and badges

FIG. 84. Seal of Thomas Beauchamp,
earl of Warwick, 1379. B.M. Harl.
ch. 83, D. 26

PLATE 73

Gates of Henry VII's Chapel, Westminster, showing Royal Badges

ginning can probably best be looked on as a special use of the
badge. When the supporters differ from those used later by
the same family (whether as supporters or badges) as do the
savages on the seal of Patrick, earl of Dunbar and March (1334),
it is less easy to be sure that they have a heraldic meaning.

In the fifteenth century true heraldic supporters were normally used by the same class who used badges—the lords and
those holding important commands or offices. In the course of
the sixteenth century their use became restricted to peers and
Knights of the Garter (Figs. 85 and 86).

(j) Badges

The hey-day of the heraldic badge falls between the late fourteenth and the early sixteenth centuries (Pl. 73). During that
period its most distinctive use was on the liveries worn by the
retainers of the great to show who their masters were and on
those masters' possessions as a mark of ownership. The mullet
of Vere, the Percy crescent, the bear (Fig. 83) and the ragged
staff of the earls of Warwick, and the Stafford knot are well-
known examples. The badges of the royal house and its
branches were numerous, and much has been written on their
complicated history. The *Sunburst* of Edward III, the *White
Hart* of Richard II, the *Tree root* of Thomas of Woodstock,
the *Antelope* of Lancaster, the *Sun* of York, the *Portcullis* of
Beaufort, and the various forms and combinations of *Falcon,
Fetterlock, Ostrich feather,* and *Rose* are among the best known.
A notable use of some of these was in the livery-collars
bestowed by royalty upon those whom they wished to honour,
as in the Lancastrian Collar of SS. (Esses) and the Yorkist
Collar of suns and roses.

The badge was always a single object or conjunction of
objects like those mentioned and was thus quite distinct from
the shield of arms, whose distinctiveness consisted in its total
pattern rather than in the individual charges forming that
pattern. The badge, however, could be and often, though by
no means always, was the same beast, bird, monster, or other
device as its owner used for crest or supporter. The history of

the badge cannot therefore be understood in isolation, and the question when it first appears in heraldry needs close definition

FIG. 85. Seal of Jasper Tudor, earl of Pembroke 1459

FIG. 86. Counterseal of Jasper Tudor, earl of Pembroke, 1459

before it can be answered. The swan on the counterseal of Humphrey de Bohun, earl of Hereford and Essex, of 1301 is

unquestionably heraldic, as are several other devices found on seals but not on shields at this date. Our earliest evidence for the household or livery badge is a good deal later, however.

In a discussion of the frontiers of heraldry Merchants' Marks must be mentioned as falling definitely beyond them, although their owners often sought to give them a heraldic air by charging them on shields. They appear in the fourteenth and fifteenth centuries and are found on seals and elsewhere down to the end of our period. They are usually somewhat cryptic combinations of crosses and letters.

2. Grammar

(a) Blazon

The modern development of heraldry, with its fine distinc- tions and extensive stock of charges, has inevitably made the technical language complicated, but the language of medieval heraldry is essentially simple and its rare difficulties spring mainly from the occasional use of obsolete words. The word blazon, meaning a shield, came to mean a heraldic shield, then its heraldic description, and finally the language of herald- ry. The descriptions of crests and shields in the romances of the late twelfth and early thirteenth centuries show a gradual increase of precision, and by about 1250, when the oldest ex- tant blazoned rolls of arms (Glover's Roll in England and the Bigot Roll in France) were compiled the chief terms and con- ventions had crystallized. At this date and until the fifteenth century the normal language of blazon in England was French.

The oldest technical terms of blazon were the colour names, the names of the linear figures which have come to be called ordinaries, and the words indicating position and relation. Special names for colours seem from the first to have been pre- ferred to commoner ones. At the very first *or* was interchange- able with *jaune* and *argent* with *blanc*. But *or* and *argent* soon won and the distinction between these two 'metals' and the re- maining 'colours' was rendered important by the convention that if the field was of a metal the charges on it must be of a colour, and vice versa. Nevertheless *or* could always be shown

as yellow and *argent* as white. Of the colour names *gules* defeated the alternatives *rouge, vermeil,* and *sinople; azure* defeated
bleu and *sable* defeated *noir.* The only other colours found in
early heraldry, and then but rarely, are *vert* and *purpure.*

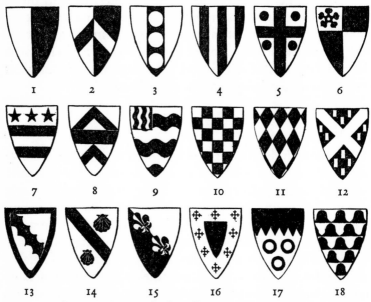

FIG. 87. Ordinaries and charges. (1) Party per pale. (2) Party per pale a chevron
counterchanged. (3) On a pale three roundels. (4) Paly of six. (5) A cross between
four roundels. (6) Quarterly a cinquefoil pierced in the canton (*or* in the first quarter
or in dexter chief). (7) Two bars and in chief three mullets (*or* molets). (8) A fess
between two chevrons (*or* chevronels). (9) Barry wavy of six a canton paly wavy of
six. (10) Checky. (11) Lozengy (*or* fusilly). (12) Billety (*or* Semée of billets) a
saltire. (13) A bend engrailed within a bordure. (14) A bend between two
escallops. (15) Per bend two fleurs-de-lys bendwise counterchanged. (16) An
escutcheon within an orle of cross crosslets. (17) Three annulets and a chief indented. (18) Vair

The names of the linear figures (Fig. 87) develop in rather
the same way. *Fesse, bende, liste, barre,* and *baston* seem to start
as interchangeable names for a horizontal band across the
shield. But they soon become specialized. A fess (to give the
word its English form) is a single broad, horizontal band across
the middle; a bar one of two or more narrower horizontal

bands; a bend a diagonal band; a baston a narrow bend; and *liste* drops out of use.

A few more linear figures, the pale and chevron, chief, pile, cross, and saltire; a few smaller figures such as crosslet, roundel, lozenge, billet, and mullet; the names for the divisions of the shield such as party, paly, barry, bendy, gyronny, lozengy, checky, and vair; of certain notched lines such as indented, engrailed, and undy; and of a few powderings such as crusilly, billety, ermine; and the conventional flowers, fleur-de-lys, tre-foil, quatrefoil, and cinquefoil almost complete the list of early terms peculiar to heraldry. The beasts, birds, and fishes bear their common names and the monsters come from bestiaries and travel books. Some of the words describing the positions in which they are shown, however, such as *rampant, passant, espanie (épanoui*: i.e. displayed (of an eagle)), have from the first a technical flavour.

The terminology of early heraldry is to be learnt from those rolls of arms (p. 381) in which the arms are blazoned instead of being (as is commoner) painted. If a blazon in one of these is hard to follow it is usually possible to interpret it by a painted example of the same man's arms found elsewhere. In rare in-stances the same roll is both painted and blazoned, and the best such example, Thomas Jenyns's Book (*c.* 1410), is a splendid textbook for the student.

A blazon begins with the tincture (metal or colour) of the field and goes on to the ordinaries and other charges, e.g.:

> *Sire Hue de Veer, quartile de or e de goules, a un molet de argent, od la bordure endente de sable.*

> Sir Hugh de Vere, Quarterly or and sable a mullet argent and a border sable indented.

Latin blazons are found occasionally in documents of the fourteenth century and in the treatises of Johannes de Bado Aureo, *c.* 1390, and Nicholas Upton, *c.* 1440. They do not depart in principle from the contemporary French convention. About 1430, however, Sicily, the herald of Alfonso V of

Aragon, invented a system substituting the names of gems for the tincture names previously in use, e.g. topaz for or, pearl for argent, ruby for gules. This had more popularity with the writers of textbooks than with practising heralds, but is oc׳ casionally found used in English armorials of the late fifteenth and early sixteenth centuries.

In the course of the fifteenth century French gave place to English as the language of blazon, though a number of French terms (e.g. azure, gules, sable, vert, fess, chevron, bend) con׳ tinued to be used in English forms. Or and *Argent*, replaced at this time by *Gold* and *Silver*, were brought back into English use in the later sixteenth century and have since remained current, though a certain school of antiquaries in the twentieth century has preferred to change over to *Gold* and *Silver* again.

The Book of St. Albans, 1486, propounds a number of fresh complications. For example, it gives twenty׳five distinct kinds of cross as against a mere ten in the treatise of Johannes de Bado Aureo. Although it is itself far outdone by the sixteenth׳ century works of Gerard Legh (1562) and others, there is ample evidence that by the middle of the fifteenth century heraldry had become a scholastic subject, made complex by lecturers for the pure pleasure of complication.

(b) Canting Arms

In most instances the reasons why particular designs for arms were chosen are altogether lost, but in certain instances they are clear or can be guessed. In many cases, as we have seen, the arms of one family were based on those of another with which it was connected. In very rare instances we can safely say that some personal feat or aspiration was referred to, as the heart in the arms of Douglas alludes to the vow of Sir James Douglas to take the heart of Bruce to the Holy Land. But the commonest explanation of heraldic design lies in the medieval fondness for a canting coat, punning on the owner's name.

Thus corbet bore corbies, Heronvile herons, Scales escallops, Warcop cups, Trumpington trumpets, Pigot and Pikworth picks, Gaunt gloves or gauntlets (*gauntz*), Mauleverer grey׳

hounds (*leverers*), and Cokerynton cocks. The pun might be in French or English; thus both Martel and Hamerton bore hammers: nor was the blazon of a coat adapted to reveal the pun. It has been suggested that the object was, if anything, to conceal it. Thus the ox-heads of Oxcliff are firmly blazoned as *testes de bœuf*, and the roots of Rotour as *racynes*.

Some puns of this kind seem obscure to us merely because the punning words are obsolete or dialectical or foreign, such as the monastery or *moustier* of Musters, the *bourdons* or staves of Burdon, the *bosons* or bird bolts of Boson, the *gurges* or whirl-pool of Gorges, and the *herisons* or hedgehogs of Herries.

Sometimes the pun's reference was not to the surname but to an office or possession. Thus Argentine probably bore covered cups in allusion to his tenure by the service of providing a silver cup for the coronation, while Butler bore them in allu-sion to the office indicated by his name, even as Chamberlain bore keys. Geneville bore brays in allusion to his kinship with the house of Broyes and Mainston bore urchins or hedgehogs for his manor of Urchinfield.

In some other cases a more recondite pun seems to be in-tended. The bands in the fretty coat of Maltravers have a bad traverse, each being crossed by others. The golden dance on blue of Delaryver may depict sparkling waves, and the bars of Grey may represent a *gré* or ladder.

(c) Differencing

Since the purpose of arms was to distinguish individuals, members of a family other than the head bore the family coat with minor differences (Fig. 88). This, at least, was the strict theory, though not always observed in practice. There was no set rule for differencing and various methods were used at different times. One of the oldest methods was to change a major charge. Thus in the middle of the thirteenth century Walter de Clifford bore *Checky or and azure with a bend gules*, while his brother Roger bore the same with a *fess gules*. An-other method was to vary the field, as when Reynold Fitz Piers (*d.* 1286) bore *Gules three lioncels or*, while his cousin

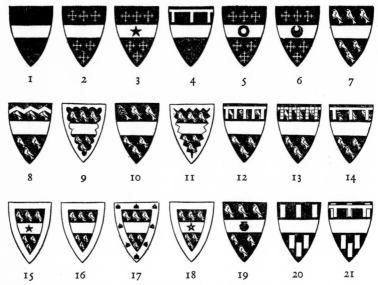

FIG. 88. The Beauchamp differences

1. Gules a fess or.
2. Gules a fess between six cross crosslets or.
3. Gules on a fess between six cross crosslets or a mullet sable.
4. Gules a fess or and a label azure.
5. Gules on a fess between six cross crosslets or an annulet sable.
6. Gules on a fess between six cross crosslets or a crescent sable.
7. Gules a fess between six martlets or.
8. Gules a fess between six martlets or, in chief a dance.
9. Gules a fess between six martlets or within a bordure engrailed argent.
10. Gules a fess between six martlets or, on the first martlet three chevrons gules.
11. Gules a fess between six martlets or within a bordure indented argent.
12. Gules a fess between six martlets or a label of five points argent.
13. Gules a fess between six martlets or a label of five points gobony argent and azure.
14. Gules a fess between six martlets, or, on the first martlet three chevrons gules, a label argent.
15. Gules on a fess between six martlets or a mullet, all within a bordure argent.
16. Gules a fess between six martlets or within a bordure argent.
17. Gules a fess between six martlets or within a bordure argent charged with tonsure caps sable (also read as bells, mitres, fleurs-de-lys, and roses).
18. Gules on a fess between six martlets or a pierced mullet sable.
19. Gules on a fess between six martlets or an escallop sable.
20. Gules a fess between six billets or.
21. Gules, a fess between six billets or a label sable.

The Beauchamp differences (see Fig. 88)

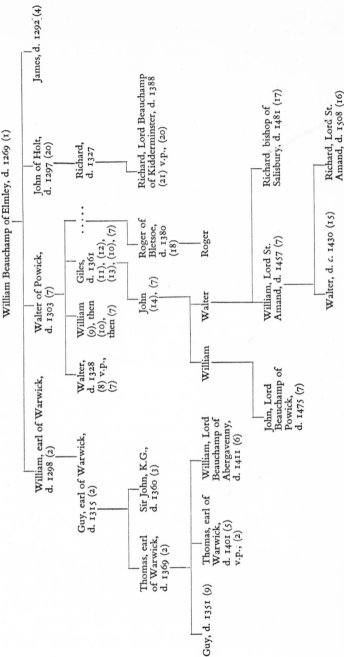

Quarterings are omitted.

v.p. = in his father's lifetime.

Changes of difference made by individuals may sometimes have been due to a personal caprice or to objection made, but probably more often followed succession to a father, or brother, or an arrangement affecting property or allegiance.

Herbert Fitz Matthew bore the same with the field *party azure and gules*. Sometimes only a change of tincture was made. Sometimes a label was charged over all, and as time went on this particular difference came to be reserved for the heir in his father's lifetime. Sometimes a canton, bendlet, or border was added, as when William Longespée bore *Azure six lioncels or*, while his brother bore the same with a *canton ermine*. Another method was to powder the field with small charges such as crosslets, fleurs-de-lys, or escallops. Thus William Bardolf bore *Azure three cinquefoils or*, while his brother Thomas bore the same with the field *semée of crosslets or*.

As time went on and the total number of arms in use grew, smaller differences between one coat and another, and still more between differenced versions of the same coat, had necessarily to be admitted. And thus during the fourteenth century a method of differencing within the family merely by addition of a single charge such as a mullet, a crescent, or annulet came into use. Out of this again, in the fifteenth century, grew the present system of differencing by fixed cadency marks, a label for the eldest son, a crescent for the second, a mullet for the third, and so forth, first found in treatises of the mid-century.

The arms of bastards (Fig. 89) were until the late fourteenth century differenced in the same ways as those of legitimate sons. Then, however, some of them are found bearing their fathers' arms on a bend, fess, chief, chevron, or quarter, with a plain or a party field. Thus Sir John Beaufort (before his legitimization in 1396) bore *Party per pale argent and azure a bend of Lancaster* (i.e. *Gules three lions passant guardant or a label of three points azure each charged with three fleurs-de-lys or*). Others were assigned new coats in which ancestral charges were to be seen in new combinations, as when Sir John Stanley, a bastard of Lord Derby's house, bore *Or three eagles' legs erased gules on a chief indented azure three stags' heads caboshed or*; thus combining his father's badge, the eagle's leg (or gripe's claw), with the stags head from his shield and the indented chief from the Lathom quartering. The border gobony, used by the

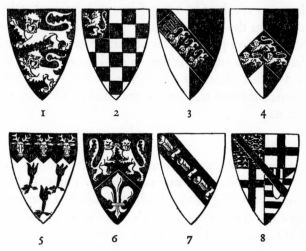

FIG. 89. Arms of Bastards

1. Richard de Dover or Fitzroy, living 1232, bastard of King John. *Gules two lions passant gardant or.* *Genealogist*, N.S., xxii. 109–10.

2. Sir Edward de Warenne, bastard of John de Warenne, earl of Surrey (d. 1347), by Maud de Nerford. *Checky or and azure on a canton gules a lion rampant argent.* i.e. Warenne with a canton of Nerford.

3. John Beaufort, marquess of Somerset, b. *c.* 1371, d. 1410. Bastard of John of Gaunt, legitimated 1397. Before legitimation, *Party per pale argent and azure a bend of Lancaster* (i.e. *a bend gules charged with three lions passant guardant or and a label of three points azure each charged with three fleurs-de-lys or*). After legitimation, Quarterly, 1 and 4. France modern, *Azure three fleurs-de-lys or*, 2 and 3. England. *Gules three lions passant guardant or. All within a bordure gobony argent and azure.*

4. Henry Beaufort, cardinal of St. Eusebius, bishop of Winchester, d. 1447. Brother of 3. At first, *Per pale argent and azure on a chevron gules three lions passant guardant or.* Later. As 3 after legitimation.

5. Sir John Stanley. *Or three eagles legs erased gules, on a chief indented azure three stags' heads caboshed or.*

6. Sir John of Clarence, bastard of Thomas, duke of Clarence (d. 1421). *Per chevron gules and azure in chief two lions combatant gardant and in base a fleur-de-lys or.*

7. Sir Roger de Clarendon, bastard of Edward the Black Prince (d. 1376). *Gules (or perhaps or) on a bend sable three ostrich feathers argent with scrolls argent* (perhaps *or*).

8. Sir Arthur Plantagenet, K.G., Viscount Lisle, d. 1542, bastard of King Edward IV. Quarterly, 1st grand quarter. Quarterly, 1 and 4. France modern. 2 and 3. England. 2nd and 3rd grand quarters. Burgh, earl of Ulster. *Or a cross gules*, 4th grand quarter. Mortimer, Over all, *a baston sinister azure.*

Beauforts as a difference *after* their legitimation, was not in the middle ages a mark of bastardy (though later used so by false inference from the Beaufort case); and the bendlet or baston, which the punning tendencies of heralds would suggest as a fit difference for bastards, is not, to my knowledge, so used in England before the time of Edward IV's bastard Arthur Plantagenet, though treatises of the middle fifteenth century mention it.

(d) Marshalling

When two lordships were combined in one hand, it was con-venient to combine their arms in one shield. This could be done in various ways (Fig. 90). Hugh de Balliol (d. before 1271) displayed the arms of his mother's lordship of Galloway on a shield in the corner of his paternal arms; and a Norman seal of 1218, that of Eudes, seigneur du Pont, shows a similar small shield in chief. When Ferdinand III of Castile suc-ceeded in 1230 through his mother to the kingdom of Leon, he combined the arms of the two kingdoms by dividing his shield into quarters with Castile in the first and fourth and Leon in the second and third. This form of combination, which became familiar in England when the future Edward I married Ferdinand's daughter Eleanor in 1254 was apparently used for a different purpose by Henry III when he permitted his uterine brother William de Valence, whom he had in-vited to England in 1247, to bear a quartered shield of Eng-land and Valence, as depicted on an enamelled shield now at Reggio Emilia. Later heralds would have called these 'arms of affection', there being no blood of the kings of England in William de Valence.

The Emperor Otto IV was the nephew of John of England, and against the account of his election in 1199 Matthew Paris depicts his shield *mutatum pro amore regis Anglie*. It is parted per pale, the dexter half showing the arms of England, the sinister those of the Empire, both dimidiated (cut in half). An early seal, that of Robert of Pinkney, c. 1195, shows an impaled or dimidiated shield, but we do not know with what

meaning. Soon after 1300 we find shields dimidiating or impaling their husbands' with their fathers' arms on the seals of
married women. When Henry Percy, earl of Northumberland,

FIG. 90. Marshalling. (1) Hugh de Balliol with a shield of Galloway in the
Canton. (2) Castile quartering Leon. (3) England quartering Valence (see *The
Coat of Arms*, 1954-5). (4) Shield of the Emperor Otto IV, *mutatum pro amore regis
Anglie*, 1199. (5) Dimidiated shield of Robert of Pinkney, *c.* 1200 (B.M. Harl. ch.
86, B. 55). (6) Richard Neville, earl of Warwick and Salisbury, the King-Maker,
d. 1471. Quarterly I. quarterly 1 and 4, Beauchamp; 2 and 3, Warwick. II. 1 and
4, Montague; 2 and 3, Monthermer. III. Neville. IV. 1 and 4, Clare; 2 and 3,
Despenser (*The Ancestor*, v. 201). (7) Hastings impaling Leybourne, 1330 (B.M.
Seal Catalogue, no. 8684)

married Maud Lucy in 1381, her lands were entailed upon
him and his descendants by a former wife on condition that he
and they should quarter the Lucy arms with those of Percy,
and so, accordingly, they did.

When more than two but not more than four lordships were
conjoined in one hand, their arms could still be shown in one

shield of four quarters if the balance given by repeating the
first and second in the fourth and third were abandoned. Thus

FIG. 91. Garter Stall Plate of John Talbot, earl of Shrewsbury, d. 1453.
Quarterly: 1, Earldom of Shrewsbury; 2, Talbot; 3, Strange; 4, Furnival

the Garter stall plate of John Talbot, earl of Shrewsbury (d.
1450) (Fig. 91) shows four different quarters for his earldom,

FIG. 92. Garter Stall Plate of Sir John Grey of Ruthin, d. 1439. Quarterly: I and IV. Grey. II and III. quarterly: 1 and 4, Hastings; 2 and 3, Valence. Over all, *a label of three points*

FIG. 93. Garter Stall Plate of Richard Beauchamp, earl of Warwick, *c.* 1423.
Quarterly: 1 and 4, Beauchamp; 2 and 3, Warwick. In pretence, Quarterly:
1 and 4, Clare; 2 and 3, Despencer

his family coat, and his baronies of Strange and Furnival. In other instances of similar date the problem is solved by charg-ing a small shield over all, which if itself quartered gives room for four coats in all without loss of symmetry (Fig. 92). Again, one or more of the quarterings may themselves be quartered. In extreme cases such as that of Richard Neville, the king-maker (Fig. 93), who had six coats to combine, all these methods could be used at once.

In this way the conjunction of many lordships produced the shield of many quarterings which in the late fifteenth century and after was put to a new use, the purely genealogical one of indicating heirship in blood without the corresponding in-heritance of lands.

3. Use and Regulation

(a) Armigers

We have seen that heraldry was in its origin a distinctive system adopted by the knights, the newly risen feudal nobility. It is unlikely that a system produced by their needs and for their use would for some time be pirated or copied by others not of their camp, and in fact there is no evidence of this occurring till well on in the thirteenth century, when arms are occasionally found on the seals of merchants and artisans. The civilian use of arms, however, begins much earlier with their adoption by ladies. Rohese de Clare, countess of Lincoln, displayed the Clare chevrons on her seal soon after 1156 (Fig. 94) and Maud of Portugal, countess of Flanders, sealed with the arms of Portugal in 1189 (Fig. 95). In the next century the seals of great ladies often display two or more shields of the arms of their fathers' and husbands' families, until near 1300, when dimidiation and impalement came in.

It is not until about the middle of the fourteenth century that English bishops, abbeys, cities, and boroughs begin to show arms on their seals, and even then the fashion spread but slowly. Many religious houses, indeed, seem to have adopted arms only near the end of their lives in the late fifteenth or early sixteenth century. The granting of arms to the incorporated trades of the

City of London began in the fifteenth century, and between the issue of the Drapers' patent in 1439 and the end of the century some thirty companies had obtained patents of arms (Fig. 96). In some parts of Europe, notably northern France and

FIG. 94. Seal of Rohese (de Clare), countess of Lincoln, 1156. *Topographer and Genealogist*, i. 318–19

FIG. 95. Seal of Maud of Portugal, countess of Flanders, 1189. D. L. Galbreath, *Manuel du Blason*, fig. 54

the Low Countries, the free cities of the Rhineland and the Swiss confederation, arms were fairly freely used on seals and otherwise by merchants, artisans, and peasants in the thirteenth, fourteenth, and fifteenth centuries. But it is also clear that this was resented by the nobility, and in consequence by 1350 there were two distinct theories of the legal status of arms. According to one school they were ensigns of nobility and could be assumed by none but the noble. According to the other any man might take arms at will. The statement of the case by Bartolus of Sassoferrato (1314–57), the great Italian

jurist, had a greater influence on the Continent than in England, though it was adopted by Nicholas Upton, who wrote about 1440 that

in these days many poor men labouring in the French wars, have become noble, some by their prudence, some by their zeal, some by their courage, some by their other virtues, which ennoble men. And many of these have by their own authority assumed arms to be borne by themselves and their heirs;

FIG. 96. John Smert, Garter King of Arms, from the initial of his grant of arms to the Tallow Chandlers' Company, 1450

adding that in his view arms so taken, if not already those of someone else, are legitimate and valid, but cannot be of such dignity or authority as arms given by the authority of sovereigns or lords. A different view is conveyed in a letter addressed by Henry V in 1417 to the sheriffs of certain counties in which he orders proclamation to be made that none of those about to take part in his French expedition should take to himself arms or tunics of arms (called *cote armures*) unless he should possess the same by ancestral right or by the grant of some person having authority sufficient thereunto. This was the doctrine enforced by authority in the next century through the heralds' visitations and Court of Chivalry, and it has recently been pointed out by Mr. H. S. London that the writer of a treatise on heraldry very little later than Upton, Richard Strangways of the Inner

Temple, who wrote about 1454, drew a sharp distinction between marks such as merchants use which anyone may adopt,
and arms which no one may take without the intervention of a
competent authority, that is, either the sovereign or a herald.

The delegation by the king to his heralds, or rather to the
senior heralds called kings of arms, of the right to grant arms to
suitable persons seems first to have taken place either in the
fifteenth or the late fourteenth century. Before this we find some

I   2   3

FIG. 97. (1) Audley, *Gules fretty or.* (2)
Touchet, *Ermine a chevron gules.* (3) *Party per
pale indented sable* and *Ermine a chevron gules
fretty or,* granted in 1404 by John Touchet,
Lord Audley, to John and Thomas Mackworth

few grants by the king himself and some by the great lords. In
most of these instances the arms granted were based on those
of the grantor. Thus Edward III granted to Peter de Maundell
the arms of England with a crown azure round the neck of each
leopard. In 1347 Lord Stafford granted arms based on his own
to Esmond de Mortayn; and in 1404 John Touchet, Lord
Audley, granted to John and Thomas Macworth arms based
on those of Audley and Touchet (Fig. 97). Earlier still, in
the thirteenth century, it is common to find the arms of feudal
tenants embodying charges from those of their lords, and it is a
plausible suggestion that in the earliest times lords conferred
arms, whether derived from their own or not, upon their
tenants on enfeoffment or knighthood, as we have seen that
Henry I did on Geoffrey Plantagenet.

The subject of armigers cannot be left without a reference to
the medieval habit of attributing arms to fabulous and pre-
heraldic personages. By the middle of the thirteenth century
arms were attributed to St. Edward the Confessor at West-

minster and Matthew Paris assigns arms to King Offa and
William the Conqueror. St. George and St. Edmund had
their arms not long after. Several Saxon founders of religious
houses had arms assigned them in the fourteenth and fifteenth
centuries, and so did the Nine Worthies, King Arthur and
some of his knights, Roland, Bevis of Hampton, and some of
the kings in the British History. Once it was taken for granted
that heraldry had existed when all these had lived, it was clear
that they must have had their arms and all that remained was to
ascertain them by one of those quasi-logical processes in which
the medieval mind was not less fertile than our own.

(b) The Court of Chivalry

The Constable and the Marshal, originating as officers of
the king's household, had become by 1200 great officers of
state. Till lately it has been held that their authority over the
army in the field led in early times to their becoming judges in
the Court of Chivalry (*Curia Militaris* = Court of the
Knighthood or Chivalry). Mr. G. D. Squibb has, however,
now shown (in 'The High Court of Chivalry', Oxford,
1959) that this court in all probability originated in a delegation to them by the Crown in 1347 or 1348. Their Court
dealt with contracts touching deeds of arms and war out of the
realm and matters touching war within the realm as well as
armorial disputes. These last, in Mr. Squibb's view, had previously been referred to commissioners specially appointed by
the Crown. They had certainly caused trouble before 1347.
On the Caerlaverock campaign in 1300 it was noted with
astonishment that Brian Fitz Alan and Hugh Poyntz bore the
same arms, *Barry or and gules*, whence a dispute arose between
them. At the siege of Calais in 1345–8 Sir Nicholas de Burnell found Sir Robert de Morley using the same arms as himself, *Argent a lion sable crowned and armed or*, and challenged him;
whereupon the Constable, the earl of Northampton, and the
Marshal, the earl of Warwick, sat 'tribunalement' in the
church of St. Peter outside Calais and gave judgement that
Morley, for his deeds of prowess performed under them, should

bear the arms for life, but after his death Burnell and Burnell's heirs should have them. It is not entirely surprising that in 1386 the same dispute arose again between the heirs, and the hearings continued over a number of years. The best-known case heard in the court was that of Scrope against Grosvenor (1385–90) for the coat, *Azure a bend or*, which was adjudged to Scrope by the Constable, the judgement being confirmed by the king on appeal.

The third great medieval plea of arms was Grey *v.* Hastings (1407–17). The proceedings in these three cases are preserved through the accident that they went to appeal, those of others which did not do so being lost, though the occurrence of a number of these is known by incidental references.

(c) The Heralds

The earliest references to heralds (or heralds of arms) yet noted belong to the late twelfth century. All the early mentions connect them not with war but with tournaments, which they proclaimed beforehand and at which they preceded champions, announced their entry, and acclaimed their victories. They became experts in the conduct of jousts (Pl. 138) and in secular pageantry in general, and were closely linked in early times with their rivals the minstrels. Since they must recognize the combatants they had to know their armorial devices, and by the fourteenth century, if not earlier, they were both recording and devising these. Hence at an early date the name heraldry was given to the study of armorial bearings.

In the thirteenth century only a fortunate few seem to have been in fixed employment. The rest followed the rumours of tournaments from place to place. By the middle fourteenth century, however, this was past. The heralds' status had risen and kings, lords, and knights had their private heralds, to whom they gave special names of office taken from their lordships, castles, badges, mottoes, or fancies. The probationer herald was called a pursuivant and the senior heralds of sovereigns were created by them kings of heralds or kings of arms (i.e. kings of heralds of arms).

Pursuivants' names of office were usually taken from badges or mottoes, as Etoile volant, Bluemantle, Rose Blanche, Secret, Endure, or Bonaventure. Heralds' names came usually from their masters' lordships or fortresses (as some pursuivants' did too), as Carlisle, Dorset, Richmond, Warwick, and Windsor. The names of the kings of arms were of all kinds. Montjoye king of arms of France had his name from his master's war-cry; Falcon king of arms in England from a royal badge; and Anjou, Aquitaine, and Guienne kings of arms from appanages of the Crown. Lancaster, Leicester, and March were the names of heralds of noblemen whose dignities passed to the Crown, whereupon these titles were given to royal kings of arms.

In the fourteenth and fifteenth centuries heralds were much employed on embassies and messages between sovereigns both in war and peace, and the heralds of all nations formed an international fraternity, the Office of Arms. Within this the heralds of the English obedience, both the king's heralds and those of noblemen, formed a smaller coherent body, which as time went on showed the same self-organizing and self-protecting tendencies as many other trades. Before 1415 different kings of arms enjoyed from time to time a pre-eminence over their fellows, as chief of the Office of Arms and King of Arms of England, but whether by appointment, election, or seniority we do not know. In 1415, however, Henry V created the new office of Garter King of Arms (Fig. 96) and gave it permanent primacy over the others. The new king of arms was an officer of the Order of the Garter and his office was from the first one of great dignity, but unhappily its relationship to those previously existing had not been clearly thought out, with the consequence that disputes arose over jurisdiction.

When disputes over the right to particular arms and the adoption of arms by men of doubtful qualification made a closer supervision of heraldic use appear desirable, it was to the heralds as the existing experts in the subject that the work was necessarily entrusted. Several documents of the fifteenth century reveal a move in this direction. Patents of arms were issued, surveys of arms were made, and in 1484 the heralds were

incorporated by Richard III and given a house in which to keep their records. The full-grown system of heraldic visitation was the creation of Henry VIII, but less formal surveys of the same kind are found fifty years or more earlier.

4. *Heraldic Art*

An instructive parallel can be drawn between the development of Gothic architecture and that of heraldic design. The composition of arms in the early centuries of heraldry develops logically from the structural facts of the shield form, which itself changes slowly from the long, pointed twelfth-century type through the perfection of the heater shape to the broader late medieval forms. The normal shield forms being triangular, three, six, or ten identical charges are common, two, four, or five very rare. Six would be placed 3, 2, 1, and ten 4, 3, 2, 1. Besides this sort of balance, symmetry and boldness are the salient qualities. Only in the later fifteenth century do we find oddities and complications creeping in, partly from a change of taste, partly to meet the growing difficulties of differencing when so many simpler patterns had been used up.

The principal surviving examples of early heraldic art are on seals, monuments, monumental brasses, and buildings, and in manuscripts, textiles, glass, and enamel. What remains is of necessity the merest vestige of what was, and inventories and descriptions indicate that we have lost much of the best. The enamelled stall plates of the Knights of the Garter in St. George's Chapel, Windsor, running in unbroken series from the reign of Henry V to the present day, comprise some of the finest extant English heraldic art. Yet it is likely that the fourteenth-century plates which have perished, all but one, were finer than those of the fifteenth century which remain.

Upon the whole finer renderings of heraldry survive in three-dimensional than in two-dimensional examples; that is to say, on seals and in carvings upon tombs and buildings.

WORKS FOR REFERENCE

The study of English medieval heraldry must rest mainly on the manuscript records called Rolls of Arms and on armorial seals, and only when these have been edited and published far more fully than at present will firm conclusions on many important points become possible.

The only full account of the former is the present writer's *A Catalogue of English Mediaeval Rolls of Arms* (Society of Antiquaries, 1950) and the best general study of the latter is the paper on 'Armorials on English Seals from the Twelfth to the Sixteenth Centuries' by C. H. Hunter Blair (*Archaeologia*, lxix, 1943). The early heraldic treatises are discussed by H. Stanford London in the *Antiquaries Journal*, xxxiii (1953), 169–83. Our present knowledge of medieval heraldry may be compared in some respects with the state of our knowledge of medieval architecture a hundred years ago. Furthermore, heraldry has attracted a number of popular writers whose conclusions have not been hampered by a close acquaintance with historical fact. Among the few general works based on a first-hand study of the source material are the *Complete Body of Heraldry*, by Joseph Edmondson (1780); *Inquiries into the Origin and Progress of the Science of Heraldry in England*, by the Rev. James Dallaway (1793); *The Pursuivant of Arms*, by J. R. Planché (1851 and 1873); the article on heraldry by Oswald Barron in the *Encyclopaedia Britannica* (11th ed., 1910); *A Grammar of English Heraldry* (1913 and 1953) and *Heraldry for Craftsmen and Designers* (1913), both by Sir William St. John Hope; *Heraldry in Scotland*, by J. H. Stevenson (1914); *Manuel du Blason*, by D. L. Galbreath (Lausanne, 1942); and the article on heraldry in *Chambers's Encyclopaedia* (1950), by A. R. Wagner, D. L. Galbreath, and H. Stanford London; J. W. Papworth, *Ordinary of British Armorials* (1874) is useful but must be used with caution. A new edition is in preparation.

PRINTED IN
GREAT BRITAIN
AT THE
UNIVERSITY PRESS
OXFORD
BY
CHARLES BATEY
PRINTER
TO THE
UNIVERSITY

PREFACE

In 1902 Dr. F. P. Barnard edited a book entitled *Companion to English History*. It was on the basis of this useful volume that in 1924 the late Professor H. W. C. Davis edited and revised for the Clarendon Press *Medieval England* to form part of the series of which *Shakespeare's England* is probably the best known. After more than half a century the original book, and indeed Davis's revised edition, have become quite out of date. In these circumstances, the new edition has been almost completely rewritten by experts in the subjects with which the chapters deal; only two of the original chapters survive and these have been carefully and thoroughly revised. Though the original plan has been retained, this book is really a new book with some additional chapters discussing aspects of history (such as Medieval Science) which were not included in previous editions. It does not aim at uniformity of treatment; each author has adopted his own arrangement of the material, and selected his own illustrations which form an important feature of the volumes. Many scholars have given me valuable advice in the preparation of the work; but I should particularly wish to thank Professor V. H. Galbraith who has been unfailing in giving me the benefit of his wide knowledge and experience.

A. L. P.

Oxford University Press, Amen House, London E.C.4

GLASGOW NEW YORK TORONTO MELBOURNE WELLINGTON
BOMBAY CALCUTTA MADRAS KARACHI KUALA LUMPUR
CAPE TOWN IBADAN NAIROBI ACCRA

PRINTED IN GREAT BRITAIN

MEDIEVAL ENGLAND

A NEW EDITION
REWRITTEN AND REVISED

EDITED BY

AUSTIN LANE POOLE
D.Litt., F.B.A.

VOLUME I

OXFORD
AT THE CLARENDON PRESS
1958

A Street Scene
Presentation of a book to the author's patron, fifteenth century.
From the miniature by Jean Foucquet

MEDIEVAL ENGLAND

942   P822m   M   v.1
POOLE
  MEDIEVAL ENGLAND
                              19.00

WITHDRAWN